Construction
Administration
in Architectural
Practice

Construction Administration in Architectural Practice

Arthur F. O'Leary
Fellow, American Institute of Architects
Member, Royal Institute of the Architects of Ireland
O'Leary Terasawa Partners
AIA Architects
Los Angeles, California

McGraw-Hill, Inc.
New York St. Louis San Francisco Auckland Bogotá
Caracas Lisbon London Madrid Mexico Milan
Montreal New Delhi Paris San Juan São Paulo
Singapore Sydney Tokyo Toronto

Library of Congress Cataloging-in-Publication Data

O'Leary, Arthur F.
    Construction administration in architectural practice / Arthur F.
O'Leary.
      p.   cm.
    Includes index.
    ISBN 0-07-047903-8
    1. Construction industry—Management.   I. Title.
TH438.O44   1992
692—dc20   91-19153

Copyright © 1992 by McGraw-Hill, Inc. All rights reserved. Printed in the United States of America. Except as permitted under the United States Copyright Act of 1976, no part of this publication may be reproduced or distributed in any form or by any means, or stored in a data base or retrieval system, without the prior written permission of the publisher.

1 2 3 4 5 6 7 8 9 0   HAL/HAL   9 7 6 5 4 3 2 1

ISBN 0-07-047903-8

The sponsoring editor for this book was Joel Stein, the editing supervisor was Stephen M. Smith, and the production supervisor was Suzanne W. Babeuf. It was set in ITC Garamond Light by McGraw-Hill's Professional Book Group composition unit.

Printed and bound by Arcata Graphics/Halliday.

Information contained in this work has been obtained by McGraw-Hill, Inc., from sources believed to be reliable. However, neither McGraw-Hill nor its authors guarantees the accuracy or completeness of any information published herein and neither McGraw-Hill nor its authors shall be responsible for any errors, omissions, or damages arising out of use of this information. This work is published with the understanding that McGraw-Hill and its authors are supplying information but are not attempting to render engineering or other professional services. If such services are required, the assistance of an appropriate professional should be sought.

Contents

Acknowledgments xiii

1 Introduction 1

Standard Construction Documents 1
Architects as Contract Administrators 2
Construction Contract Benefits Both Parties 3
Contract Administration by Contractors 4
Contract Administration in the Owner's Behalf 4
The Contract Documents 5
Contractual Relationships 6
General Principles 6

2 Selecting the Contractor 9

Negotiated Contract or Competitive Bidding 9
Establishing the Bidding Conditions 10
Bidding Practices 10
Recommended Bidding Procedures 10
Selection of Bidders 11
Invitations to Bid 12
Instructions to Bidders 12
The Bid Package 13
Bidding Period 14
Base Bid, Alternate Bids, and Unit Prices 14
Bid Bond and Proposal Form 15
Opening of Bids and Determining the Low Bidder 15
Award of Contract 16

3 The Preconstruction Jobsite Conference   19

    Commencement of the Construction Phase   19
    What Is a Successful Building Project?   19
    Preconstruction Jobsite Conference: A Communication Tool   20
    Errors in the Contract Documents   21
    Matters Pertaining to Use of the Site   21
    Contract Documents   22
    Design Intent   22
    Specification Substitutions   23
    Progress Schedules   23
    Record Keeping on the Jobsite   23
    Communications   24
    Architect's Job Visits   24
    Construction Methods and Safety Procedures   25
    Contractor's Requests for Payment   25
    Testing and Inspections   25
    Notice to Proceed   26
    Private Meeting   26
    Owner's Financial Capability   27
    Unit Prices and Allowances   27
    Contractor's Overhead and Profit   27
    Separate Contractors   28
    Preconstruction Submittals   28
    Owner's Insurance   29
    Liquidated Damages   29
    Architect's Decisions   30

4 Consultants and Advisors   31

    Liability for Mistakes of Outside Consultants   31
    Limiting Exposure to Liability   32
    Limiting Liability for Consultants' Shortcomings   33
    Owners' versus Architects' Consultants and Advisors   34

5 Construction Insurance   37

    Financial Responsibility for Accidental Losses   37
    AIA General Conditions   37
    Owner's Instructions Regarding Insurance and Bonds   38
    Certificates of Insurance   38

6 Site Observation and Administration of Construction   41

    Construction Observation: How Much Is Enough?   41
    Architectural Service Agreements   42
    Construction Phase   42
    Construction Phase Services   43
    Budgeting the Fee for Construction Phase Services   45
    Construction Observation   46
    Architect's Personnel in the Field   47
    Record Keeping During Construction Administration   47
    Keeping the Owner Informed   48
    Limitations of Architect's Authority   48

7 Construction Administration When the Contract Is Bonded — 51

Construction Bonds 51
Obligations of Surety 52
Cost of a Bond 52
Contractor Prequalification 53
Surety as Adversary 53
Surety as Ally 54
Owner's Right to Approve Contractor's Surety 54
AIA Standard Bond Forms 54
Transmitting Bond to Owner 55
Commencing Work Before Issuance of Bond 55
Keeping Surety Informed 55
Termination of the Construction Contract 56
Consent of Surety 56
Overpaying the Contractor 57
Owner's Claim against Bond 57

8 Shop Drawing Procedures — 59

Shop Drawings: Friend or Foe? 59
Shop Drawing Procedures in AIA Documents 60
Submittals Defined 60
Are Shop Drawings Really Needed? 60
Specifying Unneeded Shop Drawings 61
Contractor's Review of Shop Drawings 61
Consultants' Review of Shop Drawings 62
Monitoring Progress of Submissions 63
Keeping the Client Informed 63
Qualified Personnel 64
Shop Drawing Stamps 64
Architect's Approval of a Shop Drawing 64
Improper Use of Shop Drawings 65

9 Payment Certifications — 67

Contractor's Application for Payment 67
Representations and Limitations of Certificates 68
Decisions to Withhold Certificate 69
Overcertification 69
Certificate Must Be Fair 70
Final Payment 71
Accord and Satisfaction 71
Substantiation for Payment Requests 72

10 Change Orders — 73

Who Benefits from Changes During Construction? 73
Owner's Right to Make Changes 74
Change Orders and Construction Change Directives 74
Change Order Procedure 74
Pricing and Billing of Change Orders 76
Changes in Time 77
Acceleration and Impact Claims 77
Architect and Surety 78
Contractor's Claims for Extra Compensation 78
Architect's Minor Changes 79
Use Change Orders for All Contract Changes 79

11 Responsibilities of the Owner in a Construction Contract 81

The Owner as a Member of the Construction Team 81
AIA General Conditions 82
Owner's Responsibilities 82
Signing the Contract 83
After the Contract Is Signed 83
Owner Must Furnish Informtion 84
Insurance and Bonds 84
Payments 85
Owner's Failure to Pay 86
Owner's Right to Stop the Work 86
Owner's Right to Carry Out the Work 87
Separate Contractors 87
Owner's Claims against the Contractor 88
Defective Work 88
Owner and Architect 88
The Ideal Owner 89

12 The Contractor's Responsibilities 91

What Is Expected of the General Contractor 91
Signing of the Contract 92
Drawings and Specifications 93
Contractor Responsible for Results 93
Construction Quality 94
Taxes and Licenses 94
Safety and Accident Prevention 94
Separate Contractors 95
Communications 96
Subcontractors and Suppliers 96
Hazardous Waste Materials 97
Contractor's Warranty 97
Warranty Period 98
Architect's Services During Warranty Period 99
Contractor's Indemnification of Owner and Architect 99
Limitation on Owner's Rights to Appoint New Architect or Change Architect's Duties 99

13 Role of the Construction Superintendent 101

Contractor's Superintendent 101
Preliminary Site Visit 103
Review of Contract Documents and Field Conditions 103
Preconstruction Jobsite Conference 104
Daily Construction Log 104
Construction of the Work 105
Supervision and Construction Procedures 105
Progress Schedule 105
Documents and Samples at the Site 106
Shop Drawings, Product Data, and Samples 106
Cutting and Patching 106
Communications Facilitating Contract Administration 106
Continuing Contract Performance 107
Claims for Concealed or Unknown Conditions 107
Claims for Additional Time 107
Cooperation with Owner and Architect and with Separate Contractors 108
Changes in the Work 108
Time of Construction 108

Substantial Completion 109
  Protection of Persons and Property 109
  Asbestos and PCB 110
  Uncovering and Correction of Work 111
  Tests and Inspections 111

14 Closing Out the Job   113

  Orderly Conclusion of the Construction Contract 113
  Substantial Completion 114
  Certificate of Substantial Completion 114
  Notice of Completion (as Distinguished from Certificate of Substantial Completion) 115
  Final Submissions 116
  Final Completion 117
  Architect's Final Certificate and Final Payment 117
  Decisions to Withhold Certificate 118
  Owner's Partial Use or Occupancy 119
  Retainage 120
  Liquidated Damages 120
  Termination of the Contract 121
  Architect's Decisions 121
  Owner-Architect Relationship 121

15 Termination of the Construction Contract   123

  Termination Provisions in the Contract 123
  Termination by the Contractor 123
  Termination by the Owner for Cause 125
  Suspension by the Owner for Convenience 126
  Position of the Surety 126
  Position of the Architect 127
  Practical Considerations in the Decision to Terminate 127
  Warranty Responsibility 129

16 Architect's Decisions Based on Design Concept, Aesthetic Effect, and Intent of the Contract Documents   131

  Imprecise Standards for Architect's Decisions 131
  Intent of the Contract Documents 132
  Design Concept 133
  Architect's Decisions 133
  Minor Changes in the Work 134
  Aesthetic Effect Decisions 134

17 Resolution of Construction Disputes   137

  Misunderstandings During Construction 137
  General Conditions of the Contract 138
  Claims and Disputes 139
  Architect's Aesthetic Effect Decisions 140
  Architect's Minor Changes 141
  Assistance from Surety 141
  Architect's Failure to Render a Final Decision 141
  Alternative Dispute Resolution Methods 142
  Filing an Arbitration Demand 142
  Continuing Contract Performance 143

Arbitration Award 144
Conclusion 144

18 Preventing Time and Delay Disputes in Construction Contracts — 145

Changed Conditions 145
AIA General Conditions 145
Liquidated Damages 146
Working Days versus Calendar Days 146
Unforeseen or Differing Conditions 147
Delay Caused by Owner or Architect 147
Construction Schedule 148
Weather Delays 148
Critical Path 150
Substantial Completion 150
Delay Damages 151
The Moment of Truth 151

19 Owner's and Contractor's Legal Claims against Architects — 153

What to Do If You Get Sued 153
Arbitration Demand or Lawsuit 154
Responding to the Complaint 154
Professional Liability Insurance 155
Legal Counsel 155
Selecting a Lawyer 155
Preparations to Assist Your Lawyer 156
How Long Should Records Be Kept? 160
Statutes of Limitations 161
Settlement 162
Appearing as a Witness 162

20 Analyzing Liability for Construction Defects — 165

Types of Defects 165
Analyzing the Situation 166
Identifying the Source of Responsibility 166
Mediation, a Possible Solution 167

21 Written Communication — 169

What Must Be in Writing 169
Architect's Certifications 170
Certificates Required by the AIA General Conditions 170
Notices 171
Submittals 175
Additional Agreements 177
Orders, Authorizations, Approvals, and Objections 178
Additional Written Communications 179

Appendix A: AIA Document B141—Standard Form of Agreement Between Owner and Architect, 1987 Edition 181

Appendix B: AIA Document A101—Standard Form of Agreement Between Owner and Contractor (where the basis of payment is a Stipulated Sum), 1987 Edition 197

Appendix C: AIA Document A111—Standard Form of Agreement Between Owner and Contractor (where the basis of payment is the Cost of the Work Plus a Fee with or without a Guaranteed Maximum Price), 1987 Edition 211
Appendix D: AIA Document A201—General Conditions of the Contract for Construction, 1987 Edition 231
Appendix E: Synopses of AIA Standard Form Documents Referred to in This Book 261

Index 265

Acknowledgments

I respectfully acknowledge the early educational influence and inspiration exerted by Professor Henry Charles Burge, FAIA, at the School of Architecture, University of Southern California. He also instilled the importance of objectivity, thorough analysis, and the superiority of valid basic principles over rote and arbitrary rules.

Those who provided consultation and encouragement include my partners Toshikazu Terasawa, FAIA, Edward K. Takahashi, AIA, CCS, Rudolph V. De Chellis, FAIA, Lawrence Chaffin, Jr., AIA, and Takashi Shida, AIA; my professional associates Justin J. Gershuny, AIA, and Keith J. Randall, AIA; and my associates in forensic architecture Herbert A. Wiedoeft II, AIA, and Russell W. Hobbs, AIA, CCS.

My belief in the value and effectiveness of the arbitration process was developed from service as a construction arbitrator in over 150 arbitrations through the Los Angeles office of the American Arbitration Association since 1957.

My limited command of legal principles and construction law has been absorbed vicariously from the scores of construction industry lawyers I have consulted with through the years and especially from my close professional association with James Acret of the Los Angeles bar and his extensive writings in construction law.

Skilled assistance in preparation of the manuscript was provided by Felicity Matthews.

To Inny, my patient, beloved wife, this book is dedicated.

Arthur F. O'Leary, FAIA, MRIAI

Introduction

Standard Construction Documents

The continual evolution of the construction process in the United States has been propelled by remarkable improvements in the technology of materials, building systems, contracting methods, architectural design, and environmental and structural engineering. Concurrent with technological progress is the continuing development of administrative procedures which must always move to reflect the latest conditions of accountability, contractual considerations, liability apportionment, governmental regulation, and legal requirements.

Various construction industry organizations have been diligent in providing standard form documents which are consistent with the demands of changing requirements. For more than a century, the American Institute of Architects (AIA), through its national study committees, has responded to the needs of the industry by issuing and updating a complete range of architectural and construction forms and contracts. These documents have provided a measure of uniformity to an industry that is otherwise quite individualistic and decentralized. The contents and structure of the AIA documents and the general principles on which they are based are widely known and accepted by the industry. Members of the recognized national contracting, subcontracting, and engineering societies consult with architects and counsel of the AIA document committee in developing and revising the standard documents.

Architects across the nation do not always conform to a precisely defined, single invariable approach to construction administration, but the widespread use of standardized form documents has unquestionably resulted in a fairly high degree of uniformity. Architects tend to conduct themselves in accordance with the standard documents, and the standard documents in turn reflect current professional practices.

Thus the continual change in the standard form documents is closely parallel to the evolution in architectural practice.

Architects as Contract Administrators

Although much has been written to assist contractors in appropriate procedures needed for conducting a construction business, very little has been made available to aid architects in understanding their professional functions and responsibilities during the construction period.

This book is written primarily for architects who are faced with the necessity of performing those services which they have contracted to do during, and in anticipation of, the construction phase of the typical architectural contract. Large architectural and engineering firms generally have several projects in the construction phase at any one time and, depending on their organizational structure, may have one or more full-time architectural construction administrators on staff. These architects are in the construction phase of the firm's design contracts on a more or less continuous basis and are usually well qualified and highly experienced. They will need this book only as an occasional authoritative reference source. Some larger firms, however, if organized in separate teams for each project, may not have full-time construction administrators. This function will be fulfilled as needed by the project architect or administrator, much like principals of smaller firms.

The principals and key personnel of small and medium-sized firms must be capable of rendering the construction phase services as and when called upon, even though this might represent only a small and infrequent part of their total involvement in the firm's obligations. Ninety percent of their time might be taken up by various other pressing professional activities such as seeking new assignments; conferring with consultants, clients, and employees; designing; drafting construction documents; writing specifications; and office administration, among other equally necessary, diverse, and demanding pursuits. It is these diversified, conscientious architectural practitioners who will find this book most useful as a practical reference for guidance in carrying out their contracted responsibilities during the construction phase.

Administration of the contract provides the architect the opportunity of observing the construction as it progresses and the means to suggest adjustments as necessary to preserve the design integrity of the project. The architect will also be able to quickly recognize when contractors and suppliers have misunderstood the intent of the contract drawings and specifications. This will be beneficial to all involved, as it will often reduce the economic waste incurred in the correction of errors.

It has been a tradition during the past century for architects to administer the construction contracts under which their projects were built. But during the most recent two or three decades, some liability insurance carriers and legal advisors to the architectural profession have reasoned that there would be considerably less exposure to professional liability claims if architects had less direct involvement in the construction process. Accordingly, many architects and firms declined to render services beyond completion of the construction documents. Although this approach eliminated the possibility of some types of architectural malpractice occurrences during construction, it also removed the architect entirely from the construction scene. This resulted in a greater possibility of construction errors caused by contractors' faulty interpretation or misunderstanding of the construction documents. If the architect was not available during construction, errors or omissions in the documents were not discovered in time to be rectified in an economical manner.

In recent years, informed opinion has reverted once again to favor the architect's traditional role of monitoring the construction contract. This has several advantages which outweigh the disadvantages. With the architect more intimately involved in the conversion from drawings and specifications to physical reality, there is a greater chance of preventing contractor misconceptions and misinterpretations in a timely manner. It also affords the architect the opportunity of correcting errors and anomalies in the documents before construction progress makes them impossible, impractical, or too costly to rectify.

A significant twofold outcome of this evolution is that (1) architects now recognize that the physical construction is the contractor's sole responsibility and architects no longer interfere in the contractor's determination and control of means, methods, techniques, sequences, and procedures of construction; and (2) the architect's role during the construction period is limited to counseling, administering, monitoring, observing, and reporting. It is of extreme importance that these two general principles not be violated by architects in their preparation of construction documents or in construction administration.

Another way of distinguishing the differences in contractors' and architects' duties is that the contractor is responsible for carrying out the construction contract while the architect's role is to monitor that contract. The monitoring process includes interpreting the contract, providing technical assistance to the contractor, observing the work to determine its compliance with the contract, reporting all significant and relevant information to the owner, certifying payments to the contractor, resolving disputes, facilitating communication, and consulting with the owner.

An interesting aspect of this evolution is that the architect's construction period role used to be termed *supervision* of construction, whereas now it would be referred to as *observation* of construction. A subtle but important difference.

Construction Contract Benefits Both Parties

Owners and contractors mutually share in the benefits and burdens of their construction contracts. The failure of either to realize their expected legitimate objectives is often caused by shortcomings in carrying out the physical work of the contract. But just as often it is caused by inadequate or inefficient administration of the contract.

The contract, usually arrived at through negotiation, is the medium of expression by which each party delineates the goals it seeks to obtain. The contractor expects to secure desirable construction employment for its forces, which can be performed under favorable physical and economic conditions, with the reasonable expectation of recovering its costs and a fair profit. The owner aspires to receiving its required construction project built according to the contract drawings and specifications, available for use on or before the agreed delivery date, and to pay no more than the stipulated price.

Contract Administration by Contractors

The largest part of the operation of a construction business is concerned with administration of the contracts which form that company's portfolio of business. Numerous authoritative reference books are available to the construction industry explaining the management and operation of contracting businesses of all sizes, organizational types, and building specialties.

The procedures referred to in this book will apply primarily to construction work contracted by private parties. The general principles also apply generally to public work. However, when contracting with governmental entities, additional statutory requirements will always apply. For the protection of public funds, public works contracting is subject to a large body of specialized laws and regulations which apply to bidding procedures, forms of contracts, specifications, change orders, applications for payment, insurance, bonding, contract termination, closing out procedures, warranties, and appeal procedures.

Contract Administration in the Owner's Behalf

The owner's legitimate interests in a construction contract must be assured through knowledgeable negotiation of the contract in the first place. Many owners are quite competent and able to care for their own interests and are fully capable of negotiating on the level of the most canny of general contractors. Others will undoubtedly need the skilled assistance of their legal advisors, architects, and other construction industry experts.

After contract provisions have been completely discussed, agreed upon, and reduced to mutually acceptable written terms, and the contract has been duly signed by both parties, then only upon the diligent follow-through of capable contract administration can the owner realistically expect to fully realize the benefits offered by the contract.

Architects who administer construction contracts in behalf of owners customarily apply the principles and procedures reflected in the various forms of standard agreements of the American Institute of Architects. The owner will usually engage the architect's services for this purpose by using the appropriate owner-architect agreement and by making certain that the owner-contractor agreement contains harmonious conditions requiring the contractor's cooperation and participation. The premise of this book is that the architect's services will have been contracted for by the owner using the standard AIA form

> Standard Form of Agreement Between Owner and Architect, Fourteenth Edition, AIA Document B141, 1987 (Appendix A)

or a similar type of agreement. It is also based on the construction contract being formed substantially from one of the following two standard forms of construction agreement:

> Standard Form of Agreement Between Owner and Contractor (where the basis of payment is a Stipulated Sum), Twelfth Edition, AIA Document A101, 1987 (Appendix B)

> Standard Form of Agreement Between Owner and Contractor (where the basis of payment is the Cost of the Work Plus a Fee with or without a Guaranteed Maximum Price), Tenth Edition, AIA Document A111, 1987 (Appendix C)

The construction contract must also include the AIA General Conditions:

> General Conditions of the Contract for Construction, Fourteenth Edition, AIA Document A201, 1987 (Appendix D)

The Contract Documents

The documents which comprise a complete construction contract in the United States are called the *contract documents* and consist of the agreement between the owner and contractor (usually called the agreement), conditions of the contract (general, supplementary, and other conditions), construction drawings, and specifications.

Also included in the contract documents are addenda issued prior to execution of the contract, other documents which may be listed in the agreement, and modifications issued after execution of the contract. Examples of modifications are (1) a written amendment to the contract signed by both parties, (2) a change order, (3) a construction change directive, and (4) a written order for a minor change in the work issued by the architect.

Unless specifically enumerated in the agreement, the contract documents do not include other documents such as bidding requirements (advertisements or invitations to bid, instructions to bidders, sample forms, the contractor's bid, or portions of addenda relating to bidding requirements). Shop drawings, product data, samples, and similar submittals are not contract documents.

The foregoing understandings as to what constitutes the usual contract documents in a standard construction contract are to be found in Subparagraphs 1.1.1 and 3.12.4 of the 1987 edition of the AIA General Conditions. In addition, none of the following are contract documents: surety bonds, insurance certificates, requests for information, proposal requests, price quotations, clarification drawings, information bulletins, unexecuted change orders, and correspondence.

Contractual Relationships

The AIA standard documents are based on the contractual relationships in the conventional contracting systems prevalent in the United States and some other countries. These relationships are illustrated in Fig. 1.1. When analyzing a given situation, it is helpful to review this diagram to determine and visualize the true contractual relationships and communication links between the entities.

Although communication should flow freely along contract lines, the single exception is that the architect, as administrator of the construction contract, controls communication between the owner and contractor. All parties should respect the proper communication procedures. This will facilitate systematic administration and avoid confusion and unexpected liability consequences.

General Principles

All recommendations and procedures will be based on the use of the standard AIA documents with the objective of providing effective and efficient service to the client in full compliance with the offerings of the architectural services contract. Consideration is also given to the responsible limitation of professional liability where possible and the elimination of unnecessary risk. Unavoidable risk should be controlled and minimized. This is in the interest of both the architect and the owner.

The AIA standard documents have evolved on a continual basis over decades of practical daily usage and are periodically issued anew to reflect the developing trends in construction technology, techniques, and administration as well as legal and insurance implications and professional liability consequences. The latest issue of the core construction industry documents, all coordinated and consistent with each other, is the 1987 edition. All of the AIA documents referred to are synopsized in Appendix E.

It is always advantageous to use standard form documents where possible, as the construction industry is accustomed to their use and most participants are acquainted with their provisions and the principles upon which they are founded. Customization to reflect the peculiarities of a specific project can be accomplished by means of deleted or added paragraphs amending the standard forms. In this way only the deviations need be studied, rather than an entire new document. It is also recommended that the actual printed AIA forms be used, rather than retyping them, so that users can be confident that the basic document has not been revised. Although standard documents may be incorporated into contracts and specifications by citation, it is always preferable to physically include the actual documents for immediate reference by the user.

In this book, many of the standard AIA documents have been quoted in part or paraphrased for convenience. Architects planning to take important administrative actions on their projects are hereby not

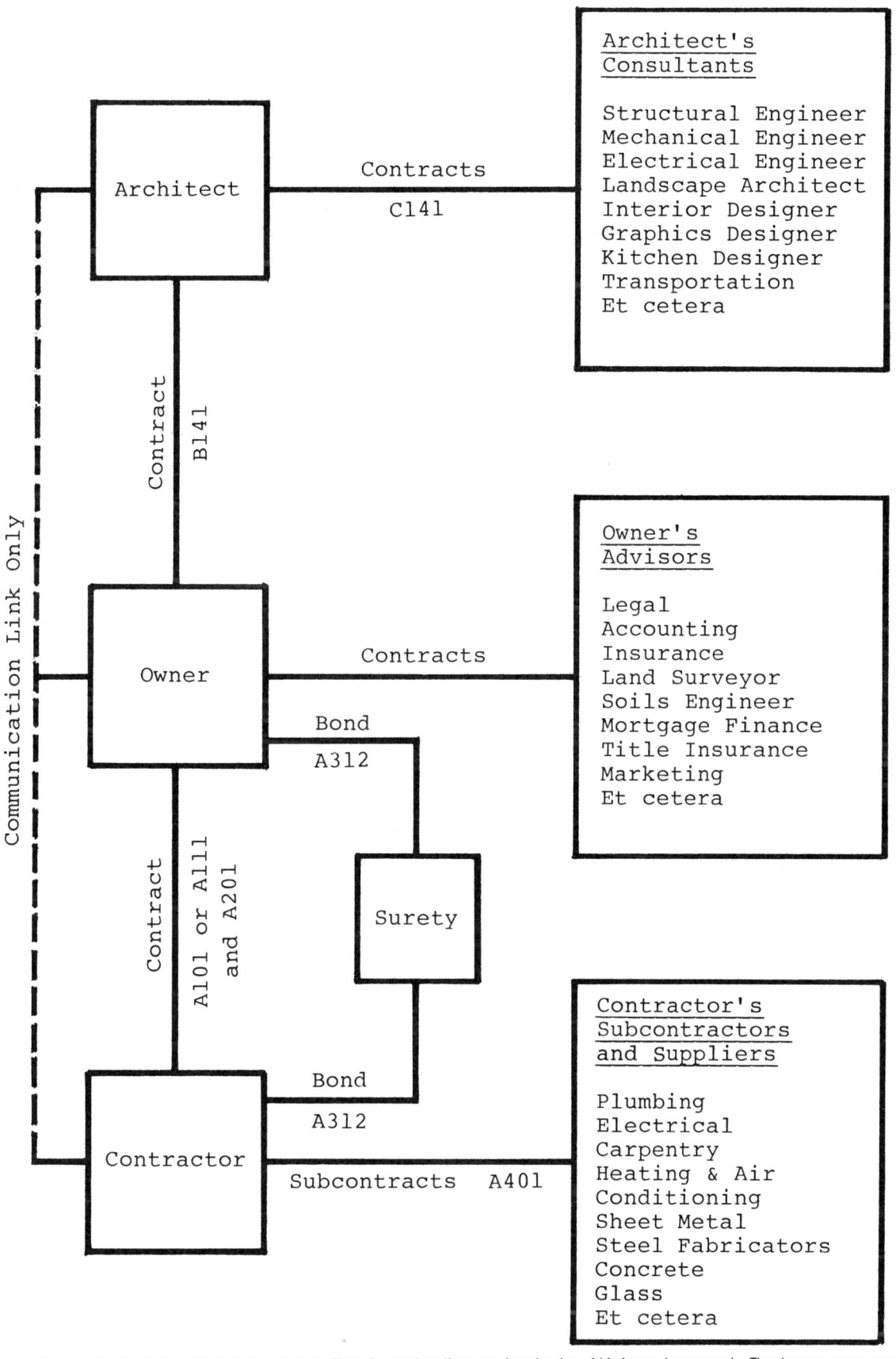

Fig. 1.1 Contractual relationships in the conventional construction contract using AIA form documents. The boxes represent the various entities involved in a typical building project. The solid lines connecting the boxes represent agreements between the entities, generally in the form of written contracts. (Note that the numbers of the appropriate AIA documents are shown.) The dashed line represents a communications link only. The solid line connecting Owner and Contractor is the *construction contract*, comprised of the contract documents. This is the contract which will be administered in the owner's behalf by the architect.

only advised but urged to refer to the actual documents in their entirety for the exact wording in proper context.

Although the opinions expressed in this book are based on many years of practical experience and on the orthodox and generally accepted interpretations of the AIA documents, they may not be directly applicable to special or peculiar situations which should be individually analyzed. Lawyers practicing in the construction industry milieu will be helpful in considering unique, complex, or unusual contractual situations which might require atypical or novel analysis.

Some of the chapters of this book have previously appeared in slightly abridged form in *Design Cost & Data for Management of Building Design* and in *L.A. Architect,* a publication of the Los Angeles chapter of the American Institute of Architects.

2

Selecting the Contractor

Negotiated Contract or Competitive Bidding

Before the contract drawings and specifications are completed, the owner and architect should start considering how to select a suitable contractor to be entrusted with the project. Often the owner will already be acquainted with a reputable competent contractor, perhaps from previously completed construction. The owner might feel very confident and secure in the hands of a familiar, tested, and trusted contractor. When the owner wishes to proceed with a known contractor, it is simply a matter of negotiation with the chosen firm to determine the contracting method, the formula for the contractor's remuneration, and the cost of the project.

A negotiated contract with a selected contractor is favored by many experienced construction owners, as it provides opportunity for the architect and owner to consult with the contractor during the design and construction document phases. This enables the owner to confirm in advance of actual construction that the architect's design is realistically constructible and that the scope and quality of the project are within budgetary limitations.

Other owners are reluctant to proceed with consideration of only one contractor because of the apparent lack of competition and the fear of overpaying. Actually, competition would not be completely lacking, as the selected contractor would obtain competitive bids from the numerous subcontractors and suppliers. A negotiated contract is advisable only when the owner has complete trust and confidence in the competence and integrity of the selected contractor.

Establishing the Bidding Conditions

For those owners who require competitive proposals from several contractors, the architect and owner should discuss the entire matter prior to establishing the bidding procedures. The architect will need to know the owner's requirements and decisions so they can be properly reflected in the supplementary conditions and bidding instructions. The owner must decide the number of bidders and who will be invited to bid.

It is the owner's prerogative to establish the insurance and bonding requirements. The owner must also decide on the contracting method and form of contract to be used. Decisions on these topics should be formed by the owner in consultation with the architect and specialized insurance, legal, and financial consultants.

Written instructions for the owner's insurance, bonding, contracting, and bidding requirements can be conveniently transmitted to the architect by use of AIA Document G612, Owner's Instructions Regarding the Construction Contract, Insurance and Bonds, and Bidding Procedures, 1987 Edition. Upon the architect's receipt of the owner's decisions on all of these matters, the contract documents and bidding documents can be completed.

Bidding Practices

Contractors do not charge a fee for preparing a competitive proposal for a construction contract, although the expense, time, and trouble of preparing a careful and responsible bid are substantial. Most contractors keep a running account of the number of unsuccessful proposals submitted for every contract successfully signed up. The wasted proposals must be charged to the contractor's general overhead, which eventually must be recovered proportionately from the active contracts undertaken.

Owners must reserve the right to reject any and all proposals submitted, as this is necessary in the event that the lowest bid exceeds the budget or if there is any suggestion or suspicion of collusion among the bidders. There is, however, an implied promise that the bidding procedure will be fair, just, and equitable and that the owner will enter into negotiations for a contract only with the lowest responsible bidder. If it were not for this tacit understanding, contractors would not be willing to commit the considerable resources necessary to prepare a competitive proposal. The owner's right to reject bids should not be used as a subterfuge for favoring a contractor who was not the low bidder or did not enter the bidding competition at all.

Recommended Bidding Procedures

In the interest of establishing uniform, ethical bidding conditions respecting the legitimate concerns and objectives of owners and contractors alike, a written standard was devised by committees of the American Institute of Architects and the Associated General Contractors in 1948. It continues to develop, has been revised and updated several times, and now exists as Recommended Guide for Competitive Bidding Procedures and Contract Awards for Building Construction, June 1982 Edition, AIA Document A501, AGC Document 325(23). Architects who wish to quickly inform their clients of accepted ethical bidding procedures should present a copy of this nominally priced booklet to each of their clients for consideration.

Architectural offices that conduct bidding procedures perceived by the construction community to be unfair or unethical have increasing difficulty finding contractors to bid their clients' work. The procedures outlined in the AIA/AGC Guide are reasonable and provide fair and equal opportunities for all bidders without compromising the interests of the owner.

The architect must obtain the owner's approval of the list of bidders, contracting method, and bidding procedures to be used. The architect and owner should review the guide together, discuss its recommendations, and resolve any owner reservations. The owner will undoubtedly recognize that adherence to the procedures will be beneficial to all concerned.

An owner might ask why negotiations should be confined solely to the low bidder when the owner may have a preference for one of the other bidders. No contracting firm should be asked to expend its resources preparing a proposal if it would not be acceptable should it become low bidder. If a particular contractor on the list is so attractive to the owner that it would be given favoritism over the low bidder, the owner should forgo the bidding procedure and enter into a negotiated contract directly with the favored contractor.

Selection of Bidders

One of the first decisions to be made is the number of contractors to be placed on the bidding list. In public work, bidding procedures are governed by law, and little discretion can be exercised by owner or architect. Generally there is no limit to the number of contractors who may bid the job. In private contracts, the owner may control the number and identity of contractors who will be allowed to submit proposals. Too few contractors on the bidding list will not provide sufficient price competition while too many diminishes the incentive for serious competition. Judgment as to the length of the bid list will depend on such factors as size, nature, and complexity of the project and current competitive conditions in the community. Usually a list of from three to five prequalified bidders will provide adequate price competition.

The contractors invited to bid should be carefully selected so that the owner would be willing to enter into a contract with whoever is low bidder. It is best to choose contractors who are appropriately experienced for the type of project and who are not too small or large for the size of project. The bidders should be approximately the same size, as overhead costs will be similar. Although contractors will not always agree, it is advantageous to select bidders reasonably closely located to the jobsite, as it stands to reason that the service will be better than that provided by remotely located contractors. A carefully screened list of prequalified contractors will save the time, inconvenience, and mutual disappointment of rejecting a low bidder for reasons that could have been discovered prior to bidding. Each prospective bidder should be required to submit evidence of relevant experience, qualifications of its personnel, equipment, and other resources, and financial capacity and stability prior to being invited to bid. A standard AIA form questionnaire, Contractor's Qualification Statement, Document A305, can be used by contractors as a uniform method of transmitting pertinent information regarding their organizations. References from financial institutions and prior owners should be verified by the owner.

The pre-bidding data received from prospective bidders should be organized and submitted to the owner for final screening and compilation of a bid list. The owner will have access to its bank and other financial advisors for credit checking and final determination of each contractor's financial stability.

Invitations to Bid

The contractors selected for inclusion in the bid list should each be sent a written invitation to bid, outlining the general scope of work and informing them that the bidding documents will be available to all of the bidders at the same hour and day. Each of the bidders who accept the invitation should be given identical information on which to base proposals.

Instructions to Bidders

In the interest of fairness, it is important that all bidders receive identical information at the same time and that sealed bids are due at the same time and place. The American Institute of Architects has developed a standard Instructions to Bidders, 1987 Edition, Document A701, which contains a set of uniform conditions and directions. The standard instructions are coordinated and consistent with the general conditions and construction contracts of the AIA. The instructions are not intended to be a contract document; therefore, any provisions of the document intended to remain in effect after execution of the contract must be included in the supplementary conditions of the contract.

The bidders are required by the instructions to bidders to examine and compare the bidding documents and the contract documents of other concurrent work on the site and to report to the architect at once any errors, inconsistencies, or ambiguities discovered. This is an idealistic requirement and impractical to enforce, particularly in respect to those who do not become low bidder.

Bidders and sub bidders requiring clarification, interpretation, or additional information must make their requests in writing to the architect at least 7 days before the bids are due. Bidders are instructed not to telephone or visit the architect's office during the bidding period. The architect will collect all requests for additional information and disseminate an addendum simultaneously to all bidders at least 4 days before bid time giving requested interpretations, clarifications, deletions, additions, and corrections of the bidding documents. The addenda should include all determinations of acceptable substitutions of specified materials, products, and equipment.

A practice favored by many architects and contractors is to have a pre-bid conference at the onset of the bidding period for general orientation, to introduce the bidders to the site, to answer questions, and to explain and identify the important features of the project. At this conference, the architect or an assistant should take notes so that any questions answered on the day or resolved later can be included in an addendum to be sent to all bidders.

The Bid Package

The miscellany of information to be distributed to each of the bidders is termed the bidding documents, also called the bid package. The Bidding Documents are defined in the AIA Instructions to Bidders, Paragraph 1.1, and "include the Bidding Requirements and the proposed Contract Documents. The Bidding Requirements consist of the Advertisement or Invitation to Bid, Instructions to Bidders, Supplementary Instructions to Bidders, the bid form, and other sample bidding and contract forms. The proposed Contract Documents consists of the form of Agreement between the Owner and Contractor, Conditions of the Contract (General, Supplementary and other Conditions), Drawings, Specifications and all Addenda issued prior to execution of the Contract."

Each bidder should receive identical bidding documents, free of charge, usually by posting a deposit, refundable when the documents are returned in good condition. The bidders should be allowed to retain the documents until after the contract is awarded or until the bidder is eliminated from the competition. The architect should determine how many sets of documents are reasonably needed by the bidders considering the type and size of work and the length of the bidding period. The bidders need sufficient sets of the bidding documents to obtain several sub bids on each subdivision of the work.

It is a faulty practice for bidders to separate the drawings and specifications of certain trades and issue only partial sets to subcontractors, as they would then not be aware of the interrelationships between their work and that of other related or adjoining trades. The bidders should also be issued the contract drawings and specifications of work to be performed concurrently on the same site by separate contractors or by the owner.

Some cities have public plan services where the bidding documents of projects being bid are on display for subcontractors and suppliers to examine them, prepare estimates, and submit proposals to the bidders. Where available, this is very beneficial to owners, as it provides greater exposure to sub bidders and a resulting diversity of sub bids.

It is false economy to tightly limit the number of bidding documents issued to each contractor. After bidding, all of the documents will be returned and can then be reissued to the awarded contractor, who will need them for construction. Any bidder who requests additional bidding documents is usually allowed to purchase them, but they still must be returned after the bidding period.

The architect should return the bidders' deposits promptly upon receipt of the returned documents, deducting only the amounts necessary to replace damaged or missing sheets of drawings or pages of specifications.

Bidding Period

The bidders require enough time to review and assimilate the great volume of documentary material, visit and examine the site, make all of their material and labor takeoffs, contact their sub bidders, coordinate their financial information, and prepare their proposals. They will also need time to work out the rationale of their construction sequences, procedures, and techniques and prepare a tentative proposed construction schedule. The architect should determine the amount of time reasonably needed by the bidders and set a date and time upon which bids will be due. Traditionally, and for practical reasons, bids should not be made due on a Monday or the day after or preceding any holiday. Afternoons are better than mornings. Bidding activities must compete with other procedures in the firm involving the same personnel. It is best to avoid having bids due on the same day as other important bid openings in the same community, as they will involve many of the same contractors, subcontractors, and suppliers.

If it becomes necessary to extend the bidding period, all bidders should be notified in writing at least 3 days before the original due date. In addition, an immediate telephone call to each bidder would be appreciated, as it provides additional notice.

Base Bid, Alternate Bids, and Unit Prices

Some owners need the flexibility of adding to or eliminating portions of the work from the base bid as a practical technique for meeting the project budget. The base bid will be the amount tendered to provide the basic specified project. Alternate bids are the sums to be added to or deducted from the base bid if certain specified work is added to or eliminated from the basic project.

Unit prices are quotations for adding or omitting specified units of certain materials, such as square feet of terrazzo flooring, cubic yards of mass excavating, or lineal feet of 4-inch-diameter vitreous clay sewer pipe. Unit prices are needed to facilitate pricing of change orders, should they occur.

Alternate and unit pricing create a certain amount of confusion in the contractor's office, particularly when sub bids are being evaluated and bid proposals compiled at the last minute before bids are due. It is best not to require any more alternate bids or unit prices than are absolutely necessary to serve the owner's legitimate purposes.

Bid Bond and Proposal Form

Part of the process of keeping conditions fair and uniform for all bidders is the usual requirement that bids be submitted in a standard format. A blank form of proposal should be included in the bid package and bidders should be instructed to submit bids filling in all blanks with typewriter or manually in ink. All bids should be submitted in an opaque sealed envelope marked on the outside with the name of the project and the bidder's name and address.

Also included in the sealed envelope, if required by the bidding documents, should be the bid security, which can be in the form of a cashier's check or a bid bond. The purpose of the security is to reimburse the owner for any losses suffered by the low bidder's refusal to enter into a contract on the terms stated in the bid and to post performance and payment bonds, if specified. Should the contractor default for any of these reasons, the bid security will be forfeited to the owner as liquidated damages, not as a penalty. The amount forfeited is limited to the difference between the low bid and the next responsible bid up to the face amount of the bid security.

The amount of the bid bond is usually a specified sum equal to approximately 10 percent of the contract budget. Sureties usually charge their principal, the contractor, nothing or a nominal annual service charge for bid bonds. However, inasmuch as they will have to furnish performance and payment bonds if their principal is low bidder, the credit and status checking of the contractor will be as thorough as if the construction bonds were being applied for. The bonding company will want to ascertain that their contractor would not become overextended or undercapitalized by obtaining new work. If a contractor is unable to obtain a bid bond, this is a good indication of that bidder's lack of financial capacity.

In the event that the bid bond becomes forfeited, the contractor will have to reimburse the surety for any funds paid out, as the contractor must indemnify the surety as a condition of obtaining the bid bond. Bid bonds should be written on AIA Document A310, Bid Bond.

A recent technological development is the submission of bids by telephonic facsimile transmission. If this is acceptable, it should be so stated in the bidding instructions and provision made for prior submission of bid bonds by mail or hand delivery.

Opening of Bids and Determining the Low Bidder

On private work it is up the owner to determine whether or not the bids are to be opened in the presence of the bidders. As a courtesy to the bidders and as a demonstration of the fairness and openness of the process, the bidders should be invited to witness the opening of the sealed bids. Prior to the opening of bids, the architect or owner should prepare a blank schedule on which to record and summarize the bids as opened. A copy of the filled-in schedule should be provided to each of the bidders whether present at the opening or not. It is not customary to make any determinations or announcements at the opening. The architect should merely thank the bidders and inform them that the owner will take the bids under advisement. It is understood that the architect or owner will contact the successful contractor after the bids have been analyzed to determine which is the lowest acceptable bid.

The low bid is the combination of base bid and alternate bids which will be actually contracted for. Thus it is possible for the contractor with the lowest base bid to lose the job if the accepted alternates are not also sufficiently low to comprise the low combination.

Negotiations leading to an executed contract should be held with the low bidder only. The low bidder may be asked to submit additional prices for adding to or deducting from the work of the project to make the contract sum fit the budget. But if the scope of the project is radically or materially changed, all bids should be rejected and the project re-bid. The owner has the right to reject all bids and to waive irregularities or informalities in any bid. It would be unethical for the owner to use these rights as a pretext to overcome the fairness of the bidding procedure, to favor, or to discriminate against any particular contractor.

Should the low bidder discover that an arithmetical or clerical error has resulted in an excessively low bid, the contractor should be allowed to withdraw the bid. In this case, the next lowest bid becomes the low bid. If the error is not arithmetical or clerical but one of judgment or misevaluation, the owner is not obligated to allow withdrawal of the bid. However, it is questionable judgment to have a contractor on the job who is facing a certain loss by proceeding with the contract. The contractor's incentive to recover the losses is in direct conflict with the owner's objective of obtaining a project of a specified quality. Many owners would find it repugnant and contrary to ethical business principles to force a contractor into an unconscionable contract even when it has the legal right to do so.

Award of Contract

The form of construction contract which the low bidder will be required to enter into is stated in the bidding instructions as AIA Document A101, Standard Form of Agreement Between Owner and Contractor (where the basis of payment is a stipulated sum). (See Appendix B.) If some other payment method or form of agreement is contemplated, it should be stated in the supplementary instructions to bidders.

In a *stipulated sum contract* the contractor guarantees the total cost of the project. If the contractor is efficient and the project runs smoothly, the profit will be as anticipated in estimating or even better. Conversely, when inefficiency and obstacles are encountered, there will be less profit and possibly out-of-pocket losses. In either case, the owner's position remains unchanged.

In *cost-plus-fee contracts*, the contractor will be allowed to recover all direct costs plus a fee for services. The most important features of a cost-plus contract are competent definitions of "costs to be reimbursed" and "costs not to be reimbursed." The second category is presumably included in the contractor's fee. The contractor's total remuneration for profit, overhead, and services is in the sum stated as the contractor's fee. It would be unethical and fraudulent of the contractor to secretly derive any fees or profit from any of the subcontractors or suppliers.

The contractor's fee in a cost-plus contract can be based on an agreed percentage of the reimbursed costs or can be an agreed fixed fee. Most cost-plus contracts are limited in amount by a stipulated guaranteed maximum price stated in the contract. Any change orders issued during the construction will serve to raise or lower the guaranteed maximum price accordingly. An excellent standard form of cost-plus-fee contract is AIA Document A111. (See Appendix C.)

3

The Preconstruction Jobsite Conference

Commencement of the Construction Phase

Effective and amicable communications are essential to the smooth-running construction process which culminates in a successful building project. Assume for the purpose of illustration that the contractor prequalification process is completed, the bidding procedures have been concluded, the low bidder has been determined, and the contract price has been established and is within the owner's budget. The owner and contractor have signed the agreement and have identified all of the other contract documents by signing them. So the physical execution of the project may now proceed.

What Is a Successful Building Project?

A construction project is a very complex organizational mechanism involving the disciplined acquisition, application, and coordination of such diverse resources as materials, equipment, trained personnel, and capital to carry out precisely the terms of a technical contract within the constraints of a rigorous time limit and an inviolable budget. So, to be considered successful, a construction project must result in faithful execution of the architect's design as expressed in the contract documents, within the owner's cost and time expectations, and must yield a reasonable profit to each of the contractors and suppliers. In most cases this is performed on a new building site utilizing an unfamiliar combination of subcontractors and suppliers that have never before worked together to produce a unique project from a heretofore unused and untested set of contract documents.

This sounds like a nearly impossible goal to achieve with an acceptable degree of precision and efficiency. However, the construction industry under these conditions routinely produces thousands of successful projects each year.

Preconstruction Jobsite Conference: A Communication Tool

In the interests of improved communications, mutual cooperation with contractors, and a heightened awareness of the contract requirements, many architects and engineers regularly schedule a conference at the jobsite before commencement of construction. The best time for this meeting is after the contract is signed, all required insurance is in effect, and the surety bond, if any, is issued, but before the owner has authorized the construction to proceed.

It would be best to announce in the specifications your intention to have this meeting, and most contractors will welcome it as an indication of impending cooperation and good will from the architect. The owner and contractor should both be invited to attend this initial site conference, and the contractor should be instructed to have the superintendent and representatives of major subcontractors and suppliers present.

In that this meeting will be the first construction phase visit for the architect, notes should be taken so that a written observation report can be promptly prepared and mailed to all participants and interested absent parties. It should cover all subjects discussed and decided. All questions or issues raised by attendees should be answered in the report.

The following items should be addressed at the preconstruction jobsite conference.

1. Errors, inconsistencies, or omissions in the contract documents which have been discovered by the contractor
2. Contractor's use of the site
3. Security provisions
4. Noise and dust control
5. Contractor's use of owner's water, power, telephone, and toilet facilities
6. Hours of operation
7. Contractor to receive property data from owner
8. Architect's explanation of dimensioning system
9. Contract documents

10. Architect's explanation of design intent
11. Specification substitutions
12. Ordering long lead items
13. Progress schedule
14. Submittal schedule
15. Shop drawings, samples, and product data
16. Weather delays
17. Jobsite record keeping
18. Communications
19. Architect's job visits
20. Construction methods
21. Safety procedures
22. Contractor's payment requests
23. Testing and inspections
24. Notice to proceed

Errors in the Contract Documents

The contractor should be asked if any errors, inconsistencies, or omissions in the contract documents have been noted by the contractor and should be reminded that as any such irregularities are discovered, the architect should be promptly notified. (AIA Document A201, Subparagraph 3.2.1)

Matters Pertaining to Use of the Site

Discussions are for the purpose of clarifying the information and requirements of the contract documents. If anything is decided which changes or extends the contract requirements, the architect should be alert to point this out to the owner and contractor so an appropriate change order can be prepared. It is poor practice to allow changes in the contract requirements to remain undiscussed, as it will usually result in misunderstanding and controversy. The owner will usually interpret silence as meaning there will be no extra cost, and the contractor will assume it means that the cost will be negotiated later. Naturally the roles and attitudes will be reversed when contract conditions are eased, which should result in a credit to the owner.

Some of the matters which should be discussed relate to the contractor's use of the site. During construction, the contractor will be in responsible charge of the site. Before construction starts, the contractor should inform the owner how the site will be organized as to general location of (1) materials storage, (2) debris storage, (3) chemical toilets, (4) jobsite office, (5) workers' parking,

(6) truck parking, (7) signs, and (8) temporary fences. The architect and owner are free to offer alternative suggestions for the contractor's consideration and to voice reasonable objections.

Security provisions and noise and dust control should be discussed, particularly in alteration and addition projects where the owner will continue to occupy some portion of the building or site. Consideration should be given to the effect of noise and dust on neighboring properties.

The conditions of the contractor's use of the owner's water, power, telephone, and toilet facilities should be discussed.

Hours of operation on the site should be discussed and reasonable limitations decided upon. If the owner was aware of the necessity of unusually restrictive working hours, this should have been specified in the supplementary conditions to enable the contractor to price the job accordingly.

The owner should provide the contractor with copies of the boundary survey, topographic survey, legal description of the property, and reports of the foundation investigation. The datum points of the land survey should be identified to the contractor. The horizontal and vertical dimensioning rationale of the contract drawings should be discussed and explained by the architect if deemed necessary by the architect or contractor.

Contract Documents

The architect should make certain that the contractor has sufficient copies of all of the contract documents so that all of the subcontractors can know the full extent of their contracted obligations and their relationships with related or adjoining trades. The owner is obligated by the AIA General Conditions (Subparagraph 2.2.5) to furnish, without cost to the contractor, such copies of the drawings and project manuals as are reasonably necessary for the execution of the work. The contractor should be reminded that a complete set of the initial drawings, specifications, and addenda should always be kept in good condition at the jobsite as well as a complete set of all change orders, construction change directives, and all other modifications. The documents should be marked currently to serve as a record of changes and selections made during construction. In addition, the contractor should maintain at the site a set of all approved shop drawings, product data, and samples. (A201, 3.11.1)

Design Intent

The architect should take this opportunity to briefly explain the design concept and objectives to the builders present. This is the time to point out and discuss the special details and features of significance and identify what is important. Models, perspective renderings, and other design presentation drawings if available will help illustrate the design intent.

Specification Substitutions

Most specifications provide that all contractor-initiated substitutions be proposed during the bidding period so that all bidders can be on an equal footing. However, sometimes that proves to be somewhat idealistic if some normally available specified item is just not obtainable. The architect should suggest to the contractor that purchase orders be placed with all subcontractors and suppliers at once so that unavailable specified items become quickly known. Also all long lead orders should be placed immediately to assure that the job will not be delayed later. The specification provision on substitutions and application of the phrases "or equal" or "equivalent" should be explained. Usually they mean that the proposed alternate item should be comparable in function, capacity, quality, and appearance and approved by the architect prior to its utilization.

Progress Schedules

The construction progress schedule required by Paragraph 3.10 of the AIA General Conditions should already have been submitted by the contractor and should now be available for discussion. If any of the subcontractors present have any doubt about the practicality of the time schedule and their own ability to comply, they should now voice such reservations.

The submittal schedule should also be discussed and the contractors advised to commence production of shop drawings in time to meet the schedule. All product data and samples should be immediately prepared or accumulated, organized, and marked for submittal on time.

In discussing time scheduling, it would be appropriate to review the contract documents in respect to allowable extensions of time for justifiable delay such as that caused by inclement weather and other events that cannot be anticipated or controlled. The AIA General Conditions, Subparagraphs 8.3.1 and 4.3.8.2, provide that the only justifiable adverse weather delay is when "weather conditions were abnormal for the period of time...." The architect's proposed administrative application of the contract for contractor's time extension requests should be discussed to avoid later arguments.

Record Keeping on the Jobsite

Most general contractors require their job superintendent to maintain a daily log on the jobsite and to record all relevant information on a current basis. The superintendent's log should be preserved as a permanent chronological record of all significant events occurring on the jobsite. In the event that the contractor on your project does not usually keep a daily log, the practice should be suggested and urged, although it cannot be absolutely required unless previously specified. (See Chap. 13, Role of the Construction Superintendent.)

Communications

Although the communication system among the parties during the construction period is defined in the AIA General Conditions, it is advisable to review the requirements so all may understand and abide by them in practice.

All communications between the owner and contractor should be channeled through the architect.

All communications by and with the architect's consultants should be through the architect.

All communications to or from the subcontractors and suppliers should be through the contractor.

All communications with separate contractors should be through the owner. (A201, 4.2.4)

The superintendent on the jobsite is a representative of the contractor, and communications given to the superintendent are as binding as if given to the contractor. (A201, 3.9.1)

All important communications should be in writing or if given orally should be confirmed in writing.

Architect's Job Visits

The architect's intentions should be expressed for the benefit of the contractor as to the scheduling of periodic jobsite visits. Some architects make it a practice to visit the site on a regular weekly, biweekly, or monthly basis. Others will plan to visit only once for each contractor's payment request or upon the completion of certain agreed stages of the work. The frequency will be based on the type and magnitude of the project, the architect's professional judgment, and the agreement between owner and architect. The contractor or superintendent should be present for all site visitations to explain conditions and operations to the architect and to receive pertinent instructions. The subcontractors who have questions or problems might plan to be present for relevant discussion and decisions.

Promptly after each site visit the architect should prepare and issue a written observation report to the owner with copies to the contractor and all other interested parties. The report should include the date, time, duration, weather conditions, persons present, work now being accomplished, percentage of work completed by trade, work progress compared to schedule, work scheduled before next visit, questions raised by contractor or owner, determinations made by the architect, and any questions or actions which remain pending for appropriate later attention. (See Chap. 6, Site Observation and Administration of Construction.)

Construction Methods and Safety Procedures

The architect must be careful not to exceed the authority bestowed by the owner-architect agreement or the contract documents. It is the contractor's sole prerogative to determine, control, and be responsible for the construction means, methods, techniques, sequences, and procedures and for coordinating the work. (A201, 3.3.1) The architect is specifically excluded from authority in these matters. (A201, 4.2.3 and 4.2.7) The architect's viewing of the work during its execution is for the purpose of determining in general if the work is being performed in a manner indicating that the work, when completed, will be in accordance with the contract documents. (A201, 4.2.2) The architect's opinion on these matters should be expressed in the periodic written observation reports.

Safety precautions and accident prevention programs on the site are the responsibility of the contractor. (A201, Article 10) The superintendent is the contractor's representative with the specific duty of carrying out all programs for personal safety and the protection of property unless the contractor designates some other person in writing to the owner and architect. (A201, 10.2.6)

Contractor's Requests for Payment

The contractor should be reminded that periodic applications for payments should be only for the percentage of work which is in place prior to or on the date of the architect's site verification. The architect cannot authorize payment of funds for work not actually observed to be in existence. Payments for the value of work in progress in fabricators' shops or stored off site cannot be authorized by the architect unless the owner and contractor have previously agreed otherwise in writing. The architect can allow the value of materials or equipment suitably stored on the site even though not yet incorporated into the work. (A201, 9.3.2)

The contractor and architect should agree on a procedure so the architect does not unexpectedly receive payment requests with the contractor's expectation of an immediate site visit and approval. The payment requests and architect's site visits could be entered in the contractor's construction schedule or submittal schedule.

The subcontractors present could be reminded that the architect, if requested, is authorized to inform them of the status of payments to the contractor in respect to the work of the subcontractors. (A201, 9.6.3)

Testing and Inspections

The contractor is responsible for paying for and making all necessary arrangements for specified materials testing and inspections, utilizing independent testing laboratories or entities acceptable to the owner. Any tests or inspection requirements imposed after bidding will be paid for by the owner. (A201, 13.5.1) The contractor should reveal the identity of the testing agencies for the owner's consideration.

A very high percentage of construction defects are associated with roofing installation. Accordingly, many owners deem it advisable to employ a separate independent roofing inspector to observe the roofing work continuously during its installation. If this is the owner's intention, the contractor should be informed so that appropriate scheduling can be provided.

Notice to Proceed

Construction on the jobsite should not "jump the gun" by commencing before all required insurance is activated, surety bond issued, and mortgage liens recorded. Should this happen, bonds and guarantees will have to be arranged for by the owner to satisfy the mortgage lenders, title guarantee companies, and surety. The events and operations expected to be covered by insurance or bonds would not have been covered. Therefore, the AIA General Conditions contains a procedure that, if followed, will obviate these serious problems. The contractor is not to start any work whatsoever on the site prior to the receipt of a written notice to proceed given by the owner. The architect, if authorized by the owner, could issue the notice to proceed. In the event that, for whatever reason, the contractor has not received a written notice to proceed, the contractor is required to give a written notice to the owner not less than 5 days before commencing work. (8.2.2)

Private Meeting

An additional meeting is needed among architect, owner, and contractor to discuss other contractual matters which are of no direct concern to the subcontractors and suppliers. This meeting could be held at the time of signing of the contract documents or at the beginning or end of the preconstruction jobsite conference. Various matters need to be discussed in the interest of avoiding future misunderstandings and mutual distrust.

The following items should be addressed at the private meeting.

1. Owner's financial arrangements
2. Unit prices and allowances
3. Contractor's overhead and profit
4. Owner's separate contractors
5. Preconstruction submittals
6. Owner's insurance
7. Contractor's insurance
8. Liquidated damages
9. Architect's decisions

Owner's Financial Capability

The contractor has the right prior to signing the agreement and from time to time during the construction to request the owner to furnish promptly reasonable evidence that adequate financial arrangements have been made to fulfill the owner's obligations under the contract. (A201, 2.2.1) Should the owner fail to furnish promptly the requested reasonable evidence, the contractor may exercise its option to refrain from executing the agreement or commencing the work or to stop the work and terminate the contract. (A201, 14.1.1.5) (See Chap. 15, Termination of the Construction Contract.)

Unit Prices and Allowances

The contractor and owner should be reminded that any unit prices quoted in the bid proposal or later negotiated before the contract was signed are subject to change under certain circumstances. If the quantities originally contemplated are so changed by a change order or construction change directive that the original unit prices become substantially inequitable to owner or contractor, the unit prices are equitably adjusted. (A201, 7.1.4) Such would be the case if too few units were actually required in which case the contractor would be undercompensated. If there were an exceptionally large number of units, it would be to the disadvantage of the owner. If the owner and contractor cannot agree on new unit prices, the architect will have to decide the matter, subject to appeal in arbitration.

Contractor's invoices for allowance items should be prepared using the general principles of Paragraph 3.8, AIA Document A201. Arguments and misunderstandings will be alleviated if both parties are aware of these provisions for the billing of allowances. The owner should be reminded that selections of materials, equipment, and vendors for allowance items should be presented promptly to the contractor to avoid being the cause of construction delay. All items for owner's selection should be entered in the contractor's construction progress schedule or submittal schedule. If the architect is to make these selections for the owner, then the architect should conform to the schedule.

Contractor's Overhead and Profit

According to Subparagraph 7.3.6 of the AIA General Conditions, the contractor is entitled to add a reasonable amount for overhead and profit when submitting prices for extra work. Each of the subcontractors will include their overhead and profit in quotations to the contractor for changes in their contracts. The architect is charged with determining what is reasonable. Future misunderstandings could be minimized if the contractor's expectations and the architect's opinions in this matter were discussed with the owner. The owner should realize that subcontractors normally use a higher markup than do general contractors. This discussion would not be necessary if the contractor's and subcontractors' overhead and profit percentages were specified by the architect or required to be submitted by the contractor as part of the bidding procedure.

Separate Contractors

It is the owner's prerogative under the contract to engage separate contractors to perform other parts of the work. The contractor is obligated to cooperate with the owner and separate contractors. It is the owner's responsibility to coordinate the separate contractors with the work of the contractor. (A201, Article 6) The owner should disclose to the contractor the likelihood and extent of separate contractors being on the premises during the work of the contractor so that related problems and costs may be anticipated.

Preconstruction Submittals

After the contract has been awarded and before any work is commenced, the contractor should promptly submit to the owner through the architect all specified submittals, including the following documents required by the AIA General Conditions:

- List of subcontractors and suppliers proposed for each principal portion of the work. The architect should respond in writing if the owner or architect, after due investigation, has reasonable objection to any proposed person or entity. Failure to promptly respond constitutes notice of no reasonable objection. (5.2.1) Should a subcontractor or supplier be eliminated, the contractor is required to submit an alternate not objectionable to the owner and architect. The contract sum must be adjusted, up or down, to account for any difference in subcontract bids. (5.2.3)

- Certificates of all required insurance. (11.1.3) The architect should refrain from offering any opinions as to the adequacy, terms, or suitability of insurance certificates or the underlying insurance policies. These are matters which the owner should take up with insurance advisors and legal counsel.

- Surety bond. Bonds covering faithful performance of the contract and payment for labor and materials, each in the full amount of the contract, if required by the owner. (11.4) If the owner required the bond before bidding, the contract bid price will include the bond premium. If the bond requirement was imposed by the owner after bidding, the premium can be billed as an extra to the contract. The owner should submit the bond to its insurance advisor or legal counsel for review.

- Schedule of values. This is a detailed cost breakdown allocating values to each trade and division of the work to be used as a basis for contractor's payment requests. The contractor's overhead and profit may appear as a segregated line item or may be proportionally distributed among each of the work items. This should be submitted by the contractor to the architect for review before the first application for payment. (9.2 and 9.3)

- Construction progress schedule, showing all construction operations and completion within the time limits of the contract. It should be revised as necessary during construction to reflect changes in conditions and should be kept current. The schedule and updated versions are to be submitted to the owner and architect for information only, not for their approval. (3.10.1)

- Submittal schedule. This is submitted for the architect's approval and should be in synchronization with the construction progress schedule. It will show when all submittals are to be forthcoming from the contractor and when the architect is expected to return them after reviewing. (3.10.2)

Owner's Insurance

The owner, if it wishes the coverage, must carry its own liability insurance. (A201, 11.2.1) The owner is required to carry property insurance to cover the perils of fire and extended coverage and physical loss or damage, boiler and machinery insurance, and loss of use insurance, including the interests of the owner, contractor, subcontractors, and sub-subcontractors in the work. The owner is required by the contract to furnish a copy of all required insurance policies to the contractor before any losses occur. Therefore, it must be done prior to start of construction. (A201, 11.3) The owner should be advised to review the entirety of Article 11, Insurance and Bonds, of AIA Document A201 with its insurance advisor or legal counsel. (See Chap. 5, Construction Insurance.)

Liquidated Damages

If the contract contains a liquidated damages provision, the contractor and owner will benefit from an open discussion of the matter. The length of time allocated for construction will in most cases have been established or accepted by the contractor, and this could usually be considered as realistic, if not too optimistic. A prudent contractor will apply for all justifiable time extensions as the construction progresses to avoid the possibility of having to pay any liquidated damages to the owner. Conversely, the owner will often take a hard line on the granting of time extensions. The architect should make it clear to the parties that all decisions on this and other matters will be fair to both parties.

Architect's Decisions

In the event of even a minor dispute between owner and contractor during these initial conferences, the architect must make the final decision as provided in Paragraph 4.3 of the AIA General Conditions. The architect can give the parties a feeling of security in the architect's hands if all such decisions and contract interpretations are handled firmly, fairly, and skillfully. To start with, both sides must always be given the opportunity to fully express their positions. The architect must set aside all perceptions of pressure from either party and make all decisions in accordance with the written provisions of the contract. All interpretations and decisions must be fair, just, and equitable, siding with neither party. If the disagreement is based on ambiguity or errors in the contract documents produced by the architect, the decision is that much more difficult. The faulty documents must usually be construed against the owner in favor of the contractor. The economic consequences of the architectural or engineering error must be taken up separately between the architect and client.

If improved communications among architect, owner, and contractor can be promoted by use of the preconstruction jobsite conference, it will be well worth the time and trouble.

4

Consultants and Advisors

Liability for Mistakes of Outside Consultants

There is no question that architects as prime design contractors bear the legal responsibility for professional malpractices committed by their hired engineers and other technical consultants. Although we cannot completely eliminate this burden, we can try to conduct our practices in a manner which will at least minimize our exposure to this contingent liability.

Individually and as a profession, we have spent decades trying to convince prospective clients that they should look to the architect as "captain of the ship" in determining the design and administering the construction on the site. Indeed, we have persuaded them that the architectural profession should decide and fashion all of the built environment. It logically follows, then, that the legal consequence of centralization of design prerogative is that clients need look no further than their architects for affixing responsibility for design errors and omissions.

We have been made increasingly and painfully aware that we can be held financially responsible for our own professional shortcomings. One way to control, but probably not eliminate, our exposure to risk of malpractice claims is to conduct our practices as carefully, diligently, and skillfully as we are able, thereby limiting the circumstances for error.

Limiting Exposure to Liability

The use of adroitly worded professional service contracts such as those provided by the American Institute of Architects is the first step in limiting liability exposure. In addition, it is logical to avoid situations which are conducive to professional negligence. The objective is to create a positive climate in which a higher quality of professional output is likely, and accordingly there should be less possibility for error. The most elementary possibilities for consideration are:

- Adequate compensation should be required for all professional assignments. If the fee is not sufficient to cover the time necessary to perform all of the contracted services competently and completely, the chances of making mistakes are greatly increased.

- All assignments should be properly analyzed, designed, and produced. All procedures and work product should be carefully monitored and checked. Slighting any of the required services on account of limitation or depletion of available fee is not a legally or ethically acceptable excuse for incomplete or hastily done work.

- Assignments should not be accepted if they are beyond the technological expertise of the available personnel. Various firms have specialized in particular building types, thereby raising the required standards for anyone performing those types of work. Misleading portrayals of a firm's experience or abilities should be avoided in making representations to prospective clients.

- Only competent personnel should be engaged. Only skilled and qualified persons should be utilized on each assignment, and they should be appropriately supervised, commensurate with their experience and ability. All assignments carried out by interns and recent graduates should be closely supervised and checked by fully qualified persons.

- All assignments should be approached skillfully and competently, exercising judgment and taste to the standard of care of architects practicing in the same community. In order to know what the standard is, it is necessary to pursue continuing education as both teacher and student, read the professional press, associate with other architects, and observe other architects' work product as well as their work. The standard of care requires that all professional activity must be pursued with due diligence and reasonable skill.

- Novel and adventurous design solutions should be undertaken only after frank and open disclosure to the client of all the attendant risks and possible disadvantages as well as the advantages. The client's informed approval should be obtained in writing. Disclosures should include the intended specification of materials and equipment which have undergone only limited field experience.

- All outside consultants should be carefully selected to assure that they possess the requisite technical competence and appropriate experience.

Limiting Liability for Consultants' Shortcomings

No matter how perfectly we are able to raise our own professional level of performance, being only human, we can still make mistakes. Added to this there still remains the risk of liability for errors made by our consultants. This underscores the necessity for cautious and discriminating choice of outside consultants. The search for competent engineers and other consultants who are suitable and acceptable as design collaborators and technicians becomes a very personal problem. Mutual trust and respect must ever be present in the relationship. Working with the same expert advisors over years and numerous projects will gradually result in the development of mutually accepted understandings and safe procedures.

Although most contracts between architects and their consultants consist merely of a scanty memo or an oral discussion, there appears to be sufficient mutual understanding between the parties to get them through most of the exigencies of the relationship. A friendly give and take attitude and professional courtesy will help maintain a climate of civility, fairness, and equity between the parties.

When a minor misunderstanding or lapse in communication occurs, there is little or no argument over the resultant redesign or redrawing required or fixing of blame. Even when larger sums of money are involved, polite negotiation will usually settle the matter based on past understandings, mutually accepted operating principles, and the expectation of a continuing relationship.

However, in the event of sizable or catastrophic errors or omissions which involve large-scale economic liability, the controversy between architect and consultant will no longer be a matter to be decided quietly between friendly and respectful colleagues. It will instead be decided by insurance carriers and by judges or arbitrators after lengthy and often heated dispute involving third parties. In this unfortunate situation the consultant relationship would have been more definitely ascertained if it had been exactly delineated, as it would be in a complete written contract.

The American Institute of Architects has over the years developed a series of standard form contracts which can be used to particularize the agreements between architects and their consultants. The AIA agreements cover the appropriate subjects peculiar to the architect-consultant relationship and establish the mutual rights and responsibilities of the parties. AIA architect-consultant agreements are in harmony with the AIA owner-architect agreements and the AIA General Conditions which is part of the usual construction contract. All of the AIA standard form agreements have uniform terminology and procedures and meshing arbitration clauses.

The most widely used of the AIA architect-consultant contracts is Document C141, Standard Form of Agreement Between Architect and

Consultant, 1987 Edition. This newly revised agreement is suitable for use when the prime owner-architect agreement is AIA Document B141, 1987 Edition. The AIA publishes three other variations of the architect-consultant agreement to accommodate situations where other versions of the prime owner-architect agreement are used.

The use of a written contract with consultants will not necessarily minimize or eliminate liability but will at least apportion unavoidable liability fairly so that the parties will generally be liable only for their own errors and omissions. Although we must answer to our clients for our consultants' shortcomings, we have legal recourse to our consultants for indemnity. This recourse is only as effective as the indemnitor's financial ability to fund it. This can be overcome if consultants carry professional liability insurance.

Owners' versus Architects' Consultants and Advisors

The principal area for minimization and possibly virtual elimination of contingent liability for certain consultants' malpractice is in prevailing upon the owner to engage some of the consultants and advisors. Those who provide information about the owner's property or advice to the owner, as contrasted to those who assist the architect in design, should be employed directly by the client. This includes land surveyors, programmers, geotechnical consultants, cost estimators, financial advisors, real estate feasibility advisors, marketing experts, insurance advisors, accountants, economists, lawyers, and construction schedulers.

Those consultants who actually participate in the design process jointly with the architect should be engaged by the architect. They should be under the direct control and direction of the architect. This includes primarily the normal engineering disciplines such as civil, structural, electrical, and mechanical engineers. In addition, landscape architects, graphic and interior designers, kitchen consultants, construction specifiers, and all others who participate in the architect's design and production of the contract documents should be hired by the architect. It is the architect's responsibility to coordinate the work of the consultants who participate in the design. All of the consultants' construction drawings and specifications must be coordination-checked to make certain that the work of each discipline is properly interfaced, mutually compatible, and not in physical conflict.

Such consultants as vertical transportation, commercial kitchen designers, acoustical engineers, hazardous substances consultants, inspectors, and materials testing laboratories, if engaged primarily in furnishing information solely on existing conditions, design criteria, or construction testing, should be employed by the owner. If these specialized consultants are to participate in the design function, they could be hired by the architect.

Consultants' work should be properly identified as to authorship by use of the usual title block credit. In the event of error in consultant work it is important that it be easily distinguishable from the architect's work or that of other consultants. If this system of assigning consultants is adopted, the architect can at least minimize if not avoid responsibility for mistakes made by the owner's advisors and information providers.

Owners often do not wish to get involved in the arcane particulars of selecting, negotiating, and hiring of technical consultants and will request the architect to administer these details. In such cases the architect should hire these consultants in the owner's name and have the owner sign the agreements. Make certain that the owner receives copies of all agreements and correspondence to and from consultants as well as copies of all consultants' reports and other work product. Instruct all owner's consultants to direct all invoices to their client, the owner.

If any portion of the work product of the owner's consultants is to be included in the contract documents produced by the architect, it should be presented with full authorship credit. No misleading impression should be given that it is part of the architect's work product.

5

Construction Insurance

Financial Responsibility for Accidental Losses

Unfortunate accidental occurrences causing severe property damage, personal injury, or death on a construction site could easily bring economic ruin to those who are financially responsible. It is customary to fund this awesome liability by means of insurance. Owners and contractors who enter into construction contracts owe each other the mutual obligation of providing insurance to cover certain specified risks.

Insurance is an extremely important element of the construction contract, so it is not surprising that over 10 percent of the text of the AIA General Conditions is devoted to this complex and inscrutable subject.

AIA General Conditions

The AIA General Conditions of the Contract for Construction, Document A201, was extensively revised in 1987 (Fourteenth Edition). The insurance portions were carefully considered, written, and edited by construction industry legal and insurance experts in consultation with architects outstanding in the field of construction administration and documentation. Architects generally are not expected to be insurance experts but need to know how to cope with the insurance aspects of construction contracts and their administration.

The AIA General Conditions specifies the insurance requirements in broad general terms, while the Supplementary Conditions written by the architect must specify the specific insurance coverage required for the project, the interests to be insured, the policy limits, the perils to be insured, the insurance contract term, and the deductible amount.

It is a very risky practice for architects to provide insurance advice to their clients. Many professional liability insurance policies carried by architects specifically exclude coverage for the furnishing of insurance advice. The architect should respectfully but firmly decline to answer any insurance questions. Should an owner rely on an architect's erroneous insurance or surety advice to its detriment, the architect would be likely to be held financially liable for the resultant damages.

Owner's Instructions Regarding Insurance and Bonds

The AIA Owner-Architect Agreement, Document B141, also revised in 1987, provides in Paragraph 4.8 that the owner will furnish all legal, accounting, and insurance services as may be necessary at any time for the project. Therefore, the architect should obtain the insurance requirements directly from the owner. Owners are not usually insurance experts either, so they will have to confer with their own legal and insurance advisors. There is a convenient form devised by the AIA entitled Owner's Instructions Regarding the Construction Contract, Insurance and Bonds, and Bidding Procedures, Document G612, 1987 Edition, which architects can present to their clients. It is in the format of a nine-page questionnaire in three parts, A, B, and C. Part B, Owner's Instructions for Insurance and Bonds, pages 4 through 7, can be used by the owner's insurance advisor to instruct the architect in respect to the owner's insurance and bond requirements. The architect can then rely on these instructions when writing the insurance specification in the Supplementary Conditions.

Certificates of Insurance

Evidence of insurance specified to be carried by owner and contractor must be provided as proof of its existence and its terms and conditions. Certificates of insurance are commonly issued free of charge by insurance carriers, agents, and brokers when requested by their insureds. Certificates of the contractor's insurance should be addressed to the owner while certificates of the owner's insurance should be addressed to the contractor. In the interest of promoting uniformity in construction industry documentation and administration, the AIA has issued a standard form of Certificate of Insurance, Document G705, which many construction insurers have adopted. This document may soon drop out of common use as a new insurance industry form is taking its place and is now recommended by the AIA. The Agency Company Organization for Research and Development issues the new form, designated as ACORD 25-S (3/88). One of the most important aspects of an insurance certificate is the statement that the policies will not be canceled or allowed to expire unless 30 days' written notice has been given to the addressee of the certificate.

According to the AIA General Conditions, Subparagraph 4.2.4, all communications between owner and contractor should be through the architect. Consequently, the insurance certificates from each party will flow through the architect's administration to the opposite party. When the architect transmits insurance certificates or surety bonds, the covering letter should merely inventory the enclosures but should not comment on the sufficiency of the carrier or surety or the adequacy or conditions of the coverage. The architect should advise the client to seek legal or insurance advice in appraising the insurance coverages underlying the certificates.

All specified insurance and bonds must be in force before any construction is undertaken at the jobsite. Insurance companies and sureties are reluctant to issue insurance coverage or bonds once construction operations are under way.

6

Site Observation and Administration of Construction

Construction Observation: How Much Is Enough?

The owners of a project under construction always seem to find time, even if it's not convenient, to make frequent visits to their construction site. Seeing their visions materialize is currently the most exhilarating and fascinating event in their lives. They do not always understand why their architect appears to be less absorbed in the physical evolvement of their undertaking than they are. The usual reason for this common misunderstanding is that their architect hasn't made it clear what they should expect during the construction period. Perhaps they would be more understanding if they were fully aware of all the behind-the-scenes activities of the architect while the construction progresses in the field.

Residence clients generally are more subjective and emotional than clients for commercial, industrial, or institutional projects. However, all clients are similar in at least one respect: their construction undertakings are very important to them. Their projects represent major commitments of funds, proportional to each client's economic situation. All clients need to be cultivated, encouraged, respected, and kept informed.

Architectural Service Agreements

The standard architectural services contract describes the basic services to be performed by the architect throughout each of the phases of professional service. The most recently revised contract is AIA Document B141, Owner-Architect Agreement, Fourteenth Edition, 1987. (See Appendix A.) This agreement is harmonious with the AIA General Conditions, which is a part of the construction contract.

Also available from the AIA are three additional variations of architectural services agreements: AIA Document B151, Abbreviated Owner-Architect Agreement, which can be used on projects of limited scope; AIA Document B161, Standard Form of Agreement Between Owner and Architect for Designated Services, which must be used with its companion AIA Document B162, Scope of Designated Services; and AIA Document B181, Standard Form of Agreement Between Owner and Architect for Housing Services with Cost Estimating Services Provided by Owner. All three of these agreements are also in congruity with the AIA General Conditions.

Unless otherwise indicated, paragraph numbers given parenthetically in this chapter refer specifically to AIA Document B141, although the commentary applies equally to architectural services provided under any of the four contract variations.

Construction Phase

According to the agreement (2.6.1) the construction phase commences with the award of the construction contract. Whether the architect is being paid on the basis of a lump-sum fee or a percentage of the cost of construction, approximately 80 to 85 percent of the total architectural fee will have been expended for all of the services performed prior to start of construction. This leaves approximately 15 to 20 percent of the fee available to cover construction phase services.

Even with hourly rate contracts, knowledgeable owners are likely to become disgruntled if fee billings during the construction phase appreciably exceed 15 to 20 percent of the total architectural fee. Architectural practices are usually conducted in a rational businesslike manner and with anticipation of a reasonable profit. The normal expectation is that preconstruction phase services will not consume more than their allotted proportion of the fee and that the 15 to 20 percent of gross fee reserved for construction phase services will be available. All too often the early phases of schematic design and design development consume more time than is allocated. The construction documents phase is not only complicated but is voluminous and not highly conducive to shortcuts or other timesaving methods. The bidding or negotiation phase will sometimes consume considerably more time than was expected, particularly when the lowest bid is in excess of the owner's budget. In this case, if a fixed limit of construction cost has been agreed upon, the architect at its own expense will have to modify the construction documents as required to comply with the fixed limit. (5.2.5) This will also entail additional dealings with the owner to determine acceptable economic alternatives and with contractors to obtain the cost differences and to finalize the construction agreement.

The honorable architect will honestly and sincerely intend to do all that is required by the contract during the final phase even if it means only breaking even or, worse, suffering an economic loss. The construction phase ends when the architect issues the final certificate for payment or 60 days after the date of substantial completion, whichever occurs first. (2.6.1)

The construction phase therefore could last up to 2 months longer than expected. The normal process of construction of an uncomplicated residence when running smoothly would take a minimum of 5 to 7 months and with some complications could require 10 to 12 months. Difficult or complex projects or those in distress will take longer. A hospital estimated to require 18 months for construction might unexpectedly take 24 to 30 months or more. A simple 5-month warehouse project might run an unanticipated 7 or 10 months.

The difficulty in estimating the actual length of the construction time complicates the process of realistically budgeting the architectural services fee during the administrative period.

Construction Phase Services

The services which the architect must provide during the construction phase are varied and numerous. The architect must always be available for advice and consultation with the owner. (2.6.4) The contract does not impose any limitation on the amount of time which might be required for this sensitive and significant duty. Some clients require considerable personal attention, explanation, and reassurance during the construction period. This time-consuming activity can seldom be completely delegated to less experienced members of the staff.

Visiting the construction site, as one of the architect's most conspicuous activities, has a great potential for causing misunderstanding with clients. According to the architectural contract, the architect must visit the site "at intervals appropriate to the stage of construction...." (2.6.5) This means that the architect must exercise professional judgment in determining frequency and timing of site visits. The architect should be present to observe work or events of major impact on the structural or design integrity of the final result. Some parts of the work need to be examined during their execution and before they are covered by subsequent operations while other components need only to be observed upon their completion. The contract further explains that the site visit is for the architect "to become generally familiar with the progress and quality of the Work completed and to determine in general if the Work is being performed in a manner indicating that the Work when completed will be in accordance with the Contract Documents." The architect is required to keep the owner informed of the progress and quality of the work. (2.6.5)

Keeping the owner informed of construction progress and quality is best accomplished by a system of regularly issued written reports. This also serves to keep the client aware of the extent of services being performed on its behalf by the architect. It will also impart to the owner the sense that the project is being properly monitored and is not out of control.

The agreement also says that the architect will "endeavor to guard the owner against defects and deficiencies in the Work." This is not a guarantee or assurance by the architect but is a promise to exercise skillful and informed observation of the contractor's work with the expectation of detecting and preventing noncompliance with requirements of the contract documents.

The owner and contractor are required by their construction agreement to channel all of their communications to each other through the architect. (General Conditions of the Contract for Construction, Fourteenth Edition, AIA Document A201, 1987, Subparagraph 4.2.4) The administrative burden generated by this provision consumes time throughout the construction period.

All payment applications made by the contractor must be reviewed, correlated with construction progress, and certified by the architect. (2.6.9) No payment certification should be issued unless based upon a concurrent site observation visit.

The architect's certificate for payment is a representation to the owner that the architect has personally conducted on-site observations, that the work has actually progressed to the point indicated, and that the work is in accordance with requirements of the contract documents, to the best of the architect's knowledge, information, and belief. (2.6.10)

During construction, the architect is also obligated to receive, review, and act upon the contractor's submittals of specified shop drawings, samples, and product data. (2.6.12) This necessitates the operation of a methodical record-keeping system to keep track of the status of all submittals received from the contractor, indicating the dates on which they were received, referred to consultants, or returned to the contractor for correction, rejected, or approved. A standard form published for this purpose is AIA Document G712, Shop Drawing and Sample Record. The contract documents should be carefully reviewed to make certain that all specified submittals have been received from the contractor.

The architect must also receive and act upon construction and submittal schedules, certificates of required insurance, and warranties tendered by the contractor. When sending along the contractor's insurance certificates and warranties to the owner, the architect should avoid giving any opinions as to their adequacy. These would be considered technical insurance and legal matters beyond the purview of normal architectural competence. Should the owner rely upon erroneous opinions to its detriment, the architect would have little if any legal defense available. If advice on these subjects is needed, the owner should be advised to consult with its own insurance or legal counsel.

Construction changes required by the owner or contractor or caused by unexpected conditions will result in change orders or construction change directives which must be prepared by and further administered by the architect. (2.6.13) (See Chap. 10, Change Orders.)

All matters in contention between the owner and contractor are to be submitted to the architect for consideration, interpretation, and decision. (2.6.15, 2.6.18, and 2.6.19) All interpretations should be based on careful study of the contract documents and consideration of all relevant factors, and the decision should be in writing. (2.6.16) (See Chap. 17, Resolution of Construction Disputes.)

Considering the wide range of time-consuming duties contractually assumed by the architect to be performed during the construction period it is usually difficult to keep the time expenditure within the fee allocated to this phase. None of these activities can be safely slighted, least of all the time which must be spent at the construction site. The architect's exhaustion of the fee reserve is not a legally or ethically acceptable excuse for failure to perform the contracted duties completely and competently.

Budgeting the Fee for Construction Phase Services

The fee available for construction phase services should be budgeted as realistically as possible, by predicting the time needed each week to perform all of the known duties and activities which have been contracted.

When the fee is determined as a percentage of construction cost, projects of lesser cost will not usually generate sufficient fee to cover all of the services promised in the AIA Owner-Architect Agreement. Architects in such cases have only two options: increase the fee or eliminate some of the services. Either option requires concurrence of the client and must be discussed and agreed upon when the contract is originally negotiated. It is too late to address these matters months later during the construction period.

Budgeting the fee is primarily a function of the length of construction time. If the construction becomes unpredictably protracted, the architectural time budget will be irretrievably compromised. Partial economic relief is offered by the agreement in Subparagraph 11.5.1 in which a time period (in months) for performance of basic services is to be inserted. Any services provided after expiration of the agreed time span would be compensated on the same basis as for additional services. (10.3.3 and 11.3.2) The value of this provision will be realized only when the time period inserted proves to be realistic, not so short as to cause client resistance or so long as to be ineffective. Even with this possibility of billing for services provided during prolongation of construction time, some clients will not take kindly to additional architectural cost. The architect must then make a business decision which could risk the continuing goodwill of the client.

Construction Observation

The architect's site visits should be regularly scheduled or at least announced in advance so the contractor is represented at the site as well as the owner if desired. The architect should keep notes of visual observations, relevant comments offered, and oral directives given by any of the parties present.

The architectural agreement indicates that the purpose of the architect's site visit is to become "generally familiar" with the progress and quality of the work and to determine if the work is being done in a manner which will yield results consistent with the contract documents. The agreement further explains that the architect is not required to make exhaustive or continuous on-site inspections. The architect is required, however, to keep the owner informed of the progress and quality of the work. (2.6.5) Most architects discharge this continuing obligation by sending the owner a written report of each site visit with a copy sent to the contractor. The report should be a complete record of the proceedings at the architect's jobsite visit and should include

1. Date
2. Time
3. Duration
4. Weather conditions
5. Persons present
6. Percentage of work completed by trade
7. Work progress compared to schedule
8. Work now being accomplished
9. Work scheduled before next visit
10. Questions raised by contractor or owner
11. Determinations made by the architect
12. Any questions or actions which remain pending for appropriate later attention

All observations and comments in the reports should be honest and complete to the best of the architect's knowledge and belief. Many architectural firms have forms which they have designed for this purpose. The AIA has a standard form (Architect's Field Report, Document G711) which is quite suitable and is widely used. The report should be written and issued promptly, preferably on the day of the visit, and certainly no later than 1 or 2 days following.

On the occasion of each site visit, the architect should specifically inquire of the contractor or the superintendent if there are any pending or unreported claims under consideration. The question and answer should be recorded in the observation report. This will serve the purpose of bringing all claims promptly to the forefront, where they can be immediately dealt with and quickly resolved, thereby preventing the accumulation of unresolved claims. It will also help to prevent old issues from being resurrected at a later time.

The architect's observation in the field is in the nature of a periodic examination or viewing of the work in process or completed as contrasted to the contractor's continuous daily superintendence and supervision of the trade workers and artisans involved in the day-to-day execution of the work. The architect should be observing and evaluating, whereas the contractor is controlling and directing the work.

The term inspection is used only twice in the architectural agreement, to describe the architect's on-site observations for determining the date or dates of substantial completion and the date of final completion. (2.6.14)

Architect's Personnel in the Field

Quite generally recent architectural graduates, trainees, or interns are assigned office tasks in design, drafting, shop drawing review, specification writing, and construction administration to fill out the architectural teams. This is important for the professional development of the individuals involved as well as for the advancement and propagation of the profession. These activities are performed under the direct supervision of experienced architects and are checked by them. Senior personnel are always available in the office for consultation and guidance of the less experienced. However, in the case of site observation duties, it is not appropriate to assign inexperienced or unqualified staff members unless accompanied by and under the close supervision of fully qualified and experienced architects.

Record Keeping During Construction Administration

The architect's basic record keeping during the construction period will consist primarily of keeping track of documentation, accounting for contract funds and time, and recording communications among the affected parties. These actions should result in a memorialization of all significant transactions growing out of the contract and the construction process. The following items should be a part of the architect's construction administration record keeping:

1. Field observation reports; follow-ups on all unresolved items
2. Shop drawings, samples, product data; checklist of all required submissions
3. Submittals; checklist of all required submittals
4. Correspondence
5. Payment requests, schedules of contract sum and time, change orders, construction change directives, bidding alternates, and reconciliation of cash allowances

6. Change orders and construction change directives
7. Drawings and revisions
8. Specifications and revisions
9. Status of requests for information and requests for quotations
10. Memos on delays caused by weather, strikes, unavailability of materials, and other things

Keeping the Owner Informed

During the construction period, the owner is frequently under considerable stress owing to the pressure of impending moving and furniture purchasing arrangements, apprehension of the vagaries of construction, economic fears, and possibly, misdoubt of the project's suitability. This is the stage of the architect's involvement with the owner when there is the greatest possibility of a major misunderstanding which could escalate to an irreconcilable difference. During the previous phases of architectural service, the architect and owner probably have worked together very closely and without much outside interference. However, previously established rapport could be seriously undermined when the owner receives conflicting information from the contractor, workers on the jobsite, and well-meaning but uninformed friends. Confidence and security in the architect may dwindle.

After the construction contract is signed, the owner will not always be completely aware of all of the architect's numerous activities being performed on the owner's behalf unless the architect makes them known. The architect should send information copies to the client of all correspondence with contractors, testing laboratories, consultants, utility companies, and governmental agencies. The owner should also be regularly receiving the field reports, insurance certificates, bonds, schedules, warranties, interpretations and decisions, change orders, construction change directives, certificates for payment, certificate of substantial completion, and certificate for final payment.

Another possible source for owner dissatisfaction during the construction phase is the architect's obligation to render fair decisions and interpretations on contentions of the owner or contractor. The architect should be meticulous in obtaining the viewpoints of both parties before deciding such issues and should be open, fair, honest, and prompt in all decision making. Some owners feel that their architect should side with them against the contractor, and when their position cannot be fairly sustained by the architect there could be a client problem.

Limitations of Architect's Authority

The architectural agreement explicitly provides that the architect is to have no control over the methods, means, and techniques of construction. These are matters strictly in the contractor's province and are so provided in the construction contract. The architect is neither in charge of nor in control of the contractor and is not responsible for the contractor's failure to properly perform the contracted duties. The contractor is solely responsible for scheduling and determining the sequences and procedures of construction. All safety precautions and programs are to be instituted and carried out by the contractor. (2.6.6) The architect should not interfere with the contractor in any of these matters and should only consult, observe, and report. The architect's authority, however, includes rejection of work which in the architect's opinion does not conform to the requirements of the contract documents and the ordering of additional inspection and testing. (B141, 2.6.11, and A201, 4.2.6)

Only the owner has the power to accept defective or nonconforming work. (A201, 12.3.1) If the architect were to do so without the owner's knowledge and concurrence, it would clearly be beyond the architect's contractual authority and could be considered a breach of the architect's fiduciary duty to the owner.

The architect may order minor changes in the work as long as they require no adjustment in the contract price or time and are not inconsistent with the contract documents. (2.6.13) Any such minor changes ordered should be immediately reported to the owner in the interest of maintaining open and amicable communications with the client.

Included in the particularization of responsibilities to be found in the architectural services agreement is Subparagraph 2.6.2, which describes the architect's duties and the limitations of authority set out in the AIA General Conditions. All of these duties must be performed with due care and reasonable diligence and to the standard of care usually exercised by architects in the community. The architect is under no legal duty to perform any work not contracted for but would be liable for any activities voluntarily assumed if the work is done negligently.

7

Construction Administration When the Contract Is Bonded

Construction Bonds

The existence of a bond on a construction project will have significant effect on the architect's administration of the contract during the construction phase.

It is the owner's prerogative, and it is so stated in the AIA General Conditions, to require the contractor to furnish a bond covering faithful performance of the contract and payment of obligations arising from the contract. (Subparagraph 11.4.1 of General Conditions of the Contract for Construction, Fourteenth Edition, AIA Document A201, 1987)

If the bond requirement is stipulated in the contract documents or bidding instructions, the contractor should include the bond cost in the bid. However, if the owner imposes the bond requirement after bidding or negotiation of the contract price, the owner must pay the cost in addition to the contract price. The bond premium must be paid in advance.

A construction contract bond guarantees that the contractor will perform the contract in full, including the usually specified warranty periods, and that the owner will receive the work free and clear of all liens and encumbrances. A bond is usually issued in the form of two separate documents, a performance bond and a labor and material payment bond, each in the full amount of the contract and referred to collectively as a bond. Bonds for construction are normally issued by corporate sureties, usually insurance companies, which are licensed and regulated by the department of insurance in each state in which they operate. Financially capable individuals can be sureties, but this is no longer common.

Obligations of Surety

A bond is a three-party instrument where the surety or guarantor (the bonding company) guarantees the performance of its principal (the contractor) for the benefit of the obligee (the owner) up to the face amount of the bond (the penalty or penal sum). The bonding company guarantees that the contractor will do all that is required of it by the contract documents and that all of the subcontractors, suppliers, and workers will be paid up to the face amount of the bond. The surety's obligations are basically the same as those of its principal. But in addition, it must conduct itself in accordance with the insurance statutes of the various states which now generally require that they make prompt investigations and that they settle claims promptly and fairly. Surety companies can be required to pay punitive damages if they fail to follow the statutory requirements. This has resulted in a dramatic change in the ways that some sureties handle claims. They can no longer stonewall without incurring a serious risk of liability for punitive damages.

If the contractor defaults, the surety may use its own judgment as to how it will complete the contract. It may elect to continue with the defaulting contractor, to hire a new contractor, to hire subcontractors and suppliers directly, or to pay money to the owner.

Cost of a Bond

Many owners consider that payment of the bond premium is good value for money in limiting or eliminating some of the financial risk of construction. Bonds cost approximately ¾ of 1 percent up to 1½ percent of the construction contract price, depending on the contractor's financial stability, building experience, business history, and size of contract. At the end of the contract the total premium will be recalculated on the final contract price including all changes. The fee paid for a bond is not based on the same concept as a casualty insurance premium where the rates are set to create a pool of funds from which to pay losses. Bonding companies do not expect to pay losses from their own funds but expect to reimburse themselves for all costs and legal expenses from the guarantees and assurances they receive from their principal. The surety will not pay any of its own funds until after the principal's assets are exhausted. The surety industry considers a bond premium as a fee for extension of credit.

Contractors normally maintain a close and continuous relationship with their bonding company. Initially they must submit an extensive application giving detailed information on their business organization, experience in various types of construction, equipment, personnel, status of work in process, and financial position. The contractor is required to keep its bonding company informed on a current basis as to all relevant changes in operating and financial conditions and status of contracts, bonded and unbonded.

Contractor Prequalification

The surety's ability to acquire relevant information in respect to its principal's financial stability far surpasses the usual owner's resources. Thus the requirement for a bond is an excellent contractor prequalification service.

When a contractor is unable to obtain a surety bond, it indicates the surety's opinion that the contractor is undercapitalized, underequipped, improperly experienced, has too much work in process, or has underbid the job. Considerable risk is undertaken by an owner who decides to go ahead with a contractor who cannot obtain a surety bond.

Some owners instruct their architects to specify in the bidding instructions that all bidders must be bondable and that a bond will be required but then do not require a bond from the successful contractor. Although the owner will save the cost of the bond, there will be no financial shoring in the event of the contractor's default. Other owners will require that bid bonds be submitted with all proposals under the theory that only bidders with a continuing satisfactory relationship with a bonding company will submit a bid. Most bonding companies make only a nominal charge or no charge for bid bonds for their regular customers. Owners who dispense with bonds altogether should be especially careful in reviewing prospective contractors' qualifications and should obtain reliable financial data, credit information, and legal advice before proceeding into a construction contract.

Surety as Adversary

Bonding an otherwise unsuitable contractor is not a good idea because the bond will not improve the contractor's capabilities or performance. A bonding company will not step into a faltering contractor's shoes or pay money to the owner until such time as the contractor has actually become incapable or insolvent. It is usually necessary for the owner to file a lawsuit or arbitration demand against the contractor and surety and obtain a court judgment or arbitrator's award before receiving any monetary relief from the surety.

When a claim is made against a bond, the surety will usually take every legal means possible to be exonerated of its obligation or to find some other party to assume some or all of the liability costs. Prime targets in this search for scapegoats are the owner and architect who might have compromised the surety's security by their departure from established procedures set out in the contract documents. The architect is particularly vulnerable if there has been any deviation from the professional standard of care. The owner will have difficulty in perfecting a bond claim if it is in default of any aspect of the construction contract.

Surety as Ally

The bonding company makes an excellent ally in situations where the contractor is exhibiting danger signs of possible impending default. When a contractor appears to be in financial difficulty, the owner is usually understandably reluctant to continue paying the contractor's invoices. To simply stop paying would seem to be financially prudent, but would be a breach of the contract. One solution to this dilemma lies in the owner's making all future payments jointly to the contractor and its surety. Although the AIA agreements do not provide for this procedure, the contractor would have difficulty objecting to it. It is in the surety's financial interest to prevent the contractor's default, and it has the legal leverage to apply appropriate pressure on the contractor. In some cases the surety will intervene, providing financial assistance and counsel to the contractor to facilitate successful completion of the contract.

Owner's Right to Approve Contractor's Surety

A surety is only as effective as its financial strength and ability to discharge its bonded obligations, so it is necessary that the owner reserve its right of approval of the contractor's bonding company. The owner should exercise its right to reject a contractor's surety only when information becomes available indicating the surety is unacceptable in some specific way such as financial incapacity or unfavorable reputation in respect to claims management. However, the architect should not specify use of a particular bonding company in the bidding instructions or elsewhere because of the close relationship that usually exists between a contractor and its surety. For a contractor to change bonding companies would necessitate filing of a new application and financial statement and a waiting period.

AIA Standard Bond Forms

In the interest of promoting uniformity and familiarity of procedures in the construction industry, the AIA has issued a standard form for a two-part Performance Bond and Payment Bond, December 1984 Edition, Document A312. This form is acceptable to and is used by most corporate sureties. It is considered good practice to specify that bonds be submitted on the standard AIA form.

Use of the AIA bond forms is particularly desirable, since some sureties would otherwise include provisions in their bonds that would severely limit the owner's rights. For example, some sureties would include a provision that the bond is exonerated if the owner and contractor agree to any change orders without the prior written consent of the surety.

Transmitting Bond to Owner

When a bond is required by the contract documents and is submitted by the contractor to the architect for transmission to the owner, the architect should refrain from expressing any opinion as to the suitability of the surety or the adequacy of the bond. To express such opinions would be in the province of legal or insurance experts and beyond the ambit of competency of architects. Should an owner rely to its detriment on erroneous opinions of its architect, the architect could become liable for resultant damages.

Commencing Work Before Issuance of Bond

If a bond is specified in the contract requirements, the architect should be particularly attentive to ascertain that the bond is received from the contractor, approved by the owner, and in effect before any work is commenced on the site. Bonding companies are extremely reluctant to issue bonds after the contract work has been started. If the contractor commences work explaining that the bond has been applied for and will be issued in due course, there is good reason to believe that the contractor is having difficulty in procuring a bond and will never succeed in obtaining it. If the contractor in this case should default, there will be no bond protection for the owner and other aggrieved claimants.

Keeping Surety Informed

Presumably, a surety has reviewed the contract documents and evaluated its risks before setting the rate and providing the bond. Thus, if the conditions of the contract are later changed in any material way without previous notification of the surety, this could release the bonding company from its obligation. The architect administering the contract should therefore keep the surety informed of any changes in conditions which would affect the surety's exposure to risk and in most cases should notify the surety or obtain its consent before proceeding.

It is a very simple matter to send a copy of all change orders and construction change directives to the bonding company. It is not necessary to obtain the surety's approval for changes made according to the procedures provided in the contract. If the contract time is altered or extended by the owner, the surety need not be notified, as this notice is specifically waived in the AIA standard bond form. However, there is no harm in giving this information to the surety.

Should the owner or architect learn directly or indirectly, through rumor or otherwise, of the contractor's failure to pay subcontractors or suppliers or other evidence of the contractor's economic distress, the owner should promptly notify the bonding company. This would allow the bonding company to take whatever steps it deems appropriate to assist the contractor and thereby prevent or limit its own losses and possibly those of the contractor. The owner should simultaneously alert and confer with its own legal advisors.

Termination of the Construction Contract

Whether or not the job is bonded, should the owner find it necessary to terminate the contract for cause as provided for in the AIA General Conditions (Subparagraph 14.2.2), the owner, upon certification by the architect that sufficient cause exists to justify such action, must give the contractor and the surety, if any, 7 days' written notice prior to terminating employment of the contractor. The architect's certification must be well founded on the reasons stated in the contract and should be based on solid documentable evidence capable of withstanding the inevitable legal challenge of the surety. (See Chap. 15, Termination of the Construction Contract.)

If the job is bonded, the previously described termination and certification procedure must be preceded by additional requirements found in the bond: The owner must give the contractor and surety written notice of a conference to be held within 15 days of the notice in which to discuss methods of performing the contract. If the owner, contractor, and surety agree, the contractor will be given a reasonable time to perform. The termination cannot be declared sooner than 20 days after the conference notice. According to bond provisions, the surety's obligations are greatly reduced when the owner is also in default. The most common owner default would be failure to pay the contract amounts certified by the architect. However, the owner could be unintentionally in default by any failure to perform and complete or comply with any other terms of the contract. The architect must be very careful in performing any of the owner's obligations, or in acting for the owner, that bond protection is not inadvertently reduced or lost.

Consent of Surety

The surety will need to know of any changes which prejudice its financial security in the contract. In the event of a default, the surety will undoubtedly attack an architect who has approved the final payment and an owner who has paid it when the defaulting contractor has dissipated the funds, lost incentive, or is insolvent. To prevent this eventuality it is important to obtain the surety's unconditional consent to the making of the final payment to the contractor. Some bonding companies have their own forms for this consent, but they usually contain objectionable conditional language such as "if in the architect's judgment." It would be more appropriate to require use of AIA Document G707, Consent of Surety to Final Payment, April 1970 Edition, which is worded as an unconditional approval.

A similar problem is associated with any reduction in or partial release of the retainage. The AIA has a standard form for this purpose, Document G707A, Consent of Surety to Reduction in or Partial Release of Retainage, June 1971 Edition.

Overpaying the Contractor

Whether the contract is bonded or not, all contractor's payment applications certified by the architect should always be carefully and fairly judged as to percentage of completion on a line-by-line basis, not allowing the amounts of understated items to offset overstated items. But in the case of a bonded contract, the bonding company will be very sensitive to any negligent overcertifying or overpaying of contractors when there later has been a default. Approving payment for materials or equipment on the site but not yet incorporated into the work, or for materials or equipment stored or being fabricated elsewhere will be considered by the surety to have lessened its security. However, if the owner and contractor had previously agreed to such payments and the surety had been informed, the surety cannot complain.

Sometimes contractors include in their payment request work which has not yet been done, with the rationale that it will soon be started and will be done by the time the payment has been received from the owner. The architect cannot approve this procedure, as the certificate is supposedly based on completion percentages in place no later than the date of the architect's site verification.

Often during the course of construction of a bonded contract, the architect will receive a form letter from the bonding company requesting such information as the percentage of completion of the work, the amount previously paid to the contractor, and the quality of workmanship. The architect owes no duty to the bonding company to fill in these forms and assumes some liability without compensation by doing so.

Owner's Claim against Bond

In the event of default by the contractor, it would be advisable for the owner to direct a prompt claim to the bonding company. Considering the widespread legal repercussions of a contractor in default, an incompleted or defective construction project, and a claim against a surety, the owner should without delay consult with its own legal counsel, preferably one with construction industry orientation and experience.

8

Shop Drawing Procedures

Shop Drawings: Friend or Foe?

To the construction industry, shop drawings seem to be a necessary evil. Contractors find them expensive to produce and architects find them unappealing to review. Both find them time-consuming and costly to administer. We seemingly cannot construct buildings without them; but they have become a perennial source of annoyance and confusion and, more importantly, a significant source of professional liability claims against architects. Undiscovered mistakes in shop drawings will often lead to unexpected or undesired construction results as well as high-ticket economic claims against architects, engineers, and contractors. Some shop drawing anomalies have resulted in costly construction defects, tragic personal injuries, and catastrophic loss of life.

In decades long past, shop drawings were treated in a fairly casual, offhand manner by contractors and architects alike. Often, to save time and trouble, contractors would instruct the subcontractor or supplier to submit the shop drawings or samples directly to the architect. The shop drawings would then appear unexpectedly in the architect's office, and they would have to sit and wait until someone got around to looking them over. If the contractor started complaining that the job was being held up, the architect would get one of the junior drafters to browse through them, mark any obvious errors, stamp them "approved," and call the subcontractor to pick them up. But it is not anything like that any more.

Shop Drawing Procedures in AIA Documents

This analysis of shop drawing problems and procedures will be based on the situations that would prevail if the owner, architect, consultants, and contractor contracted with each other using the standard form agreements issued by the American Institute of Architects. Use of the following documents will be assumed: Owner-Architect Agreement, Fourteenth Edition, AIA Document B141, 1987; Architect-Consultant Agreement, Sixth Edition, AIA Document C141, 1987; and General Conditions of the Contract for Construction, Fourteenth Edition, AIA Document A201, 1987 (incorporated as part of the Owner-Contractor Agreement).

The contractor is obligated by the contract documents to submit shop drawings, product data, and samples for certain parts of the work. The architect is obligated by the Owner-Architect Agreement to "review and approve or take other appropriate action upon Contractor's submittals such as Shop Drawings, Product Data and Samples...." (Subparagraph 2.6.12) This is included among the architect's duties during the construction phase—administration of the construction contract.

Submittals Defined

The AIA General Conditions provides definitions for each of the contractor's submittals:

> "Shop drawings are drawings, diagrams, schedules and other data specially prepared for the Work by the Contractor or a Subcontractor, Sub-subcontractor, manufacturer, supplier or distributor to illustrate some portion of the Work." (3.12.1)

> "Product Data are illustrations, standard schedules, performance charts, instructions, brochures, diagrams and other information furnished by the Contractor to illustrate materials or equipment for some portion of the Work." (3.12.2)

> "Samples are physical examples which illustrate materials, equipment or workmanship and establish standards by which the Work will be judged." (3.12.3)

These and similar submittals are not considered contract documents. They are submitted for the purpose of illustrating how the contractor proposes to conform to the requirements and the design concepts expressed in the construction drawings and specifications.

Are Shop Drawings Really Needed?

The drawings and specifications prepared by architects and engineers will show the general design concept of the project and each of the major components and their relationships to each other. Some of the subcontractors and suppliers must prepare additional drawings, diagrams, schedules, and other data to illustrate the specific way in which their particular company or shop will undertake to fabricate, assemble, or install their product.

Shop drawings are needed by the fabrication shops for their own use in instructing their own personnel how to carry out the requirements of the contract documents. Fabricators will produce the shop drawings even if they are not required to submit them for architect's approval. In many cases, the building could have been built satisfactorily even if the architect had not reviewed the shop drawings. The principal reason architects and engineers need to review the shop drawings is to ascertain that the contractor understands the architectural and engineering design concepts and to correct any misapprehensions before they are carried out in the shop or field.

Specifying Unneeded Shop Drawings

One way of lessening the exposure to risk of error in reviewing shop drawings is to refrain from specifying them in any case where the contract documents are sufficiently explicit to adequately depict the product or assemblage. If shop drawings of a certain trade have been specified, but not submitted and therefore not reviewed, the architect could be found negligent if mistakes are carried out in the construction which could have been prevented if the shop drawings had been checked. The architect's liability position would have been better if submission of the shop drawings had not been specified at all. Architects should be attentive that all specified submittals are actually received from the contractor. It is a good idea to prepare a checklist of all specified submittals at the beginning of the construction period so that each may be checked off as received. The contractor should then be reminded to submit any missing submittals.

A procedure for processing shop drawings may be inferred from various related provisions of the AIA General Conditions, Document A201. Subparagraph 3.10.2 requires the contractor to prepare and keep current a submittal schedule which is to be coordinated with the construction progress schedule. The submittal schedule should show when each shop drawing, product data, and sample is to be submitted to the architect and when the architect is expected to return it to the contractor. The schedule should allow the architect sufficient time to properly review the submittal and to refer it if necessary to the appropriate engineering consultant. Time should also be allowed in the schedule for redrawing and resubmission of shop drawings which have to be revised or replaced.

Contractor's Review of Shop Drawings

The contractor is obligated to review and approve all submittals before conveying them to the architect. (A201, 3.12.5) The contractor's review should be for compliance with all information given in the contract documents as well as for suitability to field conditions and dimensions. The contractor certainly cannot review for conformity with the design concept or the intent of the documents. The contractor is required to make such submissions to the architect with reasonable promptness, in such sequence as to cause no delay in the work, and in accordance with the submission schedule. Architects should be very strict in enforcing the requirements of Subparagraph 3.12.5, AIA Document A201. If the submittals do not exhibit a contractor's review stamp showing "approved," they should be immediately returned to the contractor. The same subparagraph also states that the architect may return without action any submittals which are not specified in the contract documents.

Consultants' Review of Shop Drawings

All submittals which further illustrate or describe work originally designed by consultants such as civil, structural, electrical, or mechanical engineers should be referred to the original designer for review. The architect should also check them to the extent of coordination requirements such as physical interrelating or meshing with work of other disciplines. Some examples:

Doors should not scrape lighting fixtures off the ceiling.

An electrical switchboard 90 inches high will not fit in a space with a 7-foot ceiling height.

In the case of highly technical matters, the architect should provide leadership in encouraging coordination among consultants. Some examples:

Low-voltage control wiring should not be specified in both electrical and air-conditioning sections.

Lighting fixtures cannot be in the same place as air-conditioning registers.

Ducts, conduits, pipes, and structural members cannot occupy the same space.

Architects, when making their agreements with consultants, should be sure that shop drawing review and coordination is included in the consultants' duties. The AIA Standard Form of Agreement Between Architect and Consultant, Sixth Edition, Document C141, 1987, provides in Subparagraph 2.6.11 for the consultant to review the contractor's submittals in respect to the portion of the work entrusted to the consultant. This subparagraph is harmonious with the comparable provision in the AIA Owner-Architect Agreement (B141, 2.6.12). However, if AIA Document C142, Abbreviated Architect-Consultant Agreement, First Edition, 1987, is used, a paragraph must be added to cover submittal review, as it is not included in the basic form.

Monitoring Progress of Submissions

Monitoring the progress of the contractor's submissions of shop drawings, product data, and samples and the review status of each can be a complicated process if not approached in a systematic manner. Many architects have custom-designed schedules which are used for this purpose. Also, the AIA has designed and issued Document G712, Shop Drawing and Sample Record, October 1972 Edition, which is suitable for the purpose. This is also a good use for the desktop personal computer. All shop drawings, product data, and samples should be registered and date stamped each time they are received, sent out, or acted upon. The important information which must be accounted for is

1. Receipt date
2. Title, trade, or item
3. Shop drawing number assigned
4. Specification section number
5. Contractor, subcontractor, or supplier
6. Number of copies received
7. Date, number of copies sent, and to whom referred for consultant review
8. Date, number of copies received from consultant, and consultant's recommendation for action
9. Architect's action as to approval, rejection, conditional approval, or request for resubmission
10. Distribution of shop drawings and copies of letters of transmittal (to contractor, jobsite, owner)

Each resubmission of a shop drawing will require a new set of entries to track its progression through the review process. Faithful attention to the schedule not only will help keep the situation straight but will yield a permanent record of the chronology. Needless to say, all submittals to and from the architect should be accompanied by letters of transmittal, which should be preserved as a further record of the process.

Keeping the Client Informed

Most clients of architects are not fully aware of the importance and role of shop drawings or of the large amount of time and effort expended in the review process and its related administration. In fact, many inexperienced clients have no reason to know of the existence of the shop drawing system or of the necessity of professional review and comment. This should be completely explained to the client. It is also appropriate to send the client copies of all shop drawing letters of transmittal to keep the client currently informed and aware of this significant behind-the-scenes process.

Qualified Personnel

In the architect's office, it is crucial that the usually unpopular and uninspiring task of shop drawing review be assigned to a qualified person, one who is intimately acquainted with the contract documents and the design concept or intent of the documents. Otherwise, how could the reviewer comply with the requirements of the Owner-Architect Agreement (Subparagraph 2.6.12) and of the AIA General Conditions (Subparagraph 4.2.7), which have similar language and both of which promise that the architect will be reviewing submittals "only for the limited purpose of checking for conformance with information given and the design concept expressed in the Contract Documents"?

Shop Drawing Stamps

Architects usually express their opinion of the shop drawings, product data, and samples by use of the rubber stamp, which usually has some exculpatory language in fine print plus some options which can be exercised by use of check marks. Often the stamp says something like "Review is for general compliance with Contract Documents. No responsibility is assumed for correctness of dimensions or details."

The various options to be selected include

- Reviewed
- Rejected
- Revise and Resubmit
- Furnish as Corrected
- No Exception Taken
- Make Corrections Noted
- Submit Specified Item

Space is also usually provided for the date of review and action and the shop drawing number. The wording on a shop drawing stamp will not serve to change or extend the meaning of Subparagraph 4.2.7 of the AIA General Conditions. Therefore, the words "Submittals have been reviewed and action taken in accordance with Subparagraph 4.2.7 of AIA General Conditions" could be used, with the appropriate options available for checking. The accompanying letter of transmittal should have additional comments which are needed to explain the reviewer's action or conditions of approval.

Architect's Approval of a Shop Drawing

The AIA General Conditions make it clear that the architect's approval of a shop drawing does not relieve the contractor of responsibility for requirements of the contract documents. The contractor is unquestionably responsible for errors or omissions in shop drawings. The contractor is relieved of responsibility for deviations from contract requirements only if the contractor specifically informs the architect of the deviations in writing and the architect has given specific approval of the deviation in writing. (A201, 3.12.18) At the same time, however, the architect should be extremely careful and thorough in checking shop drawings to minimize the possibility of error.

For years we have been reading in the professional literature that we should avoid using the word "approved" in describing the outcome of our review of a submittal. However, arbitrators and the courts have consistently rejected the idea that an architect or engineer could avoid responsibility for reviewing shop drawings merely by using some other word or an enigmatic expression such as "no exception taken." The AIA documents now accept the reality that architects really do approve (with or without conditions) or disapprove shop drawings. The AIA Owner-Architect Agreement (Subparagraph 2.6.12) and the AIA General Conditions (Subparagraph 4.2.7), using identical language, state: "The Architect shall *review* and *approve* or take other appropriate action..." (my italics). Therefore, it is my opinion that there should be no problem with having "approved" included as one of the options on the shop drawing stamp.

The architect's review is not to be taken as an approval of any safety precautions, as these are the contractor's responsibility. The review also is not intended to interfere in any way with the contractor's prerogative of determining and controlling construction means, methods, techniques, sequences, or procedures. The architect's review is limited to determining if the requirements of the contract documents are being met and that the completed work will be in compliance with the contract documents.

The most important principle to be followed at this juncture is to make sure that whatever words you use on the shop drawing stamp and the accompanying letter of transmittal are an accurate portrayal of your intended action. If your approval is in any way conditional, choose your words carefully so no one is led astray. The contractor is required to identify specifically in writing any shop drawing revisions other than those requested by the architect on previous submittals. (A201, 3.12.19)

Improper Use of Shop Drawings

The architect should not use the shop drawings as a medium for making changes in the contract requirements. If the architect needs or wants to make a change, it would be proper to initiate a change order or a construction change directive or to order a minor change (all provided in Article 7 of AIA Document A201). The only corrections which architects and engineers should make on submittals are to bring them into conformance with the requirements of the contract documents.

Various provisions of AIA standard form documents (A201, B141, C141, C142, and G712) have been quoted briefly and should be reviewed in their entirety for their complete language and context to avoid possible misinterpretation. Should anyone be contemplating changing the wording on shop drawing stamps based on my expressed opinions, they are hereby advised to first confer with their legal advisor or their liability insurance carrier.

9

Payment Certifications

Contractor's Application for Payment

When an owner and a contractor enter into a construction agreement using the standard AIA agreement and General Conditions, they thereby designate the architect to validate the contractor's periodic requisitions for funds to be paid by the owner. Both parties thereby signify their confidence in the integrity of the architect's certificate. They both rely on the architect's technical competence and integrity, with the expectation of fairness and impartiality. The contractor's surety, employees, subcontractors, and suppliers as well as the owner's insurers and lenders proceed in reliance on the certainty of a fair and objective payment system.

It is essential that architects' payment certifications be issued strictly in conformance with all applicable provisions of the construction contract. The architect's power does not include changing the payment procedures of the contract. The payment and certification system described here is based on the standard General Conditions of the Contract for Construction, Fourteenth Edition, AIA Document A201, 1987. (See Appendix D.)

Typically, construction agreements call for monthly payments for the value of all work in place or suitably stored on the site as of the last day of the month, with the payment due on or before the tenth day of the following month. The parties can agree to more or less frequent payments and any due dates they find convenient. According to the AIA General Conditions, each payment applied for by the contractor should be in the format of a schedule of values which had previously been submitted to and approved by the architect. (A201, 9.2.1 and 9.3.1) The value of each item of work is assessed as to its percentage of completion as of the last day of the month, the date of the application. The total amount of each application will be the value of all of the work completed to the application date reduced by the amount of the agreed retainage, with a credit allowed for all previous payments made by the owner.

The application for payment may be made in any format convenient to the contractor. Many contractors prefer to use the AIA standard forms or a similar format. The applicable forms are Application and Certificate for Payment, Document G702, and the Continuation Sheet, Document G703. These forms are quite convenient, as they are arranged in logical order and contain an affidavit for the contractor's signature as well as the architect's certificate for payment. If these forms are not used by the contractor, the architect must prepare a certificate form to be issued.

Upon receipt of the application, the architect must make a site examination to determine that the percentage of completion stated for each item does not exceed reality on the jobsite. (A201, 4.2.2 and 4.5.5) Each item must stand on its own with no averaging of "overs" with "unders" and without anticipating completion of any item a few days thereafter.

Representations and Limitations of Certificates

The architect's issuance of a certificate for payment is a representation to the owner that, to the architect's knowledge, information, and belief, the work has progressed to the point indicated. This must be based on the architect's physical presence and visual observation at the jobsite. The architect also represents that the quality of the work is in accordance with the contract documents and that the contractor is entitled to the sum of money stated in the certificate.

The issuance of a certificate is not a representation that the architect has

1. Made exhaustive or continuous on-site inspections to check the quality or quantity of the work
2. Reviewed construction means, methods, techniques, sequences, or procedures
3. Reviewed copies of requisitions received from subcontractors and material suppliers and other data requested by the owner to substantiate the contractor's right to payment
4. Made examination to ascertain how or for what purpose the contractor has used money previously paid on account of the contract sum (A201, 9.4.2)

Issuance of a certificate does not constitute acceptance of defective or nonconforming work. (A201, 9.6.6)

Neither the architect nor the owner has any duty under the contract to pay the subcontractors and suppliers or to see that they get paid. However, the architect may, if they request, release information to them regarding the amounts which have been paid to or withheld from the contractor for their portion of the work. (A201, 9.6.3 and 9.6.4)

During the time when a dispute has arisen or arbitration is pending, the architect must continue administering the payment procedure and issuing certificates when due. The owner must pay any amounts certified by the architect, and the contractor is obligated to continue the work of the contract. (A201, 4.3.4)

Decisions to Withhold Certificate

If it is the architect's opinion that the required representations cannot be made, the architect may decide to withhold certification in whole or in part to whatever extent is reasonably necessary to protect the owner from loss. If the architect is unable to issue a certificate in the amount applied for, the architect must notify the contractor and owner within 7 days after the date of the application. If the contractor and architect cannot agree on a revised amount, the architect will issue a certificate for an amount for which the necessary representations to the owner can be made. Additionally, the architect may decline to issue a certificate altogether or may nullify in whole or in part previously issued certificates if necessary to protect the owner from loss because of

1. Defective work not remedied
2. Third party claims filed or reasonable evidence indicating probable filing of such claims
3. Failure of the contractor to make payments properly to subcontractors or for labor, materials, or equipment
4. Reasonable evidence that the work cannot be completed for the unpaid balance of the contract sum
5. Damage to the owner or another contractor
6. Reasonable evidence that the work will not be completed within the contract time and that the unpaid balance would not be adequate to cover actual or liquidated damages for the anticipated delay
7. Persistent failure to carry out the work in accordance with the contract documents

Whenever the causes for withholding certification are removed, the architect may issue a certificate for the amounts withheld. (A201, 9.5.1)

Overcertification

The danger of an architect's overcertification of funds can arise from various sources, not the least common being a schedule of values which has been "front end loaded" by the contractor. This is the process of attributing larger than realistic amounts to the operations which will be completed first and reducing the sums for operations which will be accomplished later in the construction period. By artful adjustments in the breakdown the contractor can be paid more than the completed work justifies. By this means the retention can be defeated and will be insufficient to protect the owner from overpayment. The owner will have completely and effectively lost the advantage of the retention. A willfully distorted schedule of values is fraudulent and when skillfully contrived is not easy to detect. If the architect has any suspicion that this phenomenon is taking place, the contractor should be asked to submit substantiating data to validate the schedule of values.

A second major source of possible overcertification is in the estimation of the percentage of completion of each item. If the operation is one which lends itself to counting or calculating units or areas, then that should be done. It would not be unreasonable to ask the contractor how the figures were derived and to require evidence of the reasoning and computation. Each line item on the payment application should be separately weighed and considered and should be individually justifiable. An underestimated item cannot be used to offset an overstated item. Sometimes, at the time of compilation of the billing, certain items might have been optimistically estimated but not subsequently completed to the expected level, thereby resulting in overstated items. The architect has no choice but to mark them down to reality. Contractors often object to this treatment, arguing that the work is progressing and will be up to the stated completion by the time the bill is paid. The architect, being in a trusted fiduciary position, cannot allow this procedure. All completion percentages stated must be correct as of the date of the architect's site examination, and the certificate cannot predate the site visit.

Certificate Must Be Fair

The architect cannot arbitrarily reduce or refuse to issue a certificate. The owner and surety are relying on the architect to protect the owner from overpaying. At the same time the contractor and all who have a monetary interest in the owner's payment are relying on the architect for fair treatment. The architect must take this duty very seriously and carry it out skillfully, carefully, and honestly. It should be done strictly within the time periods set out in the contract.

It is generally accepted that an architect, when certifying payments due to a contractor, is acting in a quasi-judicial or arbitral capacity rather than in an exclusively ministerial role and thus has immunity from suit. There is little likelihood of a contractor prevailing in a legal claim against an architect for reduction in or refusal to issue a certificate or nullification of a previous certificate. However, the architect could lose immunity if the alleged professional transgressions are due to negligence, collusion, fraud, bad faith, or malicious intent. Although autocratic and inflexible architects are an eternal pain to contractors and do not necessarily best serve their clients in this way, they are within the bounds of allowable professional behavior.

If the contractor is not given opportunity to present its viewpoint before decisions are finalized, or is otherwise unfairly treated, the architect may lose immunity and be liable to the contractor for any monetary loss. The surety is rightful in expecting the architect to exercise ordinary care to assure that the contractor will not be overpaid since contract provisions for periodic payments, retentions, and other safeguards are as much for the surety's protection as the owner's. The architect may be liable to the surety if any losses are attributable to issuance of erroneous certificates if the architect is proved to have acted negligently or fraudulently.

Final Payment

When the architect has made the final inspection, if the work is found acceptable and the contract fully performed, the final certificate for payment should be issued. The certificate is a further representation to the owner that all conditions listed in the contract as precedent to the contractor's entitlement to final payment have been fulfilled. (A201, 9.10.1 and 9.10.2)

In those contracts which include provision for retainage, a further certificate for payment of the retainage will follow, usually 5 days after expiration of the lien period for employees, subcontractors, and suppliers. Substantiating data for release of retainage will include

1. A release of the contractor's own lien rights
2. Title company lien guarantee
3. Consent of surety

Contract provisions will vary, as mechanics' lien laws are not uniform in the various states.

The architect's final certificate should include reconciliation of all outstanding matters, including all pending change orders and construction change directives, allowances, determination of liquidated damages, retention, and previous payments and credits.

Accord and Satisfaction

The final payment constitutes an accord and satisfaction; that is, by paying it the owner is thereby acknowledging that there are no outstanding claims against the contractor other than those previously claimed and unsettled, those which might develop during the warranty period, and possible latent defects. (A201, 4.3.5 and 9.10.3) Similarly, the contractor, by accepting the final payment, acknowledges that there are no outstanding claims against the owner, other than any previously claimed and remaining unsettled. (A201, 9.10.4)

The architect's rendering of the certificate for final payment is the final element of service under the Owner-Architect Agreement. (AIA Document B141, Subparagraph 2.6.1) Any further services are classified as additional services subject to additional agreement and compensation. (B141, Article 3)

Substantiation for Payment Requests

The AIA General Conditions requires that each interim payment request be accompanied by such data substantiating the contractor's right to payment as the owner or architect may require, such as requisitions from subcontractors and material suppliers. (9.3.1) Substantiation for the final payment is more extensive and includes an affidavit that payrolls, bills for materials and equipment, and any other indebtedness connected with the work have been paid or otherwise satisfied, and certificates of any insurance which is required to remain in force after completion. Consent of surety, if any, to the final payment will also be required. Other substantiating data such as receipts, releases and waivers of liens, claims, security interests, or encumbrances arising out of the contract must be submitted if required by the owner. (A201, 9.3.1 and 9.10.2)

Some of the substantiating data may be submitted by the contractor by use of these standard forms of the AIA: Contractor's Affidavit of Payment of Debts and Claims, Document G706; Contractor's Affidavit of Release of Liens, Document G706A; Consent of Surety to Final Payment, Document G707; Consent of Surety to Reduction In or Partial Release Of Retainage, Document G707A.

The contractor should be made aware at the outset of the contract of the extent of substantiating data which will be required for all payment applications. It must be remembered that the certificate is not a representation that the architect has reviewed any of the owner-required substantiating data. The owner should check the substantiating data submitted for adequacy and authenticity if capable or should engage qualified advisors to do so.

10

Change Orders

Who Benefits from Changes During Construction?

Contrary to uninformed popular opinion, no one benefits from changes ordered during the construction period. They are generally disruptive of the orderly progress of the work and are usually an economic burden on both the owner and contractor. They are often symptomatic of someone's failure to properly fulfill their function in the construction process.

Changes in the scope or details of construction originate from various sources. Owners will have second thoughts or will embark on excursions of economic downgrading. Contractors will offer specification substitutions for various reasons, some more honorable than others. Sometimes faulty construction documents will generate the unexpected need for alternative materials or processes. Some changes such as those caused by unavailability of specified materials, unforeseen conditions, or changes in governmental requirements usually cannot be avoided. Practically every change in contract conditions will cost more than the same items would have cost if included in the original contract, and the full value of deducted items will not be credited to the owner.

Changes in the contract and work schedule cause confusion, and on projects with numerous changes, the job superintendent and subcontractors sometimes become uncertain of the exact state of the contract at any point in time. Add to this the uncertainty of prospective changes which have been discussed and price-quoted but not yet ordered. Sometimes they are never definitely confirmed or canceled. It would be in the best interest of all concerned if changes could be firmly controlled and severely limited in number or in rare circumstances even eliminated.

Owner's Right to Make Changes

Neither owner nor contractor has an inherent right to unilaterally change any of the terms of a validly executed contract unless the contract itself contains a provision which specifically allows for changes. A construction contract would be very impractical indeed if an owner could not make necessary changes as the construction progresses; therefore, nearly all construction contracts recognize that some degree of flexibility is a practical necessity and will include a change order procedure. The owner will have the right to order changes and the contractor will be required to carry them out in return for an equitable adjustment in the contract price and time.

Change Orders and Construction Change Directives

Construction contracts which include the AIA General Conditions, Document A201, 1987, have the advantage of a practical change procedure which properly reflects the roles, rights, and obligations of owner, contractor, and architect. The AIA General Conditions defines a change order as a written instrument prepared by the architect and signed by the owner, contractor, and architect stating their agreement on a change in the work and the amounts of adjustment, if any, in the contract sum and time. (A201, 7.2.1). Although the contract requires that change orders be in writing, judges and arbitrators are generally reluctant to strictly enforce this against contractors when the extra work has been done with the owner's or architect's knowledge and consent.

In those occasional circumstances where the owner and architect have signed the change order but the contractor will not, the contractor is required to proceed with the work, reserving resolution of the disagreed portions to a later time. A change order not agreed to and not signed by the contractor is called a construction change directive, a term coined by the AIA and first used in the 1987 AIA General Conditions. (Paragraph 7.3) At any time that the contractor later agrees to its terms or mutual agreement is obtained by adjustment of its terms, it is then deemed to be a change order.

The disputed portions of a construction change directive, if not resolved by negotiation, will be decided by the architect. If the architect's decision is not acceptable to the parties it is subject to arbitration. The contractor is not obligated to proceed without consent with construction change directives involving work relating to asbestos or polychlorinated biphenyl (PCB). (A201, 10.1.3) Change orders and construction change directives, upon their execution, become contract documents. (A201, 1.1.1)

Change Order Procedure

When a modification in the work is contemplated by the architect or owner contingent upon an acceptable price and time quotation, a request is sent to the contractor describing the proposed change. A standard form of the AIA, Proposal Request, Document G709, is suitable and may be used for this purpose. The request need be signed only by the architect, as it is simply a request for information and not an order to change the work of the contract in any way. If the quotation tendered by the contractor is acceptable to the owner, a change order may then be written and circulated for signatures. Change orders may be administered using the standard AIA Change Order, Document G701. If the contractor is not agreeable to any aspect of the proposed change, the AIA standard form, Construction Change Directive, Document G714, should be used. If the construction change directive is later found to be acceptable to the contractor, an appropriate change order should be issued. If the construction change directive continues to be unacceptable to the contractor, it becomes a claim to be decided by the architect.

Any unsolicited written demand for additional compensation or time for changed conditions received from the contractor is treated as though it were a proposal request. To whatever extent it is acceptable to the owner, as advised by the architect, it may be incorporated into a change order and submitted to the contractor for final acceptance as a change order or, if rejected in whole or in part, as a construction change directive.

A proposal request as well as the resulting change order must contain a description of the work sufficiently detailed to enable the contractor to price it accurately and to estimate the effect on the time schedule. The work description and drawings which would have been adequate for the pricing proposal may not be sufficiently detailed for construction, so additional drawings and specifications may have to be prepared after the change order is signed.

Supplementary drawings and specifications needed for the construction of changes will take the form of specifications, new drawings, or amendments to existing drawings. New specifications and drawings should be consistent with the proposal description, appropriately identified, and dated. Existing drawings amended to show changes should be carefully annotated and dated to assure that changes can be easily distinguished from the original contract. The usual practice of identifying different changes by consecutively numbered delta symbols should not be abused by the inclusion of unmarked changes or improperly described changes. For example, corrections of errors should not be labeled as clarifications. The amended or supplementary drawings and specifications are a part of the change order documentation and therefore become contract documents. The state of the drawings before the amendments should be recorded by preserving a print or a reproducible tracing. Owners, contractors, and subcontractors should always preserve all superseded drawings until after all contract billings have been rendered and all payments made. The architect should promptly notify the contractor whenever change order proposals are rejected by the owner so that any work which was being held in abeyance to accommodate the impending change can then proceed.

Pricing and Billing of Change Orders

The potential for owner misunderstanding and dissatisfaction is very high in the pricing of changes during construction. Most experienced owners realize that the contractor's costs for making changes will often be higher than the same or similar work would have cost if included in the original bid. Although all contracts include the implied covenant of fair dealing, some contractors will take advantage of the lack of competition and will unconsciously exaggerate their costs.

One way of partially controlling this problem is to require the general contract bidders to state their and their subcontractors' overhead and profit markups at the time of submitting their bids. It is also possible for the architect to specify the contractors' and subcontractors' acceptable markups in the supplementary general conditions so the contract price will be predicated on the specified markups being applied to all change orders. Another element in controlling or limiting the costs of changes is to request all bidders to quote unit costs for adding or deducting certain specified relevant materials and operations such as concrete, excavating, or painting.

Unit prices for adding many materials or operations will be different from those for deducting on account of the effect of associated fixed costs. It is quite common that unit prices for adding will be more than for deducting and higher for small quantities than for large quantities. This is a function of actual construction cost accounting and not a device for victimizing owners. For similar reasons, it is customary for contractors to attribute profit and overhead to additive but not deductive change orders.

Change order quotations submitted by contractors should be itemized to enable the architect and owner to properly review and evaluate the costs. Unless a lump sum has been negotiated and agreed upon, the detailed breakdown should include

1. Labor
2. Materials
3. Transportation
4. Subcontracts
5. Bond
6. Insurance
7. Permits
8. Testing
9. Coordination and superintendence
10. Overhead and profit

The subcontract amounts should be similarly detailed. Materials estimates should include delivery and sales taxes. Knowledgeable contractors, protective of their own economic interest, will impose an expiration date on all change quotations. This will cover their exposure to price rises but, more importantly, prevents uncontrolled open-ended disturbance to their construction scheduling.

All change orders should include the agreed adjustment to the contract time, and if there is to be no adjustment, then that should be stated. Some change orders are similar to cost-plus contracts when the scope of work cannot be ascertained in advance. In such cases, it is common to quote unit prices, labor rates, and overhead and profit markups in the approved change order. After the change work is completed, the total charge can be determined using the agreed rates.

Contractors should not proceed with any extra work for which they expect to be paid without suffering the formalities of a written change order. One notable exception to this advice is emergency work which must be commenced immediately to mitigate further damage. When the emergency work is completed, it should be billed promptly in such detail and substantiation as to enable the owner and architect to audit and approve it. Rush changes, those which must proceed immediately to avoid scheduling disruptions, will also be ahead of the paperwork. Diligent contractors will follow quickly with the change order information so the work can be promptly billed. Customarily, change order work is billed monthly for payment in the same manner as the original contract on the basis of percentage completed less the agreed retention.

Changes in Time

Most changes during construction will have some direct effect on the time of the contract, either deferring or advancing the estimated time of completion. Changes to non-critical-path work should not affect completion unless the change prolongs the activity sufficiently that it is then on the critical path.

When completion will be delayed by a change, the contractor will logically expect to be granted the extra time in the change order as well as the additional costs of extended overhead charges in the field and in the home office operation. Some changes will have the effect of extending work of the basic contract into future times of higher labor costs. This would be a proper charge on the change order even when the more costly labor is not related to the work of the change order.

Acceleration and Impact Claims

If the owner delays the contractor by failure to make portions of the work area available on time or in some other manner deprives the contractor of contract time, it constitutes acceleration of the contract. This will cause the contractor extra expense for more crews, overtime wages, or damages for late completion. In all fairness, rightful acceleration claims should be recognized immediately and the agreement formalized in a change order.

The cumulative effect of excessive or confusing changes leads to the disruption of carefully planned schedules and a loss of construction momentum. This is difficult to identify, quantify, and attribute to individual change orders as they occur. The effect will generally become apparent at or near the end of the job when the contractor is trying to account for the unexpected and mysterious schedule slippage and failure to meet the completion deadline. In most cases, when the contractor submits a claim for additional time due to this so-called "impact" effect, it is immediately rejected by the owner and architect as being vague, baseless, and unprovable. However, contractors who appeal their impact and acceleration claims to knowledgeable arbitrators and judges in an effective manner have a fairly good chance of prevailing.

Owners and architects would probably lessen the burdensome effect of these claims by initially evaluating them more realistically and by negotiating a reasonable settlement. Moderate compromises on each side will usually prove to be more economical than the costs of arbitration or litigation and the risk of a harsh award.

Architect and Surety

The architect has the basic administrative burden of keeping the contract straight and monitoring the progress and status of all changes. This is a very sensitive duty, as it occurs simultaneously with construction progress and if improperly performed could cause unnecessary confusion and construction delay.

Architectural construction administrators should devise and use methodical systems and procedures for continuous monitoring of the status and progress of change order proposal requests, quotations, approvals, and disapprovals. Contractors' demands for extra compensation or time should be processed promptly to avoid the accumulation of unresolved claims and the inevitable unpleasant confrontation with the owner.

When a project is bonded, the surety could be relieved of its responsibility if extensive or costly changes materially alter its originally assumed risk. Therefore, it is essential to keep the surety informed of change orders as they occur. Insignificant change orders could be accumulated and sent as a group with later important changes or when the aggregate of changes becomes significant.

Contractor's Claims for Extra Compensation

When contractors submit claims for extra compensation, the architect should immediately react by researching the contract documents and the circumstances giving rise to the claim and responding promptly. If "extra" work is already in the contract, no change order can be issued, and the reason should be furnished to the contractor in writing. If the claim arises from alleged imperfections in the architect's actions or documents, the architect must be deeply introspective and scrupulously fair in evaluating the claim. If the decision is in favor of the contractor, a change order must be issued charging the costs and time to the owner. The architect and owner must then resolve the issue between them.

Architect's Minor Changes

According to the General Conditions (7.4.1), the architect is entitled to order minor changes in the work not involving adjustment in the contract sum or time. Such changes must be consistent with the intent of the contract documents and must be in writing. A change order should be issued and executed to preclude later claims by the contractor or owner in respect to cost or time.

Use Change Orders for All Contract Changes

The change order process should be used to formalize all adjustments in the contract work, cost or time, such as:

Owner's carrying out of contractor's work (A201, 2.4.1)

Resolution and accounting of contract allowances (A201, 3.8.2.4)

Cost differences resulting from owner's rejection of subcontractors (A201, 5.2.3)

Cost of property insurance ordered by contractor and charged to owner (A201, 11.3.1.2)

Cost of insurance charged to contractor (A201, 11.3.4)

Cost of replacing insured damaged property (A201, 11.3.9)

Cost of uncovering and replacing work which was not required to be inspected and which after uncovering proved to be in accordance with the contract documents (A201, 12.1.2).

Owner's acceptance of uncorrected defective or nonconforming work, with or without a credit, should be formalized with a change order. (A201, 12.3.1) Architectural services provided under the Owner-Architect Agreement, Fourteenth Edition, AIA Document B141, revised in 1987, include, as a basic service, administration of the construction contract, although services connected with the change order process are classified as contingent additional services and therefore merit additional compensation.

11

Responsibilities of the Owner in a Construction Contract

The Owner as a Member of the Construction Team

Construction accomplished through written contracts requires efficient and effective teamwork. The main components of the usual team are owner, contractor, and architect. In addition, the main players have extensive teams of their own consisting of consultants, advisors, suppliers, and subcontractors. Altogether, dozens of persons and entities are required to combine their efforts and cooperation to achieve their mutual objective. (See the chart of contractual relationships, Fig. 1.1.) The main players usually comprise a new untried team, the combination having never before worked together on a single project, even though they may be highly experienced individually. Owners are often the weakest link in the team because they are not always as experienced and expert in their roles as are the contractors and architects they employ.

An effective team is heavily dependent on each member's appropriate conduct during the construction period. For guidance, contractors and architects can look to the customs and standards of their trade or profession and to the contract. However, the owner, not being organized as a part of the construction industry, is limited to reliance on the contract and on the advice of its advisors. Owners do not necessarily know how other owners conduct themselves in a given situation. The architect is always available to counsel the owner at any time it is needed.

Some owners find themselves in this unique contractual position only once or twice in a lifetime while others are constantly in the construction marketplace. Some experienced owners administer their roles very efficiently and effectively through their own construction departments, often staffed with architects, engineers, lawyers, accountants, estimators, contract administrators, and other highly skilled construction and real estate experts.

Owners generally have the highest stake in the physical development of their property and thus have the most to gain or lose by their own cooperation and appropriate behavior or the lack of it. The owner will usually pay for its bizarre, untimely, or inappropriate responses or any other unusual behavior. Inexperienced owners who choose to remain uninformed and uninvolved in the construction process will not obtain optimum results and could easily be deceived by unscrupulous contractors and unethical architects.

AIA General Conditions

The latest edition of the AIA standard form General Conditions of the Contract for Construction is a good source of information relating to the owner's rights, duties, and responsibilities under a standard construction contract. The General Conditions (or some edited version of it) is made a part of most construction contracts in the United States and therefore has become the main practical standard for judging the customary duties and practices of architects and contractors during construction. Likewise, usual owners' obligations are well presented and described in the document. (See Appendix D.)

Owner's Responsibilities

In analyzing the owner's activities under the AIA General Conditions, it is immediately apparent that some of the owner's duties could be, and often are, carried out by the architect. Indeed, Subparagraph 4.2.1 states that the architect is the owner's representative and has some limited authority to act on behalf of the owner. Most of the owner's duties, however, normally will have to be carried out personally or by legally authorized representatives. The owner will in some instances confer additional authority on the architect, and this must be carefully delineated in writing. The architect has no blanket power to act for the owner in any situation not previously authorized, preferably in writing.

Aside from any obligations imposed by the General Conditions, the owner and contractor are bound by the implied covenants of mutual cooperation and fair dealing. This implies that they must act promptly when required, abide by the terms of the contract, treat each other fairly, and avoid overreaching and other forms of sharp or deceptive practice.

Although the contract documents are technical and voluminous, the owner, in furtherance of its own interest, should reserve the necessary time and effort to read and examine them in their entirety. Anything not completely understood should be taken up with the architect for explanation and discussion. The owner should have its legal counsel review the entire contract and answer any questions remaining in the owner's comprehension of the contract. The owner should not execute the agreement without a thorough understanding of and concurrence with its contents.

Signing the Contract

After the owner has signed the agreement, an act not usually entrusted to the architect, the owner and contractor should sign all the rest of the contract documents. This is important, as it identifies the documents which comprise the contract. Often, drawings and specifications in particular undergo many revisions, and a substantial dispute could develop as to which edition of a document is the basis of the contract. In the event that the owner or contractor or both fail to sign the documents for identification, the architect is required to identify such unsigned documents upon request. (A201, 1.2.1)

After the Contract Is Signed

Prior to start of construction, the contractor will submit a list of intended subcontractors and suppliers for consideration by the owner and architect. This should be carefully reviewed and the contractor immediately notified if after due investigation the owner or architect has reasonable objection to any proposed person or entity. The contractor should then propose other names acceptable to the owner and architect. In the event the substitution requires a change in the contract sum, an appropriate change order should be issued. (A201, 5.2)

It is important that the work of the contract not be commenced prior to the effective date of all insurance and bonds or prior to the imposition of lenders' liens. All governmental approvals and permits must also have been obtained. When all these preliminary essentials have been accomplished, the owner should give written notice to the contractor that construction may commence. In the event that the owner neglects to issue the notice to proceed, the contractor must give 5 days' written notice to the owner before proceeding with work on the site. This would alert the owner in time that the contractor can still be stopped if all the preliminary technicalities have not been completed. (A201, 8.2.2)

The owner and architect must also receive the contractor's time schedule, which should indicate completion on or before the agreed completion date. (A201, 3.10) The purpose of the submittal is for receipt of scheduling information only and not for critical review and approval, as the contractor is solely responsible for construction procedures, techniques, and sequences.

The contractor will have to engage a testing laboratory acceptable to the owner to render certain specified testing, inspecting, and approval services. The owner should promptly accept or reject the nominated testing laboratory in writing. The contractor will pay for all specified testing, while the owner must pay for any additional testing. (A201, 13.5)

The various administrative notices required of the owner, such as a notice to proceed or to correct work, are usually taken care of by the architect and often are in the form of an entry in minutes of a meeting and distributed to all interested parties. Legal notices such as a demand for arbitration, notification of surety, or declaration of termination should be prepared by the owner's legal counsel.

During the construction period, the architect is required to visit the site from time to time to carry out its obligations under the owner-architect agreement and the construction contract. The architect should notify the owner in advance of all site visitations to enable the owner or its representative to be present if so desired. The owner should if possible attend the preconstruction jobsite meeting if one has been arranged. The owner has no contractual duty to visit the site at any time. (See Chap. 3, The Preconstruction Jobsite Conference.)

Owner Must Furnish Information

If requested in writing, the owner is required to furnish to the contractor information about the project site needed for giving notice and filing or enforcing of mechanics' lien rights. (A201, 2.1.2) The owner is also required to furnish promptly, if requested, reasonable evidence that the owner will be financially capable of meeting its obligations under the contract. (A201, 2.2.1)

The owner must also provide land surveys, descriptions of legal limitations, utility locations, and a legal description of the site. (A201, 2.2.2) It is the owner's responsibility to secure and pay for necessary approvals, easements, and assessments exacted by governmental regulation, except for those fees and permits specified to be the contractor's responsibility. (A201, 2.2.3) Any information or services which are the owner's responsibility must be furnished with reasonable promptness to avoid causing delay in the work. (A201, 2.2.4)

Insurance and Bonds

The owner is responsible for purchasing and maintaining owner's liability insurance, boiler and machinery insurance, and property insurance. (A201, 11.2 and 11.3) Property insurance includes fire and extended coverage and physical loss or damage including theft, vandalism, malicious mischief, collapse, falsework, temporary buildings, and debris removal including demolition occasioned by enforcement of any applicable legal requirements, and covers reasonable compensation for architect's services and expenses required as a result of such insured loss. (A201, 11.3.1.1) Although Document A201 requires copies of all specified owner's insurance policies be provided to the contractor before start of construction (11.3.6), common practice is to submit certificates of such insurance.

If the owner does not intend to purchase property insurance as specified, the contractor must be so notified prior to start of work on the site. The contractor can then arrange for the necessary insurance to cover the interests of the contractor, subcontractors, and sub-subcontractors. The architect should prepare a change order charging the costs to the owner. (A201, 11.3.1.2)

Insurance certificates, as evidence of the contractor's compliance with the insurance requirements of the contract, are collected by the architect and submitted to the owner for approval. (A201, 11.1.3) The owner should have its insurance counsel review the certificates before approving or disapproving. This should be done promptly as all insurance and bonds should be in proper form and in effect before any work of the contract is undertaken on the site.

The owner has the right to require the contractor to furnish a performance bond and payment bond, both in the full amount of the contract. If this requirement is in the bidding instructions or contract documents prior to execution of the contract, the bonds must be provided within the contract sum. If the bond requirement is imposed after the contract sum has been established, the premium will be added to the contract sum. (A201, 11.4.1)

Payments

The owner's most evident obligation is to provide the financial means for the mobilization and application of resources by the contractor. A steady, timely, and reliable flow of funds is essential to keep the personnel and materials supplied to the construction process.

Before signing the contract, if requested by the contractor, the owner must provide reasonable evidence of the financial arrangements which the owner has made to fulfill its obligations under the contract. If this is not promptly forthcoming, the contractor is not obligated to sign the contract or proceed with the work. After the work is started, the contractor can from time to time request this information and, if it is not promptly furnished by the owner, may stop the work. (A201, 2.2.1 and 14.1.1.5) (See Chap. 15, Termination of the Construction Contract.)

Prior to the first application for payment, the contractor must submit a schedule of values allocated to various portions of the work. The schedule, to be reviewed and approved by the architect, will be used as the basis for reviewing all payment applications. (A201, 9.2.1)

According to the contract, as each payment to the contractor becomes due, the contractor is to apply for it using a form similar to Application and Certificate for Payment, AIA Document G702, May 1983

Edition, and the Continuation Sheet, Document G703. The application should be made to the architect, who is obligated to make a site examination to verify the percentages of completion of all items. If the architect agrees that the stated degree of completion of each item is correct, the architect will execute the certificate on the contractor's application form. If the architect certifies a lesser amount than was applied for, an explanation should be attached. The owner then is required to pay the contractor the amount certified within the agreed time period. (A201, 9.3 and 9.4)

If any payments are paid after the due date, they should bear interest at a rate to be agreed by the parties, otherwise at the legal rate prevailing from time to time at the site of the project. (A201, 13.6.1) While any claim, including arbitration, is pending, the owner is obligated to continue making payments when due and the contractor is required to continue with the work. (A201, 4.3.4 and 4.5.3)

The contractor's payment application may include the value of materials and equipment suitably stored on the site unless the contract specifically provides otherwise. Materials and equipment stored or being fabricated off the site may be billed to the owner only if the owner and contractor have previously so agreed. Such an agreement should include location, protection of owner's title, security from fire and theft, transportation, and insurance. (A201, 9.3.2 and 10.2.1.2) Applications for payment may include amounts for the percentage of work completed on change orders and construction change directives. (A201, 9.1.1 and 9.3.1.1)

Owner's Failure to Pay

Should the architect fail to issue a certificate within 7 days after the contractor's application, through no fault of the contractor, or if the owner fails to pay the certified amount within 7 days after the date specified in the contract, then the contractor upon 7 days' additional written notice may stop the work until payment has been received. When the delinquent payment has been made and the work resumed, the architect will issue a change order charging the owner with the costs of shutdown, delay, and start-up and a corresponding extension in the contract time. (A201, 9.7.1) (See Chap. 15, Termination of the Construction Contract.)

Owner's Right to Stop the Work

When the contractor persistently fails to carry out the work in accordance with the contract documents or fails to correct improper or defective work, the owner may order the contractor to stop the work until the cause for the order has been eliminated. The stop work order must be in writing and signed personally by the owner or by an agent specifically so empowered in writing. The owner's power to stop the work does not impose a duty on the owner to exercise this power for the benefit of the contractor or anyone else. (A201, 2.3.1) The architect does not possess the power to stop the work of the contract. If in the architect's judgment the work should be stopped, it will be necessary to obtain the owner's concurrence and action. (See Chap. 15, Termination of the Construction Contract.)

Owner's Right to Carry Out the Work

If the contractor defaults or does not carry out the work in accordance with the contract documents, the owner may, with prior certified approval of the architect, give the contractor notice to correct the default or defective work within 7 days. If the contractor fails to proceed promptly and diligently, the owner must give a second written notice and 7 additional days. If the contractor after the second notice and during the second 7-day period fails to proceed and continue work diligently, the owner may correct the deficiencies and the architect will issue a change order charging the costs, including additional architectural fees, back to the contractor. If the remainder of the contract sum is insufficient to cover the costs, the contractor must pay the difference to the owner. (A201, 2.4.1)

If the contractor's performance has descended to the level that the owner must consider taking such drastic measures as stopping the work or carrying out any of the work, the owner should be in close consultation with the architect and legal counsel. In case of later legal action, which is almost certain to follow, the architect's prior approval of the owner's actions will have to be proved. The architect's approval should be based upon independent opinion and in the form of a written certificate.

If the contractor fails to keep the work site clean as required in the specifications, the owner is entitled to order the work done by others and charge it to the contractor. If a dispute develops among the owner, contractor, and owner's separate contractors as to relative responsibility for cleaning, the owner may clean up and allocate the charge to the various parties in proportions determined by the architect. (A201, 3.15 and 6.3.1)

The owner is entitled to carry out construction work or operations related to the work of the contractor utilizing its own forces or by contracting with separate contractors, and the contractor is required to cooperate in respect to use of the site and mutual scheduling. If the contractor determines that it has been caused extra expense or delay, a claim should be made which will be decided by the architect. (A201, 6.1 and 6.2)

Separate Contractors

The owner is responsible for communications and coordination among its own forces, separate contractors, and the contractor. However, the owner is required to channel all its own communications to the contractor through the architect. (A201, 4.2.4) Communication through less formal channels may lead to confusion, delay, and extra expense.

The contractor is responsible for whatever cutting, fitting, or patching is necessary to complete the work and to make the various parts of the work fit together properly. The contractor is not allowed to damage or endanger by cutting or patching the work of the owner's forces or separate contractors, and conversely they cannot cut or patch the contractor's work without prior written permission of the owner and contractor or other separate contractors. (A201, 3.14)

Owner's Claims against the Contractor

When unknown concealed conditions are uncovered during excavation or unusual physical conditions are otherwise encountered, if they are more costly than shown in the contract documents, the contractor is entitled to claim for the resulting additional expenses and time. Similarly, when the unknown conditions prove to be easier or less costly than depicted in the contract documents, the owner in some cases could be entitled to a credit on the contract price and time. In either event, the architect should investigate the situation, make a determination, and issue an appropriate change order. (A201, 4.3.6)

The architect is authorized to order minor changes in the work provided that there is no change in the contract sum or time. (A201, 7.4.1) If either owner or contractor disagrees with the architect's order for a minor change, the only relief is to arbitration, unless the architect is willing to revise the order.

Any other owner claims against the contractor should first be submitted to the architect for investigation and determination. The architect, after obtaining the contractor's viewpoint, will make a decision binding on both parties but subject to arbitration if either party wishes to contest it. All claims for the architect's decision or interpretation should be in writing.

Defective Work

The architect is the final judge of the acceptability of the contractor's workmanship and materials. The contractor is obligated to remove and replace any work which the architect deems not in compliance with requirements of the contract. However, if the owner desires to accept nonconforming work rather than have it removed and replaced, an appropriate and equitable adjustment will be made in the contract price. (A201, 12.2.3 and 12.3.1) Construction defects coming to the attention of the owner during the warranty period should be promptly reported to the contractor. (A201, 12.2.2)

Owner and Architect

By the time the project is ready for construction, the owner and architect will have been working closely together for several months or up to a year or longer. During this time the architect has been dealing with the owner on the basis of objective professional advisor to the client. Although the client will consider the architect's opinions, explanations, recommendations, and advice, the client has the last word in all matters and makes the final decisions. However, after the construction contract is signed, the relationship must change. The architect will still be the owner's professional advisor but must also be an independent judge of the performance of owner and contractor under the contract and must make fair rulings on the claims of owner and contractor alike. (A201, 4.2.12) Sometimes owners feel that their architect should side with them because they are paying the fees, but contractors would not freely enter into this form of construction agreement if the architect could not be trusted to render objective and impartial rulings, in good faith, fair to both sides.

In the event of termination of the employment of the architect, the owner is required to appoint a new architect, acceptable to the contractor, to fulfill the duties of architect in the administration of the construction contract. (A201, 4.1.3)

The Ideal Owner

The owner will receive the most from the construction process by reviewing all submittals promptly when received, making all decisions promptly, reporting all noted defects and deficiencies promptly, conferring with retained experts when necessary, and paying all payment certificates when due. Owners, particularly of larger, more costly projects, should confer with insurance counsel on all insurance and bond matters, construction industry lawyers on legal concerns, and experienced accountants on accounting subjects. In general, the owner should be responsive, cooperative, and reasonable and should not interfere with the contractor's progress.

If the owner lacks confidence in its expertise or finds these important duties onerous or excessively time-consuming, serious consideration should be given to extension of the architect's administrative duties or, alternatively, the engagement of a construction manager, either independent or on staff, to carry out some or all of the diverse owner functions required during the construction period.

12

The Contractor's Responsibilities

What Is Expected of the General Contractor

Contractors are generally very aware of the usual main features of a standard building contract, although only experienced owners would be as well informed. Essentially, the contractor is required to furnish all of the necessary labor and materials needed to erect the building and site improvements and the owner is obligated to pay for it. Time is an important element in most construction contracts, as to both the contractor's completion of the work and when payments must be made by the owner. The additional terms and conditions of the contract necessary to make it workable will vary widely depending on which of various available standard forms of agreement are used and how they are amended to suit the requirements of the situation at hand. Most of the standard form contracts issued by contractor organizations tend to be heavily slanted in favor of the contractor. The standard contract forms of the AIA are thought to be fairly written to give equal weight to the interests of owners and contractors.

The two main owner-contractor agreements issued by the American Institute of Architects are

Standard Form of Agreement Between Owner and Contractor (where the basis of payment is a Stipulated Sum), Twelfth Edition, AIA Document A101, 1987 (Appendix B)

Standard Form of Agreement Between Owner and Contractor (where the basis of payment is the Cost of the Work Plus a Fee with or without a Guaranteed Maximum Price), Tenth Edition, AIA Document A111, 1987 (Appendix C)

When either agreement is used, depending on the payment method agreed, the companion must be

> General Conditions of the Contract for Construction, Fourteenth Edition, AIA Document A201, 1987 (Appendix D)

These documents were written to respect the rights and obligations of contractors and owners alike and reflect the presence and role of the architect during the construction process.

The responsibilities of the contractor under the AIA General Conditions are in addition to the duties imposed by the usual customs and practices of contractors in the same community. Also, both parties are bound by the implied covenants of fair dealing and reasonableness present in any contract. Additionally, the architect and owner will naturally expect the contractor to provide all of the unwritten behind-the-scenes services and adjuncts customarily a part of any competent contracting business. The contracting firm should have a complete and efficient organizational structure, appropriately equipped and staffed to provide estimating, purchasing, contracting, accounting, engineering, and construction services for all projects undertaken.

The firm should have secretarial and clerical personnel and procedures sufficient to initiate and respond to all written communication requirements of the contract. The operation should be financially capable of performing any contract it undertakes and should be appropriately licensed to do business in any jurisdiction in which it operates. All of these diverse functions might be performed by a single individual in a one- or two-person firm. The firm should be able to perform all necessary bookkeeping functions to account for all funds received and disbursed and to render bills and accounts when necessary.

Signing of the Contract

The contractor should sign the contract in the proper name of the contracting firm, and the person signing should have the legal power to bind the firm. Some corporations and partnerships require signatures of two officers or partners on all agreements. The contractor, for its own protection, should make sure that the owner entity is also signing properly. In addition, owner and contractor should sign all of the contract documents for identification and each party should retain a complete set of signed documents for their own files. The architect should maintain a complete identical duplicate set, marked for identification but not necessarily signed by the parties, for use in administration of the contract. Should the parties neglect to sign all of the documents, the architect must be able to unequivocally identify the contract set if later requested to do so. (AIA Document A201, Subparagraph 1.2.1)

The contractor's signing of the contract is a representation that the contractor has visited the site, is familiar with local conditions, and has correlated visual observations with requirements of the contract documents. (A201, 1.2.1) It is also the contractor's confirmation that the specified contract time is a reasonable period for performing the work. (A201, 8.2.1)

Drawings and Specifications

When the work of the contract is finally completed, the contractor must return or suitably account for all drawings and specifications to the architect except for one record set. The contractor is not entitled to use the drawings or specifications on other projects. (A201, 1.3.1)

The contractor is required to study and compare the contract drawings and specifications and the land survey and to report any noted errors, discrepancies, or building code violations to the architect. Before starting work, the contractor must also take field measurements and compare these with the contract documents, reporting all discovered errors and discrepancies to the architect. (A201, 3.2.1, 3.2.2, and 3.7.3) The contractor has no obligation to find any errors and is not responsible for the existence of any errors or code violations in the documents, discovered or undiscovered, but could be held responsible for proceeding with work known to be erroneous or to be in violation of building codes. (A201, 3.7.4) The contractor could be held proportionately liable for failing to notice errors which should have been recognized, given the average contractor's knowledge and skill. The contractor should never proceed in uncertainty.

Errors, discrepancies, and ambiguities discovered and reported should be resolved by the architect. This might require redesign, issuance of revised drawings or specifications, and an appropriate adjustment in the contract sum and time.

Contractor Responsible for Results

The contractor has the general responsibility

To perform the work in compliance with the contract documents and approved submittals (A201, 3.2.3)

To supervise and direct the work (A201, 3.3.1)

To be responsible for the acts of its employees and subcontractors (A201, 3.3.2)

To enforce discipline on the job and not employ unfit persons (A201, 3.4.2)

To inspect the work of each trade to assure that it is suitable for subsequent work (A201, 3.3.4)

To pay for all labor and materials, tools, equipment, water, heat, utilities, and services necessary for and reasonably incidental to the proper execution and completion of the work (A201, 3.4.1)

The contractor is solely responsible for and should have control of the construction means, methods, techniques, sequences, and procedures for coordinating the work of the contract. (A201, 3.3.1) Neither the architect nor the owner should interpose its wishes or interfere with the contractor's performance of any of these functions, as this would jeopardize the objective of giving the contractor full and unrestricted control over these areas of primary responsibility. It is the contractor's prerogative to let subcontracts and purchase materials without respect to the architect's choice of arrangement of specification subdivisions or construction drawings. (A201, 1.2.4)

Construction Quality

The ultimate quality of the construction product is primarily in the control of the contractor. The contractor establishes the standard of workmanship integrity for its organization. This is enforced in many direct as well as subtle or indirect ways. The contract administrators, in negotiating subcontract agreements and purchase orders, can enforce the quality standard or can undermine it by bargaining it away. The contractor's superintendent on the job as well as the subcontractors' supervisors can insist on high workmanship standards or they can conspire to slide by on the minimums barely acceptable under the specifications. The general contractor can hold the subcontractors to the specified quality or higher or can act as the agent of mediocre or dilatory subcontractors or suppliers in persuading the architect to approve marginally acceptable work.

Taxes and Licenses

The contractor must

Pay all sales, consumer, or use taxes (A201, 3.6.1)

Secure and pay for building permits and governmental fees, licenses, and inspections (A201, 3.7.1)

Pay all royalties and license fees (A201, 3.17.1)

Comply with and give notices required by all laws, building codes, and ordinances (A201, 3.7.2)

In addition, the contractor must pay for any taxes and licenses that are specified in the supplementary or other conditions or in the trade sections of the specifications. Generally, the owner is responsible for taxes and assessments that relate to the land or its use, such as property taxes and assessments for sewers, water, street lighting, and schools, and similar fees and charges.

Safety and Accident Prevention

Safety on the construction site, provision of safeguards and warnings, and the giving of safety notices are all in the province of the contractor. (A201, 10.1.1 and 10.2.1 through 10.2.3) The contractor is required to appoint a person to be responsible for accident prevention on the jobsite, and it is understood to be the contractor's superintendent unless the contractor designates otherwise. (A201, 10.2.6)

The contractor is obligated to proceed with the work expeditiously, to assign adequate personnel, materials, and supervision, and to achieve substantial completion within the contract time. (A201, 8.2.3)

Separate Contractors

When the owner has contracted directly with more than one contractor to work simultaneously or serially on the same site, the contractors are known as separate contractors. This would be the case, for example, when one contractor has been engaged to construct the building while separate contractors have been hired for installation of utility lines or for installation of laboratory equipment or painting. In such situations, it is essential that the contractors cooperate with each other. So it is up to the owner when contracting with the separate contractors to anticipate the cooperation problems and to provide for the necessary coordination and communication. (A201, 4.2.4 and 6.1.3)

The owner should contract with each of the separate contractors on substantially the same basis to avoid conflicting provisions which would inhibit or prevent the necessary coordination and cooperation. Each separate contract should incorporate the same or similar general conditions including complementary insurance requirements. The AIA General Conditions contains appropriate provisions requiring cooperation among separate contractors and the owner's employees. (Article 6) These provisions are necessary to establish the owner's right to do work with its own forces and to award separate contracts without encountering unexpected or unreasonable objections from other contractors working simultaneously on the same site. The site and its facilities or limitations must be shared on a fair basis. Such necessities as parking, electrical, telephone and water services, storage areas, loading and unloading areas, office spaces, temporary toilets, scaffolding, shoring, and hoisting facilities must often be provided on a cooperative basis. Complete duplication of these services would be needlessly extravagant, so it is to the owner's advantage to specify which contractor is to provide each element and the basis on which the other contractors will be allowed to participate in its use.

Although each separate contractor is responsible for its own scheduling and completion dates, it is the owner's responsibility to schedule the separate contractors and its own employees and to coordinate the schedules. Where the work of the separate contractors comes together, each of the contractors is obligated to report discrepancies which prevent their work from properly fitting. It is the owner's responsibility to resolve all differences between separate contractors. The separate contractors are mutually responsible to refrain from damaging each other's work in process or the completed work and to pay for any damage which they cause. (A201, 3.14.2)

Communications

Otherwise well-managed construction and administration processes will deteriorate into misunderstanding and chaos when logical communication channels are not established and consistently utilized. Communications between owner and contractor should always be routed through the architect. Similarly, the contractor must be the conduit for all communications with subcontractors and suppliers. Communications with the architect's consultants should be through the architect, and the owner is the medium for communications with or among the separate contractors. (A201, 4.2.4) The owner must also provide the communication channel for all of the owner's consultants and advisors.

Subcontractors and Suppliers

The reputation of a general contractor in respect to meeting progress schedules and promised completion dates, providing superior workmanship, and quoting fair and competitive prices is directly related to its assemblage of subcontractors and suppliers with which it regularly does business. Well-managed contracting firms endeavor to establish and cultivate long-standing relationships with their principal subcontractors and suppliers. Thus they are assured of continuing availability of a cadre of high-quality skilled craftspeople and competent supervision under the control of financially capable subcontractors.

The general contract does not create any contractual relationship between the owner or architect and the subcontractors or suppliers. The contractual relationships between the general contractor and the subcontractors and suppliers will be created by the subcontracts and purchase orders issued by the contractor.

The contractor is required to submit a list of the proposed principal subcontractors and suppliers to the architect for transmission to the owner. The architect should respond in writing stating whether or not the architect or owner, after appropriate investigation, has any reasonable objection to the contractor's list. Should the architect fail to reply promptly, this is deemed to be acceptance of the list. (A201, 5.2.1)

The contractor cannot contract with any subcontractors or suppliers to which the architect or owner has made timely objection, and the contractor is not required to contract with any entities to which it has made reasonable objection. (A201, 5.2.2) Should the substitution by a mutually acceptable entity require a revision in the contract sum, an appropriate change order should be issued charging or crediting the difference to the owner. (A201, 5.2.3) After the subcontractor list has been established, the contractor cannot make a change in it if the owner or architect lodges a reasonable objection to such change. (A201, 5.2.4)

Hazardous Waste Materials

In decades past, certain substances were used in construction which have since been identified as injurious to health. Prominent among these hazardous materials are asbestos fibers, often used in acoustical walls and ceilings, flooring, siding, and insulation, and polychlorinated biphenyl (PCB), used in high-capacity electrical transformers. These toxic substances must be removed or rendered harmless, usually by encapsulation.

If hazardous materials such as asbestos or PCB which have not been rendered harmless are encountered on the project, the contractor is required to cease working in the affected area and to notify the owner and architect of the condition in writing. It is necessary then to determine definitely whether or not the suspected materials have been accurately identified. This requires testing, which would be at the owner's expense. (A201, 13.5.1) If the suspected materials are proved not to be hazardous, the contractor should promptly resume work. (A201, 10.1.2 through 10.1.4) However, should the materials be confirmed as hazardous, the contractor is justified in discontinuing work in the affected area until it has been made safe. The owner should then make arrangements with an experienced hazardous materials contractor competent to remove or render harmless the offensive materials. Only when the work area is considered safe and harmless should the original contractor resume the work of the contract.

Most professional liability insurance policies carried by architects exclude all activities involving asbestos or PCB. Therefore, upon the discovery or suspicion of the presence of these or other toxic materials on the site, architects should decline to render any services involving their discovery, removal, or disposal. Those architects who have made a specialty of problems dealing with toxic substances must obtain an appropriate special endorsement from their liability insurance carriers. According to Paragraph 9.8 of AIA Document B141, neither architects nor their consultants are required to assume any responsibility in respect to the discovery, presence, handling, removal, or disposal of hazardous materials or the exposure of persons to them in any form at the project site.

Contractor's Warranty

A warranty is a written statement guaranteeing the integrity of a product and promising the purchaser that the provider will be responsible for repairing or replacing the product for a period of time. In the General Conditions, the contractor warrants that the materials and equipment furnished under the contract will be new and of good quality unless otherwise specified and that the work will be free of defects and in conformance to the contract documents. The contractor's warranty naturally excludes any defects caused by the owner's neglect such as inadequate maintenance or improper operation. Normal wear and tear is also excluded. (A201, 3.5.1)

Warranty Period

The customary construction industry warranty is 1 year. There is no reason a shorter or longer period could not be specified if desired. However, substantial deviation from the norm would be likely to create strong resistance from most building contractors as well as an addition to the contract sum to cover the extended warranty time period.

Upon the owner's discovery of conditions which the contractor must repair or replace during the warranty period, the owner must give prompt written notice to the contractor. The 1-year warranty period starts to run as of the date of substantial completion. For work first performed after substantial completion, the start of the warranty period is extended to 1 year after the actual performance of the work. (A201, 12.2.2)

Warranties are not required to be in writing, but it is common practice for architects to specify that the contractor's 1-year warranty be submitted in writing. This should be submitted by the contractor along with all other specified warranties as part of the contract closing out procedures.

Architects, when transmitting the contractor's written warranties, should refrain from rendering any opinions as to the sufficiency or language of the warranties, as this would constitute a legal opinion. The transmittal letter should merely identify the warranties as to the specification section and contractor and contain a recommendation that the owner seek legal review of all warranties.

Warranties are only as good as the contractors who have executed them. If the contractor has gone bankrupt or is otherwise financially incapable of providing the warranty service at the time it is needed, the warranty is worthless. To provide a backup to the general contractor's warranty, it is standard practice to specify written warranties from the major subcontractors, manufacturers, and suppliers such as electrical, air conditioning, roofing, and plumbing. This yields a greater protection to the owner, as the general contractor's resources would then be supplemented by those of the subcontractor.

It is quite common to require a longer warranty period on roofing, such as 2 years. Should the owner require a longer warranty on roofing, a roofing bond of 10, 15, or 20 years is available through some manufacturers upon payment of a bond premium and the involvement of a surety that will issue a roofing bond. Only roofs of a specified higher quality are eligible for roofing bonds.

The contractor's faithful service during the warranty period is of extreme importance to most owners, and this is recognized by high-quality reliable contracting firms. Although the contractor has no obligation to continue rendering warranty services after expiration of the specified warranty period, many reputable firms voluntarily follow through on repair work for a longer time as a matter of public relations and as a way of cultivating prospects for future contracting work.

Some contractors are not so cooperative in performing corrective work during the warranty period, and in those cases, the owner would have had to withhold contract funds to be disbursed only after satisfactory completion of the 1-year warranty period. This lengthy retention of funds cannot be done unless the contract so provides.

When the job is bonded, the work of the warranty period is included in the bond. Should the contractor refuse to respond on warranty work, the bonding company should be notified.

Architect's Services During Warranty Period

The architect's services under AIA Document B141 terminate at the earlier of issuance to the owner of the final certificate for payment or 60 days after the date of substantial completion. (B141, 2.6.1) Thus, most of the services rendered in the owner's interest during the warranty period will have to be self-performed unless the architect is specifically retained for these functions. Among the services of value to the owner at this time would be the receiving, evaluating, and channeling of the owner's service requests to the contractor and a comprehensive examination of the premises just prior to expiration of the warranty period. Any list of warranty corrections submitted to the contractor should be carefully qualified to eliminate items which are not the contractor's responsibility. The owner is responsible for defects caused by normal wear and tear, abuse, insufficient maintenance, improper operation, and alterations to the contractor's work. (A201, 3.5.1)

Contractor's Indemnification of Owner and Architect

The AIA General Conditions contains a broad indemnification clause in which the contractor undertakes to pay any losses or claims against the owner, architect, and architect's consultants and hold them harmless from certain claims and losses arising out of the contractor's and subcontractors' negligent acts. Although the indemnification applies even when the owner, architect, or architect's consultants are partly at fault, the contractor's obligations do not extend to the liability of the design professionals arising out of

1. The preparation or approval of maps, drawings, opinions, reports, surveys, change orders, and designs
2. The giving of or failure to give directions or instructions by the design team provided such giving or failure to give is the primary cause of the injury or damage (A201, 3.18.1 through 3.18.3)

Limitation on Owner's Rights to Appoint New Architect or Change Architect's Duties

Should the owner and architect wish to agree in writing to restrict, modify, or extend the architect's construction phase duties, it will be necessary to obtain the contractor's consent, which consent must not be unreasonably withheld. (B141, 2.6.1, and A201, 4.1.2)

If the architect's employment is terminated or if the architect dies or becomes incapacitated, the owner is required to engage a replacement architect against whom the contractor has no reasonable objection. The new architect's duties and status under the contract are the same as those of the former architect. (A201, 4.1.3)

13

Role of the Construction Superintendent

Contractor's Superintendent

The AIA General Conditions, Document A201, 1987 edition, has only two explicit references to duties and responsibilities of the contractor's superintendent. Subparagraph 3.9.1 requires that

> "The Contractor shall employ a competent superintendent and necessary assistants who shall be in attendance at the Project site during performance of the Work. The superintendent shall represent the Contractor, and communications given to the superintendent shall be as binding as if given to the Contractor."

Subparagraph 10.2.6 requires that

> "The Contractor shall designate a responsible member of the Contractor's organization at the site whose duty shall be the prevention of accidents. This person shall be the Contractor's superintendent unless otherwise designated by the Contractor in writing to the Owner and Architect."

However, in analyzing the contractor's duties and responsibilities, it becomes apparent that some of those responsibilities could most conveniently be carried out by the superintendent at the jobsite, while others would more easily be carried out by the contractor's home office personnel. Obviously it is the contractor's prerogative to assign the contracted responsibilities in whatever way is deemed most expedient under the circumstances, apportioning duties variously to field and office personnel in the most strategic and advantageous manner.

Identification of the contractor's responsibilities most logically and reasonably expected to be assigned to the field superintendent is based mainly on the expectation that the superintendent will be physically present continuously at the jobsite. The General Conditions specifically require the superintendent to be "in attendance at the Project site during performance of the Work." (A201, 3.9.1) Also, the General Conditions mandate that the superintendent "represent" the contractor. (A201, 3.9.1) The term Contractor is defined as "the Contractor or the Contractor's authorized representative." (A201, 3.1.1) Therefore, the superintendent is clearly empowered to carry out all of the contractor's functions at the jobsite. In addition, the General Conditions designate the superintendent as a receiver of communications "as binding as if given to the Contractor." (A201, 3.9.1)

Except for very large and costly projects, the superintendent will not usually have a secretary or other clerical personnel present on the jobsite. Some contracting firms make a home office secretary available by telephone for the superintendent's necessary correspondence. However, in most cases the field superintendent will not become directly involved in the processes of letter writing and the giving of written notices other than oral notification of home office personnel of the circumstances giving rise to the need for written communications. The primary paperwork function will be performed by home office based contract administrators or clerical employees, depending on size of the project, resources of the contractor, and organizational structure of the contracting firm.

The superintendent has all of the traditional duties on the jobsite usually assigned by contracting firms. These include being responsible for dimensional control, scheduling of subcontractors, labor and materials, scheduling of all field operations including looking ahead, coordinating interfacing trades, quality control, maintaining jobsite records, keeping the contract documents and all modifications "straight," and in general managing the project at the site. This is a very large order and requires a person of superior technical and interpersonal skills including an intimate knowledge of the construction trades and processes, an organized mind, leadership ability, and diplomacy.

Supplementing this full agenda will be all of the contractor's responsibilities spelled out in the General Conditions which cannot be conveniently performed by the home office staff and which become by default an additional assortment of duties tacitly assigned to the superintendent in charge of the jobsite. While many of these functions are not usually expressly assigned to the superintendent, the contracting firm's leadership and staff will naturally expect them to be a part of the field operation.

Any of the duties and responsibilities of the superintendent deriving from the General Conditions can easily be eliminated or added to if desired by owner and contractor, merely by modification of the General Conditions. Be aware, however, that the AIA documents are coordinated, so it might be necessary to make appropriate changes in other companion documents to maintain consistency.

Preliminary Site Visit

Subparagraph 1.2.2 of the General Conditions states that

> "Execution of the Contract by the Contractor is a representation that the Contractor has visited the site, become familiar with local conditions under which the work is to be performed and correlated personal observations with requirements of the Contract Documents."

This site visitation could have been made by the superintendent but more likely would have been made by the contractor's estimating department personnel during the process of preparing the contract proposal. If the superintendent did not personally visit the site before the contract was executed, the site should be investigated before any work is started for familiarization with local conditions.

Review of Contract Documents and Field Conditions

The superintendent, before starting any work, should carefully study and compare the contract documents, property survey, and soil tests and correlate them with information obtained during field observations. Any errors, omissions, inconsistencies, or anomalies discovered must be reported to the architect. The contractor is under no contractual obligation to find any discrepancies but would be held financially responsible for carrying out any work knowing that it is based on erroneous information. Any damage or loss which is caused by the contractor's deliberate failure to report recognized errors or inconsistencies will be charged to the contractor. It would be extremely difficult to prove that a contractor knew about an unreported defect in the contract documents, but in certain situations a competent contractor would be assumed to have sufficient knowledge to recognize certain types of error. At all times during the construction period the contractor should report recognized errors to the architect in writing, although the general conditions do not specifically require written notice.

During the course of construction, the contractor is obliged to report to the architect any violations of building codes or other governmental regulations which are discovered in the contract documents. However, the contractor is under no contractual duty to ascertain that the contract documents are in compliance with applicable laws and ordinances. If the contractor knowingly proceeds with work in violation of building regulations without notice to the architect, the contractor will be held financially responsible for the consequent costs. (A201, 3.2.1, 3.7.3, and 3.7.4)

Before any construction activities are initiated at the site, the superintendent should take appropriate field measurements, both horizontal and vertical, and compare them with the contract documents in an attempt to discover any errors or discrepancies. Any apparent mistakes should be reported to the architect as previously discussed. (A201, 3.2.2) It is the architect's responsibility to resolve any such anomalies, inconsistencies, or errors discovered in the documents. The contractor should not proceed with construction in uncertainty. If correction of errors in the documents results in additional or less building cost or time, the architect should prepare the necessary change order documentation for the owner's and contractor's concurrence.

Preconstruction Jobsite Conference

If a preconstruction jobsite conference has been scheduled by the architect, the superintendent should attend. This will serve as a valuable orientation to the architect's personality and procedures as well as to the peculiarities and particulars of the project and site. (See Chap. 3, The Preconstruction Jobsite Conference.)

Daily Construction Log

Most organized construction companies require their superintendents to maintain a written journal of all significant events which occur on a jobsite on a daily basis. The daily log should have entries to record the following types of information:

1. Day and date
2. Weather conditions
3. Trades and personnel on the job
4. Earth, materials, and equipment received
5. Earth, debris, and excess materials removed
6. Names and roles of visitors
7. Delays and impending delays
8. Anticipated progress during next 7 days
9. Brief summary of accomplishments and difficulties
10. Inspections, rejections, and approvals received
11. Architect's instructions or interpretations received
12. Changed conditions
13. Unexpected or unforeseen conditions
14. Accidents, injuries, and property damage
15. Safety procedures initiated

The log should have an entry for every day including those not worked on account of labor disputes, adverse weather, lack of governmental approvals, owner's orders, lack of materials, or any other reason. All days should be accounted for between commencement and completion or termination of the work.

Some contracting firms allow the superintendent to telephone one of the main office secretaries each day to dictate the information for a neat typewritten daily log. The daily log should be carefully preserved at the end of the project as a reliable source of authentic information. It will be valuable if needed to substantiate the contractor's billing for extra work and in the event of future lawsuits or arbitrations.

Construction of the Work

The fundamental and by far the most all-encompassing duty of the contractor which will be carried out by the superintendent is imposed by Subparagraph 3.2.3, of the General Conditions which bureaucratically states that "The Contractor shall perform the Work in accordance with the Contract Documents and submittals approved pursuant to Paragraph 3.12." In simple language, this means, "build the building."

Supervision and Construction Procedures

The superintendent, utilizing best efforts, must skillfully and diligently supervise the construction and direct the work. An important general principle permeates the General Conditions, that it is the contractor's prerogative to determine, control, and be responsible for construction means, methods, techniques, sequences, and procedures and for coordinating all portions of the work. Many of these principles will be determined by the superintendent and all will be carried out in the field operation. (3.3.1)

On a continuous basis the superintendent must inspect the work of each trade to determine that the work is being done by skilled workers and that it will be suitable to receive subsequent operations and trades. The superintendent must enforce strict discipline and good order among all persons on the jobsite. (A201, 3.3.4, 3.4.2, 3.13.1, and 3.15.1)

The superintendent is also responsible for keeping the site neat and orderly and in conformance with applicable laws and contract requirements. The site must be kept clean and free of waste accumulations. At completion of the project, all work and the site must be cleaned to the degree specified and all excess materials, equipment, and temporary structures removed. (A201, 3.13.1 and 3.15.1)

The contractor must obtain and pay for all required governmental permits and approvals, unless otherwise specified, and arrange for all governmental inspections. (A201, 3.7.1) These significant details are usually organized by the superintendent.

Progress Schedule

The contractor is required to prepare and submit a construction progress schedule based on the agreed time limits and predicated on expeditious and practicable execution of the work. A schedule of all specified submittals, coordinated and consistent with the construction schedule, must also be submitted. The superintendent's input and assistance with the scheduling logic, proposed construction sequences, and time allowances estimated for each of the operations would be invaluable to the scheduling process and should increase the possibility of producing a realistic and attainable schedule. The construction schedule is submitted for the architect's and owner's information only, while the submittal schedule is subject to the architect's review and approval. The construction and submittal schedules must be revised from time to time as necessary to reflect the actual construction progress. (A201, 3.10.1 and 3.10.2) The work is required to conform to the most recent schedules. (A201, 3.10.3)

Documents and Samples at the Site

The superintendent is expected to maintain at the site a complete up-to-date set of all drawings, specifications, and other contract documents, change orders, addenda, and modifications as well as all approved shop drawings and samples for reference by the owner or architect. (A201, 3.11.1) Conforming to this contract requirement will enable the superintendent more easily to keep the current status of the contract straight in mind.

Shop Drawings, Product Data, and Samples

All shop drawings and other submittals from subcontractors and suppliers should be carefully checked and approved by the superintendent at the site to make sure that realistic jobsite conditions and actual field measurements are reflected and that they comply with the contract documents, before they are submitted for the architect's review. (A201, 3.12.5 and 3.12.7) Work requiring submittal of shop drawings or samples should be done in conformance with the approved submittals. (A201, 3.12.6)

Cutting and Patching

Cutting, fitting, and patching necessary to make the various parts of the work fit together properly is the contractor's responsibility. The superintendent will have to take care of all necessary coordination among the subcontractors to assure harmonious interconnections of the various trades. (A201, 3.14.1) Any cutting and patching which causes damage to the work of the owner or separate contractors will be the responsibility of the contractor. (A201, 3.14.2)

Communications Facilitating Contract Administration

Although the contract is between the owner and contractor, the line of communication is through the architect in furtherance of orderly administration. All communications with the architect's consultants should be through the architect, and similarly, all communications directed to subcontractors should be through the contractor. (A201, 4.2.4) The superintendent, being the alter ego of the contractor on the jobsite, is the proper recipient of communications directed to the contractor. (A201, 3.9.1) It is up to the contracting firm to establish its own two-way communication system between its home office and its superintendents at the various jobsites.

Continuing Contract Performance

While awaiting final resolution of contractor's or owner's claims against each other, whether submitted to arbitration or not, the contractor should continue diligently with the work and the owner is obligated to continue making payments as contracted. (A201, 4.3.4 and 4.5.3) For either to discontinue performance could be deemed a breach of the contract, thereby possibly excusing the other from any further performance.

Claims for Concealed or Unknown Conditions

Should physical conditions be encountered on the site which were concealed or unexpected, and which are materially different from those represented in the contract documents, the party discovering the conditions should notify the other party before conditions are disturbed. Notice must be given within 21 days of the first observance of the conditions. The architect will then investigate and determine whether the contract sum should be increased, decreased, or remain the same. A similar determination should be made in respect to extension of the time of performance. (A201, 4.3.6)

The superintendent should document the discovery and circumstances of all unexpected conditions and occurrences by suitable entry in the daily log as well as by photographs, notes, observations, and measurements when applicable. This will assist the contractor in properly invoicing the job or in making claims for extra compensation. It will also aid the architect in making fair and appropriate determinations.

Claims for Additional Time

Record keeping by the superintendent on the site is extremely important to the smooth-running job and to enable the contractor to be properly remunerated for changes in contract conditions and for additional contract time caused by various factors including adverse weather. All claims for additional time due to weather must be documented as to days of occurrence and the adverse effect the weather had on the scheduled construction. This information must be accumulated on a daily basis and should be faithfully entered in the daily job log. Only abnormal weather which could not have been reasonably anticipated and which had an adverse effect on the construction can be claimed for time extension. (A201, 4.3.8.2)

Cooperation with Owner and Architect and with Separate Contractors

The contractor is in full charge of the construction site and is required to provide access by the owner and architect to all parts of the work in all stages of progress of construction. (A201, 3.16.1)

The owner reserves the right to do work on the project site with its own forces and to award separate contracts for portions of the work. The contractor is obligated to cooperate with the owner and the separate contractors and to allow them reasonable use of the site and storage areas. The owner is required when contracting with separate contractors to use contract provisions similar to those used in the original owner-contractor agreement. The owner is also obligated to coordinate the work of its own forces and the work of separate contractors. The contractor is required to cooperate in the coordination of its time schedules with those of the owner and separate contractors. (A201, 6.1.1, 6.1.3, and 6.2.1)

Where any part of the contractor's work interfaces with the work done by the owner or separate contractors, the contractor should report to the architect any observed discrepancies or defects which would render the work of others unsuitable for continuation of construction. The contractor's failure to notify the architect will constitute acceptance of the owner's or separate contractor's work, except for defects not then reasonably discoverable. (A201, 6.2.2)

Changes in the Work

The owner has the right under the contract to order changes without invalidating the contract, and the contractor is required to carry out the changes. Changes, where the scope of work, price, and time are agreeable to the parties, are provided for by a written change order. Those changes that are not acceptable in whole or in part to the contractor are provided for by construction change directive, and the remaining disagreements are left for later resolution by the architect or by negotiation or arbitration. An order for a minor change in the work, not involving any change in contract sum or time schedule, may be ordered by the architect. The contractor must promptly carry out all changes ordered by the owner or architect. (A201, 7.1.1, 7.1.3, and 7.4.1) (See Chap. 10, Change Orders.)

Time of Construction

It is important to the owner's interests that no construction on the site is commenced before the mortgage liens, if any, are in place or prior to the effective dates on all insurance specified to be carried by the contractor or furnished by the owner. If the notice to the contractor to proceed with construction, preferably written, is not provided by the owner, the contractor is required to give the owner written notice no less than 5 days prior to starting work. (A201, 8.2.2) The contractor is required to pursue the work diligently and efficiently, using adequate forces, and to complete the work to substantial completion within the contract time. (A201, 8.2.3)

The superintendent should have all the preconstruction procedures organized before construction is commenced on the site. These consist of reviewing documents and site conditions, obtaining necessary governmental permits, preparing construction schedule and submittal schedule, submitting insurance certificates, and provisional mobilization of initial labor, materials, and subcontractors. The superintendent should be present and accompany the architect at all scheduled site visitations. This is for the purpose of answering any questions posed by the architect and to receive the architect's instructions and determinations.

Substantial Completion

Substantial completion is the stage of completion when the owner may occupy or make use of the work for its intended purpose even though there may be various items of incomplete or defective work. When the contractor considers that the work is substantially complete, the contractor must prepare a punch list (referred to in the AIA General Conditions as an inspection list) tabulating all remaining incomplete and defective work. The architect will review and possibly supplement the contractor's list. The superintendent must promptly organize and schedule the completion of all punch list work. The architect will then make a determination as to completion, binding on owner and contractor, by issuance of a certificate of substantial completion. The owner and contractor both sign the architect's certificate as an indication of their mutual acceptance of the responsibilities assigned to each of them in respect to such matters as utilities, insurance, security, maintenance, and damage to the work. (A201, 9.8.1 and 9.8.2)

The superintendent must then start making arrangements with the subcontractors and suppliers to obtain all specified written warranties, operating manuals and instructions, spare parts, and record drawings for submission to the architect. (See Chap. 14, Closing Out the Job.)

Protection of Persons and Property

One of the most significant responsibilities of the construction superintendent is the duty to safeguard persons and property on or about the site. The contractor's duty to provide safety and to prevent accidents is specifically assigned to the superintendent by Subparagraph 10.2.6, of the General Conditions which states, "The Contractor shall designate a responsible member of the Contractor's organization at the site whose duty shall be the prevention of accidents. This person shall be the Contractor's superintendent unless otherwise designated by the Contractor in writing to the Owner and Architect."

The superintendent must initiate, maintain, and supervise all safety precautions and programs to be carried out on the work. (A201, 10.1.1) The superintendent must take reasonable precautions for safety and provide reasonable protection to prevent damage, injury, or loss to persons on or about the site, work or materials, or adjacent property. (A201, 10.2.1) The superintendent must give any required notices and comply with all safety laws. (A201, 10.2.2)

The superintendent must erect and maintain all reasonable safeguards needed for safety and protection and post all necessary warning notices. Owners and users of adjacent properties and utilities must be warned of possible hazards. (A201, 10.2.3)

Use and storage of explosives and other hazardous materials or methods must be with the utmost of care and be supervised by competent personnel. (A201, 10.2.4) It is the superintendent's ongoing duty to take responsible managerial charge of the premises and not allow the site or structure to be damaged during construction by overloading or other misuse. (A201, 10.2.7)

In the event of emergency, it is the superintendent's responsibility to exercise discretion in acting to prevent, eliminate, limit, or mitigate threatened damage or injury to persons or property. Claims for additional compensation or time extension arising out of emergency action will be considered and decided by the architect. (A201, 10.3.1) The superintendent should keep complete, detailed, and current records, including photographs where appropriate, of all emergency activities to enable the contractor to compile and prove all incurred costs.

Asbestos and PCB

In alteration work in existing buildings it is not uncommon for the contractor unexpectedly to encounter materials reasonably believed to be asbestos or polychorinated biphenyl (PCB) which have not been rendered harmless. If this happens, the superintendent should immediately stop work in the area affected and give written notice of the condition to the owner and architect. If the materials prove to be in fact asbestos or PCB which have not been rendered harmless, the contractor is not required to continue work in the affected area unless it is further agreed in writing by the owner and contractor, or determined by the architect or by arbitration if demanded by either party. The contractor cannot be required to perform any work related to asbestos or PCB without consent, notwithstanding provisions of Article 7 of the General Conditions relating to construction change directives. (A201, 10.1.2 and 10.1.3)

It is now very difficult for architects and contractors to obtain insurance coverage for operations involving asbestos or PCB. The general conditions require the owner to indemnify and hold harmless the contractor and architect from losses arising out of work in an area affected by asbestos or PCB. (A201, 10.1.4)

Uncovering and Correction of Work

If work has been covered contrary to the specifications or architect's request before examination by the architect, it must be uncovered for observation and replaced at the contractor's expense, with no time extension allowable.

In the event work not specified to be observed before covering is requested by the architect to be uncovered for examination, the contractor is required to comply with the architect's request. However, if the uncovered work proves to have been satisfactory, the contractor will be paid for uncovering and replacing and be granted a reasonable time extension.

If the uncovered work is not in accordance with the contract documents, the contractor will be required to pay all the costs of uncovering and correction, unless the unsatisfactory condition was caused by the owner or a separate contractor, in which case the costs will be charged to the owner. (A201, 12.1.1 and 12.1.2)

All work rejected by the architect or failing to comply with contract requirements should be properly corrected by the contractor. All defective work should be removed from the site. (A201, 12.2.1 and 12.2.3)

Defective work which becomes apparent within 1 year after the date of substantial completion should be promptly corrected after receipt of owner's written notice. (A201, 12.2.2) During the 1-year warranty period, any correction notices received by the contractor will generally be referred to the superintendent for investigation, coordination, and appropriate action if the superintendent is still on the contractor's staff. Otherwise the contractor will have to assign it to other field personnel, preferably someone who is familiar with the project.

Tests and Inspections

Testing and inspections of portions of the work specified by the architect or required by public authorities must be arranged for and facilitated by the contractor to be performed by a competent independent testing agency acceptable to the owner. The superintendent must make portions of the work accessible for testing or observation by testing personnel and the architect. All required certificates or reports of testing, certification, inspection, or approval are required to be acquired by the contractor and promptly delivered to the architect. (A201, 13.5.1, 13.5.2, and 13.5.4)

14

Closing Out the Job

Orderly Conclusion of the Construction Contract

As the construction project is finally taking shape physically and the major building activity is starting to taper off, the architect responsible for the contract administration should start thinking about what is needed for the orderly conclusion of the contract.

Some projects seem to be very difficult to end gracefully, without a lot of terminal grousing and general dissatisfaction of the contractor and owner alike. The final punch list items often are still being corrected months after occupancy and the owner is never entirely pleased about paying the contractor's final bills. The paper work continues on a sporadic but gradually declining basis, and there never appears to be an actual clean finale to the whole affair. This sort of loose unraveled ending to the contract administration must not be very impressive to the client or contractor and is very time-consuming and exasperating for the architect. Additionally, some of the liability restriction offered by statutes of limitation, meager as it is, will be diluted by sloppy or nonexistent contract termination procedures.

The purpose here is to review the normal procedures which are available to architects in the efficient conclusion of the administration of a construction contract when the architect's services have been engaged under the terms of the standard AIA Owner-Architect Agreement and the construction contract includes the AIA General Conditions. These two standard AIA documents are coordinated so that all of their related provisions are in harmony. Most importantly, all of the architect's duties described in the AIA General Conditions are anticipated and included in the AIA Owner-Architect Agreement.

Substantial Completion

The first significant milestone in the closing down process is when the project reaches the point of substantial completion. This is when the project or a designated portion is practically complete so the owner can occupy or use it for its intended purpose. (AIA Document A201, Subparagraph 9.8.1) This does not mean that there is no more work to be done. There will still be minor or trivial items of incomplete work and defects to be rectified. There could also be major items of incomplete work, but if they do not prevent the owner's use of the building, the contract could still be substantially complete. When the contractor considers that the project has reached this decisive stage, the contractor is required to prepare a comprehensive list of all remaining items of work and corrections to be made to complete the work of the contract. The contractor should proceed promptly with the completion and rectification work on the list. At the same time, the list is submitted to the architect for review and further action. Failure to list an incomplete or defective item does not relieve the contractor from responsibility for its proper completion as specified.

Upon receipt of the contractor's correction list the architect is required to make an inspection to determine if the work is indeed substantially complete and in conformance with the contract requirements. If the architect's inspection discloses items, whether or not on the contractor's list, which are not in accordance with the contract documents and which would preclude substantial completion, then the contractor must rectify these items upon notification by the architect. The architect should have all design consultants examine the work which they designed such as structural, electrical, and mechanical systems and landscape installation. The architect's consultants may also find items to be added to the contractor's list. The contractor, upon completion of the items which preclude substantial completion, must again notify the architect to reinspect the work.

Certificate of Substantial Completion

The architect, upon determination that the work is substantially complete, must issue a certificate of substantial completion. (A201, 9.8.2) The certificate does not have to be in any particular form but could be on the AIA's standard form, Document G704, which contains all the necessary elements to comply with the AIA General Conditions.

The certificate of substantial completion must name a specific date as the date of substantial completion. This becomes the date of commencement of all warranties except those relating to items remaining on the contractor's correction list and as supplemented by the architect. The warranty periods on these items will commence on completion of the actual performance of the work. (A201, 12.2.2) The date of substantial completion is also the ending of the contract time period for determination of liquidated damages.

The owner and contractor must also sign the architect's certificate as an indication of their acceptance of the agreed allocation of responsibility for security, maintenance, heat, utilities, damage to the work, and insurance. The certificate also fixes the time within which the contractor is to finish all items on the correction list accompanying the certificate.

The owner may now move in and occupy or utilize the project or the designated portion covered by the certificate. The owner should be urged to make all defects and dissatisfactions immediately known to the architect. The architect should then promptly send on to the contractor all legitimate complaints, eliminating all unreasonable demands, nit-picking, and requests not within the scope of the contract documents. It is possible to have several dates of substantial completion if the project is divided into portions to be occupied progressively as the work continues.

Notice of Completion (as Distinguished from Certificate of Substantial Completion)

Certificate of substantial completion is a term coined by drafters of AIA form documents and is uniformly used in the AIA documents to describe the date determined by the architect as the day on which the project is sufficiently complete that it may be occupied or utilized by the owner for its intended purpose.

A notice of completion, on the other hand, is a legal term and is not mentioned in the AIA documents. The notice of completion is associated with requirements of state mechanics' lien laws. In some states, such as California, a notice of completion, signed by the owner or agent, must be recorded in the office of the recorder of the county in which the work of the contract is situated, within 10 days after completion of the work. The definition of completion of the work for the purpose of complying with the mechanics' lien law is not necessarily the same as for substantial completion as defined in the AIA General Conditions, although in many situations it could be the same date.

Completion for the purpose of complying with the lien law means the work is finished and the persons who have the right to lien the owner's property have no more work left to do. Some court cases have recognized completion when minor items were left to be done while others have held that similar minor items precluded completion.

The recording of a notice of completion is very important to the owner as well as to potential mechanics' lien claimants, as it shortens the claim period and establishes a definite date for measuring the time periods in the mechanics' lien law. A notice of completion in California must be recorded within 10 days after completion in the office of the recorder of the county in which the construction site is situated.

In California, original contractors (those who deal directly with the owner or owner's agent) have 60 days after the recording of a valid notice of completion to record their lien claims while subcontractors and others who work for the original contractor have 30 days in which to file their claims. If no notice of completion, or an invalid one, has been recorded, the period for all lien claimants is extended to 90 days after cessation of labor.

Some architects and contractors include as a part of their standard service the filling out of a notice of completion form for the owner's signature and recording with the county recorder's office. This entails the exercise of judgment as to the date to be stated as the completion date. Normally the date of substantial completion will be the date to be used in the notice of completion. However, it is possible that a mechanics' lien claimant might later convince a judge that minor corrections on the defect list inhibited completion of their work and that the notice of completion was therefore invalid and ineffective.

Architects who do not take care of the notice of completion for their clients should at least notify their client in sufficient time that they can contact their attorney or do it for themselves.

Final Submissions

While the final corrections are being made in the field, the contractor should start assembling the miscellany of specified final submittals:

- All specified written warranties. When transmitting them to the owner, the architect should refrain from stating any opinions as to their sufficiency but should suggest that the owner's legal counsel review all written warranties. The architect's principal function in respect to warranties is to confirm that the contractor has submitted all that were specified. The word guarantee no longer appears in AIA documents, as it is synonymous with the word warranty. (A201, 4.2.9)

- All specified operating instructions, user's manuals, wiring diagrams, parts lists, and spare parts for mechanical and electrical equipment.

- Keys and keying schedules.

- Record drawings. (A201, 3.11.1) The record drawings furnished by the contractor will consist primarily of marked-up prints, drawings, and other data showing significant changes in the work made during construction. If the owner wishes the architect to prepare a set of reproducible drawings based on the contractor's record drawings, this can be done as an optional additional service in the AIA Owner-Architect Agreement, Subparagraph 3.14.16.

- All contract drawings and specifications used by the contractor and subcontractors should be returned or suitably accounted for except for one contract record set which the contractor may retain. (A201, 1.3.1)

All of the contractor's final submissions should be sent to the owner accompanied by a written letter of transmittal inventorying all items in detail to create a permanent record for your file. The final submittal should precede the owner's final payment.

Final Completion

When the work of the combined correction lists has been finished, the contractor should notify the architect that the work is ready for final inspection and acceptance. At the same time, the contractor should submit the final application for payment.

The architect should make a careful inspection to determine that the completed work is in compliance with the contract documents. Consulting engineers and other design consultants should make their final inspections of the portions of the work which they have designed. When the architect is satisfied that the work of the contract is complete and in conformance with the contract documents, the architect's attention should be focused on the contractor's final application for payment.

If any work has been performed not in accordance with requirements of the contract documents, it is the owner's right to accept the work instead of requiring its correction or removal. In this case the contract price will be reduced as appropriate and equitable. If the owner and contractor cannot agree on a suitable credit, the architect will make a final determination. If the architect's opinion is not acceptable to both, it may be appealed to arbitration. (See Chap. 17, Resolution of Construction Disputes.)

Architect's Final Certificate and Final Payment

The contractor's final application for payment does not have to be in any particular form, but most contractors use a format similar to Application and Certificate for Payment, AIA Document G702, and the Continuation Sheet, AIA Document G703. If these forms are used, the architect's certificate which appears on G702 may be used. The wording of the certificate ties in with the wording of Subparagraph 9.10.1 of the AIA General Conditions. If the contractor does not use the AIA standard forms, the architect will have to create a form of final certificate. It could be in the form of a covering letter to the owner transmitting the contractor's payment application. The wording of the certificate could be similar to that on the AIA form. Although the payment and certificate issued at completion of the work are referred to as final, there will still be one or more additional payments to release the retainage, if any, and sums withheld to ensure completion of remaining inspection list items and unsettled claims.

As a condition precedent to the owner's making the final payment, the contractor is required by the General Conditions (9.10.2) to submit the following items:

- An affidavit that payrolls, bills for materials and equipment, and other indebtedness connected with the work for which the owner or owner's property might be responsible or encumbered (less amounts withheld by owner) have been paid or otherwise satisfied. Forms for this purpose are AIA Document G706, Contractor's Affidavit of Payment of Debts and Claims, and AIA Document G706A, Contractor's Affidavit of Release of Liens.

- A certificate evidencing that insurance required by the contract documents to remain in force after final payment is currently in effect and will not be canceled or allowed to expire until at least 30 days' prior written notice has been given to the owner. This certificate may be obtained by the contractor from its insurance agent or broker.

- A written statement that the contractor knows of no substantial reason that the insurance will not be renewable to cover the period required by the contract documents.

- Consent of surety, if any, to final payment. This should be an unconditional consent and could be submitted on AIA Document G707, Consent of Surety to Final Payment.

- If required by the owner, other data establishing payment or satisfaction of obligations, such as receipts, releases and waivers of liens, claims, security interests, or encumbrances arising out of the contract, to the extent and in such form as may be designated by the owner. The contractor must indemnify the owner against the possible liens of any subcontractors who refuse to furnish a release or waiver required by the owner and must fully reimburse the owner all sums paid out in discharging liens after the final payment is made.

All the documentation submitted by the contractor to satisfy these listed requirements should be promptly transmitted to the owner without stating any opinions as to their sufficiency but with the recommendation that they be reviewed by the owner's auditors and legal counsel. The owner should be reminded that if these additional submittals are in proper accounting and legal order, the enclosed architect's certificate for final payment should be paid.

The making of the final payment constitutes a waiver of claims by the owner except those arising from unsettled liens or claims arising out of the contract, failure of the work to comply with requirements of the contract documents, or terms of special warranties required by the contract documents. (A201, 4.3.5) Acceptance of the final payment by the contractor, a subcontractor, or a supplier constitutes a waiver of claims by that payee except those previously made in writing and identified by that payee as unsettled at the time of final application for payment. (A201, 9.10.4)

Decisions to Withhold Certificate

Within 7 days after receiving the contractor's application for payment, the architect must issue to the owner a certificate for payment, with a copy to the contractor, for such amount as the architect deems proper, or must notify the owner and contractor in writing of the reasons for withholding certification in whole or in part. (A201, 9.4.1) The issuance of a certificate for payment constitutes the architect's representation to the owner that work has progressed to the point indicated and that the quality of the work is in accordance with requirements of the contract documents, to the best of the architect's knowledge, information, and belief. These representations are based on the architect's site observations and information submitted by the contractor in the application for payment. (A201, 9.4.2)

Should the architect consider that the required representations cannot be made, the architect should withhold certification in whole or in part to the extent deemed necessary to protect the owner's interest. If this happens, the architect must so notify the owner and contractor in writing. If the contractor and architect cannot agree on a mutually acceptable amount, the architect should promptly issue a certificate in an amount for which the required representations can be made to the owner. The architect may refuse to certify any amount and may nullify previous certificates in whole or in part if in the architect's judgment this is necessary to protect the owner from loss on account of unremedied defective work, the filing or probable filing of third party claims, contractor's failure to pay construction bills, reasonable evidence that the work cannot be completed for the unpaid balance of the contract, damage to the owner or another contractor, evidence that the work will not be completed within the contract time and that anticipated liquidated damages will be greater than the unpaid balance of the contract, or persistent failure to comply with requirements of the contract documents. When these reasons for withholding a certificate are removed, the architect should promptly issue a certificate for the amounts previously withheld. (See Chap. 9, Payment Certifications.)

Owner's Partial Use or Occupancy

The owner may obtain partial use or occupancy of the project before completion upon the contractor's acquiescence and upon consent of the insurers and public authorities having jurisdiction over the work. The owner and contractor must further agree upon their respective responsibilities assigned to each of them in respect to payments, retainage, security, maintenance, heat, utilities, damage to the work, and insurance.

The agreement must also cover the period for correction of the work and commencement of specified warranties. The contractor may not unreasonably withhold consent for partial occupancy. (A201, 9.9.1) A joint inspection by the owner, contractor, and architect should be made prior to partial occupancy to record the condition of the work. (A201, 9.9.2) Partial occupancy does not constitute acceptance of work not in conformance to the contract documents unless otherwise agreed. (A201, 9.6.6 and 9.9.3)

Retainage

It is common in construction contracts that the owner need pay only 90 percent of the value of the work in place at each payment, the remaining 10 percent being withheld by the owner to be paid to the contractor at or after the completion of construction. Usually the contract provides that the retained amount will be payable after the expiration of the period during which mechanics' liens may be claimed. This period differs from state to state. In those states, such as California, where subcontractors' and suppliers' lien rights expire 30 days after recording of a valid notice of completion, the contract will provide for payment of retainage 35 days after recording of the notice of completion provided no mechanics' lien claims have been recorded. This allows 5 days after subcontractors' lien rights have expired in which to determine that no liens have been recorded. All that remains, then, is to obtain a waiver of lien rights from the general contractor, whose lien rights would otherwise continue an additional 30 days after the subcontractors' rights have expired. Then the retainage can be paid.

The retainage does not have to be 10 percent. It could be more or less and is subject to owner's requirements and contract negotiation. On projects involving large sums of money, the retainage can become very burdensome to the contractor, and therefore it is quite common to specify reduction or elimination of further retainage after it reaches a certain amount. For example, on a $1,000,000 contract, a 10 percent retainage would accumulate by the end of the work to $100,000. The contract could provide for no further retainage after the first $50,000, if it is deemed that this sum would sufficiently protect the owner's interest. It is also possible to release some of the retention at some point such as at completion. In this example, $25,000 could be released at completion, leaving $25,000 to be retained until after expiration of the lien period.

In the event that the retainage is to be reduced or partially released, if the job is bonded, it is essential to obtain the surety's prior permission. This should be obtained by the contractor and should be unconditional and in writing. A standard form is available for this purpose, AIA Document G707A, Consent of Surety to Reduction In or Partial Release Of Retainage.

Liquidated Damages

If the contract provides for payment or allowance of liquidated damages to the owner in the event of late completion, the architect will have to make a computation of the sum owing, if any, or a determination that the contract has been completed on time. The contract provision for liquidated damages should be in terms of a certain number of calendar days (to comply with the definition in Subparagraph 8.1.4 of the General Conditions) or a specified date for substantial completion. The starting date for computation will be stated in the contract. (A201, 8.1.2) The contract time is terminated on the date of substantial completion. (A201, 8.1.1 and 8.1.3) The contract time must be adjusted by all justifiable time extensions requested by the contractor and approved by the architect.

Termination of the Contract

Either owner or contractor may terminate the contract for cause under certain specified conditions. In addition, the owner may suspend the work for convenience. (A201, Article 14) In case of termination or suspension, careful compliance with all technical provisions of the contract is very important.

Unilateral terminations, whether initiated by owner or contractor, will always be under conditions of strained relationships, financial hardship, and unrealized expectations and will undoubtedly be followed by claims and counterclaims and litigation or arbitration. Therefore, any services performed by the architect during these stressful periods must be strictly in accordance with the procedures set out in the contract documents. (See Chap. 15, Termination of the Construction Contract.)

Architect's Decisions

All unsettled claims and differences between the parties should be resolved in the process of concluding the contract. The architect should attempt to obtain the viewpoints of owner and contractor on all matters remaining in contention. A thorough examination of their positions and a complete analysis of the requirements of the contract documents should be carefully made. The architect should promptly make a competent and fair determination of each issue in controversy so that the dispute resolution process can proceed to the next step, arbitration, if necessary. (A201, 4.3, 4.4, and 4.5) (See Chap. 17, Resolution of Construction Disputes.)

Owner-Architect Relationship

As part of the contract closing process the architect should make certain that the office files are complete and in proper order for permanent filing. The files will be of extreme importance in the event of a later legal claim against the architect. Even if the job has run smoothly and the client and contractor are both extremely pleased with the outcome of the contract, there is still the lurking possibility of claims being asserted by third parties, as yet unknown, such as later owners, occupants, lessees, and passersby. There is also the possibility of a latent construction defect becoming apparent years later.

The architect's responsibility to render basic services under the AIA Owner-Architect Agreement for the construction phase commences with the award of the construction contract and terminates at the earlier of issuance of the final certificate for payment or 60 days after the date of substantial completion unless extended. (B141, 2.6.1)

Many owners will wish to have the architect inspect the project prior to expiration of the various specified warranty periods. This service is not usually included in the basic architectural fee and would be the subject of an additional charge. A written detailed observation report should be issued. The architect should be meticulous in differentiating between maintenance or usage defects which are the owner's responsibility and construction defects which the contractor must rectify.

15

Termination of the Construction Contract

Termination Provisions in the Contract

The low point of an architectural construction administrator's life is when adverse circumstances result in the contractor's abandonment of the contract or the owner's ejection of the contractor. Such dire consequences are usually the eventuality of a period of gradually deteriorating conditions and are seldom completely unexpected. These extreme measures have far-reaching legal implications and financial repercussions for both parties. They should not be casually considered and should be undertaken only as a last resort. Practical and equitable termination provisions, fair to both sides, are included in the AIA General Conditions of the Contract for Construction, Fourteenth Edition, Document A201, 1987 (Appendix D).

Termination by the Contractor

At various times a contractor might conclude that mounting losses caused by rising costs, inefficiency, bad luck, or an uncooperative owner could be curtailed or eliminated by quitting the job and canceling the contract. However, these are not allowable reasons for termination. The contract provides that the contractor is justified in declaring the contract terminated only under certain limited specified conditions.

The contractor may terminate the contract if the work is stopped for a period of 30 days through no fault of the contractor or any of its suppliers, subcontractors, or employees, for any of the following reasons:

1. Issuance of an order of a court or other public authority having jurisdiction

2. An act of government, such as a declaration of national emergency, making material unavailable

3. Because the architect has not issued a certificate for payment and has not notified the contractor of the reason for withholding certification, or because the owner has not made payment within the agreed time

4. If repeated suspensions, delays, or interruptions by the owner, as allowed by the contract, constitute in the aggregate more than 100 percent of the total number of days scheduled for completion, or 120 days in any 365-day period, whichever is less

5. The owner has failed to furnish to the contractor promptly, upon request, reasonable evidence that financial arrangements have been made to fulfill the owner's obligations under the contract (AIA Document A201, Subparagraph 14.1.1)

If any of these reasons exist, the contractor may terminate the contract upon 7 additional days' written notice to the owner and architect. The contractor is then entitled to recover from the owner payment for work executed and for proved loss with respect to materials, equipment, tools, and construction equipment and machinery, including reasonable overhead, profit, and damages. (A201, 14.1.2)

The contractor may also terminate the contract if the owner or owner's agents (possibly the architect) cause the work to be stopped for 60 days by persistently failing to fulfill the owner's obligations in matters important to the progress of the work. The contractor, after giving an additional 7 days' written notice, may terminate the contract, provided the contractor, suppliers, subcontractors, or employees are not at fault. (A201, 14.1.3) Matters important to the progress of the work include such owner shortcomings as

1. Failure to make the site or work areas available when needed

2. Failure to obtain necessary easements, party line agreements, utilities, and governmental approvals

3. Failure to make necessary decisions such as those relating to color and material selections and other options

4. Failure to provide owner-furnished materials, equipment, services, or separate contractors

5. Failure to respond to shop drawing submittals or other requests for information or direction

Downside risks for the contractor who opts for termination are the negative effect on its reputation in the community, the possibility that a court or arbitrator will not agree that sufficient cause existed for termination, and the distinct likelihood of monetary loss.

Termination by the Owner for Cause

When symptoms of a contractor's impending default begin to appear, owners, their architects, and legal advisors should start considering the options and whether or not to terminate the contract. It is very unsettling to an owner when the contractor is not making satisfactory progress or the workmanship is substandard, or both. Subcontractors' complaints of not being paid and the emergence of mechanics' liens are of serious concern. Often these indications are accompanied by desperate claims for extra time and compensation on flimsy pretexts or nonexistent grounds.

The owner and architect will often consider the possibility of terminating the contract, particularly if the contractor has not reacted favorably to repeated admonitions. This is allowable under the contract only under carefully defined circumstances. The owner may terminate the contract if the contractor

1. Persistently or repeatedly refuses or fails to supply enough properly skilled workers or proper materials

2. Fails to make payment to subcontractors for materials or labor in accordance with the respective agreements between the contractor and the subcontractors

3. Persistently disregards laws, ordinances, or rules, regulations, or orders of a public authority having jurisdiction

4. Otherwise is guilty of a substantial breach of a provision of the contract documents (A201, 14.2.1)

The architect must find that one or more of these reasons exists and must certify in writing that there is sufficient cause to justify termination of the contract. The owner must give the contractor and the surety, if any, 7 days' written notice. Then the owner, subject to any prior rights of the surety, may

1. Take possession of the site and of all materials, equipment, tools, and construction equipment and machinery thereon owned by the contractor

2. Accept assignment of subcontracts, as provided in the contract

3. Finish the work by whatever reasonable method the owner may deem expedient (A201, 14.2.2)

The owner, after termination, is not obligated to make any further payments to the contractor until after the work is finished. (A201, 14.2.3) If the costs to complete the work exceed the amount remaining in the contractor's account, the contractor must pay the deficiency to the owner. The contractor is entitled to any sums remaining in the account after the costs of completion have been paid. In either case, the architect's additional services and expenses made necessary by the termination are paid by the owner and charged to the contractor. The final sum to be paid to the owner or contractor should be certified by the architect. (A201, 14.2.4)

Suspension by the Owner for Convenience

Owners often require the flexibility of suspending a construction contract in order to accommodate other unpredictable factors or events such as changes in cash availability or business requirements. The contract allows the owner at any time, without stating any cause, to order the contractor to suspend, delay, or interrupt the work of the contract for any length of time suitable to the owner's requirements. If this occurs, the owner must reimburse the contractor for the extra costs of performing the contract plus an agreed fixed or percentage fee. The owner's order must be in writing. (A201, 14.3)

Position of the Surety

If the contract is bonded using the AIA standard bond form (Performance Bond and Payment Bond, Document A312, December 1984 Edition), the surety and contractor must be given a chance to cure the deficiencies and reinstate the contractor. The bond agreement requires the owner to give the surety and contractor written notice of a conference, to be held within 15 days of the notice, to discuss methods of the contractor's performing of the contract. If the owner, contractor, and surety can agree, the contractor will be given a reasonable time to perform the contract. In the event of no such agreement or if the contractor fails to properly resume production, the owner's declaration of termination cannot be made sooner than 20 days after the conference notice. (A312, 3.1 and 3.2)

One of the principal advantages of the conference will be to enlist the aid of the surety in motivating the contractor to rehabilitate its organization and finances and to reestablish its workmanship standard, coordination, and scheduling. The surety can exercise considerable financial pressure on the contractor and will prove to be very helpful to both parties. In some cases, to protect its own investment, the surety will provide financial advice and assistance to the contractor.

If the original contractor cannot by itself satisfactorily proceed with the work of the contract, the surety may use its own judgment and exercise its own choice as to method of completing the contract. It may hire a new contractor, use the original contractor, contract directly with subcontractors and suppliers, or pay monetary damages to the owner. (A312, Paragraph 4) The owner should insist that a completion and payment bond equivalent to the original bond be in effect for the completion of the contract. The owner must continue paying the balance of the contract price to the bonding company or to its designated contractor. (See Chap. 7, Construction Administration When the Contract Is Bonded.)

Position of the Architect

The periods leading up to and following termination are generally very stressful for all involved parties including the architect. Opportunities for maladministration by the architect are profuse, and the professional liability implications are limited only by the creative imaginations of lawyers hired by the owner, contractor, and surety.

All professional ministrations of the architect must be performed with deliberation and in strict accordance with the owner-architect and construction agreements and the standard of care for architects in the community. The architect should try to keep the lines of communication open among the parties, insist that all actions be in writing, and carefully maintain and preserve all documentation. The architect should avoid being a bottleneck, impeding rapid and open communication.

An architect's certificate of sufficient cause upon which an owner will base its right of termination must be an independent opinion founded on solid provable evidence. If later a court or arbitrator deems that sufficient cause is lacking, the owner may be assessed damages in favor of the contractor.

Practical Considerations in the Decision to Terminate

When the contractor is gone from the jobsite, whether by voluntary abandonment or owner's ejection, the owner is faced with the serious problem of protecting the work in process, the site, materials, and equipment until such time as a replacement contractor has been engaged. It is usually very difficult, often impossible, to find a new contractor who will complete the work for the remaining contract sum or, for that matter, for any fixed sum. It is almost always necessary to contract on a cost-plus-fee basis without a guaranteed maximum price. Time will always be lost, as it will be necessary for the new contractor to become intimately acquainted with the contract requirements as well as with the status of all aspects of the work in the field. All the subcontractors and suppliers must be contacted and decisions made as to which to retain and which to replace. The architect must ascertain the methods and extent of correcting all defective work. If any defective work is to remain uncorrected, the owner's concurrence must be obtained for any compromise of the original contract standards. Budgets and time schedules must be reestablished. The subcontractors, employees, and materials must be remobilized and bonds and insurance must be in place before the new operation can commence.

The inevitable late completion will create additional expenses and duties for the owner: deferral of furniture, stock and equipment, and machinery deliveries, or if it is too late for postponement, provisions for receiving, protecting, and temporary storage; deferral of new or transferred employees; and notification of governmental authority and customers. Alternate financial arrangements may have to be provided.

It is usually only a remote possibility at best that the work can be completed on time or for the funds remaining in the contract. In those situations where the contractor has been involuntarily removed and thus financially responsible for the construction cost overrun there will almost always be an economic shortfall. There is little likelihood that a contractor in those circumstances will willingly pay the difference. Even though the owner may not be sympathetically disposed toward the contractor, there remains a serious duty to the contractor to eliminate waste, to exercise conservative administration of the funds, and to mitigate damages. Any contract changes which amount to economic upgrading or betterment of the project cannot be charged to the discharged contractor.

From the contractor's standpoint, the decision to abandon the contract is potentially costly, as the losses could be considerably more than the mere loss of a job. Usually the reason the owner has defaulted is insurmountable financial or legal obstacles, and the owner will not be able or willing to pay its obligations to the contractor.

Whether the owner or contractor has initiated the termination procedure, both sides will be exposed to financial losses, legal claims and counterclaims, legal fees, attacks on reputations, and considerable loss of time and effort. No termination should be initiated before complete analysis and advice from legal counsel. If after thorough consideration of the consequences and alternatives termination is deemed to be the least onerous option, it should be cautiously undertaken. Termination of a construction contract is a technical legal procedure and must be pursued strictly in accordance with the contract. Obviously, all aspects of the termination procedure should be in writing.

If the defaulting owner or contractor happens to be in or on the verge of bankruptcy proceedings, this will have a profound impact on the termination procedure. Permission of the bankruptcy court will be required for any moves against the financial interests of the bankrupt party. It is not possible to predict whether the trustee acting for the bankrupt will approve continuation of the contract or will favor the termination procedure. The decision will depend on which course would, in the trustee's judgment, yield the maximum conservation of the bankrupt's assets and the impartial treatment of all the creditors. Legal advice necessary for dealing with the bankrupt contractor should be furnished by the owner. In the event that the architect's client (the owner) is the bankrupt, the architect might have to confer with its own legal counsel.

Warranty Responsibility

The changing of contractors before completion of the contract raises a knotty problem relating to responsibility for warranties required by the contract. Confusion will arise as to which contractor is responsible, particularly for latent defects, those which are not known at the time of the change of contractors. The first contractor will always claim that the second contractor damaged or destroyed the original work while the second contractor will claim that the work of the first contractor was unsuitable or defective. Written and photographic records which describe the precise condition of the project at the time of changeover will be invaluable in determining the validity of buck-passing arguments.

16

Architect's Decisions Based on Design Concept, Aesthetic Effect, and Intent of the Contract Documents

Imprecise Standards for Architect's Decisions

Construction contracts include an impressive assemblage of documents drafted with all of the precision and technology available to informed architects and engineers and experienced construction industry lawyers. The construction drawings precisely delineate complex physical structures and operations, and the specifications accurately describe particular procedures and specific materials. The agreement exactly specifies the contract time to the day and the contract sum to the dollar. The supplementary conditions particularize the unique contract conditions for the specific project at hand. The AIA General Conditions is a collection of highly coordinated and interrelated contract conditions based on the principles that form the very essence of most construction contracts in the United States. It clearly reflects the standard and customary procedures of the U.S. construction industry.

With all this graphic and verbal technological and legal precision it would no doubt be surprising to the uninitiated to find in the AIA General Conditions that owners and contractors routinely agree to abide by the architect's decisions in some extremely abstract, nebulous, and undefined areas. It is particularly surprising that contractors, noted for their practicality, would agree to be bound by such indefinite provisions.

Intent of the Contract Documents

The cryptic phrase "intent of the contract documents" is defined in an uncertain manner in Subparagraph 1.2.3 of the AIA General Conditions: "The *intent* of the Contract Documents is to include all items necessary for the proper execution and completion of the Work by the Contractor." Further, in the same paragraph, "performance by the Contractor shall be required only to the extent consistent with the Contract Documents and *reasonably inferable* from them as being necessary to produce the *intended results*." (All italics have been supplied by me for emphasis. The AIA General Conditions has no italics.)

Only the architect can supply a definitive answer as to what physical results were actually intended. It would be far better if architects could always express their design intentions by specific contract requirements that would produce the desired results. Then the contractor would know exactly what was expected and could provide for it in the construction scheduling and the cost breakdown. As to what precisely is "reasonably inferable," there can be many an honest disagreement between well-intentioned competent contractors and fair-minded owners. If anything of substantial economic consequence is left off the drawings or omitted from the specifications, it is not proper to charge the contractor for it merely by the owner's or architect's declaration that it was reasonably inferable and should be included in the contract price. An architect, making a ruling to decide this disagreement (AIA Document A201, Subparagraph 2.6.15), must often rule in favor of the contractor. The term "reasonably inferable from the contract documents" means that the architect's opinion or conclusion must be well-balanced, rational, logically reasoned, and based on the existence of some reasonable evidence. The architect is justifiable in relying on this catchall phrase only in such situations where all of the pieces and parts customarily included in a specified installation or assembly are normally expected to be supplied without naming each part. For example, the contractor should include all fastenings, washers, gaskets, adhesives, lubricants, tools, and equipment normally incidental to the installation of the object or assembly specified.

Items are not reasonably inferable if the specification is written in such a way that competent experienced bidders would not normally include them in their cost breakdown. If they have been truly omitted from the contractor's cost breakdown, then the owner has not paid for them.

The architect is authorized to order additional testing or inspection of the work "Whenever the Architect considers it necessary or advisable for implementation of the *intent of the Contract Documents....*" (A201, 4.2.6) Clearly, any testing ordered under this provision will be chargeable to the owner unless the tests disclose defective or nonconforming work, in which case the testing would be charged to the contractor. (A201, 13.5.1, 13.5.2, and 13.5.3)

Design Concept

Another vague expression used in the AIA General Conditions is the term "design concept," which appears in Subparagraphs 3.12.4 and 4.2.7, in both cases relating to the contractor's submittals. The purpose of submitting shop drawings, product data, and samples "is to demonstrate...the way the Contractor proposes to conform to...the *design concept* expressed in the Contract Documents"; and "The Architect will review and approve...the Contractor's submittals...but only for the limited purpose of checking for conformance with...the *design concept* expressed in the Contract Documents." In each of these subparagraphs, the architect is limited by what is actually expressed in the contract documents. Regardless of the architect's mental image of the "design concept," no more can be required of the contractor than is actually explicitly stated in the contract documents.

If the architect wishes to extend the contract requirements by means of the shop drawing process, a change order should be initiated to cover the cost of any variations or elaborations. By use of the term "reasonably inferable," these two subparagraphs do not extend the meaning of design concept beyond what is specifically shown in the contract documents.

Architect's Decisions

During the construction period, when differences of opinion arise between owner and contractor, the architect is invested with the duty of interpreting the documents and rendering a decision. The decision will be final and binding upon the parties if not appealed to the arbitration process within 30 days. (A201, 4.3 and 4.4) (See Chap. 17, Resolution of Construction Disputes.)

The AIA General Conditions, Subparagraph 4.2.12, requires "Interpretations and decisions of the Architect will be consistent with the *intent* of and *reasonably inferable* from the Contract

Documents...." This places the burden of impartiality and intellectual honesty squarely on the architect's shoulders. This is particularly true if the disagreement between the owner and contractor is related to shortcomings in the contract documents prepared by the architect. If the architect is not scrupulously fair in making such decisions, an impartial arbitrator will later find no difficulty in reversing or revising the decision.

Minor Changes in the Work

Another area of inexactitude in the AIA General Conditions is to be found in Subparagraph 7.4.1, which provides that "The Architect will have authority to order minor changes in the Work not involving adjustment in the Contract Sum or extension of the Contract Time and not inconsistent with the *intent* of the Contract Documents." This particular provision would not usually impose any economic hardship on the contractor or owner beyond possibly some administrative or coordination inconvenience.

The architect cannot order workmanship to be performed or materials to be supplied to a higher standard or quality than was originally specified. To do so would be a justifiable extra cost to the contract. The architect cannot order the revision or removal of something that is already constructed or installed in accordance with requirements of the contract documents. This would also be a justifiable addition to the contract sum as well as the contract time.

Should the contractor claim that the ordered "minor" change has some effect on the contract sum or contract time, the architect will have to make a ruling. If the ruling is in favor of the contractor, the architect will have to convince the client that the minor change is worthwhile and worth paying the extra cost. If the ruling is against the contractor, the architect will not have to trouble the owner for concurrence but might later have to justify the ruling to arbitrators. In either event, the architect must be fair and just in the rulings and must not penalize the contractor if the architect's documents are at fault.

Aesthetic Effect Decisions

A unique characteristic of construction contracts which include the AIA General Conditions is the power given to the architect to make quasi-judicial determinations on the claims of the contracting parties. This is a practical procedure and a necessity to keep the work of the contract moving expeditiously in the field. However, it relies heavily on the competence, honesty, and professional integrity of the architect. The architect must also possess the ability to resist pressure from either the client or the contractor. The contractual procedure must also be capable of functioning in the rare event that an architect is unable to render objective decisions acceptable to the parties or to summon the necessary courage to rule against the intimidations of an outraged client or a threatening contractor.

If either party is dissatisfied with the architect's determination, it can be appealed to arbitration. If the arbitrators deem that the architect's decision was ill-founded or erroneous in any way, they have the power to revise or reverse it when promulgating their own award. The arbitrators' award will be final and binding if not appealed within 100 days (in California) to the court having jurisdiction in the matter. The grounds for setting aside an arbitration award are few and are limited to matters relating to fraud, corruption, and fairness of the procedure. Judges will not hear appeals based on the merits of the controversy.

All appeals from the architect's decisions as well as other controversies not submitted to the architect will ultimately be referred to arbitration as set out in Subparagraph 4.5.1 of the General Conditions, which states in part that "Any controversy or Claim arising out of or related to the Contract, or the breach thereof, shall be settled by arbitration..., except controversies or claims relating to *aesthetic effect*...."

Closely related to this is Subparagraph 4.2.13, which provides that "The Architect's decisions on matters relating to *aesthetic effect* will be final if consistent with the intent expressed in the Contract Documents." Aesthetic effect is not defined in the AIA General Conditions, so we must rely on the dictionary, which defines aesthetic as "relating to the beautiful as distinguished from the merely pleasing...the useful and utilitarian." It is synonymous with artistic.

The purpose of these seemingly loose aesthetic effect provisions is to protect the integrity of the architectural design and the design judgment and decisions of the architect. Someone has to be the final authority in everything, and it would be inappropriate for an arbitrator, even if an architect, to have final design prerogative superior to that of the design architect.

Practical application of the relevant contract provisions provides ample protection to the owner and contractor in the unlikely but possible event that an architect would get outrageously out of hand. If the owner and contractor are in unanimous opposition to the architect's aesthetic effect decisions, the architect will simply be bypassed. They will do whatever they mutually agree to do without regard to the architect's wishes.

Aesthetic effect decisions are final, not subject to arbitration, but with two notable exceptions: first, when the decision is ruled to be not consistent with the intent expressed in the contract drawings, and second, when the arbitrators rule that the determination was not strictly an aesthetic effect decision but was artfully so classified by the architect to place it beyond the reach of arbitrators.

Consequently, architects who wish to make aesthetic effect decisions which will remain in effect must adhere strictly to the terms of the contract. The decision must be in writing. (A201, 4.4.4) The decision must be consistent with the intent expressed in the contract documents. (A201, 4.2.13) It must be expressed, not merely reasonably inferable. The decision must be actually an aesthetic effect matter, not just so classified for strategic reasons or for convenience.

The newly issued General Conditions of the Contract for Construction, Fourteenth Edition, AIA Document A201, although substantially revised in 1987, is not materially different from the previous edition (1976) in respect to the matters covered in this chapter. Various provisions of the new edition have been incompletely cited or paraphrased for brevity and should be reviewed in their entirety and in proper context. (See Appendix D.)

17

Resolution of Construction Disputes

Misunderstandings During Construction

Even under the most favorable of circumstances, contractors and owners will not always be able to agree immediately when confronted with unexpected claims or demands from each other during the construction period. When the owner is disappointed in workmanship standards or other contract performance, the contractor might not be sympathetic with the owner's expectations, criticisms, and demands. The contractor might feel that the owner is unrealistic, unjust, or overreaching. When contract conditions vary from the contractor's expectations, the owner might be shocked and appalled upon receiving the contractor's claim for additional compensation or contract time. Honest, conscientious contractors and high-principled, fair-minded owners sometimes do not see things in the same way.

Construction contracts are lengthy and complex written agreements, including numerous detailed drawings and voluminous technical specifications, describing the conduct of owner and contractor and their relationship during the period of construction and for a time thereafter. The simplest of projects require contract documents detailing all of the contractor's and owner's respective responsibilities and their duties to each other. No matter how carefully drawn the contract documents may be, situations can and usually do arise which were not exactly as expected by the parties, even though they might have been contemplated in principle by the contract documents, for example, the encountering of unexpected subsurface conditions not revealed by foundation investigations or soil tests. The contractor will rightfully expect to be reimbursed for all extra labor and materials as well as overhead and profit, and will want an appropriate contract time extension to make up for any time lost in the operation. The owner will often be stunned or even outraged over these unanticipated and unbudgeted costs which will adversely impact the building's economics, possibly for years to come. The owner could be somewhat resentful toward the contractor for apparent profiting from the owner's bad luck. And the time schedule is placed in arrears at the very beginning of the project. Under these circumstances, many owners will find it hard to readily and cheerfully accede to the contractor's claim for additional compensation and time. The contractor would be adamant in its demand for compensation because the costs and time were incurred in good faith, were unavoidable, and were not in the cost or time estimates. If the owner refuses to pay this legitimate bill and to grant the necessary time extension, the owner's ill fortune will become the contractor's loss. The contractor is not likely to give in. Many other realistic examples could be cited to illustrate the areas in which construction disputes can arise.

General Conditions of the Contract

The AIA General Conditions of the Contract for Construction, Fourteenth Edition, Document A201, published in 1987, continues to provide for a system of dispute resolution mechanisms in which the architect is the central element. The system is based on the concept that the agreement between the owner and contractor will be administered by the architect. (Subparagraph 4.2.1) The owner and contractor agree to route all communications to each other through the architect. (4.2.4) Furthermore, the architect is authorized to "interpret and decide matters concerning performance under and requirements of the Contract Documents on written request of either the Owner or Contractor." (4.2.11) Thus all claims or demands of the parties against each other will first be presented to the architect for consideration and a decision. Under certain circumstances, the architect's decision will be final and binding and not subject to appeal.

This decision-making process embraces all manner of claims including those based on alleged errors or omissions by the architect. (4.3.2) When performing the quasi-judicial function of interpreting and deciding all matters submitted, the architect is under the pressure of the owner's and contractor's critical and sometimes skeptical scrutiny. They have the right to expect the ultimate in fairness and impartiality from the architect. These duties can be extremely onerous to the architect when the proper decision has to be against the owner, who after all is paying the architect's fees. The weight of responsibility is particularly oppressive when the architect must render a decision in which defective drawings or specifications or other imperfections of the architect's own actions must be acknowledged. Extra construction costs caused by errors in the architect's work product in most cases must be charged to the owner, not the contractor. The architect will then have to deal separately with the owner to apportion the liability for the error.

In many situations, both owner and contractor will be dissatisfied to some degree with the decision. The contract provides that the architect will not be liable for results of interpretations or decisions rendered in good faith. (4.2.12) The architect must have confidence in the righteousness of decisions and remain resolute against any clandestine lobbying by contractor or owner. The administrative burden on the architect imposed by the General Conditions implies that the architect should keep all of the claim processes moving and watch the time limits so the parties will not lose important or valuable rights through inadvertence.

Claims and Disputes

In general there is a 21-day maximum time limit for the parties to make a claim, each against the other. The time is measured from the date of the first occurrence or discovery of the event, whichever is later. Each claim must be in writing and be submitted to the architect within the 21-day limitation, or presumably the right to the claim is lost. (A201, 4.3.3, 4.3.6 through 4.3.9, and 4.4.1) All time limitations are expressed in calendar days. (A201, 8.1.4)

For the dispute resolution process to function efficiently, the architect must act diligently upon receipt of a written claim from either party. The architect must render the decision in writing with "reasonable promptness" or within a time limit mutually agreed upon between the parties and the architect. If no time limit has been agreed upon, the architect has an indefinite period but is still required to act with reasonable promptness. Neither owner nor contractor can create pressure on the architect for interpretation or decision by claiming delay until 15 days after the written claim is made. (A201, 4.2.11) The architect can, however, within 10 days after the claim is made, take one or more of five preliminary actions:

1. Request additional supporting data from the claimant
2. Submit a schedule to the parties indicating when the architect expects to take action
3. Reject the claim in whole or in part, stating reasons for rejection
4. Recommend approval of the claim by the other party
5. Suggest a compromise

The architect may also, but is not obligated to, notify the surety, if any, of the nature and amount of the claim. (A201, 4.4.1)

At any time that a claim has been satisfactorily concluded the architect is required to prepare or obtain appropriate documentation for execution by the parties. (A201, 4.4.2) If a claim has not been resolved after the architect has taken the preliminary actions, the claimant, within 10 days thereafter, is required to take one or more of three possible further actions:

1. Submit additional supporting data requested by the architect
2. Modify the initial claim
3. Notify the architect that the initial claim stands (A201, 4.4.3)

After an unspecified time, but presumably with reasonable promptness, the architect after reviewing any further responses from either of the parties will give written notice that the decision will be forthcoming within 7 days. The notice should state that the decision will be final and binding on the parties but is subject to arbitration. (A201, 4.4.4) The architect in preparation for rendering the decision should be extremely careful to obtain each party's full position and should carefully and completely review the contract documents so that the decision is technically competent as well as fair. The decision should be dispositive of all elements of the claim to avoid the necessity of amending the decision after review by the parties. The decision should include all appropriate monetary and time adjustments to the contract.

The architect's final decision should be properly drafted to comply with the specific requirements of Subparagraph 4.5.4.1 of the General Conditions. The decision should specifically state that the decision is final but subject to arbitration and that a demand for arbitration of the matter included in the decision must be made within 30 days after the date on which the arbitration claimant received the final written decision. If an arbitration demand is not made by either party within the 30-day period, the architect's decision becomes final and binding upon the parties. (A201, 4.5.4.1) The mere written or oral objection of owner or contractor to the decision is not sufficient to prevent the final decision from becoming binding; it is necessary that arbitration proceedings be initiated by the filing of a demand.

Architect's Aesthetic Effect Decisions

Decisions made by the architect on matters relating to aesthetic effect will be final and not subject to any further review by arbitrators if they are consistent with the intent expressed in the contract documents. (A201, 4.2.13) This places a burden of intellectual honesty on the architect to refrain from classifying questionable decisions as aesthetic when they are not. Although arbitrators are not entitled to review and possibly redecide aesthetic effect decisions, they might be called upon to rule on whether the architect has properly classified a decision as an aesthetic effect matter. The architect's mere classification of a decision as aesthetic does not necessarily place it beyond the purview of arbitrators or judges.

Should an arbitrator or judge decide that an architect's aesthetic effect decision was not consistent with the intent expressed in the contract documents or that it was not in fact a matter of aesthetic effect, the decision would no longer be final and might be reversed or modified. (See Chap. 16, Architect's Decisions Based on Design Concept, Aesthetic Effect, and Intent of the Contract Documents.)

Architect's Minor Changes

The architect has authority to order minor changes in the work not involving any change in the contract sum or time and not inconsistent with the intent of the contract documents. Such orders must be in writing and are binding on the owner and contractor. (A201, 7.4.1) The owner or contractor or both may disagree with the architect's exercise of this prerogative, in which case the only appeal is to arbitration unless the architect is willing to amend or withdraw the order.

Assistance from Surety

If the contractor has furnished a performance bond and a labor and material payment bond, the parties will find the surety a helpful ally in the search for a solution of certain types of controversies. If a claim has been ruled upon by the architect and acceptance by the parties is not forthcoming, and there appears to be a possibility of a contractor's default, the architect may, but is not obligated to, notify the surety to request assistance in resolving the controversy. (A201, 4.4.4) The surety will have some economic leverage upon the contractor. It is in the surety's financial interest to prevent the default of the contractor. The surety will often provide their contractors with helpful economic advice and assistance.

Architect's Failure to Render a Final Decision

The architect has the role, assigned by the General Conditions, of quasi-judicial interpreter and decision maker for the owner and contractor during the construction period. This duty must be promptly and competently carried out to satisfy the expectations of the parties to the contract. In most cases the architect will discharge this contracted professional responsibility with proficiency and fairness. On those rare occasions where the post of architect becomes vacant or if the architect, for other reasons, has not rendered the required written interpretation or final decision within 45 days after the initial written claim to the architect, then either party may initiate arbitration proceedings, but not before. (A201, 4.5.1)

Alternative Dispute Resolution Methods

Upon the emergence of an apparently irresolvable difference, the first resort of a typical business-oriented person will be negotiation. This is the process of rational discussion, compromise, and, ultimately, agreement. This is in the recognition that sums conceded in negotiation will more than offset the legal and administrative costs of proceeding to a more formal forum for dispute resolution. If concurrence can be reached by normal business negotiation, time, effort, and money will usually be saved. Negotiation will not yield satisfactory results when both sides persist in clinging tenaciously to firm or extreme positions and refuse to enter into the spirit of mutual concessions.

Should negotiation fail to resolve the matter, the parties could agree to mediation. This is a procedure in which a mutually acceptable impartial intermediary talks to both sides, together and separately, and assists them in their negotiations. The mediator will privately advise each side of the strengths and weaknesses of their respective positions and attempt to get the parties to see their positions more objectively. The mediator does not impose any decisions on the parties but instead helps them to arrive at their own voluntary resolution.

In some cases, the project architect, being intimately acquainted with the background information vital to understanding the dispute, will prove to be the ideal mediator. This is assuming that the architect is respected by and acceptable to both sides. The parties must also consider the architect to be trustworthy, technically competent, unprejudiced, and of the temperament to counsel both sides in a negotiation likely to result in an amicable accord.

Like negotiation, mediation is voluntary and not provided for in most construction agreements. Negotiation and mediation can take place before the arbitration demand is filed or while waiting for the first arbitration hearing to take place. If the dispute can be resolved in this way, the time, trouble, and expense of the arbitration can be avoided. Otherwise, the arbitration will proceed in accordance with the contruction agreement.

Filing an Arbitration Demand

Arbitration is a method of dispute resolution which is voluntarily selected by the parties and agreed to in a contract as an alternative to using the court system. All AIA form agreements, including the General Conditions, contain arbitration clauses. Where both parties would prefer using the court system, the arbitration clause can be eliminated at any time either before or after the contract is signed. However, after the agreement is signed, the arbitration clause will prevail if only one party wishes to eliminate it. If the construction agreement does not contain an arbitration clause, and the parties later wish to submit their dispute to arbitration, this is accomplished by execution of a submission agreement signed by both owner and contractor.

Arbitration required by the AIA form documents will be in accordance with the Construction Industry Arbitration Rules of the American Arbitration Association (AAA). The decision of the arbitrator or arbitrators, called an award, may be entered in any court having jurisdiction. (A201, 4.5.1) A copy of the Construction Industry Arbitration Rules may be obtained at no cost from any AAA regional office. All architectural construction administrators should have a copy of the rules at hand for reference.

To initiate an arbitration, notice must be given by the claimant to the other party, called the respondent. The notice can be given on a form printed by the AAA called a Demand for Arbitration or simply by writing a letter addressed to the respondent. The demand must include a statement setting forth the nature of the dispute, the amount involved, and the remedy sought. This should be sent to the other party, and three copies should be sent to the regional office of the AAA together with three copies of the arbitration provisions of the contract and the appropriate filing fee. The filing fees are quite nominal and currently are 3 percent for the first $25,000 of claim or counterclaim with a $300 minimum. Thereafter, the fee is on a sliding scale varying from 2 percent down to ¼ percent for claims of up to $5,000,000. The AAA has 35 regional offices spread across the continental United States, Hawaii, and Puerto Rico.

The AAA, in addition to administering arbitrations, also administers mediation proceedings and will assist in the selection of a suitable experienced mediator. Upon receipt of the demand, copies of the arbitration provisions of the contract, and the filing fee, the AAA will start the administration process leading to the selection of arbitrators and setting of the first hearing date. In the event that the architect renders the final decision after arbitration proceedings have been initiated, the decision may be used as evidence in the arbitration, but the arbitrator's decision will take precedence unless the architect's decision is acceptable to all parties concerned. (A201, 4.5.4.1)

Any demand for arbitration must include all arbitrable claims then known to the party making the demand. The arbitrator or arbitrators may allow later amendment of a demand to include any claims omitted through inadvertence, oversight, or excusable neglect. Claims which arise subsequently may be added by amendment. (A201, 4.5.6) The arbitration process allows for the submission of counterclaims by the respondent.

Continuing Contract Performance

While awaiting the outcome of an architect's decision or an arbitrator's award, the contractor is required to continue with performance of the construction and the owner is obligated to continue making payments, unless the parties agree in writing to suspend construction and/or payments. (A201, 4.3.4)

Arbitration Award

The arbitrator's award, in accordance with the Construction Industry Arbitration Rules, must be in writing and should be made promptly and no later than 30 days after close of hearings or, if oral hearings have been waived, from the date of submission of final written statements and proofs to the arbitrator.

The award will be final and binding on the parties, with no appeal available on the merits of the arguments. The only legal grounds for overturning of an award are based on fraud or corruption of the arbitrator, the arbitrator's refusal to accept relevant evidence, and an award which does not dispose of all issues or which makes rulings on matters not submitted. When heard by AAA arbitrators and administered by the AAA, an arbitration award would seldom be deficient in form or technicality.

Conclusion

The foregoing analysis of the dispute resolution system provided in the new AIA General Conditions is presented from the vantage point of a practicing architect. For convenience, many of the provisions of the General Conditions have been partially quoted or paraphrased. The reader is advised to refer to the complete texts of the AIA General Conditions and Construction Industry Arbitration Rules of the AAA to obtain the complete language in its proper context.

The architect engaged in construction contract administration would be well advised to recommend the owner and contractor to consult with their respective legal counsel whenever project conditions and business relationships have deteriorated to the point that the architect's interpretations and final decisions are no longer acceptable to the parties. Although it is not absolutely necessary or legally required for the parties to be represented by counsel in an arbitration proceeding, there is no question that experienced construction industry lawyers are well equipped to represent owners and contractors in arbitrations under the Construction Industry Arbitration Rules.

18

Preventing Time and Delay Disputes in Construction Contracts

Changed Conditions

Most day-to-day construction industry disputes are readily resolved by the owner and contractor or acceptably decided by the architect. Those that are not are usually based on the presence of conditions not exactly as contemplated in the drafting of the contract documents. Unforeseen or changed conditions generally have an adverse impact on the time needed to accomplish the work of the contract. Loss of time will nearly always result in economic loss accompanied by disagreement as to which party should be required to bear the burden of unexpected loss.

AIA General Conditions

The AIA General Conditions of the Contract for Construction provide contractual requirements for the owner's and the contractor's conduct and practical procedures for the architect's administration of the construction contract. Compliance with the specified procedures will not guarantee freedom from disputes but should reduce the frequency and magnitude of contention. Methodical, timely, and even-handed architectural administration should lessen owner and contractor apprehension of the risks and vagaries of the construction process. Meticulous following of the contractually mandated procedures, particularly when completely and properly documented, concurrent with construction, will serve the parties well in the event of subsequent claims to higher authority, such as submission to arbitration. All procedures described here will be those of the AIA General Conditions.

Liquidated Damages

Most owners need or want their building projects available for use at a particular time. Owners, as a basic premise, expect the contractor to start the construction promptly when ordered, to pursue the work diligently, competently, and purposefully, and to complete the work on or before the promised due date. Usually they will have made major financial commitments based on reasonable expectation of completion on the scheduled date. Failure to have use of the building when anticipated will result in losses of rentals and profits and incurred costs such as interest on invested capital, rents on duplicate facilities, and other costs. Thus construction contracts usually have provisions relating to when the construction should start, how long the construction process should take, and when the work should be completed.

Owners expect to suffer economic loss if the building is not available for use when contractually promised, so contracts often include payments to the owner from the contractor to compensate for monetary losses caused by the contractor's failure to complete on time. Payments, called "liquidated damages," imposed on the contractor for late completion of construction are not to be construed as a penalty, as the courts and arbitrators are reluctant to enforce penalties. Liquidated damages, estimated and established as realistically as possible, represent the best ascertainment of the actual losses which the owner will suffer if the completed construction is not delivered on time. Liquidated damages may be expressed as lump sum amounts and/or as a certain amount per day, with or without a maximum cumulative limitation. When a contract contains liquidated damages provisions, the architect is under serious obligation to administer the time provisions of the contract fairly and equitably to both owner and contractor.

Working Days versus Calendar Days

Time provisions expressed anywhere in the contract documents should be well thought out and written as clearly as possible. Expressing time lapse for construction in terms of working days is ambiguous and usually causes arguments in calculation as well as concept. It is more certain to express all time periods in terms of calendar days. It is easy enough to make the necessary adjustments to account for Saturdays, Sundays, and holidays when determining the number of calendar days to allow for a certain operation. When possible, it is advisable to express starting and completion times as exact calendar dates, using month, day, and year. Calendar days are used in the AIA General Conditions. (Subparagraph 8.1.4)

Construction contracts must contain adequate provision to accommodate the inevitable changes in conditions from those upon which the contract was originally based. Any change order procedure should have provision for the number of calendar days to be added to or deducted from the contract in addition to any change in the contract price. If a change affects price only and there is to be no change in contract time, the change order should state zero days (or no time adjustment) in writing. A change order silent on time will merely provoke contention because the owner will assume that silence connotes no time extension will be allowed while the contractor will assume that silence means the time extension is still open to discussion. A change order based on a condition or event which affects time only should be prepared and executed even though there is no change in contract price.

Unforeseen or Differing Conditions

Unforeseen conditions, such as those encountered during subterranean excavation, or differing conditions, such as are frequently found in alteration of existing buildings, will usually result in justifiable contract time extensions. Time extensions should always be formalized by written change orders. Occasionally unforeseen conditions will prove to be easier or less complex than expected and, if it shortens the critical path, should result in a time credit change order in fairness to the owner. In a lump sum contract the cost advantage of performing such simpler conditions will accrue to the contractor if the subterranean risk of higher cost is assumed by the contractor. The owner will benefit by cost savings in unexpectedly easier conditions only when contractually exposed to the extra cost of unexpectedly difficult conditions.

Delay Caused by Owner or Architect

Actions of the owner or architect which create delay should be promptly quantified and an appropriate time change order should be executed. Materials, services, or separate contractors to be supplied or coordinated by the owner, if not provided in time to suit the prime contractor, will adversely impact the overall time schedule. Sometimes delay is caused by the owner's inability to make available the complete site and all rights of way and easements. The owner's failure to obtain all necessary governmental approvals can also cause delay. Architects can be and sometimes are the cause of construction delay by failure to provide timely reviews of submittals, failure to make required determinations or decisions in a reasonable length of time, and furnishing defective contract documents.

Construction Schedule

In liquidated damages contracts, the construction time schedule is an extremely important document. The General Conditions (3.10) requires the contractor, prior to starting work, to prepare a construction schedule to be submitted for the owner's and architect's information. The architect is not asked to approve or disapprove it; however, it would be good practice, in the very least, to review it and be acquainted with its provisions. Without a time schedule it would be practically impossible to objectively measure whether certain events are on time, early, or late. The contractor is required to revise the schedule periodically to conform with the actual progress and conditions of the project. The contractor is also required to submit at the same time, for the architect's approval, a schedule of submittals which has been coordinated with the construction schedule. (A201, 3.10.2) All duties of the owner or architect upon which the contractor will claim reliance should be entered in the time schedules. For example, the dates on which each of the various shop drawings are supposed to be submitted to the architect should be scheduled as well as the dates on which the architect is expected to send them back to the contractor. The architect's review of the submittal schedule provides opportunity for comment in advance of unrealistic time allowances for submittal review. The schedule might later have to be adjusted by the contractor to accommodate redrafting and resubmittal of rejected shop drawings. The submittal schedule will also enable the architect to know in advance when to schedule personnel and review time in the architect's own office. Often contractors will unexpectedly submit shop drawings at the last minute, informing the architect that the shop drawing review is holding up the job. The process of scheduling shop drawing submittals and reviews should be helpful in clarifying the time responsibilities of both contractor and architect. Delays caused by outside agencies, such as government, beyond the control of owner, contractor, or architect, will give rise to justifiable extensions of contract time.

Weather Delays

Delays caused by adverse weather are a major source of dispute in claims for construction time extension. Inclement weather conditions including rain, snow, wind, and excessively high or low temperatures are clearly beyond anyone's control, although they could be reasonably expected to occur. Some construction contracts allow time extension for any and all weather delays, whereas others allow only for abnormal weather or adverse weather conditions not reasonably anticipatable. The AIA General Conditions provides in Clause 4.3.8.2 that

"If adverse weather conditions are the basis for a Claim for additional time, such Claim shall be documented by data substantiating that weather conditions were abnormal for the period of time and could not have been reasonably anticipated, and that weather conditions had an adverse effect on the scheduled construction."

In everyday practice, this provision could cause as many disputes as it was intended to resolve. Moreover, it creates administrative headaches for architects and contractors alike. This clause, in its attempt to provide certainty, fairness, and equity, creates a procedure which is too unwieldy for all but the largest, most costly projects and seems more appropriate for the courtroom or arbitration hearing rather than routine construction administration. In any event, compliance with this clause makes it difficult to comply with Subparagraph 4.3.3, which requires written notice within 21 days after occurrence of the event giving rise to such claim, and Clause 4.3.8.1, which requires the claim to include an estimate of cost and of probable effect of delay on progress of the work.

In the circumstances prevailing in more mundane projects, it would seem preferable to employ a simpler procedure. One possibility would be for the contractor to state the number of days of adverse weather anticipated and included in its base bid and time schedule. The architect would then authorize time extensions for all adverse weather which impacts construction time after allowing for the number of days initially stated by the contractor. Another possibility is to specify that the construction time schedule be prepared to reflect only actual estimated construction time without allowance for any adverse weather conditions. In this situation, the contractor would be entitled to time extension for all adverse weather which impacts construction. These circumstances would then reflect actual weather conditions, would not give the contractor a windfall profit in case of exceptionally fine weather, and would be fair to owner and contractor. Ideally, the contractor should not profit from fine weather at the owner's expense or suffer a loss from adverse weather. In effect, weather should be the owner's risk. There is no logical reason why a contractor should be considered to be an accurate long-range weather prophet. Why should a contractor be expected to pay for the inability to accurately predict the weather months or even years in advance? Naturally, the parties can reverse the risk situation by contract provision.

Whatever method of measuring time is used, an additional source of weather-based dispute is the muddy, impassable site which prevails for several days following each rainfall. When site paving and landscape work are completed and the main work is under cover, time extensions for rain and mud would be inappropriate and should not be allowed. Rain which occurs on weekends or holidays or during other concurrent delays (such as labor union stoppages) does not extend the contract time except for the resultant muddy site conditions affecting normal working days. Windy days will cause postponement of certain operations such as roofing or exterior painting and will thus affect the contractor's schedule accordingly. Adjustment for adverse weather which has no impact on the critical path cannot be allowed.

Critical Path

Analysis of the effects of adverse weather on the critical path from the opposing viewpoints of owner and contractor will reveal yet another source of dispute: To which party does the "float" in the critical path belong? There appears to be no industrywide settled answer as to who has the right to the float. Therefore, this type of question will have to be resolved by the architect on the basis of specific project circumstances and application of common sense, fairness, and equity to both parties to the contract.

Should the contractor receive additional time on the entire project to perform an operation added by change order which can be achieved simultaneously with previously scheduled activities? If the whole added operation can be performed in a simultaneous manner, obviously the contract time should not be extended. However, if a portion of the work impacts the critical path, the change order should provide accordingly for an appropriate time extension.

The contractor, according to the AIA General Conditions, is entitled to a time extension for delay in progress of the work caused by the owner's or architect's act or neglect, labor disputes, and other causes beyond control of the contractor. (8.3.1)

Substantial Completion

In construction contracts governed by the AIA General Conditions, the ending date of the construction time schedule is the date of substantial completion. (8.1.1) The AIA General Conditions defines substantial completion as "the stage in the progress of the Work when the Work or designated portion thereof is sufficiently complete in accordance with the Contract Documents so the Owner can occupy or utilize the Work for its intended use." (9.8.1) This generalized definition provides a good conceptual impression of what constitutes substantial completion but is not sufficiently complete and certain to eliminate disputes in specific situations between owners and contractors. The AIA General Conditions leaves it to the judgment of the architect for determination of the date of substantial completion. (8.1.3) The architect should look to the definition for guidance in making the determination and in issuing the certificate. The determination of specific starting and ending dates as well as the number of authorized days of time extension is crucial to the avoidance of controversy in the calculation of liquidated damages. The architect should treat these obligations very seriously and should make all required determinations fairly, promptly, and in writing.

Delay Damages

When the total elapsed construction time period is extended appreciably beyond the time initially allotted, the contractor's overhead costs will undoubtedly be increased. Among those direct and indirect costs are the wages of supervisorial and administrative personnel, rental value of facilities and equipment on the jobsite, interest on invested capital, and extended involvement of the contractor's organization, thereby causing possible loss of alternative business opportunities. The contractor may also have incurred similar obligations to subcontractors or suppliers for their similar costs during the same delays.

Whether change orders for changed conditions can include any element of delay cost in addition to the mere time extension is a matter for contract interpretation and analysis of the specific circumstances prevailing on the project. The AIA General Conditions "does not preclude recovery of damages for delay by either party under other provisions of the Contract Documents." (8.3.3) The contractor should not recover for any delay costs when the delay was caused by or could have been prevented by the contractor.

Time delay caused by the contractor can expose the owner to additional losses and expenses such as loss of interest, increased rental expense or loss of rental income, and increased personnel and other costs. However, these costs all merge into and are limited by the agreed sum expressed in the liquidated damages clause. In contracts without provision for liquidated damages, the owner could claim without limit the actual amount of all proved damages caused by the contractor.

In the event of a delay claim which cannot be amicably resolved by the owner and contractor, the architect is obligated by the AIA General Conditions to make a determination. The architect's decision will become final and binding on the parties if not contested by the timely filing of a demand for arbitration in accordance with the procedures set out in Article 4 of the General Conditions. Some contracts contain carefully drafted "no damages for delay" clauses in an attempt by owners to eliminate the possibility of damage claims by contractors for certain delay causes such as acts of the owner or architect. The AIA General Conditions does not include such a clause.

The Moment of Truth

In all situations in which the architect is obligated to make determinations or render decisions the architect should obtain the positions of both of the parties, preferably in writing, before deciding such matters. All decisions must be fair, just, and equitable and be arrived at with meticulous impartiality. This is often an unpleasant and difficult task, particularly when the decision must run counter to the interest of the architect's client.

All extra costs, time, or delay damages caused by the architect's shortcomings must be charged to the owner, not the contractor, and later resolved between the owner and architect. Such determinations are the ultimate test of an architect's professionalism, fairness, and objectivity.

19

Owner's and Contractor's Legal Claims against Architects

What to Do If You Get Sued

Notwithstanding the noblest efforts to conduct one's architectural practice to the highest attainable standards, occasionally an owner or contractor will perceive, rightly or wrongly, that the architect is the cause of their problems. They might feel that the architect improperly administered the contract or furnished defective construction documents. Consultation with their legal counsel and other advisors will often confirm their perceptions, and the architect is then faced with a formalized claim in the form of an arbitration demand or a lawsuit.

It is seldom that the formal claim arrives without some form of prior warning. Except in the case of a personal injury or a construction defect that has suddenly manifested itself, there was most likely a period of gradual deterioration of the relationships among the architect, owner, and contractor. A lapse in communication or a declining tolerance of each other's singularities can lead to reciprocal loss of respect and mutual hardening of attitudes. Flexible dispositions, reasonable discussion, and friendly negotiation will no longer be possible. One or more of the parties will then confer with counsel, thereby transferring the controversy to the arena of legal compulsion.

After the initial shock has worn off and you have sufficiently dealt with such mental images as the ungrateful client or the grasping contractor, the feelings of recrimination toward colleagues and associates, the self-pity, the unfairness of it all, and "why me?" you must do something positive. You must start organizing your response and establishing your legal position.

Arbitration Demand or Lawsuit

If the claim against you is being made by someone with whom you have a written agreement, such as a client or consulting engineer, and if the agreement contained an arbitration clause, you will have received a demand for arbitration. In an arbitration the parties are called claimant and respondent. All standard form contracts of the American Institute of Architects contain arbitration clauses naming the American Arbitration Association as administrator and incorporating the AAA Construction Industry Arbitration Rules.

If the claim is being made by someone with whom you have not contracted or by someone with whom your agreement did not have an arbitration clause, you will have been served with a lawsuit. In a lawsuit the parties are called plaintiff and defendant.

Responding to the Complaint

In either event you will have to answer the demand or complaint in a legally sufficient manner and in proper time to protect your rights. If you are being sued in the public court system you must engage legal counsel, and it should be done promptly. Time will be needed to confer with your lawyer and for preparation of the legal response to the lawsuit or arbitration demand within the time constraints of the court or arbitration system.

If you have received an arbitration demand, you are not required to be represented by a lawyer. Legally, you are entitled to represent yourself. In some situations where the issues are straightforward and the stakes not excessive, an articulate architect with an organized mind, a businesslike practice, and enough free time can self-represent and can often prevail. This of course also presupposes a detached objectivity and freedom from emotional involvement. However, this would be the exceptional case. In the event that you lose an arbitration, for all practical purposes there is no appeal. Most architects will find more comfort and security in hiring an experienced construction industry lawyer for sound and objective legal advice, to answer the arbitration claim, to organize the case, and to present it to the arbitrators.

Professional Liability Insurance

If you have a professional liability insurance policy, you should notify your insurer immediately upon receipt of an arbitration demand or lawsuit. The insurance company will promptly assign your case to an attorney, usually one in your own town or vicinity. The assigned lawyer will need to confer with you to become acquainted with the subject matter and to gather sufficient information to analyze the legal issues and answer the arbitration demand or lawsuit.

Even if you do not carry professional liability insurance, you should have your legal or insurance counsel carefully examine any general liability policy you may have had in effect at the time of the alleged negligence and at the time of the alleged loss. In rare cases, they will find some insurance coverage for cost of defense or payment of loss.

Legal Counsel

Insurance companies in the professional liability field generally hire competent lawyers or law firms with considerable experience in architectural, engineering, and construction industry matters. The main problem associated with the insurance company's selection of your attorney is the matter of possible conflict of interest. Sometimes the interests of insurer and insured are not in all ways identical, in which case you would be better served with your own independent counsel. An example of a conflict of interest is where an architect's client has made a claim alleging professional negligence and has refused to pay the architectural fee. The insurance company would consider bargaining away the architectural fee to settle the negligence claim. Independent counsel might be more diligent in asserting the fee claim as well as defending against the negligence claim. Also, in situations where the insurer is trying to deny coverage, your assigned lawyer might find something in your files which would aid the insurer in this regard. Your business secret would be handled with confidentiality by your own lawyer but not necessarily by the lawyer you share with your insurance company. It is customary for the insurer-assigned lawyer to make periodic confidential progress reports to the insurance company. In cases where there is a conflict of interest between yourself and your insurance carrier, most states require the insurer to pay the fees of independent counsel selected by the insured.

Selecting a Lawyer

In your quest for independent legal counsel it is best to seek a lawyer or law firm with prior experience in the representation of architects and engineers as well as other segments of the building industry. Avoid lawyers who express an ingrained prejudice against arbitration, as you will not receive a balanced judgment when there is a choice between arbitration and litigation in the court system. Many lawyers specialize in construction industry litigation and professional liability matters and will not need extensive familiarization with background information in preparation for your representation.

After you have retained legal counsel or it has been assigned by your insurer, it is important that you conduct yourself in accordance with your attorney's advice. In particular, you should not discuss your case with anyone without your lawyer's prior knowledge and concurrence. If you are being sued by your client or the contractor while the construction progresses, you must continue to render the contracted professional services and advice to which your client is entitled, although the relationship might be strained.

Preparations to Assist Your Lawyer

If your case is to be heard by an arbitration panel, your attorney must be prepared and ready for the first hearing in as little as 30 days up to seldom longer than 6 months. Lawsuits tried in the courts do not usually come up for trial any sooner than 3 to 5 years, depending on the trial backlog of the jurisdiction.

As time passes, it becomes more difficult and time-consuming to gather all of the relevant documents and to preserve the testimony of the people involved in the circumstances. If the claim is made during the construction period or shortly thereafter, all of the project records will still be in use and most of the concerned personnel still in the vicinity. The records which will be helpful in proving your position must be collected and presented for your lawyer's examination, evaluation, case preparation, and, ultimately, trial of the matter. The materials which should be collected will depend to a great extent on the type of claim which is being made.

Claims made against architects are of many varieties and occur at various times. The list in recent years has become longer, broader, and more innovative. Construction defects based on alleged design error are sometimes discovered while the construction is still in progress, while others are not noticed for years. Claims based on maladministration of the construction contract, such as overcertifying contractor's payments, are usually made promptly either during or directly upon completion of the construction. Claims for construction-related personal injuries will be made during or shortly after the construction period. Some personal injury claims will surface after many years of use of the project.

When a claim is made years later, as would be the case when a building defect suddenly becomes apparent or if someone is injured on the premises, it will be more difficult if not impossible to find all of the relevant records and the persons who have useful information, helpful to your defense, regarding the events which occurred many years previously. The following checklists are offered as a general guide to the types of records and documentation which would be of interest to your attorney acting on your behalf. Some of these items will be more relevant to one type of claim than to another.

If the controversy relates to events occurring prior to start of construction:

Owner-Architect Agreement and all amendments and early drafts

Maps, photographs, drawings, logs, and reports received from owner describing the site

Photographs of existing site conditions before construction

Minutes and informal notes of all meetings with owner, material and equipment manufacturers, and consultants

Owner's design program and criteria

All design criteria developed by architect or consultants

Copies of all disclaimers and disclosures sent to owner by architect or consultants

Boundary and topographic surveys and all reports and calculations received from consultants in all disciplines including but not limited to geotechnical, civil, structural, electrical, mechanical, and acoustical engineers

Reports received from building cost consultants and construction schedulers

Correspondence to and from owner and all owner's advisors such as lawyers, accountants, financial, real estate lenders, marketing, and advertising

Environmental impact statements

Memoranda to file

Insurance policies

Applicable building codes, zoning ordinances, and other governmental regulations

Building department plan correction lists

Industry standards and manufacturer's literature for relevant materials

Representations made by material and equipment manufacturers in respect to sizes, capacities, models, variations, recommended uses, and limitations

Approvals from building department and other governmental agencies

Correspondence to and from utility companies serving the site

Appointment books, telephone logs, and itemized telephone bills

Building cost estimates

Design sketches, presentation drawings, and presentation writings

Construction drawings and specifications and all early drafts and check prints

Building code analyses and research notes

Time cards of all involved personnel

(*See also other lists for relevant items*)

If the controversy relates to events occurring during the construction period:

Construction contract documents including owner-contractor agreement, general, supplementary, and special conditions, construction drawings, specifications, and all addenda; early drafts of all contract documents

Modifications to the construction contract documents such as contract amendments, change orders, construction change directives, and architect's written orders for minor changes

Advertisement for bids, bidding instructions, and sample forms

Contractor's proposal and proposals received from unsuccessful bidders, résumés and promotional literature submitted by contractors

Contractor's surety bond and bid bond

Certificates of insurance submitted by contractor or owner

Minutes and informal notes of all meetings with contractors, subcontractors, and suppliers

Shop drawings, both rejected and approved; product data and samples submitted by the contractor

Correspondence and memoranda to and from contractors, subcontractors, and suppliers

Reports of all materials sampling, testing, and inspection

Engineering calculations and certificates submitted by materials suppliers

Architect's site observation reports

Contractor's daily log

Requests for information, memoranda of architect's decisions, and interpretations

Reports, notices, and memoranda from building inspectors and all other governmental agents

Construction progress and submittal schedules, outdated and interim, as well as final

Contractor's payment requests and architect's certificates for payment

Contractor's schedule of values

Lists of subcontractors and suppliers submitted by contractor

Architect's certificates of substantial completion and final completion

Reconciliation of cash allowances

Computation of liquidated damages

Architect's inspection lists, contractor's inspection lists

Photographs and videos taken during construction

(*See also other lists for relevant items*)

If the controversy relates to events occurring after completion of the construction:

Contractor's written guarantees and mechanics' lien releases

Correspondence relating to owner's requests for warranty service

Operating instructions and equipment lists submitted by contractor

Record drawings and marked-up prints and specifications submitted by contractor

Photographs of completed project, photographs illustrating maintenance standards

Articles or advertisements from periodicals offering or describing the project

Certificate of occupancy issued by building department or other governmental agency

Notice of completion

Bids or contracts for maintenance services

(*See also other lists for relevant items*)

If the controversy involves owner's advisors or architect's consultants:

Agreements with advisors and consultants and all amendments and early drafts, accounting for all fee charges and payments

Certificates of insurance submitted by consultants

Minutes and informal notes of all meetings with advisors and consultants, correspondence and memoranda to and from all advisors and consultants

Proposals and professional résumés submitted by consultants

Reports, calculations, sketches, drawings, specifications, and other work product of consultants

All representations and disclosures received from consultants relating to materials, systems, and equipment to be used and to design criteria

Building department plan check correction lists relating to work of consultants

Applicable building codes, governmental regulations, industry standards, and design criteria relating to work designed by consultants

Reports of site observation examinations made by consultants

Photographs and videos taken by consultants

(*See also other lists for relevant items*)

If the controversy involves general business matters of the architectural firm:

Insurance policies

Financial statements

Partnership agreements, articles of incorporation, and corporation minutes

Purchase and rental agreements

Check records, paid bills, accounts with clients, consultants, suppliers, lessor, accountant, lawyer, insurance agent, and other advisors; correspondence to and from all of the preceding

Employee records including applications for employment, résumés, time cards, and payroll records; records of vacations, holidays, sick leaves, and leaves of absence; reprimands and probation periods; statements of personnel policy; policies for affirmative action, antidiscrimination, and equal employment opportunities

(See also other lists for relevant items)

In addition to gathering the relevant documents for your lawyer, it would also be helpful to prepare a chronology of events as soon as possible before the subject matter becomes too stale. This will assist your attorney to become quickly oriented and to assimilate the circumstances which comprise the background setting of your problem. Another useful tool which you can prepare for your lawyer is a list of all of the persons, firms, and agencies and their roles involved in your situation. Include names, addresses, and telephone numbers.

When the claim against you concerns a premises which you have not seen for several months or years, it would be beneficial to visit the building or site to observe and record present conditions and to obtain current photographs. However, this will require permission from the owner and/or occupant as well as prior approval from your lawyer.

How Long Should Records Be Kept?

It is very burdensome and space-consuming to preserve the vast volume of original drawings, prints, papers, and records which seem to clutter our offices; and the volume continues to proliferate. There are various and sundry governmental laws and regulations requiring the maintenance of records for periods of time differing from 4 to 7 years. However, if certain records in your possession would be useful (or even crucial) for your defense or in the assertion of a claim, it would be in your interest to have the record or document available whenever the need arises. This merely emphasizes the advisability of preserving all of your records and documents for a period considerably longer than required by law. Needless to say, you should have not only an efficient and convenient filing system but one which is not allowed to fall into a state of ill maintenance. There is no point in saving reams, rolls, bundles, and piles of documentation if it is not properly categorized, marked, indexed, and carefully preserved, so it may be efficiently and promptly retrieved. Improperly organized materials will waste your own time as well as that of highly paid legal advisors.

Statutes of Limitations

So how long should records really be kept? One hears of legal claims being made against architects, engineers, and contractors for damages caused by alleged design or construction defects or for personal injuries as long as 10 or 15 years after design of the project. The problem lies with the statutes of limitations for commencing legal action which apply in the various states. A statute of limitation defines a time period within which a particular type of lawsuit must be filed. There is not complete uniformity in application of the laws, and the time periods vary from state to state. In some states, as in California, there is a 4-year limit on patent construction defects. These are defects which would be apparent to a prudent observer. The time limit in California is increased to 10 years in the case of latent defects, that is, defects which are hidden or at least not apparent upon reasonable inspection. There are other time limits for initiating lawsuits, depending upon the specific type of legal action.

One of the problems associated with the time limits imposed by these statutes is the difficulty in determining the time from which the right of legal action is measured. For example, in an alleged design defect, the starting time could be when the mistake was made on the drawings, or when the project was completed, or when the damage was discovered.

Architects who use the AIA Standard Form of Agreement Between Owner and Architect, Fourteenth Edition, Document B141, 1987, will find that the starting time for statutes of limitations is defined in Paragraph 9.3. Construction agreements which include the AIA General Conditions of the Contract for Construction, Fourteenth Edition, Document A201, 1987, have the starting time defined in Paragraph 13.7. Also included in both form contracts is a stipulation that arbitration demands must be made no later than a lawsuit on the same matter could have been filed. (Document B141, Paragraph 7.2, and Document A201, Subparagraph 4.5.4.2) These contract stipulations will be very helpful in limiting the time in which legal action may be initiated if the dispute is among contracting parties. They will not be of much use when the claim is initiated by third parties such as lessees, later owners, occupants, and passersby.

An additional serious problem with statutes of limitation is that some judges and juries look at them as a way of depriving innocent and deserving plaintiffs of their recourse at law. Some also feel that the defendant's risk is very likely covered by insurance and that this is a desirable method of spreading the risk of bad luck. Skillful plaintiff's attorneys have kept the risk of liability open for periods longer than would seem possible under the statutes of limitation. Regardless of statutes of limitations, *never* discard any insurance policy or certificate of insurance that covers property damage, builder's risk, professional liability, or general liability.

Settlement

See Chap. 17, Resolution of Construction Disputes, for a discussion of alternative dispute resolution methods. Often a lawsuit or arbitration can be avoided by a mutually acceptable settlement arrived at through negotiation or mediation. These alternatives should be carefully investigated and seriously considered by you and your lawyer. After the formality of an arbitration demand or a lawsuit filing, your lawyer will take the lead in initiating all compromise discussions and settlement procedures. If a negotiated or mediated settlement is reached, it is important that its terms are properly documented and formally agreed to. Any pending legal proceedings must then be terminated in a legally effective manner. All of these legal formalities will be administered by your lawyer.

Appearing as a Witness

If a legal claim has been made against you, it will usually be necessary for you to testify in your own behalf in the ensuing legal proceeding, in either an arbitration hearing or a court trial. Before appearing to testify, you should have had a complete discussion with your attorney so you are properly prepared. Attorneys generally will explain the purpose and value of your testimony and the types of questions which will be asked in your direct testimony. Your attorney will also be able to predict the types of questions which are likely to be asked by opposing counsel during your cross examination.

Arbitration hearings and court trials are similar in that testimony of witnesses is usually elicited in question and answer format. Trials are more formal than arbitrations and strictly follow rules of evidence. Arbitrators may relax or eliminate the rules and may conduct their hearings in whatever manner they find most efficient.

During your testimony, you should listen very attentively to the questions which are asked and should not answer if you do not thoroughly understand the question as asked. If the question is not completely unambiguous and understandable to you, do not answer it but ask that it be rephrased or explained. Do not guess what the attorney is trying to get at. If the question is compound, that is, requiring two answers, ask that it be separated before answering.

Answer all questions honestly, openly, and completely. Address your answers to the judge or arbitrators. All of your answers should be succinct and directly to the point of the questions. Do not ramble on beyond the actual question asked.

If you do not know or cannot remember the answer, you should reply, "I do not know" or "I do not remember." You are not required to know and remember everything.

When a question is asked, hesitate slightly before answering to make sure you have properly digested the question and to give the lawyers a chance to object if it is deemed necessary. If an objection is made, do not answer until after the judge or arbitrator has ruled on it.

Take your files and notes with you if necessary to refresh your memory. But remember, if you testify from a file or notes, opposing counsel may ask to see the entire file.

If a question is asked that involves documents, such as drawings, specifications, change orders, or contracts, ask to see them before answering. Sometimes a question will be asked with a demand for a yes or no answer which you feel must be explained. The best way to answer is to state that the answer must be explained, then answer yes or no, then explain the answer. If the cross-examining lawyer will not allow an explanation, do not be concerned because your own attorney will later ask for the explanation during redirect examination, if it is considered relevant and necessary.

In the event that an owner and contractor of one of your projects resort to arbitration or litigation against each other, you will undoubtedly be called upon to testify as a witness. The advice for testifying is basically the same as above. However, you should always keep in mind that the lawyers retained by your client and the contractor are not your lawyers, and if you find that taking their advice would be injurious to your interest in any way, you should confer with your own counsel for unbiased opinions and recommendations.

20

Analyzing Liability for Construction Defects

Types of Defects

While the vast majority of construction defects are not dramatic ones leading to total collapse or loss of human life, considerable sums of money are often involved, necessitating appropriate action by the owner. Building and site development defects appear in a multitude of forms and variations, including

- Inadequate strength or stiffness, structural instability, settling of foundations, or distressed structural members as evidenced by cracking, movement, and excessive deflection
- Unsightly or dangerous cracking, crazing, scaling, peeling, discoloring, swelling, blisters, or excessive smoothness or roughness
- Weather and moisture intrusion caused by failure of roofing, exterior walls, floors, or openings
- Premature depreciation such as abnormal wear, decay, erosion, corrosion, or disintegration, beyond the effects of normal wear and tear

- Inadequate capacity or function of electrical, mechanical, vertical transportation, or environmental systems including wiring, piping, ducts, devices, and equipment

Some of these defects will result in buildings or parts of buildings that are unsuitable or unusable. Others will result in excessive operating and maintenance costs, premature replacement costs, or depreciated or unacceptable appearance—and sometimes property damage, personal injury, or death.

Analyzing the Situation

It is usually difficult for an owner to know how to go about rectifying the situation and to whom to look for redress. Someone has to analyze the situation and provide answers to the following key questions:

- What is the phenomenon? How can it be described and explained? What is its exact cause?
- How can it be remedied? By removal and replacement? By repair? By recoating? By strengthening? By recognizing shortened life and the necessity of premature replacement? By acceptance of the defect and a monetary adjustment? By some equivalent to the originally specified product or procedure? Or by some creative or innovative procedure?
- What are the costs of remedial work? Of analysis and recommendation? Of redesign? Of inspection and testing? Of labor, materials, tools, equipment, coordination, and supervision?
- What are the costs of consequential damages? Interior damage caused by roofing and enclosure leaks? Value of loss of use of the building, in whole or in part? Damages for personal injuries?

This analysis can be performed by a qualified and knowledgeable architect or engineer experienced in forensic analyses of construction problems. If there is a combination of problems, your advisor-analyst will usually consult with other appropriate technical experts. Sampling, testing, examining, and research might have to be performed in identifying the problem and devising a solution. If arbitration or litigation is in the offing, the analysis and the standards upon which it is based should be presented in writing with all supporting materials such as descriptions, measurements, photographs, cost estimates, specifications, and remedial recommendations.

Identifying the Source of Responsibility

The final question which must be answered is, Who is responsible for the failure? There are only three possibilities in determining the basic responsibility:

- Is it a *design* problem? Was the construction project properly designed, devised, selected, or specified in the first place? Was it engineered properly? Were the contract documents faulty?

- Is it a *construction* problem? Was the project built in accordance with the contract requirements? Was it properly constructed? Were the workmanship practices at fault? Were the materials and equipment furnished as specified and in accordance with industry standards?

- Is it a *maintenance* or *usage* problem? Has the project and all its systems been properly cared for? Has the project been abused or vandalized by its users? Has the project been used improperly?

Design problems are the responsibility of the architects and engineers of record. Design adequacy must be gauged by the opinions of other professionals in the same discipline. If the design flaw is founded on a deviation from accepted standards and practices of design, care, and diligence for that profession, the designer could be held liable. However, if the basis of the defect is faulty judgment, there might not be liability and the owner's recourse will be severely limited or nonexistent. Each case must be considered on its own facts and merits.

Construction problems are the prime responsibility of the general contractor. The actual party at fault might be an employee, a subcontractor, a supplier, or a manufacturer of building materials or equipment. When a contractor fails to follow the requirements of the contract documents, or unilaterally decides to deviate therefrom or make substitutions, any unsuitable or defective result is the responsibility of the contractor. If the contractor faithfully carries out the dictates of erroneous construction drawings or specifications, the contractor should not be held liable but could be held partly liable if the error is of a type that could have been recognized by a competent contractor.

Maintenance or usage problems are the owner's responsibility. Sometimes owners of a new facility are lulled into inaction by the newness of materials and systems and do not commence their maintenance programs soon enough. Some maintenance personnel are not properly trained and cause damage by improper or negligent actions. The occupants and users of buildings often abuse them by rough or inappropriate usage or vandalism. Normal wear and tear is not a construction defect. Sometimes the answer springs from a combination of causative factors in which more than one party is proportionately responsible.

Mediation, a Possible Solution

Identifying the culpable party can be difficult for an owner when the explanations and excuses offered by the involved contractors and architects are expressed in plausible-sounding but arcane terminology. To bring all parties into litigation or arbitration in an indiscriminate manner, hoping to snare the responsible one, could be inefficient, costly, unjust, and time-consuming and would be counterproductive should the owner be found responsible for the defects. A more satisfactory course would be to persuade the parties to submit the issue to an experienced neutral mediator, familiar with standard construction industry customs and practices and the standard of care of architects and engineers. The mediator can examine the contract documentation, the construction project, and the alleged defects and will evaluate the viewpoints of the owner, contractor, and architect. The mediator can then offer an impartial, informed assessment of proportionate liability for consideration by the parties. In the event that a voluntary, mutually acceptable settlement cannot be then effected, the owner will at least be in a position to proceed with confidence and certainty to negotiate, arbitrate, or litigate with those liable without any further inconvenience to the blameless party.

21

Written Communication

What Must Be in Writing

The AIA General Conditions provides that various administrative functions must be performed in writing. They may be conveniently classified in five general categories:

1. Certificates given by architect or contractor
2. Notices to and from owner, contractor, architect, surety, and others
3. Submittals to and from owner and contractor
4. Additional agreements needed to facilitate progress or the work of the original contract
5. Orders, authorizations, approvals, and objections, and miscellaneous communications among the owner, contractor, and architect

In most cases, there are no special forms which must be followed. There are a few standard AIA forms which may be used, and some construction industry textbooks and legal formbooks provide additional formats and guidelines. In writing or devising your own documents, it is important to use plain, unambiguous, direct English. Check the relevant contract provisions to make certain that all of the requirements are met.

Architect's Certifications

In the case of architect's certifications, make sure that the wording is realistic and does not assert facts beyond your ability to know, or promise results beyond your capacity to deliver. For example, some lenders and owners ask architects to sign a certificate similar to the following: "I hereby certify that the work was completed in strict compliance with the contract documents and in conformance with all applicable zoning laws and building codes."

This is much too broad and very likely would be construed as a warranty which would be excluded from the coverage of most professional liability insurance policies. There is no way an architect could possibly know all applicable zoning laws and building codes, let alone know whether all aspects of the work are in conformance. A more realistic and acceptable wording would be the following: "Based on my on-site observations, I hereby certify that to the best of my knowledge, information, and belief, the work was completed in compliance with the contract documents and applicable zoning laws and building codes except for (list exceptions)."

Certifications should always have all necessary modifying or limiting conditions completely described and should be dated. An architect could be found liable for losses incurred by anyone who places reliance on an architect's certificate which later proves to be erroneous or misleading. This is particularly true with respect to lenders, sureties, and owners when the architect has overcertified payments to contractors. If you are not absolutely certain of the suitability of the wording of a certification of any sort, the safest course is to review it with your legal counsel before signing.

Certificates Required by the AIA General Conditions

The Application and Certificate for Payment, AIA Document G702, submitted by the contractor for each payment requested, contains the following certificate to be signed by the contractor and sworn to before a notary public:

> "The undersigned Contractor certifies that to the best of the Contractor's knowledge, information and belief the Work covered by this Application for Payment has been completed in accordance with the Contract Documents, that all amounts have been paid by the Contractor for Work for which previous Certificates for Payment were issued and payments received from the Owner and that current payment shown herein is now due."

The contractor's application and certificate are in conformance with the payment procedure set out in Paragraph 9.3 of AIA Document A201.

The same application form (G702) contains an architect's certificate for payment which states:

"In accordance with the Contract Documents, based on on-site observations and the data comprising the above application, the Architect certifies to the Owner that to the best of the Architect's knowledge, information and belief the Work has progressed as indicated, and the Contractor is entitled to payment of the AMOUNT CERTIFIED."

The architect's payment certificate is in conformance with the certification procedure set out in Paragraph 9.4 of A201.

It is of fundamental significance that the date of substantial completion be conclusively established, as this is the starting date for the warranty period and the ending date of the construction period for computing liquidated damages. The date is to be determined through the independent judgment of the architect and is transmitted to the parties by means of a certificate. (A201, 4.2.9 and 9.8) A convenient form for expressing this determination is the Certificate of Substantial Completion, AIA Document G704.

The architect is also obligated to determine that the construction is completed. Upon reaching this determination, the architect should approve the contractor's final application for payment by executing the architect's certificate for payment on the application form. This constitutes the certificate of final completion. (A201, 4.2.9 and 9.10.1) When a retention has been withheld from the contractor's payments, an additional payment application and certificate will be issued when the retainage is due.

In the event that the contractor defaults or neglects to carry out the work of the contract, the owner after observing the requirement of two consecutive 7-day notice periods may correct such deficiencies and charge the costs to the contractor. The owner, however, must obtain the architect's prior approval of both the owner's action and the amount to be charged to the contractor. (A201, 2.4.1) This approval should be in the form of a certificate.

The owner may terminate the contract for cause under conditions listed in Subparagraph 14.2.1 (A201) provided all notice requirements have been complied with. The owner must obtain the architect's prior certificate that sufficient cause exists to justify the owner's action. (A201, 14.2.2)

Considering the easily predictable repercussions of either of the two foregoing certifications, the wording is of extreme importance. The certificates should be based on the architect's independent knowledge and opinion and on provable evidence of the specified facts. The architect should make a thorough examination of the conditions, should memorialize them in appropriate documentation, notes, and photographs, and should obtain the viewpoints of both owner and contractor before issuing the certificate. All certificates should be dated.

Notices

Notices include all communications transmitting information, demands, and claims. Notices required by the AIA General Conditions must be in writing. Occasionally it will be expedient or convenient to give notice orally, and it would legally suffice, although its terms might be difficult to establish later if it became necessary. Therefore, all oral notices should be followed promptly by a confirmation in writing.

All notices should be carefully worded for accurate expression to avoid ambiguity and should always be dated. According to the General Conditions, written notice is deemed to have been duly served when it is delivered in person to the individual, firm, or entity or if delivered or sent by registered or certified mail to the last business address known to the party giving notice. (A201, 13.3.1) This is a checklist of the written notices required or allowed by the AIA General Conditions:

Owner's order to the contractor to stop the work for any of the specified causes (A201, 2.3.1)

Owner's 7-day notice to the contractor of contractor's default and neglect to carry out the work of the contract (2.4.1)

Owner's second 7-day notice to the contractor of contractor's default and neglect to carry out the work of the contract (2.4.1)

Contractor's report to the architect of errors, inconsistencies, or omissions discovered in the contract drawings and information furnished by the owner (3.2.1)

Contractor's report to the architect of errors, inconsistencies, or omissions discovered in field measurements, field conditions, and other information known to the contractor, compared with the contract drawings (3.2.2)

Contractor's giving of notices required by laws, ordinances, rules, regulations, and lawful orders of public authorities bearing on performance of the work (3.7.2)

Contractor's notification of architect and owner of violations of applicable laws, statutes, ordinances, building codes, and rules and regulations found in the contract documents (3.7.3)

Contractor's informing the architect of specific deviations in the shop drawings from requirements of the contract documents (3.12.8)

Contractor's direction of architect's specific attention on resubmitted shop drawings to revisions other than those requested by the architect on previous submittals (3.12.9)

Contractor's notification of architect that the required design, process, or product is an infringement of a patent (3.17.1)

Architect's informing the owner of the progress of the work (4.2.2)

Request of owner or contractor for architect's interpretation and decision concerning performance under and requirements of the contract documents (4.2.11)

Architect's response to owner's or contractor's request for interpretation and decision concerning performance under and requirements of the contract documents (4.2.11)

Owner's or contractor's claims for adjustment or interpretation of contract terms, payment of money, extension of time, or other relief (4.3.1)

Notice by the observing party of concealed or unknown conditions differing materially from those indicated in the contract documents or those ordinarily found to exist (4.3.6)

Contractor's claims for an increase in the contract sum (4.3.7)

Contractor's claim for an increase in the contract time (4.3.8.1)

Contractor's or owner's notice of injury or damage to person or property because of act or omission of the other party (4.3.9)

Architect's initial response to contractor's or owner's claims (4.4.1)

Architect's notification of surety (not obligatory) of the nature and amount of claim (4.4.1)

Architect's notification of owner and contractor that decision on claim will be made within 7 days (4.4.4)

Architect's written decision on claim of owner or contractor (4.4.4)

Architect's notification of surety (not obligatory) of decision on claim of owner or contractor and request for the surety's assistance in resolving the controversy (4.4.4)

Owner's or contractor's demand for arbitration (4.5.1)

Owner's or contractor's amendment of demand for arbitration (4.5.6)

Contractor's report to the architect of apparent discrepancies or defects in other construction by owner or separate contractors which would render it unsuitable for contractor's further work (6.2.2)

Owner's notice to contractor to proceed with construction (8.2.2)

Contractor's notice to owner of proceeding with construction (in absence of owner's notice) (8.2.2)

Architect's notification to the contractor and owner of the architect's reasons for withholding of certificate for contractor's payment (9.4.1 and 9.5.1)

Owner's notification to the architect that the certified payment to the contractor has been made (9.6.1)

Architect's notification of contractor to complete or correct items remaining on the punch list prior to substantial completion (9.8.2)

Contractor's notice that the work is ready for architect's final inspection (9.10.1)

Architect's confirmation that material delay of final completion of the work is not the fault of the contractor (9.10.3)

Contractor's report to the owner and architect of the encountering of asbestos or PCB in the work area (10.1.2)

Architect's final determination in respect to asbestos or PCB (10.1.2)

Contractor's giving of notices complying with applicable laws, ordinances, rules, regulations, and lawful orders of public authorities bearing on safety of persons or property or their protection from damage, injury, or loss (10.2.2)

Contractor's posting of danger signs and other warnings against hazards, promulgating safety regulations, and notifying owners and users of adjacent sites and utilities (10.2.3)

Insurer's notice to owner 30 days prior to canceling insurance coverage (11.1.3)

Owner's notice to contractor that it does not intend to purchase property insurance with all of the specified coverages required by the contract (11.3.1.2)

Contractor's request for additional property insurance coverage (11.3.4)

Architect's request for contractor to uncover work which was specified to be available for observation (12.1.1)

Architect's request for contractor to uncover work which was not specified to be available for observation (12.1.2)

Owner's notice to contractor during warranty period to rectify work not in accordance with the contract documents (12.2.2)

Architect's notice to contractor fixing reasonable time to correct nonconforming work during warranty period (12.2.4)

Contractor's timely notice to architect of when and where tests and inspections are to be made (13.5.1 and 13.5.2)

Contractor's notice to the owner and architect of contractor's termination of the contract for any reason listed in Subparagraph 14.1.1 (14.1.2 and 9.7.1)

Contractor's notice to the owner and architect of contractor's termination of the contract because of owner's persistent failure to fulfill its obligations with respect to matters important to the progress of the work (14.1.3)

Owner's notice to the contractor and surety of owner's termination of the contract for any reason listed in Subparagraph 14.2.1 (14.2.2)

Owner's order to the contractor to suspend, delay, or interrupt the work in whole or in part for such period of time as the owner may determine, with cause, for the convenience of the owner (14.3.1)

Notices required by AIA Document A312, Performance Bond and Payment Bond

Submittals

Submittals are written information presented by the contractor or owner to the other such as site information, shop drawings, product data, samples, schedules, and lists. This is a checklist of submittals required by the AIA General Conditions:

Contractor's returning to the architect or suitably accounting for all of the contract documents, except one record set, upon completion of the work (A201, 1.3.1)

Owner's furnishing to the contractor information which is necessary and relevant for the contractor to evaluate, give notice of, or enforce mechanics' lien rights (2.1.2)

Owner's furnishing to the contractor of reasonable evidence that financial arrangements have been made to fulfill the owner's obligations under the contract (2.2.1)

Owner's furnishing to the contractor of surveys, soil tests, legal limitations, utility locations, and legal description of the site (2.2.2)

Owner's furnishing to the contractor of such copies of drawings and project manuals as are reasonably necessary for execution of the work (2.2.5)

Contractor's furnishing of satisfactory evidence as to the kind and quality of materials and equipment (3.5.1)

Contractor's submission of a construction schedule for the work (3.10.1)

Contractor's submission of a schedule of submittals (3.10.2)

Contractor's delivery to the architect at completion of the work of one record copy of the drawings, specifications, addenda, change orders, and other modifications marked to record changes and selections made during constructions, and in addition approved shop drawings, product data, samples, and similar required submittals (3.11.1)

Architect's submittal to owner of preceding items (3.11.1)

Contractor's submission of shop drawings, product data, samples, and similar submittals required by the contract documents (3.12.5)

Contractor's submission of professional certification of performance criteria of materials, systems, or equipment required by the contract documents (3.12.11)

Architect's forwarding to the owner of written warranties and related documents required by the contract when received from the contractor (4.2.9)

Contractor's or owner's submission to the architect of additional data supporting their claim for architect's decision (4.4.3)

Contractor's submission to the architect of list of names of persons or entities proposed for each principal portion of the work (subcontractors and suppliers) (5.2.1)

Contractor's submission to the architect of names of subcontractors or suppliers to replace those rejected by the owner or architect (5.2.3)

Contractor's submission to the architect of an itemized accounting and supporting data to substantiate pricing of construction change directives (7.3.6)

Contractor's submission to the architect of a schedule of values (9.2.1)

Contractor's submission of application for payment and its supporting data (9.3.1)

Owner's making of payments to the contractor (9.6.1)

Contractor's submission to the architect of a request for inspection accompanied by a comprehensive list of items to be completed or corrected (punch list) to achieve substantial completion (9.8.2 and 9.9.1)

Contractor's request for reinspection to determine substantial completion (9.8.2)

Contractor's submittal to architect of prerequisites to final payment itemized in 9.10.2

Contractor's submittal to architect of prerequisites to partial final payment itemized in 9.10.3

Contractor's designation of a responsible member of the contractor's organization at the site, other than the superintendent, whose duty shall be the prevention of accidents (10.2.6)

Contractor's submission of certificates of required insurance (11.1.3)

Contractor's submission of certificates of insurance required to remain in effect after the final payment (11.1.3)

Owner's filing with contractor of certificates of required insurance (11.3.6)

Owner's furnishing of a surety bond for proper performance of owner's duties as fiduciary in case of an insured loss (11.3.9)

Contractor's furnishing of bonds to the owner covering faithful performance of the contract and payment for labor and material (11.4.1)

Contractor's submitting to the architect of required certificates of testing, inspection, or approval (13.5.4)

Additional Agreements

From time to time during construction, unexpected conditions or circumstances will require the parties to make further agreements in order to facilitate construction progress. As it would be nearly impossible to write a contract that would anticipate all possible occurrences, the AIA General Conditions require the parties to further agree in writing when necessary. In the event the parties cannot agree, the architect will provide the decision subject to arbitration if the determination is unacceptable to either or both parties.

This checklist summarizes further written agreements anticipated by the AIA General Conditions:

Contractor's, owner's, and architect's agreement on time limits for architect's decision on claims submitted by contractor and owner (A201, 4.2.11)

Contractor's and owner's agreement to suspend contractor's performance and/or owner's contract payments pending final resolution of a claim (4.3.4)

Owner's, contractor's, and architect's mutual agreement to allow consolidation or joinder of the architect and the architect's employees or consultants in an arbitration between owner and contractor (4.5.5)

Owner's, contractor's, and architect's mutual agreement for change orders (7.2)

Owner's and architect's agreement to proceed with a construction change directive in the absence of contractor's concurrence (7.3)

Contractor's and owner's agreement to start construction prior to effective date of insurance (8.2.2)

Contractor's and owner's agreement of an off-site location where materials and equipment may be stored to qualify for progress payments (9.3.2)

Contractor's and owner's written acceptance of responsibilities assigned to them in the architect's certificate of substantial completion (9.8.2 and 9.9.1)

Contractor's and owner's agreement to owner's occupancy of any portion of the work (9.9.1)

Contractor's and owner's agreement for terms of contractor's resumption of work after asbestos or PCB has been encountered in the work area (10.1.2)

Contractor's and owner's agreement in respect to changes in insurance requirements prior to final payment (11.3.1)

Contractor's and owner's agreement as to distribution of insurance proceeds received in insured loss (11.3.9)

Contractor's and owner's agreement to permit assignment of the contract as a whole (13.2.1)

Contractor's and owner's agreement to a breach of the contract (13.4.2)

Contractor's and owner's agreement to the amount of a fixed or percentage fee for the increased cost of work caused by owner's suspension for convenience (14.3.3)

Orders, Authorizations, Approvals, and Objections

In the process of carrying out the contract or administering it, owner, contractor, and architect all must exercise their rights of approval or disapproval and powers to order, authorize, or consent to various proposals, issues, or submissions. These decisions and determinations should be presented to the affected parties in writing and should be dated.

The various written authorizations, approvals, and objections provided for in the AIA General Conditions are summarized in this checklist:

Architect's and owner's specific written consent to the contractor for use of the contract documents on other work (A201, 1.3.1)

Architect's approval of contractor's schedule of submittals (3.10.2)

Contractor's approval of shop drawings, product data, samples, and similar submittals prior to submission to architect (3.12.5 and 3.12.7)

Architect's approval of contractor's deviations in shop drawings, product data, or samples (3.12.8)

Owner's and separate contractor's consent for contractor to cut or alter work of the owner or separate contractor (3.14.2)

Contractor's consent for owner or separate contractor to cut or alter work of the contractor (3.14.2)

Owner's, contractor's, and architect's mutual consent to modify, restrict, or extend the duties, responsibilities, and limitations of authority of the architect (4.1.2)

Contractor's reasonable objection to appointment of replacement architect (4.1.3)

Owner's, contractor's, or architect's special authorization of direct communications rather than using the formal communications channels described in Subparagraph 4.2.4

Architect's review and approval or other appropriate action upon the contractor's submittals (4.2.7)

Architect's interpretations of and decisions on matters concerning performance under and requirements of the contract documents (4.2.11 and 4.2.12)

Architect's and owner's approval of or reasonable objection to contractor's list of subcontractors and suppliers (5.2.1)

Architect's ordering of minor changes in the work (7.4.1)

Owner's approval in advance for payment to the contractor for materials stored off the site (9.3.2)

Insurer's consent to owner's partial occupancy of the work (9.9.1 and 11.3.11)

Public authorities' authorization of owner's partial occupancy of the work (9.9.1)

Surety's consent to final payment (9.10.2)

Surety's consent to partial final payment (9.10.3)

Contractor's objection to owner's acting as fiduciary in adjusting insurance proceeds in an insured loss (11.3.10)

Additional Written Communications

Other contract documents such as the supplementary or other conditions or the trade sections of the specifications may contain additional requirements for written submissions, notices, authorizations, approvals, or objections. At any time that any of the interested parties wish to communicate with each other for any purpose, the contractual communications channels should be respected. Whenever casual communication such as face-to-face discussions or telephone conversations are used, the importance of the matter should be evaluated. In the very least, a note in your own file will memorialize the particulars and the date. If the subject matter is of greater importance, oral communications should be confirmed to all interested parties in writing.

Appendix A:
AIA Document B141 – Standard Form of Agreement Between Owner and Architect, 1987 Edition

THE AMERICAN INSTITUTE OF ARCHITECTS

1. AIA copyrighted material has been reproduced with the permission of the American Institute of Architects under license number 90011. Permission expires December 31, 1991. FURTHER REPRODUCTION IS PROHIBITED.

2. Because AIA Documents are revised from time to time, users should ascertain from the AIA the current edition of this document.

3. Copies of the current edition of this AIA document may be purchased from The American Institute of Architects or its local distributors.

4. This document is intended for use as a "consumable" (consumables are further defined by Senate Report 94-473 on the Copyright Act of 1976). This document is not intended to be used as "model language" (language taken from an existing document and incorporated, without attribution, into a newly-created document.) Rather, it is a standard form which is intended to be modified by appending separate amendment sheets and/or fill in provided blank spaces.

AIA Document B141

Standard Form of Agreement Between Owner and Architect

1987 EDITION

THIS DOCUMENT HAS IMPORTANT LEGAL CONSEQUENCES; CONSULTATION WITH AN ATTORNEY IS ENCOURAGED WITH RESPECT TO ITS COMPLETION OR MODIFICATION.

AGREEMENT

made as of the   day of   in the year of
Nineteen Hundred and

BETWEEN the Owner:
(Name and address)

and the Architect:
(Name and address)

For the following Project:
(Include detailed description of Project, location, address and scope.)

The Owner and Architect agree as set forth below.

Copyright 1917, 1926, 1948, 1951, 1953, 1958, 1961, 1963, 1966, 1967, 1970, 1974, 1977, ©1987 by The American Institute of Architects, 1735 New York Avenue, N.W., Washington, D.C. 20006. Reproduction of the material herein or substantial quotation of its provisions without written permission of the AIA violates the copyright laws of the United States and will be subject to legal prosecution.

AIA DOCUMENT B141 • OWNER-ARCHITECT AGREEMENT • FOURTEENTH EDITION • AIA® • ©1987
THE AMERICAN INSTITUTE OF ARCHITECTS, 1735 NEW YORK AVENUE, N.W., WASHINGTON, D.C. 20006

B141-1987 1

182 / Appendix A

TERMS AND CONDITIONS OF AGREEMENT BETWEEN OWNER AND ARCHITECT

ARTICLE 1
ARCHITECT'S RESPONSIBILITIES

1.1 ARCHITECT'S SERVICES

1.1.1 The Architect's services consist of those services performed by the Architect, Architect's employees and Architect's consultants as enumerated in Articles 2 and 3 of this Agreement and any other services included in Article 12.

1.1.2 The Architect's services shall be performed as expeditiously as is consistent with professional skill and care and the orderly progress of the Work. Upon request of the Owner, the Architect shall submit for the Owner's approval a schedule for the performance of the Architect's services which may be adjusted as the Project proceeds, and shall include allowances for periods of time required for the Owner's review and for approval of submissions by authorities having jurisdiction over the Project. Time limits established by this schedule approved by the Owner shall not, except for reasonable cause, be exceeded by the Architect or Owner.

1.1.3 The services covered by this Agreement are subject to the time limitations contained in Subparagraph 11.5.1.

ARTICLE 2
SCOPE OF ARCHITECT'S BASIC SERVICES

2.1 DEFINITION

2.1.1 The Architect's Basic Services consist of those described in Paragraphs 2.2 through 2.6 and any other services identified in Article 12 as part of Basic Services, and include normal structural, mechanical and electrical engineering services.

2.2 SCHEMATIC DESIGN PHASE

2.2.1 The Architect shall review the program furnished by the Owner to ascertain the requirements of the Project and shall arrive at a mutual understanding of such requirements with the Owner.

2.2.2 The Architect shall provide a preliminary evaluation of the Owner's program, schedule and construction budget requirements, each in terms of the other, subject to the limitations set forth in Subparagraph 5.2.1.

2.2.3 The Architect shall review with the Owner alternative approaches to design and construction of the Project.

2.2.4 Based on the mutually agreed-upon program, schedule and construction budget requirements, the Architect shall prepare, for approval by the Owner, Schematic Design Documents consisting of drawings and other documents illustrating the scale and relationship of Project components.

2.2.5 The Architect shall submit to the Owner a preliminary estimate of Construction Cost based on current area, volume or other unit costs.

2.3 DESIGN DEVELOPMENT PHASE

2.3.1 Based on the approved Schematic Design Documents and any adjustments authorized by the Owner in the program, schedule or construction budget, the Architect shall prepare, for approval by the Owner, Design Development Documents consisting of drawings and other documents to fix and describe the size and character of the Project as to architectural, structural, mechanical and electrical systems, materials and such other elements as may be appropriate.

2.3.2 The Architect shall advise the Owner of any adjustments to the preliminary estimate of Construction Cost.

2.4 CONSTRUCTION DOCUMENTS PHASE

2.4.1 Based on the approved Design Development Documents and any further adjustments in the scope or quality of the Project or in the construction budget authorized by the Owner, the Architect shall prepare, for approval by the Owner, Construction Documents consisting of Drawings and Specifications setting forth in detail the requirements for the construction of the Project.

2.4.2 The Architect shall assist the Owner in the preparation of the necessary bidding information, bidding forms, the Conditions of the Contract, and the form of Agreement between the Owner and Contractor.

2.4.3 The Architect shall advise the Owner of any adjustments to previous preliminary estimates of Construction Cost indicated by changes in requirements or general market conditions.

2.4.4 The Architect shall assist the Owner in connection with the Owner's responsibility for filing documents required for the approval of governmental authorities having jurisdiction over the Project.

2.5 BIDDING OR NEGOTIATION PHASE

2.5.1 The Architect, following the Owner's approval of the Construction Documents and of the latest preliminary estimate of Construction Cost, shall assist the Owner in obtaining bids or negotiated proposals and assist in awarding and preparing contracts for construction.

2.6 CONSTRUCTION PHASE—ADMINISTRATION OF THE CONSTRUCTION CONTRACT

2.6.1 The Architect's responsibility to provide Basic Services for the Construction Phase under this Agreement commences with the award of the Contract for Construction and terminates at the earlier of the issuance to the Owner of the final Certificate for Payment or 60 days after the date of Substantial Completion of the Work.

2.6.2 The Architect shall provide administration of the Contract for Construction as set forth below and in the edition of AIA Document A201, General Conditions of the Contract for Construction, current as of the date of this Agreement, unless otherwise provided in this Agreement.

2.6.3 Duties, responsibilities and limitations of authority of the Architect shall not be restricted, modified or extended without written agreement of the Owner and Architect with consent of the Contractor, which consent shall not be unreasonably withheld.

2.6.4 The Architect shall be a representative of and shall advise and consult with the Owner (1) during construction until final payment to the Contractor is due, and (2) as an Additional Service at the Owner's direction from time to time during the correction period described in the Contract for Construction. The Architect shall have authority to act on behalf of the Owner only to the extent provided in this Agreement unless otherwise modified by written instrument.

2.6.5 The Architect shall visit the site at intervals appropriate to the stage of construction or as otherwise agreed by the Owner and Architect in writing to become generally familiar with the progress and quality of the Work completed and to determine in general if the Work is being performed in a manner indicating that the Work when completed will be in accordance with the Contract Documents. However, the Architect shall not be required to make exhaustive or continuous on-site inspections to check the quality or quantity of the Work. On the basis of on-site observations as an architect, the Architect shall keep the Owner informed of the progress and quality of the Work, and shall endeavor to guard the Owner against defects and deficiencies in the Work. *(More extensive site representation may be agreed to as an Additional Service, as described in Paragraph 3.2.)*

2.6.6 The Architect shall not have control over or charge of and shall not be responsible for construction means, methods, techniques, sequences or procedures, or for safety precautions and programs in connection with the Work, since these are solely the Contractor's responsibility under the Contract for Construction. The Architect shall not be responsible for the Contractor's schedules or failure to carry out the Work in accordance with the Contract Documents. The Architect shall not have control over or charge of acts or omissions of the Contractor, Subcontractors, or their agents or employees, or of any other persons performing portions of the Work.

2.6.7 The Architect shall at all times have access to the Work wherever it is in preparation or progress.

2.6.8 Except as may otherwise be provided in the Contract Documents or when direct communications have been specially authorized, the Owner and Contractor shall communicate through the Architect. Communications by and with the Architect's consultants shall be through the Architect.

2.6.9 Based on the Architect's observations and evaluations of the Contractor's Applications for Payment, the Architect shall review and certify the amounts due the Contractor.

2.6.10 The Architect's certification for payment shall constitute a representation to the Owner, based on the Architect's observations at the site as provided in Subparagraph 2.6.5 and on the data comprising the Contractor's Application for Payment, that the Work has progressed to the point indicated and that, to the best of the Architect's knowledge, information and belief, quality of the Work is in accordance with the Contract Documents. The foregoing representations are subject to an evaluation of the Work for conformance with the Contract Documents upon Substantial Completion, to results of subsequent tests and inspections, to minor deviations from the Contract Documents correctable prior to completion and to specific qualifications expressed by the Architect. The issuance of a Certificate for Payment shall further constitute a representation that the Contractor is entitled to payment in the amount certified. However, the issuance of a Certificate for Payment shall not be a representation that the Architect has (1) made exhaustive or continuous on-site inspections to check the quality or quantity of the Work, (2) reviewed construction means, methods, techniques, sequences or procedures, (3) reviewed copies of requisitions received from Subcontractors and material suppliers and other data requested by the Owner to substantiate the Contractor's right to payment or (4) ascertained how or for what purpose the Contractor has used money previously paid on account of the Contract Sum.

2.6.11 The Architect shall have authority to reject Work which does not conform to the Contract Documents. Whenever the Architect considers it necessary or advisable for implementation of the intent of the Contract Documents, the Architect will have authority to require additional inspection or testing of the Work in accordance with the provisions of the Contract Documents, whether or not such Work is fabricated, installed or completed. However, neither this authority of the Architect nor a decision made in good faith either to exercise or not to exercise such authority shall give rise to a duty or responsibility of the Architect to the Contractor, Subcontractors, material and equipment suppliers, their agents or employees or other persons performing portions of the Work.

2.6.12 The Architect shall review and approve or take other appropriate action upon Contractor's submittals such as Shop Drawings, Product Data and Samples, but only for the limited purpose of checking for conformance with information given and the design concept expressed in the Contract Documents. The Architect's action shall be taken with such reasonable promptness as to cause no delay in the Work or in the construction of the Owner or of separate contractors, while allowing sufficient time in the Architect's professional judgment to permit adequate review. Review of such submittals is not conducted for the purpose of determining the accuracy and completeness of other details such as dimensions and quantities or for substantiating instructions for installation or performance of equipment or systems designed by the Contractor, all of which remain the responsibility of the Contractor to the extent required by the Contract Documents. The Architect's review shall not constitute approval of safety precautions or, unless otherwise specifically stated by the Architect, of construction means, methods, techniques, sequences or procedures. The Architect's approval of a specific item shall not indicate approval of an assembly of which the item is a component. When professional certification of performance characteristics of materials, systems or equipment is required by the Contract Documents, the Architect shall be entitled to rely upon such certification to establish that the materials, systems or equipment will meet the performance criteria required by the Contract Documents.

2.6.13 The Architect shall prepare Change Orders and Construction Change Directives, with supporting documentation and data if deemed necessary by the Architect as provided in Subparagraphs 3.1.1 and 3.3.3, for the Owner's approval and execution in accordance with the Contract Documents, and may authorize minor changes in the Work not involving an adjustment in the Contract Sum or an extension of the Contract Time which are not inconsistent with the intent of the Contract Documents.

2.6.14 The Architect shall conduct inspections to determine the date or dates of Substantial Completion and the date of final completion, shall receive and forward to the Owner for the Owner's review and records written warranties and related documents required by the Contract Documents and assembled by the Contractor, and shall issue a final Certificate for Payment upon compliance with the requirements of the Contract Documents.

2.6.15 The Architect shall interpret and decide matters concerning performance of the Owner and Contractor under the requirements of the Contract Documents on written request of either the Owner or Contractor. The Architect's response to such requests shall be made with reasonable promptness and within any time limits agreed upon.

2.6.16 Interpretations and decisions of the Architect shall be consistent with the intent of and reasonably inferable from the Contract Documents and shall be in writing or in the form of drawings. When making such interpretations and initial decisions, the Architect shall endeavor to secure faithful performance by both Owner and Contractor, shall not show partiality to either, and shall not be liable for results of interpretations or decisions so rendered in good faith.

2.6.17 The Architect's decisions on matters relating to aesthetic effect shall be final if consistent with the intent expressed in the Contract Documents.

2.6.18 The Architect shall render written decisions within a reasonable time on all claims, disputes or other matters in question between the Owner and Contractor relating to the execution or progress of the Work as provided in the Contract Documents.

2.6.19 The Architect's decisions on claims, disputes or other matters, including those in question between the Owner and Contractor, except for those relating to aesthetic effect as provided in Subparagraph 2.6.17, shall be subject to arbitration as provided in this Agreement and in the Contract Documents.

ARTICLE 3
ADDITIONAL SERVICES

3.1 GENERAL

3.1.1 The services described in this Article 3 are not included in Basic Services unless so identified in Article 12, and they shall be paid for by the Owner as provided in this Agreement, in addition to the compensation for Basic Services. The services described under Paragraphs 3.2 and 3.4 shall only be provided if authorized or confirmed in writing by the Owner. If services described under Contingent Additional Services in Paragraph 3.3 are required due to circumstances beyond the Architect's control, the Architect shall notify the Owner prior to commencing such services. If the Owner deems that such services described under Paragraph 3.3 are not required, the Owner shall give prompt written notice to the Architect. If the Owner indicates in writing that all or part of such Contingent Additional Services are not required, the Architect shall have no obligation to provide those services.

3.2 PROJECT REPRESENTATION BEYOND BASIC SERVICES

3.2.1 If more extensive representation at the site than is described in Subparagraph 2.6.5 is required, the Architect shall provide one or more Project Representatives to assist in carrying out such additional on-site responsibilities.

3.2.2 Project Representatives shall be selected, employed and directed by the Architect, and the Architect shall be compensated therefor as agreed by the Owner and Architect. The duties, responsibilities and limitations of authority of Project Representatives shall be as described in the edition of AIA Document B352 current as of the date of this Agreement, unless otherwise agreed.

3.2.3 Through the observations by such Project Representatives, the Architect shall endeavor to provide further protection for the Owner against defects and deficiencies in the Work, but the furnishing of such project representation shall not modify the rights, responsibilities or obligations of the Architect as described elsewhere in this Agreement.

3.3 CONTINGENT ADDITIONAL SERVICES

3.3.1 Making revisions in Drawings, Specifications or other documents when such revisions are:

.1 inconsistent with approvals or instructions previously given by the Owner, including revisions made necessary by adjustments in the Owner's program or Project budget;

.2 required by the enactment or revision of codes, laws or regulations subsequent to the preparation of such documents; or

.3 due to changes required as a result of the Owner's failure to render decisions in a timely manner.

3.3.2 Providing services required because of significant changes in the Project including, but not limited to, size, quality, complexity, the Owner's schedule, or the method of bidding or negotiating and contracting for construction, except for services required under Subparagraph 5.2.5.

3.3.3 Preparing Drawings, Specifications and other documentation and supporting data, evaluating Contractor's proposals, and providing other services in connection with Change Orders and Construction Change Directives.

3.3.4 Providing services in connection with evaluating substitutions proposed by the Contractor and making subsequent revisions to Drawings, Specifications and other documentation resulting therefrom.

3.3.5 Providing consultation concerning replacement of Work damaged by fire or other cause during construction, and furnishing services required in connection with the replacement of such Work.

3.3.6 Providing services made necessary by the default of the Contractor, by major defects or deficiencies in the Work of the Contractor, or by failure of performance of either the Owner or Contractor under the Contract for Construction.

3.3.7 Providing services in evaluating an extensive number of claims submitted by the Contractor or others in connection with the Work.

3.3.8 Providing services in connection with a public hearing, arbitration proceeding or legal proceeding except where the Architect is party thereto.

3.3.9 Preparing documents for alternate, separate or sequential bids or providing services in connection with bidding, negotiation or construction prior to the completion of the Construction Documents Phase.

3.4 OPTIONAL ADDITIONAL SERVICES

3.4.1 Providing analyses of the Owner's needs and programming the requirements of the Project.

3.4.2 Providing financial feasibility or other special studies.

3.4.3 Providing planning surveys, site evaluations or comparative studies of prospective sites.

3.4.4 Providing special surveys, environmental studies and submissions required for approvals of governmental authorities or others having jurisdiction over the Project.

3.4.5 Providing services relative to future facilities, systems and equipment.

3.4.6 Providing services to investigate existing conditions or facilities or to make measured drawings thereof.

3.4.7 Providing services to verify the accuracy of drawings or other information furnished by the Owner.

3.4.8 Providing coordination of construction performed by separate contractors or by the Owner's own forces and coordination of services required in connection with construction performed and equipment supplied by the Owner.

3.4.9 Providing services in connection with the work of a construction manager or separate consultants retained by the Owner.

3.4.10 Providing detailed estimates of Construction Cost.

3.4.11 Providing detailed quantity surveys or inventories of material, equipment and labor.

3.4.12 Providing analyses of owning and operating costs.

3.4.13 Providing interior design and other similar services required for or in connection with the selection, procurement or installation of furniture, furnishings and related equipment.

3.4.14 Providing services for planning tenant or rental spaces.

3.4.15 Making investigations, inventories of materials or equipment, or valuations and detailed appraisals of existing facilities.

3.4.16 Preparing a set of reproducible record drawings showing significant changes in the Work made during construction based on marked-up prints, drawings and other data furnished by the Contractor to the Architect.

3.4.17 Providing assistance in the utilization of equipment or systems such as testing, adjusting and balancing, preparation of operation and maintenance manuals, training personnel for operation and maintenance, and consultation during operation.

3.4.18 Providing services after issuance to the Owner of the final Certificate for Payment, or in the absence of a final Certificate for Payment, more than 60 days after the date of Substantial Completion of the Work.

3.4.19 Providing services of consultants for other than architectural, structural, mechanical and electrical engineering portions of the Project provided as a part of Basic Services.

3.4.20 Providing any other services not otherwise included in this Agreement or not customarily furnished in accordance with generally accepted architectural practice.

ARTICLE 4
OWNER'S RESPONSIBILITIES

4.1 The Owner shall provide full information regarding requirements for the Project, including a program which shall set forth the Owner's objectives, schedule, constraints and criteria, including space requirements and relationships, flexibility, expandability, special equipment, systems and site requirements.

4.2 The Owner shall establish and update an overall budget for the Project, including the Construction Cost, the Owner's other costs and reasonable contingencies related to all of these costs.

4.3 If requested by the Architect, the Owner shall furnish evidence that financial arrangements have been made to fulfill the Owner's obligations under this Agreement.

4.4 The Owner shall designate a representative authorized to act on the Owner's behalf with respect to the Project. The Owner or such authorized representative shall render decisions in a timely manner pertaining to documents submitted by the Architect in order to avoid unreasonable delay in the orderly and sequential progress of the Architect's services.

4.5 The Owner shall furnish surveys describing physical characteristics, legal limitations and utility locations for the site of the Project, and a written legal description of the site. The surveys and legal information shall include, as applicable, grades and lines of streets, alleys, pavements and adjoining property and structures; adjacent drainage; rights-of-way, restrictions, easements, encroachments, zoning, deed restrictions, boundaries and contours of the site; locations, dimensions and necessary data pertaining to existing buildings, other improvements and trees; and information concerning available utility services and lines, both public and private, above and below grade, including inverts and depths. All the information on the survey shall be referenced to a project benchmark.

4.6 The Owner shall furnish the services of geotechnical engineers when such services are requested by the Architect. Such services may include but are not limited to test borings, test pits, determinations of soil bearing values, percolation tests, evaluations of hazardous materials, ground corrosion and resistivity tests, including necessary operations for anticipating subsoil conditions, with reports and appropriate professional recommendations.

4.6.1 The Owner shall furnish the services of other consultants when such services are reasonably required by the scope of the Project and are requested by the Architect.

4.7 The Owner shall furnish structural, mechanical, chemical, air and water pollution tests, tests for hazardous materials, and other laboratory and environmental tests, inspections and reports required by law or the Contract Documents.

4.8 The Owner shall furnish all legal, accounting and insurance counseling services as may be necessary at any time for the Project, including auditing services the Owner may require to verify the Contractor's Applications for Payment or to ascertain how or for what purposes the Contractor has used the money paid by or on behalf of the Owner.

4.9 The services, information, surveys and reports required by Paragraphs 4.5 through 4.8 shall be furnished at the Owner's expense, and the Architect shall be entitled to rely upon the accuracy and completeness thereof.

4.10 Prompt written notice shall be given by the Owner to the Architect if the Owner becomes aware of any fault or defect in the Project or nonconformance with the Contract Documents.

4.11 The proposed language of certificates or certifications requested of the Architect or Architect's consultants shall be submitted to the Architect for review and approval at least 14 days prior to execution. The Owner shall not request certifications that would require knowledge or services beyond the scope of this Agreement.

ARTICLE 5
CONSTRUCTION COST

5.1 DEFINITION

5.1.1 The Construction Cost shall be the total cost or estimated cost to the Owner of all elements of the Project designed or specified by the Architect.

5.1.2 The Construction Cost shall include the cost at current market rates of labor and materials furnished by the Owner and equipment designed, specified, selected or specially provided for by the Architect, plus a reasonable allowance for the Contractor's overhead and profit. In addition, a reasonable allowance for contingencies shall be included for market conditions at the time of bidding and for changes in the Work during construction.

5.1.3 Construction Cost does not include the compensation of the Architect and Architect's consultants, the costs of the land, rights-of-way, financing or other costs which are the responsibility of the Owner as provided in Article 4.

5.2 RESPONSIBILITY FOR CONSTRUCTION COST

5.2.1 Evaluations of the Owner's Project budget, preliminary estimates of Construction Cost and detailed estimates of Construction Cost, if any, prepared by the Architect, represent the Architect's best judgment as a design professional familiar with the construction industry. It is recognized, however, that neither the Architect nor the Owner has control over the cost of labor, materials or equipment, over the Contractor's methods of determining bid prices, or over competitive bidding, market or negotiating conditions. Accordingly, the Architect cannot and does not warrant or represent that bids or negotiated prices will not vary from the Owner's Project budget or from any estimate of Construction Cost or evaluation prepared or agreed to by the Architect.

5.2.2 No fixed limit of Construction Cost shall be established as a condition of this Agreement by the furnishing, proposal or establishment of a Project budget, unless such fixed limit has been agreed upon in writing and signed by the parties hereto. If such a fixed limit has been established, the Architect shall be permitted to include contingencies for design, bidding and price escalation, to determine what materials, equipment, component systems and types of construction are to be included in the Contract Documents, to make reasonable adjustments in the scope of the Project and to include in the Contract Documents alternate bids to adjust the Construction Cost to the fixed limit. Fixed limits, if any, shall be increased in the amount of an increase in the Contract Sum occurring after execution of the Contract for Construction.

5.2.3 If the Bidding or Negotiation Phase has not commenced within 90 days after the Architect submits the Construction Documents to the Owner, any Project budget or fixed limit of Construction Cost shall be adjusted to reflect changes in the general level of prices in the construction industry between the date of submission of the Construction Documents to the Owner and the date on which proposals are sought.

5.2.4 If a fixed limit of Construction Cost (adjusted as provided in Subparagraph 5.2.3) is exceeded by the lowest bona fide bid or negotiated proposal, the Owner shall:

.1 give written approval of an increase in such fixed limit;

.2 authorize rebidding or renegotiating of the Project within a reasonable time;

.3 if the Project is abandoned, terminate in accordance with Paragraph 8.3; or

.4 cooperate in revising the Project scope and quality as required to reduce the Construction Cost.

5.2.5 If the Owner chooses to proceed under Clause 5.2.4.4, the Architect, without additional charge, shall modify the Contract Documents as necessary to comply with the fixed limit, if established as a condition of this Agreement. The modification of Contract Documents shall be the limit of the Architect's responsibility arising out of the establishment of a fixed limit. The Architect shall be entitled to compensation in accordance with this Agreement for all services performed whether or not the Construction Phase is commenced.

ARTICLE 6
USE OF ARCHITECT'S DRAWINGS, SPECIFICATIONS AND OTHER DOCUMENTS

6.1 The Drawings, Specifications and other documents prepared by the Architect for this Project are instruments of the Architect's service for use solely with respect to this Project and, unless otherwise provided, the Architect shall be deemed the author of these documents and shall retain all common law, statutory and other reserved rights, including the copyright. The Owner shall be permitted to retain copies, including reproducible copies, of the Architect's Drawings, Specifications and other documents for information and reference in connection with the Owner's use and occupancy of the Project. The Architect's Drawings, Specifications or other documents shall not be used by the Owner or others on other projects, for additions to this Project or for completion of this Project by others, unless the Architect is adjudged to be in default under this Agreement, except by agreement in writing and with appropriate compensation to the Architect.

6.2 Submission or distribution of documents to meet official regulatory requirements or for similar purposes in connection with the Project is not to be construed as publication in derogation of the Architect's reserved rights.

ARTICLE 7
ARBITRATION

7.1 Claims, disputes or other matters in question between the parties to this Agreement arising out of or relating to this Agreement or breach thereof shall be subject to and decided by arbitration in accordance with the Construction Industry Arbitration Rules of the American Arbitration Association currently in effect unless the parties mutually agree otherwise.

7.2 Demand for arbitration shall be filed in writing with the other party to this Agreement and with the American Arbitration Association. A demand for arbitration shall be made within a reasonable time after the claim, dispute or other matter in question has arisen. In no event shall the demand for arbitration be made after the date when institution of legal or equitable proceedings based on such claim, dispute or other matter in question would be barred by the applicable statutes of limitations.

7.3 No arbitration arising out of or relating to this Agreement shall include, by consolidation, joinder or in any other manner, an additional person or entity not a party to this Agreement, except by written consent containing a specific reference to this Agreement signed by the Owner, Architect, and any other person or entity sought to be joined. Consent to arbitration involving an additional person or entity shall not constitute consent to arbitration of any claim, dispute or other matter in question not described in the written consent or with a person or entity not named or described therein. The foregoing agreement to arbitrate and other agreements to arbitrate with an additional person or entity duly consented to by the parties to this Agreement shall be specifically enforceable in accordance with applicable law in any court having jurisdiction thereof.

7.4 The award rendered by the arbitrator or arbitrators shall be final, and judgment may be entered upon it in accordance with applicable law in any court having jurisdiction thereof.

ARTICLE 8
TERMINATION, SUSPENSION OR ABANDONMENT

8.1 This Agreement may be terminated by either party upon not less than seven days' written notice should the other party fail substantially to perform in accordance with the terms of this Agreement through no fault of the party initiating the termination.

8.2 If the Project is suspended by the Owner for more than 30 consecutive days, the Architect shall be compensated for services performed prior to notice of such suspension. When the Project is resumed, the Architect's compensation shall be equitably adjusted to provide for expenses incurred in the interruption and resumption of the Architect's services.

8.3 This Agreement may be terminated by the Owner upon not less than seven days' written notice to the Architect in the event that the Project is permanently abandoned. If the Project is abandoned by the Owner for more than 90 consecutive days, the Architect may terminate this Agreement by giving written notice.

8.4 Failure of the Owner to make payments to the Architect in accordance with this Agreement shall be considered substantial nonperformance and cause for termination.

8.5 If the Owner fails to make payment when due the Architect for services and expenses, the Architect may, upon seven days' written notice to the Owner, suspend performance of services under this Agreement. Unless payment in full is received by the Architect within seven days of the date of the notice, the suspension shall take effect without further notice. In the event of a suspension of services, the Architect shall have no liability to the Owner for delay or damage caused the Owner because of such suspension of services.

8.6 In the event of termination not the fault of the Architect, the Architect shall be compensated for services performed prior to termination, together with Reimbursable Expenses then due and all Termination Expenses as defined in Paragraph 8.7.

8.7 Termination Expenses are in addition to compensation for Basic and Additional Services, and include expenses which are directly attributable to termination. Termination Expenses shall be computed as a percentage of the total compensation for Basic Services and Additional Services earned to the time of termination, as follows:

.1 Twenty percent of the total compensation for Basic and Additional Services earned to date if termination occurs before or during the predesign, site analysis, or Schematic Design Phases; or

.2 Ten percent of the total compensation for Basic and Additional Services earned to date if termination occurs during the Design Development Phase; or

.3 Five percent of the total compensation for Basic and Additional Services earned to date if termination occurs during any subsequent phase.

ARTICLE 9
MISCELLANEOUS PROVISIONS

9.1 Unless otherwise provided, this Agreement shall be governed by the law of the principal place of business of the Architect.

9.2 Terms in this Agreement shall have the same meaning as those in AIA Document A201, General Conditions of the Contract for Construction, current as of the date of this Agreement.

9.3 Causes of action between the parties to this Agreement pertaining to acts or failures to act shall be deemed to have accrued and the applicable statutes of limitations shall commence to run not later than either the date of Substantial Completion for acts or failures to act occurring prior to Substantial Completion, or the date of issuance of the final Certificate for Payment for acts or failures to act occurring after Substantial Completion.

9.4 The Owner and Architect waive all rights against each other and against the contractors, consultants, agents and employees of the other for damages, but only to the extent covered by property insurance during construction, except such rights as they may have to the proceeds of such insurance as set forth in the edition of AIA Document A201, General Conditions of the Contract for Construction, current as of the date of this Agreement. The Owner and Architect each shall require similar waivers from their contractors, consultants and agents.

9.5 The Owner and Architect, respectively, bind themselves, their partners, successors, assigns and legal representatives to the other party to this Agreement and to the partners, successors, assigns and legal representatives of such other party with respect to all covenants of this Agreement. Neither Owner nor Architect shall assign this Agreement without the written consent of the other.

9.6 This Agreement represents the entire and integrated agreement between the Owner and Architect and supersedes all prior negotiations, representations or agreements, either written or oral. This Agreement may be amended only by written instrument signed by both Owner and Architect.

9.7 Nothing contained in this Agreement shall create a contractual relationship with or a cause of action in favor of a third party against either the Owner or Architect.

9.8 Unless otherwise provided in this Agreement, the Architect and Architect's consultants shall have no responsibility for the discovery, presence, handling, removal or disposal of or exposure of persons to hazardous materials in any form at the Project site, including but not limited to asbestos, asbestos products, polychlorinated biphenyl (PCB) or other toxic substances.

9.9 The Architect shall have the right to include representations of the design of the Project, including photographs of the exterior and interior, among the Architect's promotional and professional materials. The Architect's materials shall not include the Owner's confidential or proprietary information if the Owner has previously advised the Architect in writing of the specific information considered by the Owner to be confidential or proprietary. The Owner shall provide professional credit for the Architect on the construction sign and in the promotional materials for the Project.

ARTICLE 10
PAYMENTS TO THE ARCHITECT

10.1 DIRECT PERSONNEL EXPENSE

10.1.1 Direct Personnel Expense is defined as the direct salaries of the Architect's personnel engaged on the Project and the portion of the cost of their mandatory and customary contributions and benefits related thereto, such as employment taxes and other statutory employee benefits, insurance, sick leave, holidays, vacations, pensions and similar contributions and benefits.

10.2 REIMBURSABLE EXPENSES

10.2.1 Reimbursable Expenses are in addition to compensation for Basic and Additional Services and include expenses incurred by the Architect and Architect's employees and consultants in the interest of the Project, as identified in the following Clauses.

10.2.1.1 Expense of transportation in connection with the Project; expenses in connection with authorized out-of-town travel; long-distance communications; and fees paid for securing approval of authorities having jurisdiction over the Project.

10.2.1.2 Expense of reproductions, postage and handling of Drawings, Specifications and other documents.

10.2.1.3 If authorized in advance by the Owner, expense of overtime work requiring higher than regular rates.

10.2.1.4 Expense of renderings, models and mock-ups requested by the Owner.

10.2.1.5 Expense of additional insurance coverage or limits, including professional liability insurance, requested by the Owner in excess of that normally carried by the Architect and Architect's consultants.

10.2.1.6 Expense of computer-aided design and drafting equipment time when used in connection with the Project.

10.3 PAYMENTS ON ACCOUNT OF BASIC SERVICES

10.3.1 An initial payment as set forth in Paragraph 11.1 is the minimum payment under this Agreement.

10.3.2 Subsequent payments for Basic Services shall be made monthly and, where applicable, shall be in proportion to services performed within each phase of service, on the basis set forth in Subparagraph 11.2.2.

10.3.3 If and to the extent that the time initially established in Subparagraph 11.5.1 of this Agreement is exceeded or extended through no fault of the Architect, compensation for any services rendered during the additional period of time shall be computed in the manner set forth in Subparagraph 11.3.2.

10.3.4 When compensation is based on a percentage of Construction Cost and any portions of the Project are deleted or otherwise not constructed, compensation for those portions of the Project shall be payable to the extent services are performed on those portions, in accordance with the schedule set forth in Subparagraph 11.2.2, based on (1) the lowest bona fide bid or negotiated proposal, or (2) if no such bid or proposal is received, the most recent preliminary estimate of Construction Cost or detailed estimate of Construction Cost for such portions of the Project.

10.4 PAYMENTS ON ACCOUNT OF ADDITIONAL SERVICES

10.4.1 Payments on account of the Architect's Additional Services and for Reimbursable Expenses shall be made monthly upon presentation of the Architect's statement of services rendered or expenses incurred.

10.5 PAYMENTS WITHHELD

10.5.1 No deductions shall be made from the Architect's compensation on account of penalty, liquidated damages or other sums withheld from payments to contractors, or on account of the cost of changes in the Work other than those for which the Architect has been found to be liable.

10.6 ARCHITECT'S ACCOUNTING RECORDS

10.6.1 Records of Reimbursable Expenses and expenses pertaining to Additional Services and services performed on the basis of a multiple of Direct Personnel Expense shall be available to the Owner or the Owner's authorized representative at mutually convenient times.

ARTICLE 11
BASIS OF COMPENSATION

The Owner shall compensate the Architect as follows:

11.1 AN INITIAL PAYMENT of   Dollars ($)
shall be made upon execution of this Agreement and credited to the Owner's account at final payment.

11.2 BASIC COMPENSATION

11.2.1 FOR BASIC SERVICES, as described in Article 2, and any other services included in Article 12 as part of Basic Services, Basic Compensation shall be computed as follows:

(Insert basis of compensation, including stipulated sums, multiples or percentages, and identify phases to which particular methods of compensation apply, if necessary.)

11.2.2 Where compensation is based on a stipulated sum or percentage of Construction Cost, progress payments for Basic Services in each phase shall total the following percentages of the total Basic Compensation payable:
(Insert additional phases as appropriate.)

Schematic Design Phase:	percent (%)
Design Development Phase:	percent (%)
Construction Documents Phase:	percent (%)
Bidding or Negotiation Phase:	percent (%)
Construction Phase:	percent (%)
Total Basic Compensation:	one hundred percent (100%)

11.3 COMPENSATION FOR ADDITIONAL SERVICES

11.3.1 FOR PROJECT REPRESENTATION BEYOND BASIC SERVICES, as described in Paragraph 3.2, compensation shall be computed as follows:

11.3.2 FOR ADDITIONAL SERVICES OF THE ARCHITECT, as described in Articles 3 and 12, other than (1) Additional Project Representation, as described in Paragraph 3.2, and (2) services included in Article 12 as part of Basic Services, but excluding services of consultants, compensation shall be computed as follows:
(Insert basis of compensation, including rates and/or multiples of Direct Personnel Expense for Principals and employees, and identify Principals and classify employees, if required. Identify specific services to which particular methods of compensation apply, if necessary.)

11.3.3 FOR ADDITIONAL SERVICES OF CONSULTANTS, including additional structural, mechanical and electrical engineering services and those provided under Subparagraph 3.4.19 or identified in Article 12 as part of Additional Services, a multiple of ( ) times the amounts billed to the Architect for such services.
(Identify specific types of consultants in Article 12, if required.)

11.4 REIMBURSABLE EXPENSES

11.4.1 FOR REIMBURSABLE EXPENSES, as described in Paragraph 10.2, and any other items included in Article 12 as Reimbursable Expenses, a multiple of ( ) times the expenses incurred by the Architect, the Architect's employees and consultants in the interest of the Project.

11.5 ADDITIONAL PROVISIONS

11.5.1 IF THE BASIC SERVICES covered by this Agreement have not been completed within ( ) months of the date hereof, through no fault of the Architect, extension of the Architect's services beyond that time shall be compensated as provided in Subparagraphs 10.3.3 and 11.3.2.

11.5.2 Payments are due and payable ( ) days from the date of the Architect's invoice. Amounts unpaid ( ) days after the invoice date shall bear interest at the rate entered below, or in the absence thereof at the legal rate prevailing from time to time at the principal place of business of the Architect.
(Insert rate of interest agreed upon.)

(Usury laws and requirements under the Federal Truth in Lending Act, similar state and local consumer credit laws and other regulations at the Owner's and Architect's principal places of business, the location of the Project and elsewhere may affect the validity of this provision. Specific legal advice should be obtained with respect to deletions or modifications, and also regarding requirements such as written disclosures or waivers.)

11.5.3 The rates and multiples set forth for Additional Services shall be annually adjusted in accordance with normal salary review practices of the Architect.

ARTICLE 12
OTHER CONDITIONS OR SERVICES

(Insert descriptions of other services, identify Additional Services included within Basic Compensation and modifications to the payment and compensation terms included in this Agreement.)

This Agreement entered into as of the day and year first written above.

OWNER   ARCHITECT

_____   _____
(Signature)   *(Signature)*

_____   _____
(Printed name and title)   *(Printed name and title)*

AIA DOCUMENT B141 • OWNER-ARCHITECT AGREEMENT • FOURTEENTH EDITION • AIA® • ©1987
THE AMERICAN INSTITUTE OF ARCHITECTS, 1735 NEW YORK AVENUE, N.W., WASHINGTON, D.C. 20006

B141-1987   10

INSTRUCTION SHEET
FOR AIA DOCUMENT B141, STANDARD FORM OF AGREEMENT BETWEEN OWNER AND ARCHITECT—1987 EDITION

A. GENERAL INFORMATION

1. Purpose

AIA Document B141 is a standard form of agreement between Owner and Architect intended for use on construction projects where services are based on the customary five phases: Schematic Design, Design Development, Construction Documents, Bidding or Negotiation, and Construction.

2. Related Documents

B141 is intended to be used in conjunction with AIA Document A201, General Conditions of the Contract for Construction, which it incorporates by reference. It can be used with Architect-Consultant agreements such as AIA Documents C141, C142, C161, C431 or C727.

Other AIA Owner-Architect Agreements available for use in connection with customary services or in special circumstances include:

B141/CM	Owner-Architect Agreement, Construction Management Edition
B151	Abbreviated Owner-Architect Agreement for Projects of Limited Scope
B161	Owner-Architect Agreement for Designated Services
B161/CM	Owner-Architect Agreement for Designated Services, Construction Management Edition
B162	Scope of Designated Services (to be used in conjunction with B161 or B161/CM)
B171	Interior Design Services Agreement
B177	Abbreviated Interior Design Services Agreement
B181	Owner-Architect Agreement for Housing Services
B727	Owner-Architect Agreement for Special Services
B801	Owner-Construction Manager Agreement
B901	Design/Builder-Architect Agreement

3. Arbitration

This document incorporates ARBITRATION by adoption of the Construction Industry Arbitration Rules of the American Arbitration Association. Arbitration is BINDING AND MANDATORY in most states and under the federal Arbitration Act. In a minority of states, arbitration provisions relating to future disputes are not enforceable, but arbitration is enforceable if agreed to after the dispute arises. A few states require that the contracting parties be especially notified that the written contract contains an arbitration provision by: a warning on the face of the document, specific placement of the arbitration provision within the document or specific discussions among the parties prior to signing the document.

Arbitration provisions have been included in most AIA contract forms since 1888 in order to encourage alternative dispute resolution procedures and to provide users of AIA documents with legally enforceable arbitration provisions when the parties choose to adopt arbitration into their contract. Individuals may, however, choose to delete the arbitration provisions based upon their business decisions with the advice of counsel. To obtain a copy of the Construction Industry Arbitration Rules, write the American Arbitration Association, 140 West 51st Street, New York, NY 10020.

4. Use of Non-AIA Forms

If a combination of AIA documents and non-AIA documents is to be used, particular care must be taken to achieve consistency of language and intent. Certain owners require the use of owner-architect agreements and other contract forms which they prepare. Such forms should be carefully compared to the standard AIA forms for which they are being substituted before execution of an agreement. If there are any significant omissions, additions or variances from the terms of the related standard AIA forms, both legal and insurance counsel should be consulted. Of particular concern is the need for consistency between the Owner-Architect Agreement and the anticipated General Conditions of the Contract for Construction in the delineation of the Architect's Construction Phase services and responsibilities.

5. Letter Forms of Agreement

Letter forms of agreement are generally discouraged by the AIA, as is the performance of a part or the whole of professional services based on oral agreements or understandings. The standard AIA agreement forms have been developed through more than seventy-five years of experience and have been tested repeatedly in the courts. In addition, the standard forms have been carefully coordinated with other AIA documents.

6. Use of Current Documents

Prior to using any AIA document, the user should consult the AIA, an AIA component chapter or a current AIA Documents Price List to determine the current edition of each document.

7. Limited License for Reproduction

AIA Document B141 is a copyrighted work and may not be reproduced or excerpted from in substantial part without the express written permission of the AIA. The B141 document is intended to be used as a consumable—that is, the original document purchased by the user is intended to be consumed in the course of being used. There is no implied permission to reproduce this document, nor does membership in The American Institute of Architects confer any further rights to reproduce them.

A limited license is hereby granted to retail purchasers to reproduce a maximum of ten copies of a completed or executed B141, but only for use in connection with a particular Project. Further reproductions are prohibited without the express written permission of the AIA.

B. CHANGES FROM THE PREVIOUS EDITION

1. Format Changes

Former Article 1, Architect's Services and Responsibilities, has been subdivided into three new articles. All provisions dealing with payments to the Architect, including Direct Personnel Expense, Reimbursable Expenses and Architect's Accounting Records, have been consolidated and moved to the end of the document.

2. Changes in Content

The 1987 edition of B141 has been revised to reflect changes made in the 1987 edition of AIA Document A201, General Conditions of the Contract for Construction. The following changes in content have been made on the recommendation of owners, AIA members, committees and the AIA board of directors.

Article 2: Scope of Architect's Basic Services

Subparagraphs 2.2.4, 2.3.2 and 2.4.3
The term "Statement of Probable Construction Cost" has been changed to "preliminary estimate of Construction Cost" to simplify the terminology of the document.

Subparagraph 2.6.5
New language has been added to indicate that the Architect's on-site visits are for the purpose of determining that the Work, when completed, will be in accordance with the Contract Documents. A note has been added to alert users of the form that more extensive site representation is available under Additional Services.

Subparagraph 2.6.6
It is noted that the Contractor, not the Architect, is responsible for construction means, methods and schedules.

Subparagraph 2.6.9
During construction, communications between the Owner and Contractor are to be directed through the Architect.

Subparagraph 2.6.10
The Architect's Certificates for Payment are further qualified as not indicating a review of construction means or methods or review of Subcontractors' requisitions.

Subparagraph 2.6.11
It is specifically noted that the Architect's authority to reject Work is not intended to be exercised for the benefit of the Contractor, Subcontractors, suppliers, or their agents or employees.

Subparagraph 2.6.12
The Architect's review of submittals is further qualified to limit such review to the information and design concepts expressed in the Contract Documents. When professional certificates of performance are required from the Contractor, the Architect shall be entitled to rely upon them.

Subparagraph 2.6.13
Preparation of Change Orders and Construction Change Directives by the Architect is a Basic Service, but preparation of supporting documentation and data is now an Additional Service.

Article 3: Additional Services
Three new categories of Additional Services have been consolidated under this new article. The Contingent Additional Services are commenced upon notification of the Owner by the Architect of the need for such services. The other two categories, Project Representation Beyond Basic Services and Optional Additional Services, require the Owner's written approval before or after their commencement to authorize payment for those Additional Services.

Article 4: Owner's Responsibilities
A new Paragraph 4.3 has been added requiring the Owner to furnish evidence that financial arrangements have been made to pay the Architect. The Owner is now required to furnish tests for hazardous materials at the Owner's expense. If the Owner requires the Architect to provide certificates or certifications, the Owner must allow the Architect 14 days for review.

Article 6: Use of Architect's Drawings, Specifications and Other Documents
It is noted that documents prepared by the Architect in addition to the Drawings and Specifications are also the property of the Architect, who retains all common law, statutory and other reserved rights.

Article 8: Termination, Suspension or Abandonment
New provisions allow the Architect to terminate the Agreement if the Owner abandons the Project for more than 90 days or fails to make payments to the Architect.

Article 9: Miscellaneous Provisions
Provisions have been added noting that the Architect has no responsibility for the discovery, removal or disposal of toxic or hazardous substances encountered on the site. Another provision allows the Architect to use representations of the Project in promotional and professional materials.

Article 10: Payments to the Architect
Computer-aided drafting has been added to the list of Reimbursable Expenses.

Article 11: Basis of Compensation
A new provision has been added to indicate when payments are due and payable.

C. COMPLETING THE B141 FORM

1. Modifications

Users are encouraged to consult an attorney before completing an AIA document. Particularly with respect to professional licensing laws, duties imposed by building codes, interest charges, arbitration and indemnification, this document may require modification with the assistance of legal counsel to fully comply with state or local laws regulating these matters.

Generally, necessary modifications may be accomplished by writing or typing the appropriate terms in the blank spaces provided on the form, or by supplementary conditions, special conditions or amendments referenced in this document. The form may also be modified by striking out language directly on the pre-printed form. Care must be taken in making these kinds of deletions, however. Under NO circumstances should pre-printed language be struck out in such a way as to render it illegible (as, for example, with blocking tape, correction fluid or X's that completely obscure the text). This may raise suspicions of fraudulent concealment, or suggest that the completed and signed document has been tampered with. Handwritten changes should be initialed by both parties to the contract.

It is definitely not recommended practice to retype the standard document. Besides being outside the limited license for reproduction granted under these Instructions, retyping can introduce typographical errors and cloud the legal interpretation given to a standard clause when blended with modifications.

Retyping eliminates one of the principal advantages of the standard form documents. By merely reviewing the modifications to be made to a standard form document, parties familiar with that document can quickly understand the essence of the proposed relationship. Commercial exchanges are greatly simplified and expedited, good-faith dealing is encouraged, and otherwise latent clauses are exposed for scrutiny. In this way, contracting parties can more fairly measure their risks.

2. Cover Page

Date: The date represents the date the Agreement becomes effective. It may be the date that an oral agreement was reached, the date the Agreement was originally submitted to the Owner, the date authorizing action was taken or the date of actual execution. Professional services should not be performed prior to the effective date of the Agreement.

Identification of Parties: Parties to this Agreement should be identified using the full legal name under which the Agreement is to be executed, including a designation of the legal status of both parties (sole proprietorship, partnership, joint venture, unincorporated association, limited partnership or corporation [general, closed or professional], etc.). Where appropriate, a copy of the resolution authorizing the individual to act on behalf of the firm or entity should be attached.

Project Description: The proposed Project should be described in sufficient detail to identify (1) the official name or title of the facility, (2) the location of the site, if known, (3) the proposed building type and usage, and (4) the size, capacity or scope of the Project, if known.

3. Article 11—Basis of Compensation

Paragraph 11.1
Insert the dollar amount of the initial payment.

Subparagraph 11.2.1
Sample language is provided below for describing four methods of computing compensation.

Compensation—Multiple of Direct Personnel Expense: "Compensation for services rendered by Principals, employees and professional consultants shall be based on a Multiple of Direct Personnel Expense in the same manner as described in Subparagraph 11.3.2."

Compensation—Professional Fee Plus Expenses: "Compensation shall be a Fixed Fee of   Dollars ($) plus compensation for services rendered by Principals, employees and professional consultants, in the same manner as described in Subparagraph 11.3.2."

Compensation—Stipulated Sum: "Compensation shall be a stipulated sum of   Dollars ($)."

Compensation—Percentage of Construction Cost: "Compensation shall be based on one of the following Percentages of Construction Cost, as defined in Article 5:

For portions of the Project to be awarded under:

A single stipulated-sum construction contract:	percent (%)
Separate stipulated-sum construction contracts:	percent (%)
A single cost-plus construction contract:	percent (%)
Separate cost-plus construction contracts:	percent (%)"

Subparagraph 11.2.2
Only for compensation based on stipulated sum or percentage of Construction Cost, insert the percentages of total payment payable for each separate phase of services. These percentages may vary with each Project and do not necessarily have a direct relationship to the time and efforts of the Architect.

Because phases may overlap in time, these percentages have been expressed separately for each phase, rather than cumulatively. This facilitates billing when services are being provided in more than one phase at a time.

Subparagraph 11.3.1
Insert the basis of compensation for Project Representation Beyond Basic Services.

Subparagraph 11.3.2
If billing rates are used and professional consultants are classified in accordance with the AIA publication *Compensation Guidelines for Architectural/Engineering Services,* insert:

(a) Principals' time at the fixed rate of Dollars ($) per hour.
For the purposes of this Agreement, the Principals are: (list Principals)

(b) Supervisory time at the fixed rate of Dollars ($) per hour.
For the purposes of this Agreement, supervisory personnel include: (Describe supervisory personnel by job title, such as Project Architect.)

(c) Technical Level I time at the fixed rate of Dollars ($) per hour.
For the purposes of this Agreement, Technical Level I personnel include: (Describe by job title, such as Senior Designer, Specifier, etc.)

(d) Technical Level II time at the fixed rate of Dollars ($) per hour.
For the purposes of this Agreement, Technical Level II personnel include: (Describe by job title, such as Junior Designer, Senior Draftsman, etc.)

(e) Technical Level III and clerical time at the fixed rate of Dollars ($) per hour.
For the purposes of this Agreement, Technical Level III and clerical personnel include: (Describe by job title, such as Junior Draftsman, Secretary, etc.)

If a multiple of Direct Personnel Expense is used, insert: "Principals', employees' and professional consultants' time at a multiple of ( ) times their Direct Personnel Expense as defined by the AIA publication *Compensation Guidelines for Architectural/Engineering Services.*"

If a multiple of direct salaries is used, the term "Direct Salaries" should be substituted for Direct Personnel Expense above.

Subparagraph 11.3.3
Insert the multiple to be used to determine the cost to the Architect of Additional Services of consultants as defined in Article 3 or Article 12.

Subparagraph 11.4.1
Insert the multiple to be used to determine the amount due the Architect, Architect's employees or consultants for Reimbursable Expenses as described in Paragraph 10.2 or Article 12.

Subparagraph 11.5.1
Insert the number of months beyond which the Architect shall be compensated for Basic Services on the same basis as for Additional Services.

Paragraph 11.5.2
Insert the percentage rate and basis (monthly, annual) of interest charges.

Article 12—Other Conditions or Services
Insert provisions, if any, on additional phases of services, Additional Services, special compensation arrangements, other consultants, the choice of project delivery method or any other conditions.

D. EXECUTION OF THE AGREEMENT

Each person executing the Agreement should indicate the capacity in which they are acting (i.e., president, secretary, partner, etc.) and the authority under which they are executing the Agreement. Where appropriate, a copy of the resolution authorizing the individual to act on behalf of the firm or entity should be attached.

Appendix B:
AIA Document A101 — Standard Form of Agreement Between Owner and Contractor (where the basis of payment is a Stipulated Sum), 1987 Edition

THE AMERICAN INSTITUTE OF ARCHITECTS

1. AIA copyrighted material has been reproduced with the permission of the American Institute of Architects under license number 90011. Permission expires December 31, 1991. FURTHER REPRODUCTION IS PROHIBITED.

2. Because AIA Documents are revised from time to time, users should ascertain from the AIA the current edition of this document.

3. Copies of the current edition of this AIA document may be purchased from The American Institute of Architects or its local distributors.

4. This document is intended for use as a "consumable" (consumables are further defined by Senate Report 94-473 on the Copyright Act of 1976). This document is not intended to be used as "model language" (language taken from an existing document and incorporated, without attribution, into a newly - created document.) Rather, it is a standard form which is intended to be modified by appending separate amendment sheets and/or fill in provided blank spaces.

AIA Document A101

Standard Form of Agreement Between Owner and Contractor

where the basis of payment is a
STIPULATED SUM

1987 EDITION

THIS DOCUMENT HAS IMPORTANT LEGAL CONSEQUENCES; CONSULTATION WITH AN ATTORNEY IS ENCOURAGED WITH RESPECT TO ITS COMPLETION OR MODIFICATION.
The 1987 Edition of AIA Document A201, General Conditions of the Contract for Construction, is adopted in this document by reference. Do not use with other general conditions unless this document is modified.
This document has been approved and endorsed by The Associated General Contractors of America.

AGREEMENT

made as of the   day of   in the year of
Nineteen Hundred and

BETWEEN the Owner:
(Name and address)

and the Contractor:
(Name and address)

The Project is:
(Name and location)

The Architect is:
(Name and address)

The Owner and Contractor agree as set forth below.

Copyright 1915, 1918, 1925, 1937, 1951, 1958, 1961, 1963, 1967, 1974, 1977, ©1987 by The American Institute of Architects, 1735 New York Avenue, N.W., Washington, D.C. 20006. Reproduction of the material herein or substantial quotation of its provisions without written permission of the AIA violates the copyright laws of the United States and will be subject to legal prosecution.

AIA DOCUMENT A101 • OWNER-CONTRACTOR AGREEMENT • TWELFTH EDITION • AIA® • ©1987
THE AMERICAN INSTITUTE OF ARCHITECTS, 1735 NEW YORK AVENUE, N.W., WASHINGTON, D.C. 20006   A101-1987 1

ARTICLE 1
THE CONTRACT DOCUMENTS

The Contract Documents consist of this Agreement, Conditions of the Contract (General, Supplementary and other Conditions), Drawings, Specifications, Addenda issued prior to execution of this Agreement, other documents listed in this Agreement and Modifications issued after execution of this Agreement; these form the Contract, and are as fully a part of the Contract as if attached to this Agreement or repeated herein. The Contract represents the entire and integrated agreement between the parties hereto and supersedes prior negotiations, representations or agreements, either written or oral. An enumeration of the Contract Documents, other than Modifications, appears in Article 9.

ARTICLE 2
THE WORK OF THIS CONTRACT

The Contractor shall execute the entire Work described in the Contract Documents, except to the extent specifically indicated in the Contract Documents to be the responsibility of others, or as follows:

ARTICLE 3
DATE OF COMMENCEMENT AND SUBSTANTIAL COMPLETION

3.1 The date of commencement is the date from which the Contract Time of Paragraph 3.2 is measured, and shall be the date of this Agreement, as first written above, unless a different date is stated below or provision is made for the date to be fixed in a notice to proceed issued by the Owner.

(Insert the date of commencement, if it differs from the date of this Agreement or, if applicable, state that the date will be fixed in a notice to proceed.)

Unless the date of commencement is established by a notice to proceed issued by the Owner, the Contractor shall notify the Owner in writing not less than five days before commencing the Work to permit the timely filing of mortgages, mechanic's liens and other security interests.

3.2 The Contractor shall achieve Substantial Completion of the entire Work not later than

(Insert the calendar date or number of calendar days after the date of commencement. Also insert any requirements for earlier Substantial Completion of certain portions of the Work, if not stated elsewhere in the Contract Documents.)

subject to adjustments of this Contract Time as provided in the Contract Documents.

(Insert provisions, if any, for liquidated damages relating to failure to complete on time.)

ARTICLE 4
CONTRACT SUM

4.1 The Owner shall pay the Contractor in current funds for the Contractor's performance of the Contract the Contract Sum of   Dollars ($), subject to additions and deductions as provided in the Contract Documents.

4.2 The Contract Sum is based upon the following alternates, if any, which are described in the Contract Documents and are hereby accepted by the Owner:

(State the numbers or other identification of accepted alternates. If decisions on other alternates are to be made by the Owner subsequent to the execution of this Agreement, attach a schedule of such other alternates showing the amount for each and the date until which that amount is valid.)

4.3 Unit prices, if any, are as follows:

ARTICLE 5
PROGRESS PAYMENTS

5.1 Based upon Applications for Payment submitted to the Architect by the Contractor and Certificates for Payment issued by the Architect, the Owner shall make progress payments on account of the Contract Sum to the Contractor as provided below and elsewhere in the Contract Documents.

5.2 The period covered by each Application for Payment shall be one calendar month ending on the last day of the month, or as follows:

5.3 Provided an Application for Payment is received by the Architect not later than the   day of a month, the Owner shall make payment to the Contractor not later than the   day of the   month. If an Application for Payment is received by the Architect after the application date fixed above, payment shall be made by the Owner not later than   days after the Architect receives the Application for Payment.

5.4 Each Application for Payment shall be based upon the Schedule of Values submitted by the Contractor in accordance with the Contract Documents. The Schedule of Values shall allocate the entire Contract Sum among the various portions of the Work and be prepared in such form and supported by such data to substantiate its accuracy as the Architect may require. This Schedule, unless objected to by the Architect, shall be used as a basis for reviewing the Contractor's Applications for Payment.

5.5 Applications for Payment shall indicate the percentage of completion of each portion of the Work as of the end of the period covered by the Application for Payment.

5.6 Subject to the provisions of the Contract Documents, the amount of each progress payment shall be computed as follows:

5.6.1 Take that portion of the Contract Sum properly allocable to completed Work as determined by multiplying the percentage completion of each portion of the Work by the share of the total Contract Sum allocated to that portion of the Work in the Schedule of Values, less retainage of   percent (%). Pending final determination of cost to the Owner of changes in the Work, amounts not in dispute may be included as provided in Subparagraph 7.3.7 of the General Conditions even though the Contract Sum has not yet been adjusted by Change Order;

5.6.2 Add that portion of the Contract Sum properly allocable to materials and equipment delivered and suitably stored at the site for subsequent incorporation in the completed construction (or, if approved in advance by the Owner, suitably stored off the site at a location agreed upon in writing), less retainage of   percent (%);

5.6.3 Subtract the aggregate of previous payments made by the Owner; and

5.6.4 Subtract amounts, if any, for which the Architect has withheld or nullified a Certificate for Payment as provided in Paragraph 9.5 of the General Conditions.

5.7 The progress payment amount determined in accordance with Paragraph 5.6 shall be further modified under the following circumstances:

5.7.1 Add, upon Substantial Completion of the Work, a sum sufficient to increase the total payments to   percent (%) of the Contract Sum, less such amounts as the Architect shall determine for incomplete Work and unsettled claims; and

5.7.2 Add, if final completion of the Work is thereafter materially delayed through no fault of the Contractor, any additional amounts payable in accordance with Subparagraph 9.10.3 of the General Conditions.

5.8 Reduction or limitation of retainage, if any, shall be as follows:

(If it is intended, prior to Substantial Completion of the entire Work, to reduce or limit the retainage resulting from the percentages inserted in Subparagraphs 5.6.1 and 5.6.2 above, and this is not explained elsewhere in the Contract Documents, insert here provisions for such reduction or limitation.)

ARTICLE 6
FINAL PAYMENT

Final payment, constituting the entire unpaid balance of the Contract Sum, shall be made by the Owner to the Contractor when (1) the Contract has been fully performed by the Contractor except for the Contractor's responsibility to correct nonconforming Work as provided in Subparagraph 12.2.2 of the General Conditions and to satisfy other requirements, if any, which necessarily survive final payment; and (2) a final Certificate for Payment has been issued by the Architect; such final payment shall be made by the Owner not more than 30 days after the issuance of the Architect's final Certificate for Payment, or as follows:

ARTICLE 7
MISCELLANEOUS PROVISIONS

7.1 Where reference is made in this Agreement to a provision of the General Conditions or another Contract Document, the reference refers to that provision as amended or supplemented by other provisions of the Contract Documents.

7.2 Payments due and unpaid under the Contract shall bear interest from the date payment is due at the rate stated below, or in the absence thereof, at the legal rate prevailing from time to time at the place where the Project is located.

(Insert rate of interest agreed upon, if any.)

(Usury laws and requirements under the Federal Truth in Lending Act, similar state and local consumer credit laws and other regulations at the Owner's and Contractor's principal places of business, the location of the Project and elsewhere may affect the validity of this provision. Legal advice should be obtained with respect to deletions or modifications, and also regarding requirements such as written disclosures or waivers.)

7.3 Other provisions:

ARTICLE 8
TERMINATION OR SUSPENSION

8.1 The Contract may be terminated by the Owner or the Contractor as provided in Article 14 of the General Conditions.

8.2 The Work may be suspended by the Owner as provided in Article 14 of the General Conditions.

AIA DOCUMENT A101 • OWNER-CONTRACTOR AGREEMENT • TWELFTH EDITION • AIA® • ©1987
THE AMERICAN INSTITUTE OF ARCHITECTS, 1735 NEW YORK AVENUE, N.W., WASHINGTON, D.C. 20006

ARTICLE 9
ENUMERATION OF CONTRACT DOCUMENTS

9.1 The Contract Documents, except for Modifications issued after execution of this Agreement, are enumerated as follows:

9.1.1 The Agreement is this executed Standard Form of Agreement Between Owner and Contractor, AIA Document A101, 1987 Edition.

9.1.2 The General Conditions are the General Conditions of the Contract for Construction, AIA Document A201, 1987 Edition.

9.1.3 The Supplementary and other Conditions of the Contract are those contained in the Project Manual dated   , and are as follows:

Document	Title	Pages

9.1.4 The Specifications are those contained in the Project Manual dated as in Subparagraph 9.1.3, and are as follows:
(Either list the Specifications here or refer to an exhibit attached to this Agreement.)

Section	Title	Pages

9.1.5 The Drawings are as follows, and are dated   unless a different date is shown below:
(Either list the Drawings here or refer to an exhibit attached to this Agreement.)

Number   **Title**   **Date**

9.1.6 The Addenda, if any, are as follows:

Number   **Date**   **Pages**

Portions of Addenda relating to bidding requirements are not part of the Contract Documents unless the bidding requirements are also enumerated in this Article 9.

AIA DOCUMENT A101 • OWNER-CONTRACTOR AGREEMENT • TWELFTH EDITION • AIA® • ©1987
THE AMERICAN INSTITUTE OF ARCHITECTS, 1735 NEW YORK AVENUE, N.W., WASHINGTON, D.C. 20006   A101-1987 **7**

9.1.7 Other documents, if any, forming part of the Contract Documents are as follows:

(List here any additional documents which are intended to form part of the Contract Documents. The General Conditions provide that bidding requirements such as advertisement or invitation to bid, Instructions to Bidders, sample forms and the Contractor's bid are not part of the Contract Documents unless enumerated in this Agreement. They should be listed here only if intended to be part of the Contract Documents.)

This Agreement is entered into as of the day and year first written above and is executed in at least three original copies of which one is to be delivered to the Contractor, one to the Architect for use in the administration of the Contract, and the remainder to the Owner.

OWNER   CONTRACTOR

_____   _____
(Signature)   *(Signature)*

_____   _____
(Printed name and title)   *(Printed name and title)*

AIA DOCUMENT A101 • OWNER-CONTRACTOR AGREEMENT • TWELFTH EDITION • AIA® • ©1987
THE AMERICAN INSTITUTE OF ARCHITECTS, 1735 NEW YORK AVENUE, N.W., WASHINGTON, D.C. 20006   **A101-1987 8**

INSTRUCTION SHEET

FOR AIA DOCUMENT A101, STANDARD FORM OF AGREEMENT BETWEEN OWNER AND CONTRACTOR where the Basis of Payment is a STIPULATED SUM—1987 EDITION

A. GENERAL INFORMATION

1. Purpose

AIA Document A101 is intended for use on construction projects where the basis of payment is a stipulated sum (fixed price). It is suitable for any arrangement between the Owner and Contractor where the cost has been set in advance, either by bidding or by negotiation.

2. Related Documents

This document has been prepared for use in conjunction with the 1987 edition of AIA Document A201, General Conditions of the Contract for Construction, which is adopted into A101 by a specific reference. This integrated set of documents is suitable for most projects; however, for projects of limited scope, use of AIA Document A107 may be considered.

The A101 document may be used as one part of the Contract Documents which record the Contract for Construction between the Owner and the Contractor. The other Contract Documents are:

General Conditions (i.e., A201)
Supplementary Conditions
Drawings
Specifications
Modifications

Although the AIA does not produce standard documents for Supplementary Conditions, Drawings or Specifications, a variety of model and guide documents are available, including AIA's MASTERSPEC.

3. Arbitration

This document incorporates ARBITRATION by adoption of AIA Document A201, which provides for arbitration according to the Construction Industry Arbitration Rules of the American Arbitration Association. Arbitration is BINDING AND MANDATORY in most states and under the federal Arbitration Act. In a minority of states, arbitration provisions relating to future disputes are not enforceable, but arbitration is enforceable if agreed to after the dispute arises. A few states require that the contracting parties be especially notified that the written contract contains an arbitration provision by: a warning on the face of the document, specific placement of the arbitration provision within the document or specific discussions among the parties prior to signing the document.

Arbitration provisions have been included in most AIA contract forms since 1888 in order to encourage alternative dispute resolution procedures and to provide users of AIA documents with legally enforceable arbitration provisions when the parties choose to adopt arbitration into their contract. Individuals may, however, choose to delete the arbitration provisions based upon their business decisions with the advice of counsel. To obtain a copy of the Construction Industry Arbitration Rules, write the American Arbitration Association, 140 West 51st Street, New York, NY 10020.

4. Use of Non-AIA Forms

If a combination of AIA documents and non-AIA documents is to be used, particular care must be taken to achieve consistency of language and intent. Certain owners require the use of owner-contractor agreements and other contract forms which they prepare. Such forms should be carefully compared with the standard AIA forms for which they are being substituted before execution of an agreement. If there are any significant omissions, additions or variances from the terms of the related standard AIA forms, both legal and insurance counsel should be consulted.

5. Letter Forms of Agreement

Letter forms of agreement are generally discouraged by the AIA, as is the performance of a part or the whole of the Work on the basis of oral agreements or understandings. The standard AIA agreement forms have been developed through more than seventy-five years of experience and have been tested repeatedly in the courts. In addition, the standard forms have been carefully coordinated with other AIA documents.

6. Use of Current Documents

Prior to using any AIA document, the user should consult the AIA, an AIA component chapter or a current AIA Documents Price List to determine the current edition of each document.

7. Limited License for Reproduction

AIA Document A101 is a copyrighted work and may not be reproduced or excerpted from in substantial part without the express written permission of the AIA. The A101 document is intended to be used as a consumable—that is, the original document purchased by the user is intended to be consumed in the course of being used. There is no implied permission to reproduce this document, nor does membership in The American Institute of Architects confer any further rights to reproduce them.

A limited license is hereby granted to retail purchasers to reproduce a maximum of ten copies of a completed or executed A101, but only for use in connection with a particular Project. A101 may not be reproduced for Project Manuals. Rather, if a user wishes to include it as an example in a Project Manual, the normal practice is to purchase a quantity of the pre-printed forms and bind one in each of the Project Manuals. Partial modifications, if any, may be accomplished without completing the form by using separate Supplementary Conditions.

Upon reaching agreement concerning the Contract Sum and other conditions, the form may be removed from the manual and such information, except for the signatures, may be added to the blank spaces of the form. The user may then reproduce up to ten copies to facilitate the execution (signing) of multiple original copies of the form, or for other administrative purposes in connection with a particular Project. Please note that at least three original copies of A101 should be signed by the parties as required by the last provision of A101.

B. CHANGES FROM THE PREVIOUS EDITION

1. Format Changes

Two new articles have been added: Article 8, Termination or Suspension; and Article 9, Enumeration of Contract Documents.

2. Changes in Content

The 1987 edition of A101 revises the 1977 edition to reflect changes made in the most recent (1987) edition of A201. It incorporates alterations proposed by architects, contractors, owners and professional consultants. The following are some of the significant changes made to the contents from the 1977 edition of A101:

Article 1: A specific statement has been added that the Contract represents the entire agreement between the parties, superseding previous negotiations and writings.

Article 2: Space has been provided to describe any exceptions to the description of Contractor's scope of Work.

Article 3: In the title of this article, "Time of Commencement" has been changed to "Date of Commencement."

Article 4: Space has been provided for insertion of the amounts relating to alternates and unit prices.

Article 5: The Progress Payments article has been substantially rewritten and expanded. Detailed directions have been added on how and when payments shall be calculated and applied for.

Article 6: Further details have been added to clarify the conditions under which final payment shall be made by the Owner.

Article 7: The reference to definitions contained in the Conditions of the Contract has been deleted because the A201 document is now specifically adopted by reference under Article 9.

Article 8: This is a new article containing references to the General Conditions.

Article 9: This article is new. The A101 Document and the A201 Document are explicitly enumerated as parts of the Contract Documents. Spaces are provided for information specifically identifying the other Contract Documents, including the Supplementary Conditions, Specifications, Drawings and Addenda, if any.

Signature Page: It is noted above the signature lines that this agreement is executed on at least three original copies. See the instructions pertaining to Limited License for Reproduction.

C. COMPLETING THE A101 FORM

1. Prospective bidders should be informed of any additional provisions which may be included in A101, such as liquidated damages or provisions for stored materials, by an appropriate notice in the Bidding Documents and the Supplementary Conditions.

2. Modifications

Users are encouraged to consult an attorney before completing an AIA document. Particularly with respect to contractor's licensing laws, duties imposed by building codes, interest charges, arbitration and indemnification, this document may require modification with the assistance of legal counsel to fully comply with state or local laws regulating these matters.

Generally, necessary modifications may be accomplished by writing or typing the appropriate terms in the blank spaces provided on the form or by Supplementary Conditions, special conditions or amendments included in the Project Manual and referenced in this document. The form may also be modified by striking out language directly on the original pre-printed form. Care must be taken in making these kinds of deletions, however. Under NO circumstances should pre-printed language be struck out in such a way as to render it illegible (as, for example, with blocking tape, correction fluid or X's that completely obscure the text). This may raise suspicions of fraudulent concealment or suggest that the completed and signed document has been tampered with. Handwritten changes should be initialed by both parties to the contract.

It is definitely not recommended practice to retype the standard document. Besides being outside the Limited License for Reproduction granted under these Instructions, retyping can introduce typographical errors and cloud the legal interpretation given to a standard clause when blended with modifications.

Retyping eliminates one of the principal advantages of the standard form documents. By merely reviewing the modifications to be made to a standard form document, parties familiar with that document can quickly understand the essence of the proposed relationship. Commercial exchanges are greatly simplified and expedited, good-faith dealing is encouraged, and otherwise latent clauses are exposed for scrutiny. In this way, contracting parties can more fairly measure their risks.

3. Cover Page

Date: The date represents the date the Agreement becomes effective. It may be the date that an oral agreement was reached, the date the Agreement was originally submitted to the owner, the date authorizing action was taken or the date of actual execution. It will be the date from which the Contract Time is measured unless a different date is inserted under Paragraph 3.1.

Identification of Parties: Parties to this Agreement should be identified using the full address and legal name under which the Agreement is to be executed, including a designation of the legal status of both parties (sole proprietorship, partnership, joint venture, unincorporated association, limited partnership or corporation [general, closed or professional], etc.). Where appropriate, a copy of the resolution authorizing the individual to act on behalf of the firm or entity should be attached.

Project Description: The proposed Project should be described in sufficient detail to identify (1) the official name or title of the facility, (2) the location of the site, if known, (3) the proposed building type and usage, and (4) the size, capacity or scope of the Project, if known.

Architect: As in the other Contract Documents, the Architect's full legal or corporate titles should be used.

4. **Article 1—The Contract Documents**

   The Contract Documents must be enumerated in detail in Article 9. The Contractor's bid itself may be incorporated into the Contract; similarly, other bidding documents, bonds, etc., may be incorporated, especially in public work.

5. **Article 2—The Work of This Contract**

   Portions of the Work which are the responsibility of persons other than the Contractor and which have not been otherwise indicated should be listed here.

6. **Article 3—Date of Commencement and Substantial Completion**

   The following items should be included as appropriate:

   Paragraph 3.1
   The date of commencement of the Work should be inserted if it is different from the date of the Agreement. It should not be earlier than the date of execution (signing) of the Contract. After the first sentence, enter either the specific date of commencement of the Work, or if a notice to proceed is to be used, enter the sentence, "The date of commencement shall be stipulated by the notice to proceed." When time of performance is to be strictly enforced, the statement of starting time should be carefully weighed.

   Paragraph 3.2
   The time within which Substantial Completion of the Work is to be achieved may be expressed as a number of days (preferably calendar days) or as a specified date. Any requirements for earlier Substantial Completion of portions of the Work should be entered here if not specified elsewhere in the Contract Documents.

   Also insert any provisions for liquidated damages relating to failure to complete on time. Liquidated damages are not a penalty to be inflicted on the Contractor, but must bear an actual and reasonably estimable relationship to the Owner's loss if construction is not completed on time. If liquidated damages are to be assessed because delayed construction will result in actual loss to the Owner, the amount of damages due for each day lost should be entered in the Supplementary Conditions or the Agreement. Factors such as confidentiality or the need to inform Subcontractors about the amount of liquidated damages will help determine the location chosen.

   The provision for liquidated damages, which should be carefully reviewed or drafted by the Owner's attorney, may be as follows:

   > The Contractor and the Contractor's surety, if any, shall be liable for and shall pay the Owner the sums hereinafter stipulated as liquidated damages for each calendar day of delay until the Work is substantially complete: Dollars ($).

   For further information on liquidated damages, penalties and bonus provisions, see AIA Document A511, Guide for Supplementary Conditions, Paragraph 9.11.

7. **Article 4—Contract Sum**

   Paragraph 4.1
   Enter the Contract Sum payable to the Contractor.

   Paragraph 4.2
   Identify any alternates described in the Contract Documents and accepted by the Owner. If decisions on alternates are to be made subsequent to execution of A101, attach a schedule showing the amount of each alternate and the date until which that amount is valid.

   Paragraph 4.3
   Enter any unit prices, cash allowances or cash contingency allowances.

   If unit prices are not covered in greater detail elsewhere in the Contract Documents, the following provision for unit prices is suggested:

   > The unit prices listed below shall determine the value of extra Work or changes in the Work, as applicable. They shall be considered complete and shall include all material and equipment, labor, installation costs, overhead and profit. Unit prices shall be used uniformly for additions or deductions.

   Specific allowances for overhead and profit on Change Orders may be included under this paragraph to forestall disputes over future Change Order costs.

8. **Article 5—Progress Payments**

   Paragraph 5.2
   Insert the time period covered by each Application for Payment if it differs from the one given.

Paragraph 5.3

Insert the time schedule for presenting Applications for Payment. Insert the day of the month progress payments are due, indicating whether such day is to be in the same or the following month after receipt by the Architect of the relevant Application for Payment.

The last day upon which Work may be included in an Application should normally be no less than 14 days prior to the payment date, in consideration of the 7 days required for the Architect's evaluation of an Application and issuance of a Certificate for Payment and the time subsequently accorded the Owner to make payment in Article 9 of A201. The Contractor may prefer a few additional days to prepare the Application.

Due dates for payment should be acceptable to both the Owner and Contractor. They should allow sufficient time for the Contractor to prepare an Application for Payment, for the Architect to certify payment, and for the Owner to make payment. They should also be in accordance with time limits established by this Article and Article 9 of A201.

Subparagraph 5.6.1

Indicate the percent retainage, if any, to be withheld when computing the amount of each progress payment.

The Owner frequently pays the Contractor 90 percent of the earned sum when payments fall due, retaining 10 percent to ensure faithful performance. These percentages may vary with circumstances and localities. The AIA endorses the practice of reducing retainage as rapidly as possible, consistent with the continued protection of all affected parties. See AIA Document A511, Guide for Supplementary Conditions, for a complete discussion.

Subparagraph 5.6.2

Insert any additional retainage to be withheld from that portion of the Contract Sum allocable to materials and equipment stored at the site.

Payment for materials stored off the site should be provided for in a specific agreement and enumerated in Paragraph 7.3. Provisions regarding transportation to the site and insurance protecting Owner's interests should be included.

Subparagraph 5.7.1

Enter the percentage of the Contract Sum to be paid to the Contractor upon Substantial Completion.

Paragraph 5.8

Describe any arrangements to reduce or limit retainages indicated in Subparagraphs 5.6.1 and 5.6.2, if not explained elsewhere in the Contract Documents.

A provision for reducing retainage should provide that the reduction will be made only if the Architect judges that the Work is progressing satisfactorily. If the Contractor has furnished a bond, demonstration of the surety's consent to reduction in or partial release of retainage must be provided before such reduction is effected. Use of AIA Document G707A is recommended.

9. **Article 6—Final Payment**

   Insert the date by which Owner shall make final payment, if it differs from the one stated.

   When final payment is requested, the Architect should ascertain that all claims have been settled or should define those which remain unsettled. The Architect should obtain the Contractor's certification required by Article 9 of A201 and must determine that, to the best of the Architect's knowledge and belief and according to final inspection, the requirements of the Contract have been fulfilled.

10. **Article 7—Miscellaneous Provisions**

    Paragraph 7.2

    Enter any agreed-upon interest rate due on overdue payments.

    Paragraph 7.3

    Insert other provisions here.

11. **Article 9—Enumeration of Contract Documents**

    A detailed enumeration of all Contract Documents must be made in this Article.

D. **EXECUTION OF THE AGREEMENT**

The Agreement should be executed in not less than triplicate by the Owner and the Contractor. Each person executing the Agreement should indicate the capacity in which they are acting (i.e., president, secretary, partner, etc.) and the authority under which they are executing the Agreement. Where appropriate, a copy of the resolution authorizing the individual to act on behalf of the firm or entity should be attached.

Appendix C:
AIA Document A111 – Standard Form of Agreement Between Owner and Contractor (where the basis of payment is the Cost of the Work Plus a Fee with or without a Guaranteed Maximum Price), 1987 Edition

THE AMERICAN INSTITUTE OF ARCHITECTS

1. AIA copyrighted material has been reproduced with the permission of the American Institute of Architects under license number 90011. Permission expires December 31, 1991. FURTHER REPRODUCTION IS PROHIBITED.

2. Because AIA Documents are revised from time to time, users should ascertain from the AIA the current edition of this document.

3. Copies of the current edition of this AIA document may be purchased from The American Institute of Architects or its local distributors.

4. This document is intended for use as a "consumable" (consumables are further defined by Senate Report 94-473 on the Copyright Act of 1976). This document is not intended to be used as "model language" (language taken from an existing document and incorporated, without attribution, into a newly-created document.) Rather, it is a standard form which is intended to be modified by appending separate amendment sheets and/or fill in provided blank spaces.

AIA Document A111

Standard Form of Agreement Between Owner and Contractor

where the basis of payment is the
COST OF THE WORK PLUS A FEE
with or without a Guaranteed Maximum Price

1987 EDITION

THIS DOCUMENT HAS IMPORTANT LEGAL CONSEQUENCES; CONSULTATION WITH AN ATTORNEY IS ENCOURAGED WITH RESPECT TO ITS COMPLETION OR MODIFICATION.

The 1987 Edition of AIA Document A201, General Conditions of the Contract for Construction, is adopted in this document by reference. Do not use with other general conditions unless this document is modified.

This document has been approved and endorsed by The Associated General Contractors of America.

AGREEMENT

made as of the   day of   in the year of
Nineteen Hundred and

BETWEEN the Owner:
(Name and address)

and the Contractor:
(Name and address)

the Project is:
(Name and address)

the Architect is:
(Name and address)

The Owner and Contractor agree as set forth below.

Copyright 1920, 1925, 1951, 1958, 1961, 1963, 1967, 1974, 1978, ©1987 by The American Institute of Architects, 1735 New York Avenue, N.W., Washington, D.C. 20006. Reproduction of the material herein or substantial quotation of its provisions without written permission of the AIA violates the copyright laws of the United States and will be subject to legal prosecution.

AIA DOCUMENT A111 • OWNER-CONTRACTOR AGREEMENT • TENTH EDITION • AIA® • ©1987 • THE AMERICAN INSTITUTE OF ARCHITECTS, 1735 NEW YORK AVENUE, N.W., WASHINGTON, D.C. 20006   A111-1987   **1**

ARTICLE 1
THE CONTRACT DOCUMENTS

1.1 The Contract Documents consist of this Agreement, Conditions of the Contract (General, Supplementary and other Conditions), Drawings, Specifications, Addenda issued prior to execution of this Agreement, other documents listed in this Agreement and Modifications issued after execution of this Agreement; these form the Contract, and are as fully a part of the Contract as if attached to this Agreement or repeated herein. The Contract represents the entire and integrated agreement between the parties hereto and supersedes prior negotiations, representations or agreements, either written or oral. An enumeration of the Contract Documents, other than Modifications, appears in Article 16. If anything in the other Contract Documents is inconsistent with this Agreement, this Agreement shall govern.

ARTICLE 2
THE WORK OF THIS CONTRACT

2.1 The Contractor shall execute the entire Work described in the Contract Documents, except to the extent specifically indicated in the Contract Documents to be the responsibility of others, or as follows:

ARTICLE 3
RELATIONSHIP OF THE PARTIES

3.1 The Contractor accepts the relationship of trust and confidence established by this Agreement and covenants with the Owner to cooperate with the Architect and utilize the Contractor's best skill, efforts and judgment in furthering the interests of the Owner; to furnish efficient business administration and supervision; to make best efforts to furnish at all times an adequate supply of workers and materials; and to perform the Work in the best way and most expeditious and economical manner consistent with the interests of the Owner. The Owner agrees to exercise best efforts to enable the Contractor to perform the Work in the best way and most expeditious manner by furnishing and approving in a timely way information required by the Contractor and making payments to the Contractor in accordance with requirements of the Contract Documents.

ARTICLE 4
DATE OF COMMENCEMENT AND SUBSTANTIAL COMPLETION

4.1 The date of commencement is the date from which the Contract Time of Subparagraph 4.2 is measured; it shall be the date of this Agreement, as first written above, unless a different date is stated below or provision is made for the date to be fixed in a notice to proceed issued by the Owner.

(Insert the date of commencement, if it differs from the date of this Agreement or, if applicable, state that the date will be fixed in a notice to proceed.)

Unless the date of commencement is established by a notice to proceed issued by the Owner, the Contractor shall notify the Owner in writing not less than five days before commencing the Work to permit the timely filing of mortgages, mechanic's liens and other security interests.

4.2 The Contractor shall achieve Substantial Completion of the entire Work not later than

(Insert the calendar date or number of calendar days after the date of commencement. Also insert any requirements for earlier Substantial Completion of certain portions of the Work, if not stated elsewhere in the Contract Documents.)

, subject to adjustments of this Contract Time as provided in the Contract Documents.

(Insert provisions, if any, for liquidated damages relating to failure to complete on time.)

ARTICLE 5
CONTRACT SUM

5.1 The Owner shall pay the Contractor in current funds for the Contractor's performance of the Contract the Contract Sum consisting of the Cost of the Work as defined in Article 7 and the Contractor's Fee determined as follows:

(State a lump sum, percentage of Cost of the Work or other provision for determining the Contractor's Fee, and explain how the Contractor's Fee is to be adjusted for changes in the Work.)

5.2 GUARANTEED MAXIMUM PRICE (IF APPLICABLE)

5.2.1 The sum of the Cost of the Work and the Contractor's Fee is guaranteed by the Contractor not to exceed _____ Dollars ($ _____), subject to additions and deductions by Change Order as provided in the Contract Documents. Such maximum sum is referred to in the Contract Documents as the Guaranteed Maximum Price. Costs which would cause the Guaranteed Maximum Price to be exceeded shall be paid by the Contractor without reimbursement by the Owner.

(Insert specific provisions if the Contractor is to participate in any savings.)

AIA DOCUMENT A111 • OWNER-CONTRACTOR AGREEMENT • TENTH EDITION • AIA® • ©1987 • THE AMERICAN INSTITUTE OF ARCHITECTS, 1735 NEW YORK AVENUE, N.W., WASHINGTON, D.C. 20006

5.2.2 The Guaranteed Maximum Price is based upon the following alternates, if any, which are described in the Contract Documents and are hereby accepted by the Owner:

(State the numbers or other identification of accepted alternates, but only if a Guaranteed Maximum Price is inserted in Subparagraph 5.2.1. If decisions on other alternates are to be made by the Owner subsequent to the execution of this Agreement, attach a schedule of such other alternates showing the amount for each and the date until which that amount is valid.)

5.2.3 The amounts agreed to for unit prices, if any, are as follows:

(State unit prices only if a Guaranteed Maximum Price is inserted in Subparagraph 5.2.1.)

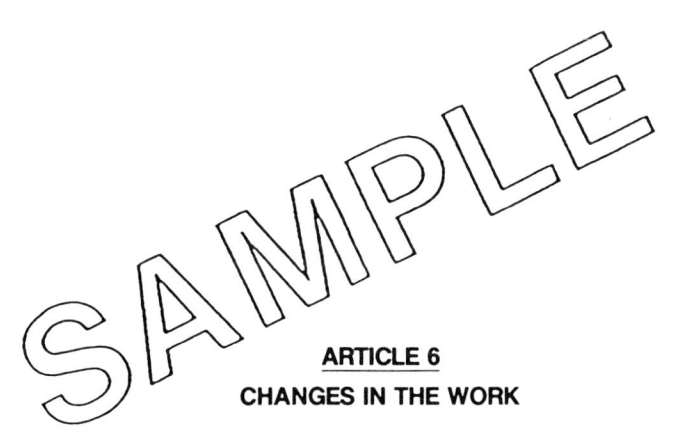

ARTICLE 6
CHANGES IN THE WORK

6.1 CONTRACTS WITH A GUARANTEED MAXIMUM PRICE

6.1.1 Adjustments to the Guaranteed Maximum Price on account of changes in the Work may be determined by any of the methods listed in Subparagraph 7.3.3 of the General Conditions.

6.1.2 In calculating adjustments to subcontracts (except those awarded with the Owner's prior consent on the basis of cost plus a fee), the terms "cost" and "fee" as used in Clause 7.3.3.3 of the General Conditions and the terms "costs" and "a reasonable allowance for overhead and profit" as used in Subparagraph 7.3.6 of the General Conditions shall have the meanings assigned to them in the General Conditions and shall not be modified by Articles 5, 7 and 8 of this Agreement. Adjustments to subcontracts awarded with the Owner's prior consent on the basis of cost plus a fee shall be calculated in accordance with the terms of those subcontracts.

6.1.3 In calculating adjustments to this Contract, the terms "cost" and "costs" as used in the above-referenced provisions of the General Conditions shall mean the Cost of the Work as defined in Article 7 of this Agreement and the terms "fee" and "a reasonable allowance for overhead and profit" shall mean the Contractor's Fee as defined in Paragraph 5.1 of this Agreement.

6.2 CONTRACTS WITHOUT A GUARANTEED MAXIMUM PRICE

6.2.1 Increased costs for the items set forth in Article 7 which result from changes in the Work shall become part of the Cost of the Work, and the Contractor's Fee shall be adjusted as provided in Paragraph 5.1.

6.3 ALL CONTRACTS

6.3.1 If no specific provision is made in Paragraph 5.1 for adjustment of the Contractor's Fee in the case of changes in the Work, or if the extent of such changes is such, in the aggregate, that application of the adjustment provisions of Paragraph 5.1 will cause substantial inequity to the Owner or Contractor, the Contractor's Fee shall be equitably adjusted on the basis of the Fee established for the original Work.

ARTICLE 7
COSTS TO BE REIMBURSED

7.1 The term Cost of the Work shall mean costs necessarily incurred by the Contractor in the proper performance of the Work. Such costs shall be at rates not higher than the standard paid at the place of the Project except with prior consent of the Owner. The Cost of the Work shall include only the items set forth in this Article 7.

7.1.1 LABOR COSTS

7.1.1.1 Wages of construction workers directly employed by the Contractor to perform the construction of the Work at the site or, with the Owner's agreement, at off-site workshops.

7.1.1.2 Wages or salaries of the Contractor's supervisory and administrative personnel when stationed at the site with the Owner's agreement.

(If it is intended that the wages or salaries of certain personnel stationed at the Contractor's principal or other offices shall be included in the Cost of the Work, identify in Article 14 the personnel to be included and whether for all or only part of their time.)

7.1.1.3 Wages and salaries of the Contractor's supervisory or administrative personnel engaged, at factories, workshops or on the road, in expediting the production or transportation of materials or equipment required for the Work, but only for that portion of their time required for the Work.

7.1.1.4 Costs paid or incurred by the Contractor for taxes, insurance, contributions, assessments and benefits required by law or collective bargaining agreements and, for personnel not covered by such agreements, customary benefits such as sick leave, medical and health benefits, holidays, vacations and pensions, provided such costs are based on wages and salaries included in the Cost of the Work under Clauses 7.1.1.1 through 7.1.1.3.

7.1.2 SUBCONTRACT COSTS

Payments made by the Contractor to Subcontractors in accordance with the requirements of the subcontracts.

7.1.3 COSTS OF MATERIALS AND EQUIPMENT INCORPORATED IN THE COMPLETED CONSTRUCTION

7.1.3.1 Costs, including transportation, of materials and equipment incorporated or to be incorporated in the completed construction.

7.1.3.2 Costs of materials described in the preceding Clause 7.1.3.1 in excess of those actually installed but required to provide reasonable allowance for waste and for spoilage. Unused excess materials, if any, shall be handed over to the Owner at the completion of the Work or, at the Owner's option, shall be sold by the Contractor; amounts realized, if any, from such sales shall be credited to the Owner as a deduction from the Cost of the Work.

7.1.4 COSTS OF OTHER MATERIALS AND EQUIPMENT, TEMPORARY FACILITIES AND RELATED ITEMS

7.1.4.1 Costs, including transportation, installation, maintenance, dismantling and removal of materials, supplies, temporary facilities, machinery, equipment, and hand tools not customarily owned by the construction workers, which are provided by the Contractor at the site and fully consumed in the performance of the Work; and cost less salvage value on such items if not fully consumed, whether sold to others or retained by the Contractor. Cost for items previously used by the Contractor shall mean fair market value.

7.1.4.2 Rental charges for temporary facilities, machinery, equipment, and hand tools not customarily owned by the construction workers, which are provided by the Contractor at the site, whether rented from the Contractor or others, and costs of transportation, installation, minor repairs and replacements, dismantling and removal thereof. Rates and quantities of equipment rented shall be subject to the Owner's prior approval.

7.1.4.3 Costs of removal of debris from the site.

7.1.4.4 Costs of telegrams and long-distance telephone calls, postage and parcel delivery charges, telephone service at the site and reasonable petty cash expenses of the site office.

7.1.4.5 That portion of the reasonable travel and subsistence expenses of the Contractor's personnel incurred while traveling in discharge of duties connected with the Work.

7.1.5 MISCELLANEOUS COSTS

7.1.5.1 That portion directly attributable to this Contract of premiums for insurance and bonds.

7.1.5.2 Sales, use or similar taxes imposed by a governmental authority which are related to the Work and for which the Contractor is liable.

7.1.5.3 Fees and assessments for the building permit and for other permits, licenses and inspections for which the Contractor is required by the Contract Documents to pay.

7.1.5.4 Fees of testing laboratories for tests required by the Contract Documents, except those related to defective or nonconforming Work for which reimbursement is excluded by Subparagraph 13.5.3 of the General Conditions or other provisions of the Contract Documents and which do not fall within the scope of Subparagraphs 7.2.2 through 7.2.4 below.

7.1.5.5 Royalties and license fees paid for the use of a particular design, process or product required by the Contract Documents; the cost of defending suits or claims for infringement of patent rights arising from such requirement by the Contract Documents; payments made in accordance with legal judgments against the Contractor resulting from such suits or claims and payments of settlements made with the Owner's consent; provided, however, that such costs of legal defenses, judgment and settlements shall not be included in the calculation of the Contractor's Fee or of a Guaranteed Maximum Price, if any, and provided that such royalties, fees and costs are not excluded by the last sentence of Subparagraph 3.17.1 of the General Conditions or other provisions of the Contract Documents.

7.1.5.6 Deposits lost for causes other than the Contractor's fault or negligence.

7.1.6 OTHER COSTS

7.1.6.1 Other costs incurred in the performance of the Work if and to the extent approved in advance in writing by the Owner.

7.2 EMERGENCIES: REPAIRS TO DAMAGED, DEFECTIVE OR NONCONFORMING WORK

The Cost of the Work shall also include costs described in Paragraph 7.1 which are incurred by the Contractor:

7.2.1 In taking action to prevent threatened damage, injury or loss in case of an emergency affecting the safety of persons and property, as provided in Paragraph 10.3 of the General Conditions.

7.2.2 In repairing or correcting Work damaged or improperly executed by construction workers in the employ of the Contractor, provided such damage or improper execution did not result from the fault or negligence of the Contractor or the Contractor's foremen, engineers or superintendents, or other supervisory, administrative or managerial personnel of the Contractor.

7.2.3 In repairing damaged Work other than that described in Subparagraph 7.2.2, provided such damage did not result from the fault or negligence of the Contractor or the Contractor's personnel, and only to the extent that the cost of such repairs is not recoverable by the Contractor from others and the Contractor is not compensated therefor by insurance or otherwise.

7.2.4 In correcting defective or nonconforming Work performed or supplied by a Subcontractor or material supplier and not corrected by them, provided such defective or nonconforming Work did not result from the fault or neglect of the Contractor or the Contractor's personnel adequately to supervise and direct the Work of the Subcontractor or material supplier, and only to the extent that the cost of correcting the defective or nonconforming Work is not recoverable by the Contractor from the Subcontractor or material supplier.

ARTICLE 8
COSTS NOT TO BE REIMBURSED

8.1 The Cost of the Work shall not include:

8.1.1 Salaries and other compensation of the Contractor's personnel stationed at the Contractor's principal office or offices other than the site office, except as specifically provided in Clauses 7.1.1.2 and 7.1.1.3 or as may be provided in Article 14.

8.1.2 Expenses of the Contractor's principal office and offices other than the site office.

8.1.3 Overhead and general expenses, except as may be expressly included in Article 7.

8.1.4 The Contractor's capital expenses, including interest on the Contractor's capital employed for the Work.

8.1.5 Rental costs of machinery and equipment, except as specifically provided in Clause 7.1.4.2.

8.1.6 Except as provided in Subparagraphs 7.2.2 through 7.2.4 and Paragraph 13.5 of this Agreement, costs due to the fault or negligence of the Contractor, Subcontractors, anyone directly or indirectly employed by any of them, or for whose acts any of them may be liable, including but not limited to costs for the correction of damaged, defective or nonconforming Work, disposal and replacement of materials and equipment incorrectly ordered or supplied, and making good damage to property not forming part of the Work.

8.1.7 Any cost not specifically and expressly described in Article 7.

8.1.8 Costs which would cause the Guaranteed Maximum Price, if any, to be exceeded.

ARTICLE 9
DISCOUNTS, REBATES AND REFUNDS

9.1 Cash discounts obtained on payments made by the Contractor shall accrue to the Owner if (1) before making the payment, the Contractor included them in an Application for Payment and received payment therefor from the Owner, or (2) the Owner has deposited funds with the Contractor with which to make payments; otherwise, cash discounts shall accrue to the Contractor. Trade discounts, rebates, refunds and amounts received from sales of surplus materials and equipment shall accrue to the Owner, and the Contractor shall make provisions so that they can be secured.

9.2 Amounts which accrue to the Owner in accordance with the provisions of Paragraph 9.1 shall be credited to the Owner as a deduction from the Cost of the Work.

ARTICLE 10
SUBCONTRACTS AND OTHER AGREEMENTS

10.1 Those portions of the Work that the Contractor does not customarily perform with the Contractor's own personnel shall be performed under subcontracts or by other appropriate agreements with the Contractor. The Contractor shall obtain bids from Subcontractors and from suppliers of materials or equipment fabricated especially for the Work and shall deliver such bids to the Architect. The Owner will then determine, with the advice of the Contractor and subject to the reasonable objection of the Architect, which bids will be accepted. The Owner may designate specific persons or entities from whom the Contractor shall obtain bids; however, if a Guaranteed Maximum Price has been established, the Owner may not prohibit the Contractor from obtaining bids from others. The Contractor shall not be required to contract with anyone to whom the Contractor has reasonable objection.

10.2 If a Guaranteed Maximum Price has been established and a specific bidder among those whose bids are delivered by the Contractor to the Architect (1) is recommended to the Owner by the Contractor; (2) is qualified to perform that portion of the Work; and (3) has submitted a bid which conforms to the requirements of the Contract Documents without reservations or exceptions, but the Owner requires that another bid be accepted; then the Contractor may require that a Change Order be issued to adjust the Guaranteed Maximum Price by the difference between the bid of the person or entity recommended to the Owner by the Contractor and the amount of the subcontract or other agreement actually signed with the person or entity designated by the Owner.

10.3 Subcontracts or other agreements shall conform to the payment provisions of Paragraphs 12.7 and 12.8, and shall not be awarded on the basis of cost plus a fee without the prior consent of the Owner.

ARTICLE 11
ACCOUNTING RECORDS

11.1 The Contractor shall keep full and detailed accounts and exercise such controls as may be necessary for proper financial management under this Contract; the accounting and control systems shall be satisfactory to the Owner. The Owner and the Owner's accountants shall be afforded access to the Contractor's records, books, correspondence, instructions, drawings, receipts, subcontracts, purchase orders, vouchers, memoranda and other data relating to this Contract, and the Contractor shall preserve these for a period of three years after final payment, or for such longer period as may be required by law.

ARTICLE 12
PROGRESS PAYMENTS

12.1 Based upon Applications for Payment submitted to the Architect by the Contractor and Certificates for Payment issued by the Architect, the Owner shall make progress payments on account of the Contract Sum to the Contractor as provided below and elsewhere in the Contract Documents.

12.2 The period covered by each Application for Payment shall be one calendar month ending on the last day of the month, or as follows:

12.3 Provided an Application for Payment is received by the Architect not later than the   day of a month, the Owner shall make payment to the Contractor not later than the   day of the   month. If an Application for Payment is received by the Architect after the application date fixed above, payment shall be made by the Owner not later than   days after the Architect receives the Application for Payment.

12.4 With each Application for Payment the Contractor shall submit payrolls, petty cash accounts, receipted invoices or invoices with check vouchers attached, and any other evidence required by the Owner or Architect to demonstrate that cash disbursements already made by the Contractor on account of the Cost of the Work equal or exceed (1) progress payments already received by the Contractor; less (2) that portion of those payments attributable to the Contractor's Fee; plus (3) payrolls for the period covered by the present Application for Payment; plus (4) retainage provided in Subparagraph 12.5.4, if any, applicable to prior progress payments.

12.5 CONTRACTS WITH A GUARANTEED MAXIMUM PRICE

12.5.1 Each Application for Payment shall be based upon the most recent schedule of values submitted by the Contractor in accordance with the Contract Documents. The schedule of values shall allocate the entire Guaranteed Maximum Price among the various portions of the Work, except that the Contractor's Fee shall be shown as a single separate item. The schedule of values shall be prepared in such form and supported by such data to substantiate its accuracy as the Architect may require. This schedule, unless objected to by the Architect, shall be used as a basis for reviewing the Contractor's Applications for Payment.

12.5.2 Applications for Payment shall show the percentage completion of each portion of the Work as of the end of the period covered by the Application for Payment. The percentage completion shall be the lesser of (1) the percentage of that portion of the Work which has actually been completed or (2) the percentage obtained by dividing (a) the expense which has actually been incurred by the Contractor on account of that portion of the Work for which the Contractor has made or intends to make actual payment prior to the next Application for Payment by (b) the share of the Guaranteed Maximum Price allocated to that portion of the Work in the schedule of values.

12.5.3 Subject to other provisions of the Contract Documents, the amount of each progress payment shall be computed as follows:

12.5.3.1 Take that portion of the Guaranteed Maximum Price properly allocable to completed Work as determined by multiplying the percentage completion of each portion of the Work by the share of the Guaranteed Maximum Price allocated to that portion of the Work in the schedule of values. Pending final determination of cost to the Owner of changes in the Work, amounts not in dispute may be included as provided in Subparagraph 7.3.7 of the General Conditions, even though the Guaranteed Maximum Price has not yet been adjusted by Change Order.

12.5.3.2 Add that portion of the Guaranteed Maximum Price properly allocable to materials and equipment delivered and suitably stored at the site for subsequent incorporation in the Work or, if approved in advance by the Owner, suitably stored off the site at a location agreed upon in writing.

12.5.3.3 Add the Contractor's Fee, less retainage of _____ percent (___ %). The Contractor's Fee shall be computed upon the Cost of the Work described in the two preceding Clauses at the rate stated in Paragraph 5.1 or, if the Contractor's Fee is stated as a fixed sum in that Paragraph, shall be an amount which bears the same ratio to that fixed-sum Fee as the Cost of the Work in the two preceding Clauses bears to a reasonable estimate of the probable Cost of the Work upon its completion.

12.5.3.4 Subtract the aggregate of previous payments made by the Owner.

12.5.3.5 Subtract the shortfall, if any, indicated by the Contractor in the documentation required by Paragraph 12.4 to substantiate prior Applications for Payment, or resulting from errors subsequently discovered by the Owner's accountants in such documentation.

12.5.3.6 Subtract amounts, if any, for which the Architect has withheld or nullified a Certificate for Payment as provided in Paragraph 9.5 of the General Conditions.

12.5.4 Additional retainage, if any, shall be as follows:

(If it is intended to retain additional amounts from progress payments to the Contractor beyond (1) the retainage from the Contractor's Fee provided in Clause 12.5.3.3, (2) the retainage from Subcontractors provided in Paragraph 12.7 below, and (3) the retainage, if any, provided by other provisions of the Contract, insert provision for such additional retainage here. Such provision, if made, should also describe any arrangement for limiting or reducing the amount retained after the Work reaches a certain state of completion.)

12.6 CONTRACTS WITHOUT A GUARANTEED MAXIMUM PRICE

12.6.1 Applications for Payment shall show the Cost of the Work actually incurred by the Contractor through the end of the period covered by the Application for Payment and for which the Contractor has made or intends to make actual payment prior to the next Application for Payment.

12.6.2 Subject to other provisions of the Contract Documents, the amount of each progress payment shall be computed as follows:

12.6.2.1 Take the Cost of the Work as described in Subparagraph 12.6.1.

12.6.2.2 Add the Contractor's Fee, less retainage of _____ percent (___ %). The Contractor's Fee shall be computed upon the Cost of the Work described in the preceding Clause 12.6.2.1 at the rate stated in Paragraph 5.1 or, if the Contractor's Fee is stated as a fixed sum in that Paragraph, an amount which bears the same ratio to that fixed-sum Fee as the Cost of the Work in the preceding Clause bears to a reasonable estimate of the probable Cost of the Work upon its completion.

12.6.2.3 Subtract the aggregate of previous payments made by the Owner.

12.6.2.4 Subtract the shortfall, if any, indicated by the Contractor in the documentation required by Paragraph 12.4 or to substantiate prior Applications for Payment or resulting from errors subsequently discovered by the Owner's accountants in such documentation.

12.6.2.5 Subtract amounts, if any, for which the Architect has withheld or withdrawn a Certificate for Payment as provided in the Contract Documents.

12.6.3 Additional retainage, if any, shall be as follows:

12.7 Except with the Owner's prior approval, payments to Subcontractors included in the Contractor's Applications for Payment shall not exceed an amount for each Subcontractor calculated as follows:

12.7.1 Take that portion of the Subcontract Sum properly allocable to completed Work as determined by multiplying the percentage completion of each portion of the Subcontractor's Work by the share of the total Subcontract Sum allocated to that portion in the Subcontractor's schedule of values, less retainage of   percent (%). Pending final determination of amounts to be paid to the Subcontractor for changes in the Work, amounts not in dispute may be included as provided in Subparagraph 7.3.7 of the General Conditions even though the Subcontract Sum has not yet been adjusted by Change Order.

12.7.2 Add that portion of the Subcontract Sum properly allocable to materials and equipment delivered and suitably stored at the site for subsequent incorporation in the Work or, if approved in advance by the Owner, suitably stored off the site at a location agreed upon in writing, less retainage of   percent (%).

12.7.3 Subtract the aggregate of previous payments made by the Contractor to the Subcontractor.

12.7.4 Subtract amounts, if any, for which the Architect has withheld or nullified a Certificate for Payment by the Owner to the Contractor for reasons which are the fault of the Subcontractor.

12.7.5 Add, upon Substantial Completion of the entire Work of the Contractor, a sum sufficient to increase the total payments to the Subcontractor to   percent (%) of the Subcontract Sum, less amounts, if any, for incomplete Work and unsettled claims; and, if final completion of the entire Work is thereafter materially delayed through no fault of the Subcontractor, add any additional amounts payable on account of Work of the Subcontractor in accordance with Subparagraph 9.10.3 of the General Conditions.

(If it is intended, prior to Substantial Completion of the entire Work of the Contractor, to reduce or limit the retainage from Subcontractors resulting from the percentages inserted in Subparagraphs 12.7.1 and 12.7.2 above, and this is not explained elsewhere in the Contract Documents, insert here provisions for such reduction or limitation.)

The Subcontract Sum is the total amount stipulated in the subcontract to be paid by the Contractor to the Subcontractor for the Subcontractor's performance of the subcontract.

12.8 Except with the Owner's prior approval, the Contractor shall not make advance payments to suppliers for materials or equipment which have not been delivered and stored at the site.

12.9 In taking action on the Contractor's Applications for Payment, the Architect shall be entitled to rely on the accuracy and completeness of the information furnished by the Contractor and shall not be deemed to represent that the Architect has made a detailed examination, audit or arithmetic verification of the documentation submitted in accordance with Paragraph 12.4 or other supporting data; that the Architect has made exhaustive or continuous on-site inspections or that the Architect has made examinations to ascertain how or for what purposes the Contractor has used amounts previously paid on account of the Contract. Such examinations, audits and verifications, if required by the Owner, will be performed by the Owner's accountants acting in the sole interest of the Owner.

ARTICLE 13
FINAL PAYMENT

13.1 Final payment shall be made by the Owner to the Contractor when (1) the Contract has been fully performed by the Contractor except for the Contractor's responsibility to correct defective or nonconforming Work, as provided in Subparagraph 12.2.2 of the General Conditions, and to satisfy other requirements, if any, which necessarily survive final payment; (2) a final Application for Payment and a final accounting for the Cost of the Work have been submitted by the Contractor and reviewed by the Owner's accountants; and (3) a final Certificate for Payment has then been issued by the Architect; such final payment shall be made by the Owner not more than 30 days after the issuance of the Architect's final Certificate for Payment, or as follows:

13.2 The amount of the final payment shall be calculated as follows:

13.2.1 Take the sum of the Cost of the Work substantiated by the Contractor's final accounting and the Contractor's Fee; but not more than the Guaranteed Maximum Price, if any.

13.2.2 Subtract amounts, if any, for which the Architect withholds, in whole or in part, a final Certificate for Payment as provided in Subparagraph 9.5.1 of the General Conditions or other provisions of the Contract Documents.

13.2.3 Subtract the aggregate of previous payments made by the Owner.

If the aggregate of previous payments made by the Owner exceeds the amount due the Contractor, the Contractor shall reimburse the difference to the Owner.

13.3 The Owner's accountants will review and report in writing on the Contractor's final accounting within 30 days after delivery of the final accounting to the Architect by the Contractor. Based upon such Cost of the Work as the Owner's accountants report to be substantiated by the Contractor's final accounting, and provided the other conditions of Paragraph 13.1 have been met, the Architect will, within seven days after receipt of the written report of the Owner's accountants, either issue to the Owner a final Certificate for Payment with a copy to the Contractor, or notify the Contractor and Owner in writing of the Architect's reasons for withholding a certificate as provided in Subparagraph 9.5.1 of the General Conditions. The time periods stated in this Paragraph 13.3 supersede those stated in Subparagraph 9.4.1 of the General Conditions.

13.4 If the Owner's accountants report the Cost of the Work as substantiated by the Contractor's final accounting to be less than claimed by the Contractor, the Contractor shall be entitled to demand arbitration of the disputed amount without a further decision of the Architect. Such demand for arbitration shall be made by the Contractor within 30 days after the Contractor's receipt of a copy of the Architect's final Certificate for Payment; failure to demand arbitration within this 30-day period shall result in the substantiated amount reported by the Owner's accountants becoming binding on the Contractor. Pending a final resolution by arbitration, the Owner shall pay the Contractor the amount certified in the Architect's final Certificate for Payment.

13.5 If, subsequent to final payment and at the Owner's request, the Contractor incurs costs described in Article 7 and not excluded by Article 8 to correct defective or nonconforming Work, the Owner shall reimburse the Contractor such costs and the Contractor's Fee applicable thereto on the same basis as if such costs had been incurred prior to final payment, but not in excess of the Guaranteed Maximum Price, if any. If the Contractor has participated in savings as provided in Paragraph 5.2, the amount of such savings shall be recalculated and appropriate credit given to the Owner in determining the net amount to be paid by the Owner to the Contractor.

ARTICLE 14
MISCELLANEOUS PROVISIONS

14.1 Where reference is made in this Agreement to a provision of the General Conditions or another Contract Document, the reference refers to that provision as amended or supplemented by other provisions of the Contract Documents.

14.2 Payments due and unpaid under the Contract shall bear interest from the date payment is due at the rate stated below, or in the absence thereof, at the legal rate prevailing from time to time at the place where the Project is located.

(Insert rate of interest agreed upon, if any.)

(Usury laws and requirements under the Federal Truth in Lending Act, similar state and local consumer credit laws and other regulations at the Owner's and Contractor's principal places of business, the location of the Project and elsewhere may affect the validity of this provision. Legal advice should be obtained with respect to deletions or modifications, and also regarding requirements such as written disclosures or waivers.)

14.3 Other provisions:

ARTICLE 15
TERMINATION OR SUSPENSION

15.1 The Contract may be terminated by the Contractor as provided in Article 14 of the General Conditions; however, the amount to be paid to the Contractor under Subparagraph 14.1.2 of the General Conditions shall not exceed the amount the Contractor would be entitled to receive under Paragraph 15.3 below, except that the Contractor's Fee shall be calculated as if the Work had been fully completed by the Contractor, including a reasonable estimate of the Cost of the Work for Work not actually completed.

15.2 If a Guaranteed Maximum Price is established in Article 5, the Contract may be terminated by the Owner for cause as provided in Article 14 of the General Conditions; however, the amount, if any, to be paid to the Contractor under Subparagraph 14.2.4 of the General Conditions shall not cause the Guaranteed Maximum Price to be exceeded, nor shall it exceed the amount the Contractor would be entitled to receive under Paragraph 15.3 below.

15.3 If no Guaranteed Maximum Price is established in Article 5, the Contract may be terminated by the Owner for cause as provided in Article 14 of the General Conditions; however, the Owner shall then pay the Contractor an amount calculated as follows:

15.3.1 Take the Cost of the Work incurred by the Contractor to the date of termination.

15.3.2 Add the Contractor's Fee computed upon the Cost of the Work to the date of termination at the rate stated in Paragraph 5.1 or, if the Contractor's Fee is stated as a fixed sum in that Paragraph, an amount which bears the same ratio to that fixed-sum Fee as the Cost of the Work at the time of termination bears to a reasonable estimate of the probable Cost of the Work upon its completion.

15.3.3 Subtract the aggregate of previous payments made by the Owner.

The Owner shall also pay the Contractor fair compensation, either by purchase or rental at the election of the Owner, for any equipment owned by the Contractor which the Owner elects to retain and which is not otherwise included in the Cost of the Work under Subparagraph 15.3.1. To the extent that the Owner elects to take legal assignment of subcontracts and purchase orders (including rental agreements), the Contractor shall, as a condition of receiving the payments referred to in this Article 15, execute and deliver all such papers and take all such steps, including the legal assignment of such subcontracts and other contractual rights of the Contractor, as the Owner may require for the purpose of fully vesting in the Owner the rights and benefits of the Contractor under such subcontracts or purchase orders.

15.4 The Work may be suspended by the Owner as provided in Article 14 of the General Conditions; in such case, the Guaranteed Maximum Price, if any, shall be increased as provided in Subparagraph 14.3.2 of the General Conditions except that the term "cost of performance of the Contract" in that Subparagraph shall be understood to mean the Cost of the Work and the term "profit" shall be understood to mean the Contractor's Fee as described in Paragraphs 5.1 and 6.3 of this Agreement.

ARTICLE 16
ENUMERATION OF CONTRACT DOCUMENTS

16.1 The Contract Documents, except for Modifications issued after execution of this Agreement, are enumerated as follows:

16.1.1 The Agreement is this executed Standard Form of Agreement Between Owner and Contractor, AIA Document A111, 1987 Edition.

16.1.2 The General Conditions are the General Conditions of the Contract for Construction, AIA Document A201, 1987 Edition.

16.1.3 The Supplementary and other Conditions of the Contract are those contained in the Project Manual dated   , and are as follows:

Document	Title	Pages

16.1.4 The Specifications are those contained in the Project Manual dated as in Paragraph 16.1.3, and are as follows:
(Either list the Specifications here or refer to an exhibit attached to this Agreement.)

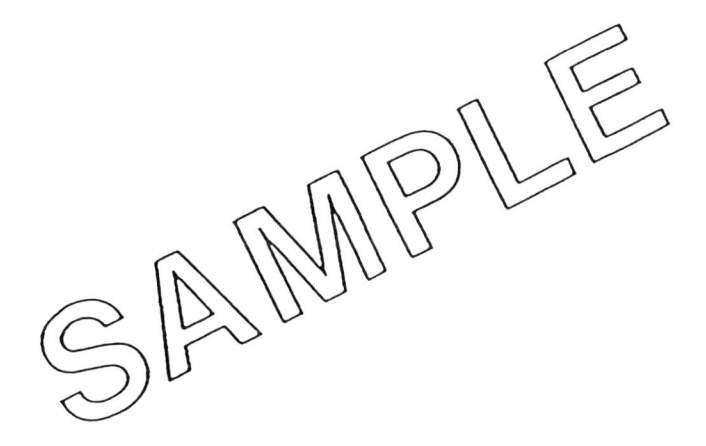

Section	Title	Pages

16.1.5 The Drawings are as follows, and are dated　　　　　　　　　　unless a different date is shown below:
(Either list the Drawings here or refer to an exhibit attached to this Agreement.)

Number　　　　　　　　　　　　　　**Title**　　　　　　　　　　　　　　**Date**

16.1.6 The Addenda, if any, are as follows:

Number　　　　　　　　　　　　　　**Date**　　　　　　　　　　　　　　**Pages**

Portions of Addenda relating to bidding requirements are not part of the Contract Documents unless the bidding requirements are also enumerated in this Article 16.

AIA DOCUMENT A111 • OWNER-CONTRACTOR AGREEMENT • TENTH EDITION • AIA® • ©1987 • THE AMERICAN INSTITUTE OF ARCHITECTS, 1735 NEW YORK AVENUE, N.W., WASHINGTON, D.C. 20006　　　A111-1987　**13**

16.1.7 Other Documents, if any, forming part of the Contract Documents are as follows:

(List here any additional documents which are intended to form part of the Contract Documents. The General Conditions provide that bidding requirements such as advertisement or invitation to bid, Instructions to Bidders, sample forms and the Contractor's bid are not part of the Contract Documents unless enumerated in this Agreement. They should be listed here only if intended to be part of the Contract Documents.)

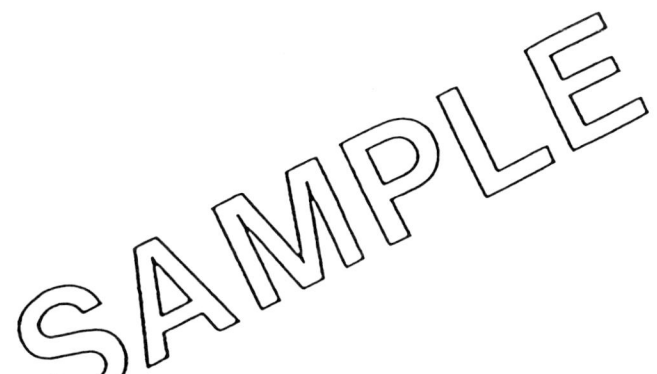

This Agreement is entered into as of the day and year first written above and is executed in at least three original copies of which one is to be delivered to the Contractor, one to the Architect for use in the administration of the Contract, and the remainder to the Owner.

OWNER   CONTRACTOR

_____   _____
(Signature)   *(Signature)*

_____   _____
(Printed name and title)   *(Printed name and title)*

AIA DOCUMENT A111 • OWNER-CONTRACTOR AGREEMENT • TENTH EDITION • AIA® • ©1987 • THE AMERICAN INSTITUTE OF ARCHITECTS, 1735 NEW YORK AVENUE, N.W., WASHINGTON, D.C. 20006

A111-1987 14

INSTRUCTION SHEET

FOR AIA DOCUMENT A111, STANDARD FORM OF AGREEMENT BETWEEN OWNER AND CONTRACTOR where the basis of payment is the COST OF THE WORK PLUS A FEE with or without a Guaranteed Maximum Price—1987 EDITION

A. GENERAL INFORMATION

1. Purpose

AIA Document A111 is intended for use on construction projects where the basis of payment is the cost of the Work plus a fixed or percentage fee. While the cost-plus-fee arrangement lacks the financial certainty of a lump-sum agreement, it may be desirable when fixed prices on portions of the Work cannot be obtained, when construction must be started before Drawings and Specifications are completed, or under other circumstances.

2. Related Documents

This document has been prepared for use in conjunction with the 1987 edition of AIA Document A201, General Conditions of the Contract for Construction, which is adopted into A111 by a specific reference. This integrated set of documents is suitable for most projects; however, for projects of limited scope, use of AIA Document A117 may be considered.

The A111 document may be used as one part of the Contract Documents which record the Contract for Construction between the Owner and the Contractor. The other Contract Documents are:

General Conditions (i.e., A201)
Supplementary Conditions
Drawings
Specifications
Modifications

Although the AIA does not produce standard documents for Supplementary Conditions, Drawings or Specifications, a variety of model and guide documents are available, including AIA's MASTERSPEC.

3. Arbitration

This document incorporates ARBITRATION by adoption of AIA Document A201, which provides for arbitration according to the Construction Industry Arbitration Rules of the American Arbitration Association. Arbitration is BINDING AND MANDATORY in most states and under the federal Arbitration Act. In a minority of states, arbitration provisions relating to future disputes are not enforceable, but arbitration is enforceable if agreed to after the dispute arises. A few states require that the contracting parties be especially notified that the written contract contains an arbitration provision by: a warning on the face of the document, specific placement of the arbitration provision within the document or specific discussions among the parties prior to signing the document.

Arbitration provisions have been included in most AIA contract forms since 1888 in order to encourage alternative dispute resolution procedures and to provide users of AIA documents with legally enforceable arbitration provisions when the parties choose to adopt arbitration into their contract. Individuals may, however, choose to delete the arbitration provisions based upon their business decisions with the advice of counsel. To obtain a copy of the Construction Industry Arbitration Rules, write to the American Arbitration Association, 140 West 51st Street, New York, NY 10020.

4. Use of Non-AIA Forms

If a combination of AIA documents and non-AIA documents is to be used, particular care must be taken to achieve consistency of language and intent. Certain owners require the use of owner-contractor agreements and other contract forms which they prepare. Such forms should be carefully compared to the standard AIA forms for which they are being substituted before execution of an agreement. If there are any significant omissions, additions or variances from the terms of the related standard AIA forms, both legal and insurance counsel should be consulted.

5. Letter Forms of Agreement

Letter forms of agreement are generally discouraged by the AIA, as is the performance of a part or the whole of the Work on the basis of oral agreements or understandings. The standard AIA agreement forms have been developed through more than seventy-five years of experience and have been tested repeatedly in the courts. In addition, the standard forms have been carefully coordinated with other AIA documents.

6. Use of Current Documents

Prior to using any AIA document, the user should consult the AIA, an AIA component chapter or a current AIA Documents Price List to determine the current edition of each document.

7. Limited License for Reproduction

AIA Document A111 is a copyrighted work and may not be reproduced or excerpted from in substantial part without the express written permission of the AIA. The A111 document is intended to be used as a consumable—that is, the original document purchased by the user is intended to be consumed in the course of being used. There is no implied permission to reproduce this document, nor does membership in The American Institute of Architects confer any further rights to reproduce them.

A limited license is hereby granted to retail purchasers to reproduce a maximum of ten copies of a completed or executed A111, but only for use in connection with a particular Project. A111 may not be reproduced for Project Manuals. Rather, if a user wishes to include it as an example in a Project Manual, the normal practice is to purchase a quantity of the pre-printed forms and bind one in each of the Project Manuals. Partial modifications, if any, may be accomplished without completing the form by using separate Supplementary Conditions.

Upon reaching agreement concerning the Contract Sum and other conditions, the form may be removed from the manual and such information, except for the signatures, may be added to the blank spaces of the form. The user may then reproduce up to ten copies to facilitate the execution (signing) of multiple original copies of the form, or for other administrative purposes in connection with a particular Project. Please note that at least three original copies of A111 should be signed by the parties as required by the last provision of A111.

B. CHANGES FROM THE PREVIOUS EDITION

1. Format Changes

The titles of Articles 3, 4, 5, 12 and 13 have been changed; a new Article 16, Enumeration of Contract Documents, has been added; and former Articles 5 and 6 have been combined into a new Article 5, Contract Sum.

2. Changes in Content

The 1987 edition of A111 revises the 1978 edition to reflect changes made in the most recent (1987) edition of AIA Document A201, General Conditions of the Contract for Construction, and to incorporate alterations proposed by architects, owners, contractors and professional consultants.

Article 2: Space has been provided to describe any exceptions to the description of the Contractor's scope of Work.

Article 3: Language has been added requiring the Owner to excercise best efforts to enable the Contractor to perform the Work.

Article 4: The title of this article now refers to the date rather than the time of commencement. The Contractor is now required to notify the Owner before commencing the Work to permit the timely filing of mortgages and other security interests.

Article 5: This article, entitled Contract Sum, combines the former article on Cost of the Work and Guaranteed Maximum Cost and the former article on Contractor's Fee. The provisions on Guaranteed Maximum Price have been expanded to include further details on Change Orders.

Article 6: This article has been substantially revised to allow for changes in the Work with or without a Guaranteed Maximum Price.

Article 7: Costs to be reimbursed now include payment for customary medical health benefits, costs of waste and spoilage, costs of testing and payment of royalties or fees for use of patentable materials, and costs of emergencies and repairs to defective Work not caused by the Contractor.

Article 8: Two new exceptions are made as to costs that will not be reimbursed. One is to allow payment of the Contractor's personnel at the principal office when specifically provided for under Article 7 or 14; the other allows payment for costs of correction when the cause is not the Contractor or the Contractor's supervisory personnel.

Article 9: Rebates and discounts accruing to the Owner are credited to the Owner as a deduction from the Cost of the Work.

Article 10: The Owner may designate specific Subcontractors from whom the Contractor must obtain bids. If a Guaranteed Maximum Price is provided, however, the Contractor may obtain a Change Order if the Owner rejects a Subcontractor selected by the Contractor.

Article 12: This article combines two former articles on payments to the Contractor. Separate payment procedures are provided for contracts with and contracts without a Guaranteed Maximum Price.

Article 13: The article on final payment has been substantially rewritten to parallel the provisions of AIA Document A201. Further detail has been added on the procedures for calculating final payment, including a requirement that the Owner's accountant review the Contractor's final accounting.

Article 14: The reference to the definition of terms contained in the A201 document has been deleted; A201 is now specifically adopted by reference into A111. A new sentence has been added noting that references to a specific provision of the General Conditions or another Contract Document include any amendment or supplement to that provision. The provision on interest for overdue payments has been moved to this article from the former article on payments to the Contractor.

Article 15: Provisions have been added concerning termination of contracts with a Guaranteed Maximum Price and suspension of the Project.

Article 16: This new article contains cross-references to the General Conditions.

C. COMPLETING THE A111 FORM

1. Modifications

Users are encouraged to consult an attorney before completing an AIA document. Particularly with respect to contractor's licensing laws, duties imposed by building codes, interest charges, arbitration and indemnification, this document may require modification with the assistance of legal counsel to fully comply with state or local laws regulating these matters.

Generally, necessary modifications may be accomplished by writing or typing the appropriate terms in the blank spaces provided on the form or by Supplementary Conditions, special conditions or amendments included in the Project Manual and referenced in this document. The form may also be modified by striking out language directly on the original pre-printed form. Care must be taken in making these kinds of deletions, however. Under NO circumstances should pre-printed language be struck out in such a way as to render it illegible (as, for example, with blocking tape, correction fluid or X's that completely obscure the text). This may raise suspicions of fraudulent concealment, or suggest that the completed and signed document has been tampered with. Handwritten changes should be initialed by both parties to the contract.

It is definitely not recommended practice to retype the standard document. Besides being outside the limited license for reproduction granted under these Instructions, retyping can introduce typographical errors and cloud the legal interpretation given to a standard clause when blended with modifications.

Retyping eliminates one of the principal advantages of the standard form documents. By merely reviewing the modifications to be made to a standard form document, parties familiar with that document can quickly understand the essence of the proposed relationship. Commercial exchanges are greatly simplified and expedited, good-faith dealing is encouraged, and otherwise latent clauses are exposed for scrutiny. In this way, contracting parties can more fairly measure their risks.

2. Cover Page

Date: The date represents the date the Agreement becomes effective. It may be the date an oral agreement was reached, the date the Agreement was originally submitted to the Owner, the date authorizing action was taken or the date of actual execution. It will be the date from which the Contract Time is measured unless a different date is inserted under Paragragh 4.1.

Identification of Parties: Parties to this Agreement should be identified using the full legal name under which the Agreement is to be executed, including a designation of the legal status of both parties (sole proprietorship, partnership, joint venture, unincorporated association, limited partnership or corporation [general, closed or professional], etc.). Where appropriate, a copy of the resolution authorizing the individual to act on behalf of the firm or entity should be attached.

Project Description: The proposed Project should be described in sufficient detail to identify (1) the official name or title of the facility, (2) the location of the site, if known, (3) the proposed building type and usage, and (4) the size, capacity or scope of the Project, if known.

Architect: As in the other Contract Documents, the Architect's full legal or corporate titles should be used.

3. Article 2—The Work of This Contract

Portions of the Work which are the responsibility of persons other than the Contractor and which have not been otherwise indicated should be listed here.

4. Article 4—Date of Commencement and Substantial Completion

Paragraph 4.1

The date of commencement of the Work should be inserted if it is different from the date of the Agreement. It should not be earlier than the date of execution (signing) of the Contract. After the first sentence, enter either the specific date of commencement of the Work, or if a notice to proceed is to be used, enter the sentence, "The date of commencement shall be stipulated by the notice to proceed." When time of performance is to be strictly enforced, the statement of starting time should be carefully considered.

Paragraph 4.2

The time within which Substantial Completion of the Work is to be achieved may be expressed as a number of days (preferably calendar days) or as a specified date. Any requirements for earlier Substantial Completion of portions of the Work should be entered here if not specified elsewhere in the Contract Documents.

Also insert any provisions for liquidated damages relating to failure to complete on time. Liquidated damages are not a penalty to be inflicted on the Contractor, but must bear an actual and reasonably estimable relationship to the Owner's loss if construction is not completed on time. If liquidated damages are to be assessed because delayed construction will result in actual loss to the Owner, the amount of damages due for each day lost should be entered in the Supplementary Conditions or the Agreement. Factors such as confidentiality or the need to inform Subcontractors about the amount of liquidated damages will help determine the location chosen.

The provision for liquidated damages, which should be carefully reviewed or drafted by the Owner's attorney, may be as follows:

> The Contractor and the Contractor's surety, if any, shall be liable for and shall pay the Owner the sums hereinafter stipulated as liquidated damages for each calendar day of delay until the Work is substantially completed: _____ ($_____).

For further information on liquidated damages, penalties and bonus provisions, see AIA Document A511, Guide for Supplementary Conditions, Paragraph 9.11.

5. Article 5—Contract Sum

Paragraph 5.1

Enter the method used for determining the Contractor's Fee (lump sum, percentage of Cost of the Work or other method) and explain how the Contractor's Fee is to be adjusted for changes in the Work.

Subparagraph 5.2.1

If applicable, insert a Guaranteed Maximum Price for the Cost of the Work and the Contractor's Fee. Insert specific provisions if the Contractor is to participate in any savings when the final Cost of the Work is below the Guaranteed Maximum Price.

Subparagraph 5.2.2

If a Guaranteed Maximum Price is given in Subparagraph 5.2.1, identify any alternates described in the Contract Documents and accepted by the Owner. If decisions on alternates are to be made subsequent to execution of A111, attach a schedule showing the amount of each alternate and the date until which that amount is valid.

Subparagraph 5.2.3
If a Guaranteed Maximum Price is given in Subparagraph 5.2.1, state any amounts agreed for unit prices.

6. Article 7—Costs To Be Reimbursed
Article 8—Costs Not To Be Reimbursed
Modifications to these articles should be included in Paragraph 14.3. Such modifications should be carefully coordinated to ensure consistency between these two articles.

7. Article 12—Progress Payments
Paragraph 12.2
Insert the time period covered by each Application for Payment if it differs from the one given.

Paragraph 12.3
Insert the time schedule for presenting Applications for Payment. Insert the day of the month progress payments are due, indicating whether such day is to be in the same or the following month after receipt by the Architect of the relevant Application for Payment.

The last day upon which Work may be included in an Application should normally be no less than 14 days prior to the payment date, in consideration of the 7 days required for the Architect's evaluation of an Application and issuance of a Certificate for Payment and the time subsequently accorded the Owner to make payment in Article 9 of A201. The Contractor may prefer a few additional days to prepare the Application.

Due dates for payment should be acceptable to both the Owner and Contractor. They should allow sufficient time for the Contractor to prepare an Application for Payment, for the Architect to certify payment, and for the Owner to make payment. They should also be in accordance with time limits established by this Article and Article 9 of A201.

Clause 12.5.3.3
In contracts with a Guaranteed Maximum Price, indicate the percent retainage, if any, to be withheld from the Contractor's Fee when computing the amount of each progress payment.

Subparagraph 12.5.4
In contracts with a Guaranteed Maximum Price, insert additional retainage, if any, from progress payments to the Contractor above that indicated in Clause 12.5.3.3 or elsewhere in A111. Describe arrangements for limiting or reducing such additional retainage as the Work progresses.

Clause 12.6.2.2
In contracts without a Guaranteed Maximum Price, indicate the percent retainage to be withheld from Contractor's Fee when computing the amount of each progress payment.

Subparagraph 12.6.3
In contracts without a Guaranteed Maximum Price, insert additional retainage, if any, from progress payments to the Contractor above that indicated in Subparagraph 12.6.2 or elsewhere in A111. Describe arrangements for limiting or reducing such additional retainage as the Work progresses.

Subparagraph 12.7.1
Insert the percent retainage, if any, to be subtracted from the share of the total Subcontract Sum in the Subcontractor's schedule of values when determining the maximum amount of payment per Subcontractor to be included in each of the Contractor's Applications for Payment.

Subparagraph 12.7.2
Insert the percent retainage, if any, to be subtracted from the portion of the Subcontract Sum allocable to materials and equipment stored at the site when calculating the maximum payment per Subcontractor to be included in each of the Contractor's Applications for Payment.

Subparagraph 12.7.5
Insert the percentage of the Subcontract Sum to be paid to the Subcontractor upon Substantial Completion. Describe any arrangements to reduce or limit any retainages indicated in Subparagraphs 12.7.1 and 12.7.2, if not explained elsewhere.

8. Article 14—Miscellaneous Provisions
Paragraph 14.2
Insert any agreed-upon rate of interest chargeable on overdue payments to the Contractor.

Paragraph 14.3
Insert any other provisions which may apply and which are not mentioned elsewhere in the Contract Documents.

9. Article 16—Enumeration of Contract Documents
A detailed enumeration of all Contract Documents must be made in this article.

D. EXECUTION OF THE AGREEMENT
The Agreement should be executed in not less than triplicate by the Owner and the Contractor. Each person executing the Agreement should indicate the capacity in which they are acting (i.e., president, secretary, partner, etc.) and the authority under which they are executing the Agreement. Where appropriate, a copy of the resolution authorizing the individual to act on behalf of the firm or entity should be attached.

Appendix D:
AIA Document A201 — General Conditions of the Contract for Construction, 1987 Edition

THE AMERICAN INSTITUTE OF ARCHITECTS

1. AIA copyrighted material has been reproduced with the permission of the American Institute of Architects under license number 90011. Permission expires December 31, 1991. FURTHER REPRODUCTION IS PROHIBITED.

2. Because AIA Documents are revised from time to time, users should ascertain from the AIA the current edition of this document.

3. Copies of the current edition of this AIA document may be purchased from The American Institute of Architects or its local distributors.

4. This document is intended for use as a "consumable" (consumables are further defined by Senate Report 94-473 on the Copyright Act of 1976). This document is not intended to be used as "model language" (language taken from an existing document and incorporated, without attribution, into a newly-created document.) Rather, it is a standard form which is intended to be modified by appending separate amendment sheets and/or fill in provided blank spaces.

AIA Document A201

General Conditions of the Contract for Construction

THIS DOCUMENT HAS IMPORTANT LEGAL CONSEQUENCES; CONSULTATION WITH AN ATTORNEY IS ENCOURAGED WITH RESPECT TO ITS MODIFICATION

1987 EDITION
TABLE OF ARTICLES

1. GENERAL PROVISIONS
2. OWNER
3. CONTRACTOR
4. ADMINISTRATION OF THE CONTRACT
5. SUBCONTRACTORS
6. CONSTRUCTION BY OWNER OR BY SEPARATE CONTRACTORS
7. CHANGES IN THE WORK
8. TIME
9. PAYMENTS AND COMPLETION
10. PROTECTION OF PERSONS AND PROPERTY
11. INSURANCE AND BONDS
12. UNCOVERING AND CORRECTION OF WORK
13. MISCELLANEOUS PROVISIONS
14. TERMINATION OR SUSPENSION OF THE CONTRACT

This document has been approved and endorsed by the Associated General Contractors of America.

Copyright 1911, 1915, 1918, 1925, 1937, 1951, 1958, 1961, 1963, 1966, 1967, 1970, 1976, ©1987 by The American Institute of Architects, 1735 New York Avenue, N.W., Washington, D.C., 20006. Reproduction of the material herein or substantial quotation of its provisions without written permission of the AIA violates the copyright laws of the United States and will be subject to legal prosecutions.

AIA DOCUMENT A201 • GENERAL CONDITIONS OF THE CONTRACT FOR CONSTRUCTION • FOURTEENTH EDITION
AIA® • ©1987 THE AMERICAN INSTITUTE OF ARCHITECTS, 1735 NEW YORK AVENUE, N.W., WASHINGTON, D.C. 20006   A201-1987   1

INDEX

Acceptance of Nonconforming Work	9.6.6, 9.9.3, **12.3**
Acceptance of Work	9.6.6, 9.8.2, 9.9.3, 9.10.1, 9.10.3
Access to Work	**3.16**, 6.2.1, 12.1
Accident Prevention	4.2.3, 10
Acts and Omissions	3.2.1, 3.2.2, 3.3.2, 3.12.8, 3.18, 4.2.3, 4.3.2, 4.3.9, 8.3.1, 10.1.4, 10.2.5, 13.4.2, 13.7, 14.1
Addenda	1.1.1, 3.11
Additional Cost, Claims for	4.3.6, 4.3.7, 4.3.9, 6.1.1, 10.3
Additional Inspections and Testing	4.2.6, 9.8.2, 12.2.1, 13.5
Additional Time, Claims for	4.3.6, 4.3.8, 4.3.9, 8.3.2
ADMINISTRATION OF THE CONTRACT	3.3.3, **4**, 9.4, 9.5
Advertisement or Invitation to Bid	1.1.1
Aesthetic Effect	4.2.13, 4.5.1
Allowances	**3.8**
All-risk Insurance	11.3.1.1
Applications for Payment	4.2.5, 7.3.7, 9.2, **9.3**, 9.4, 9.5.1, 9.6.3, 9.8.3, 9.10.1, 9.10.3, 9.10.4, 11.1.3, 14.2.4
Approvals	2.4, 3.3.3, 3.5, 3.10.2, 3.12.4 through 3.12.8, 3.18.3, 4.2.7, 9.3.2, 11.3.1.4, 13.4.2, 13.5
Arbitration	4.1.4, 4.3.2, 4.3.4, 4.4.4, **4.5**, 8.3.1, 10.1.2, 11.3.9, 11.3.10
Architect	**4.1**
Architect, Definition of	4.1.1
Architect, Extent of Authority	2.4, 3.12.6, 4.2, 4.3.2, 4.3.6, 4.4, 5.2, 6.3, 7.1.2, 7.2.1, 7.3.6, 7.4, 9.2, 9.3.1, 9.4, 9.5, 9.6.3, 9.8.2, 9.8.3, 9.10.1, 9.10.3, 12.1, 12.2.1, 13.5.1, 13.5.2, 14.2.2, 14.2.4
Architect, Limitations of Authority and Responsibility	3.3.3, 3.12.8, 3.12.11, 4.1.2, 4.2.1, 4.2.2, 4.2.3, 4.2.6, 4.2.7, 4.2.10, 4.2.12, 4.2.13, 4.3.2, 5.2.1, 7.4, 9.4.2, 9.6.4, 9.6.6
Architect's Additional Services and Expenses	2.4, 9.8.2, 11.3.1.1, 12.2.1, 12.2.4, 13.5.2, 13.5.3, 14.2.4
Architect's Administration of the Contract	**4.2**, 4.3.6, 4.3.7, 4.4, 9.4, 9.5
Architect's Approvals	2.4, 3.5.1, 3.10.2, 3.12.6, 3.12.8, 3.18.3, 4.2.7
Architect's Authority to Reject Work	3.5.1, 4.2.6, 12.1.2, 12.2.1
Architect's Copyright	1.3
Architect's Decisions	4.2.6, 4.2.7, 4.2.11, 4.2.12, 4.2.13, 4.3.2, 4.3.6, 4.4.1, 4.4.4, 4.5, 6.3, 7.3.6, 7.3.8, 8.1.3, 8.3.1, 9.2, 9.4, 9.5.1, 9.8.2, 9.9.1, 10.1.2, 13.5.2, 14.2.2, 14.2.4
Architect's Inspections	4.2.2, 4.2.9, 4.3.6, 9.4.2, 9.8.2, 9.9.2, 9.10.1, 13.5
Architect's Instructions	4.2.6, 4.2.7, 4.2.8, 3.7, 7.4.1, 12.1, 13.5.2
Architect's Interpretations	4.2.11, 4.2.12, 4.3.7
Architect's On-Site Observations	4.2.2, 4.2.5, 4.3.6, 9.4.2, 9.5.1, 9.10.1, 13.5
Architect's Project Representative	4.2.10
Architect's Relationship with Contractor	1.1.2, 3.2.1, 3.2.2, 3.3.3, 3.5.1, 3.7.3, 3.11, 3.12.8, 3.12.11, 3.16, 3.18, 4.2.3, 4.2.4, 4.2.6, 4.2.12, 5.2, 6.2.2, 7.3.4, 9.8.2, 11.3.7, 12.1, 13.5
Architect's Relationship with Subcontractors	1.1.2, 4.2.3, 4.2.4, 4.2.6, 9.6.3, 9.6.4, 11.3.7
Architect's Representations	9.4.2, 9.5.1, 9.10.1
Architect's Site Visits	4.2.2, 4.2.5, 4.2.9, 4.3.6, 9.4.2, 9.5.1, 9.8.2, 9.9.2, 9.10.1, 13.5
Asbestos	10.1
Attorneys' Fees	3.18.1, 9.10.2, 10.1.4
Award of Separate Contracts	6.1.1
Award of Subcontracts and Other Contracts for Portions of the Work	**5.2**
Basic Definitions	**1.1**
Bidding Requirements	1.1.1, 1.1.7, 5.2.1, 11.4.1
Boiler and Machinery Insurance	**11.3.2**
Bonds, Lien	9.10.2
Bonds, Performance and Payment	7.3.6.4, 9.10.3, 11.3.9, 11.4
Building Permit	3.7.1
Capitalization	**1.4**
Certificate of Substantial Completion	9.8.2
Certificates for Payment	4.2.5, 4.2.9, 9.3.3, **9.4**, 9.5, 9.6.1, 9.6.6, 9.7.1, 9.8.3, 9.10.1, 9.10.3, 13.7, 14.1.1.3, 14.2.4
Certificates of Inspection, Testing or Approval	3.12.11, 13.5.4
Certificates of Insurance	9.3.2, 9.10.2, 11.1.3
Change Orders	1.1.1, 2.4.1, 3.8.2.4, 3.11, 4.2.8, 4.3.3, 5.2.3, 7.1, **7.2**, 7.3.2, 8.3.1, 9.3.1.1, 9.10.3, 11.3.1.2, 11.3.4, 11.3.9, 12.1.2
Change Orders, Definition of	7.2.1
Changes	**7.1**
CHANGES IN THE WORK	3.11, 4.2.8, **7**, 8.3.1, 9.3.1.1, 10.1.3
Claim, **Definition** of	**4.3.1**
Claims and Disputes	**4.3**, 4.4, 4.5, 6.2.5, 8.3.2, 9.3.1.2, 9.3.3, 9.10.4, 10.1.4
Claims and Timely Assertion of Claims	**4.5.6**
Claims for Additional Cost	4.3.6, **4.3.7**, 4.3.9, 6.1.1, 10.3
Claims for Additional Time	4.3.6, **4.3.8**, 4.3.9, 8.3.2
Claims for Concealed or Unknown Conditions	**4.3.6**
Claims for Damages	3.18, 4.3.9, 6.1.1, 6.2.5, 8.3.2, 9.5.1.2, 10.1.4
Claims Subject to Arbitration	4.3.2, 4.4.4, 4.5.1
Cleaning Up	**3.15**, 6.3
Commencement of Statutory Limitation Period	**13.7**
Commencement of the Work, Conditions Relating to	2.1.2, 2.2.1, 3.2.1, 3.2.2, 3.7.1, 3.10.1, 3.12.6, 4.3.7, 5.2.1, 6.2.2, 8.1.2, 8.2.2, 9.2, 11.1.3, 11.3.6, 11.4.1
Commencement of the Work, Definition of	8.1.2
Communications Facilitating Contract Administration	3.9.1, 4.2.4, 5.2.1
Completion, Conditions Relating to	3.11, 3.15, 4.2.2, 4.2.9, 4.3.2, 9.4.2, 9.8, 9.9.1, 9.10, 11.3.5, 12.2.2, 13.7
COMPLETION, PAYMENTS AND	**9**
Completion, Substantial	4.2.9, 4.3.5.2, 8.1.1, 8.1.3, 8.2.3, 9.8, 9.9.1, 12.2.2, 13.7
Compliance with Laws	1.3, 3.6, 3.7, 3.13, 4.1.1, 10.2.2, 11.1, 11.3, 13.1, 13.5.1, 13.5.2, 13.6, 14.1.1, 14.2.1.3
Concealed or Unknown Conditions	4.3.6
Conditions of the Contract	1.1.1, 1.1.7, 6.1.1
Consent, Written	1.3.1, 3.12.8, 3.14.2, 4.1.2, 4.3.4, 4.5.5, 9.3.2, 9.8.2, 9.9.1, 9.10.2, 9.10.3, 10.1.2, 10.1.3, 11.3.1, 11.3.1.4, 11.3.11, 13.2, 13.4.2
CONSTRUCTION BY OWNER OR BY SEPARATE CONTRACTORS	**1.1.4, 6**
Construction Change Directive, Definition of	7.3.1
Construction Change Directives	1.1.1, 4.2.8, 7.1, **7.3**, 9.3.1.1
Construction Schedules, Contractor's	3.10, 6.1.3
Contingent Assignment of Subcontracts	**5.4**
Continuing Contract Performance	**4.3.4**
Contract, Definition of	1.1.2
CONTRACT, TERMINATION OR SUSPENSION OF THE	4.3.7, 5.4.1.1, **14**
Contract Administration	3.3.3, 4, 9.4, 9.5
Contract Award and Execution, Conditions Relating to	3.7.1, 3.10, 5.2, 9.2, 11.1.3, 11.3.6, 11.4.1
Contract Documents, The	**1.1**, 1.2; 7
Contract Documents, Copies Furnished and Use of	1.3, 2.2.5, 5.3
Contract Documents, Definition of	1.1.1
Contract Performance During Arbitration	4.3.4, 4.5.3
Contract Sum	3.8, 4.3.6, 4.3.7, 4.4.4, 5.2.3, 6.1.3, 7.2, 7.3, **9.1**, 9.7, 11.3.1, 12.2.4, 12.3, 14.2.4
Contract Sum, **Definition** of	**9.1**
Contract Time	4.3.6, 4.3.8, 4.4.4, 7.2.1.3, 7.3, 8.2.1, 8.3.1, 9.7, 12.1.1
Contract Time, **Definition** of	**8.1.1**

CONTRACTOR **3**	**Emergencies** 4.3.7, **10.3**
Contractor, **Definition** of **3.1**, 6.1.2	Employees, Contractor's 3.3.2, 3.4.2, 3.8.1, 3.9, 3.18.1,
Contractor's Bid 1.1.1	3.18.2, 4.2.3, 4.2.6, 8.1.2, 10.2, 10.3, 11.1.1, 14.2.1.1
Contractor's Construction Schedules **3.10**, 6.1.3	Equipment, Labor, Materials and 1.1.3, 1.1.6, 3.4, 3.5.1,
Contractor's Employees 3.3.2, 3.4.2, 3.8.1, 3.9, 3.18, 4.2.3,	3.8.2, 3.12.3, 3.12.7, 3.12.11, 3.13, 3.15.1, 4.2.7,
4.2.6, 8.1.2, 10.2, 10.3, 11.1.1, 14.2.1.1	6.2.1, 7.3.6, 9.3.2, 9.3.3, 11.3, 12.2.4, 14
Contractor's Liability Insurance **11.1**	Execution and Progress of the Work 1.1.3, 1.2.3, 3.2, 3.4.1,
Contractor's Relationship with Separate Contractors	3.5.1, 4.2.2, 4.2.3, 4.3.4, 4.3.8, 6.2.2, 7.1.3,
and Owner's Forces 2.2.6, 3.12.5, 3.14.2, 4.2.4, 6, 12.2.5	7.3.9, 8.2, 8.3, 9.5, 9.9.1, 10.2, 14.2, 14.3
Contractor's Relationship with Subcontractors 1.2.4, 3.3.2,	**Execution, Correlation and Intent** of the
3.18.1, 3.18.2, 5.2, 5.3, 5.4, 9.6.2, 11.3.7, 11.3.8, 14.2.1.2	Contract Documents **1.2**, 3.7.1
Contractor's Relationship with the Architect 1.1.2, 3.2.1, 3.2.2,	Extensions of Time 4.3.1, 4.3.8, 7.2.1.3, 8.3, 10.3.1
3.3.3, 3.5.1, 3.7.3, 3.11, 3.12.8 3.16, 3.18, 4.2.3, 4.2.4, 4.2.6,	Failure of Payment by Contractor 9.5.1.3, 14.2.1.2
4.2.12, 5.2, 6.2.2, 7.3.4, 9.8.2, 11.3.7, 12.1, 13.5	Failure of Payment by Owner 4.3.7, 9.7, 14.1.3
Contractor's Representations .. 1.2.2, 3.5.1, 3.12.7, 6.2.2, 8.2.1, 9.3.3	Faulty Work (See Defective or Nonconforming Work)
Contractor's Responsibility for Those	**Final Completion and Final Payment** 4.2.1, 4.2.9, 4.3.2,
Performing the Work 3.3.2, 3.18, 4.2.3, 10	4.3.5, **9.10**, 11.1.2, 11.1.3, 11.3.5, 12.3.1, 13.7
Contractor's Review of Contract Documents 1.2.2, 3.2, 3.7.3	Financial Arrangements, Owner's 2.2.1
Contractor's Right to Stop the Work 9.7	Fire and Extended Coverage Insurance 11.3
Contractor's Right to Terminate the Contract 14.1	**GENERAL PROVISIONS** **1**
Contractor's Submittals 3.10, 3.11, 3.12, 4.2.7, 5.2.1, 5.2.3,	**Governing Law** **13.1**
7.3.6, 9.2, 9.3.1, 9.8.2, 9.9.1, 9.10.2,	Guarantees (See Warranty and Warranties)
9.10.3, 10.1.2, 11.4.2, 11.4.3	Hazardous Materials 10.1, 10.2.4
Contractor's Superintendent 3.9, 10.2.6	Identification of Contract Documents 1.2.1
Contractor's Supervision and Construction Procedures 1.2.4,	Identification of Subcontractors and Suppliers 5.2.1
3.3, 3.4, 4.2.3, 8.2.2, 8.2.3, 10	**Indemnification** 3.17, **3.18**, 9.10.2, 10.1.4, 11.3.1.2, 11.3.7
Contractual Liability Insurance 11.1.1.7, 11.2.1	**Information and Services Required of the Owner** 2.1.2, **2.2**,
Coordination and Correlation 1.2.2, 1.2.4, 3.3.1,	4.3.4, 6.1.3, 6.1.4, 6.2.6, 9.3.2, 9.6.1, 9.6.4, 9.8.3, 9.9.2,
3.10, 3.12.7, 6.1.3, 6.2.1	9.10.3, 10.1.4, 11.2, 11.3, 13.5.1, 13.5.2
Copies Furnished of Drawings and Specifications ... 1.3, 2.2.5, 3.11	**Injury or Damage to Person or Property** **4.3.9**
Correction of Work 2.3, 2.4, 4.2.1, 9.8.2,	Inspections 3.3.3, 3.3.4, 3.7.1, 4.2.2,
9.9.1, 12.1.2, 12.2, 13.7.1.3	4.2.6, 4.2.9, 9.4.2, 9.8.2, 9.9.2, 9.10.1, 13.5
Cost, Definition of 7.3.6, 14.3.5	Instructions to Bidders 1.1.1
Costs 2.4, 3.2.1, 3.7.4, 3.8.2, 3.15.2, 4.3.6, 4.3.7, 4.3.8.1, 5.2.3,	Instructions to the Contractor 3.8.1, 4.2.8, 5.2.1, 7, 12.1, 13.5.2
6.1.1, 6.2.3, 6.3, 7.3.3.3, 7.3.6, 7.3.7, 9.7, 9.8.2, 9.10.2, 11.3.1.2,	Insurance 4.3.9, 6.1.1, 7.3.6.4, 9.3.2, 9.8.2, 9.9.1, 9.10.2, 11
11.3.1.3, 11.3.4, 11.3.9, 12.1, 12.2.1, 12.2.4, 12.2.5, 13.5, 14	**Insurance, Boiler and Machinery** **11.3.2**
Cutting and Patching **3.14**, 6.2.6	**Insurance, Contractor's Liability** **11.1**
Damage to Construction of Owner or Separate Contractors 3.14.2,	Insurance, Effective Date of 8.2.2, 11.1.2
6.2.4, 9.5.1.5, 10.2.1.2, 10.2.5, 10.3, 11.1, 11.3, 12.2.5	**Insurance, Loss of Use** 11.3.3
Damage to the Work 3.14.2, 9.9.1, 10.2.1.2, 10.2.5, 10.3, 11.3	**Insurance, Owner's Liability** **11.2**
Damages, Claims for .. 3.18, 4.3.9, 6.1.1, 6.2.5, 8.3.2, 9.5.1.2, 10.1.4	**Insurance, Property** 10.2.5, **11.3**
Damages for Delay 6.1.1, 8.3.3, 9.5.1.6, 9.7	Insurance, Stored Materials 9.3.2, 11.3.1.4
Date of Commencement of the Work, Definition of 8.1.2	**INSURANCE AND BONDS** **11**
Date of Substantial Completion, Definition of 8.1.3	Insurance Companies, Consent to Partial Occupancy .. 9.9.1, 11.3.11
Day, Definition of 8.1.4	Insurance Companies, Settlement with 11.3.10
Decisions of the Architect 4.2.6, 4.2.7, 4.2.11, 4.2.12, 4.2.13,	Intent of the Contract Documents 1.2.3, 3.12.4,
4.3.2, 4.3.6, 4.4.1, 4.4.4, 4.5, 6.3, 7.3.6, 7.3.8, 8.1.3, 8.3.1, 9.2,	4.2.6, 4.2.7, 4.2.12, 4.2.13, 7.4
9.4, 9.5.1, 9.8.2, 9.9.1, 10.1.2, 13.5.2, 14.2.2, 14.2.4	**Interest** **13.6**
Decisions to Withhold Certification **9.5**, 9.7, 14.1.1.3	**Interpretation** 1.2.5, 1.4, **1.5**, 4.1.1, 5.1, 6.1.2, 8.1.4
Defective or Nonconforming Work, Acceptance,	Interpretations, Written 4.2.11, 4.2.12, 4.3.7
Rejection and Correction of 2.3, 2.4, 3.5.1, 4.2.1,	Joinder and Consolidation of Claims Required 4.5.6
4.2.6, 4.3.5, 9.5.2, 9.8.2, 9.9.1, 10.2.5, 12, 13.7.1.3	**Judgment on Final Award** 4.5.1, 4.5.4.1, **4.5.7**
Defective Work, Definition of 3.5.1	**Labor and Materials,** Equipment 1.1.3, 1.1.6, **3.4**, 3.5.1, 3.8.2,
Definitions 1.1, 2.1.1, 3.1, 3.5.1, 3.12.1, 3.12.2, 3.12.3, 4.1.1,	3.12.2, 3.12.3, 3.12.7, 3.12.11, 3.13, 3.15.1,
4.3.1, 5.1, 6.1.2, 7.2.1, 7.3.1, 7.3.6, 8.1, 9.1, 9.8.1	4.2.7, 6.2.1, 7.3.6, 9.3.2, 9.3.3, 12.2.4, 14
Delays and Extensions of Time 4.3.1, 4.3.8.1, 4.3.8.2,	Labor Disputes 8.3.1
6.1.1, 6.2.3, 7.2.1, 7.3.1, 7.3.4, 7.3.5, 7.3.8,	Laws and Regulations 1.3, 3.6, 3.7, 3.13, 4.1.1, 4.5.5, 4.5.7,
7.3.9, 8.1.1, **8.3**, 10.3.1, 14.1.1.4	9.9.1, 10.2.2, 11.1, 11.3, 13.1, 13.4, 13.5.1, 13.5.2, 13.6
Disputes 4.1.4, 4.3, 4.4, 4.5, 6.2.5, 6.3, 7.3.8, 9.3.1.2	Liens 2.1.2, 4.3.2, 4.3.5.1, 8.2.2, 9.3.3, 9.10.2
Documents and Samples at the Site 3.11	**Limitation on Consolidation or Joinder** **4.5.5**
Drawings, Definition of 1.1.5	Limitations, Statutes of 4.5.4.2, 12.2.6, 13.7
Drawings and Specifications, Use and Ownership of 1.1.1, 1.3,	Limitations of Authority 3.3.1, 4.1.2, 4.2.1,
2.2.5, 3.11, 5.3	4.2.3, 4.2.7, 4.2.10, 5.2.2, 5.2.4, 7.4, 11.3.10
Duty to Review Contract Documents and Field Conditions 3.2	
Effective Date of Insurance 8.2.2, 11.1.2	

234 / Appendix D

Limitations of Liability	2.3, 3.2.1, 3.5.1, 3.7.3, 3.12.8, 3.12.11, 3.17, 3.18, 4.2.6, 4.2.7, 4.2.12, 6.2.2, 9.4.2, 9.6.4, 9.10.4, 10.1.4, 10.2.5, 11.1.2, 11.2.1, 11.3.7, 13.4.2, 13.5.2
Limitations of Time, General	2.2.1, 2.2.4, 3.2.1, 3.7.3, 3.8.2, 3.10, 3.12.5, 3.15.1, 4.2.1, 4.2.7, 4.2.11, 4.3.2, 4.3.3, 4.3.4, 4.3.6, 4.3.9, 4.5.4.2, 5.2.1, 5.2.3, 6.2.4, 7.3.4, 7.4, 8.2, 9.5, 9.6.2, 9.8, 9.9, 9.10, 11.1.3, 11.3.1, 11.3.2, 11.3.5, 11.3.6, 12.2.1, 12.2.2, 13.5, 13.7
Limitations of Time, Specific	2.1.2, 2.2.1, 2.4, 3.10, 3.11, 3.15.1, 4.2.1, 4.2.11, 4.3, 4.4, 4.5, 5.3, 5.4, 7.3.5, 7.3.9, 8.2, 9.2, 9.3.1, 9.3.3, 9.4.1, 9.6.1, 9.7, 9.8.2, 9.10.2, 11.1.3, 11.3.6, 11.3.10, 11.3.11, 12.2.2, 12.2.6, 13.7, 14
Loss of Use Insurance	**11.3.3**
Material Suppliers	1.3.1, 3.12.1, 4.2.4, 4.2.6, 5.2.1, 9.3.1, 9.3.1.2, 9.3.3, 9.4.2, 9.6.5, 9.10.4
Materials, Hazardous	10.1, 10.2.4
Materials, Labor, Equipment and	1.1.3, 1.1.6, 3.4, 3.5.1, 3.8.2, 3.12.2, 3.12.3, 3.12.7, 3.12.11, 3.13, 3.15.1, 4.2.7, 6.2.1, 7.3.6, 9.3.2, 9.3.3, 12.2.4, 14
Means, Methods, Techniques, Sequences and Procedures of Construction	3.3.1, 4.2.3, 4.2.7, 9.4.2
Minor Changes in the Work	1.1.1, 4.2.8, 4.3.7, 7.1, **7.4**
MISCELLANEOUS PROVISIONS	**13**
Modifications, Definition of	1.1.1
Modifications to the Contract	1.1.1, 1.1.2, 3.7.3, 3.11, 4.1.2, 4.2.1, 5.2.3, 7, 8.3.1, 9.7
Mutual Responsibility	**6.2**
Nonconforming Work, Acceptance of	**12.3**
Nonconforming Work, Rejection and Correction of	2.3.1, 4.3.5, 9.5.2, 9.8.2, 12, 13.7.1.3
Notice	2.3, 2.4, 3.2.1, 3.2.2, 3.7.3, 3.7.4, 3.9, 3.12.8, 3.12.9, 3.17, 4.3, 4.4.4, 4.5, 5.2.1, 5.3, 5.4.1.1, 8.2.2, 9.4.1, 9.5.1, 9.6.1, 9.7, 9.10, 10.1.2, 10.2.6, 11.1.3, 11.3, 12.2.2, 12.2.4, 13.3, 13.5.1, 13.5.2, 14
Notice, Written	2.3, 2.4, 3.9, 3.12.8, 3.12.9, 4.3, 4.4.4, 4.5, 5.2.1, 5.3, 5.4.1.1, 8.2.2, 9.4.1, 9.5.1, 9.7, 9.10, 10.1.2, 10.2.6, 11.1.3, 11.3, 12.2.2, 12.2.4, **13.3**, 13.5.2, 14
Notice of Testing and Inspections	13.5.1, 13.5.2
Notice to Proceed	8.2.2
Notices, Permits, Fees and	2.2.3, **3.7**, 3.13, 7.3.6.4, 10.2.2
Observations, Architect's On-Site	4.2.2, 4.2.5, 4.3.6, 9.5.1, 9.10.1, 13.5
Observations, Contractor's	1.2.2, 3.2.2
Occupancy	9.6.6, 9.8.1, 9.9, 11.3.11
On-Site Inspections by the Architect	4.2.2, 4.2.9, 4.3.6, 9.4.2, 9.8.2, 9.9.2, 9.10.1
On-Site Observations by the Architect	4.2.2, 4.2.5, 4.3.6, 9.4.2, 9.5.1, 9.10.1, 13.5
Orders, Written	2.3, 3.9, 4.3.7, 7, 8.2.2, 11.3.9, 12.1, 12.2, 13.5.2, 14.3.1
OWNER	**2**
Owner, **Definition** of	**2.1**
Owner, Information and Services Required of the	**2.1.2, 2.2**, 4.3.4, 6, 9, 10.1.4, 11.2, 11.3, 13.5.1, 14.1.1.5, 14.1.3
Owner's Authority	3.8.1, 4.1.3, 4.2.9, 5.2.1, 5.2.4, 5.4.1, 7.3.1, 8.2.2, 9.3.1, 9.3.2, 11.4.1, 12.2.4, 13.5.2, 14.2, 14.3.1
Owner's Financial Capability	2.2.1, 14.1.1.5
Owner's Liability Insurance	**11.2**
Owner's Loss of Use Insurance	11.3.3
Owner's Relationship with Subcontractors	1.1.2, 5.2.1, 5.4.1, 9.6.4
Owner's Right to Carry Out the Work	2.4, 12.2.4, 14.2.2.2
Owner's Right to Clean Up	**6.3**

Owner's Right to Perform Construction and to Award Separate Contracts	**6.1**
Owner's Right to Stop the Work	**2.3**, 4.3.7
Owner's Right to Suspend the Work	14.3
Owner's Right to Terminate the Contract	14.2
Ownership and Use of Architect's Drawings, Specifications and Other Documents	1.1.1, **1.3**, 2.2.5, 5.3
Partial Occupancy or Use	9.6.6, **9.9**, 11.3.11
Patching, Cutting and	**3.14**, 6.2.6
Patents, Royalties and	**3.17**
Payment, Applications for	4.2.5, 9.2, **9.3**, 9.4, 9.5.1, 9.8.3, 9.10.1, 9.10.3, 9.10.4, 14.2.4
Payment, Certificates for	4.2.5, 4.2.9, 9.3.3, **9.4**, 9.5, 9.6.1, 9.6.6, 9.7.1, 9.8.3, 9.10.1, 9.10.3, 13.7, 14.1.1.3, 14.2.4
Payment, Failure of	4.3.7, 9.5.1.3, **9.7**, 9.10.2, 14.1.1.3, 14.2.1.2
Payment, Final	4.2.1, 4.2.9, 4.3.2, 4.3.5, 9.10, 11.1.2, 11.1.3, 11.3.5, 12.3.1
Payment Bond, Performance Bond and	7.3.6.4, 9.10.3, 11.3.9, **11.4**
Payments, Progress	4.3.4, 9.3, 9.6, 9.8.3, 9.10.3, 13.6, 14.2.3
PAYMENTS AND COMPLETION	**9**, 14
Payments to Subcontractors	5.4.2, 9.5.1.3, 9.6.2, 9.6.3, 9.6.4, 11.3.8, 14.2.1.2
PCB	10.1
Performance Bond and Payment Bond	7.3.6.4, 9.10.3, 11.3.9, 11.4
Permits, Fees and Notices	2.2.3, **3.7**, 3.13, 7.3.6.4, 10.2.2
PERSONS AND PROPERTY, PROTECTION OF	**10**
Polychlorinated Biphenyl	10.1
Product Data, Definition of	3.12.2
Product Data and Samples, Shop Drawings	3.11, **3.12**, 4.2.7
Progress and Completion	4.2.2, 4.3.4, **8.2**
Progress Payments	4.3.4, 9.3, 9.6, 9.8.3, 9.10.3, 13.6, 14.2.3
Project, Definition of the	1.1.4
Project Manual, Definition of the	1.1.7
Project Manuals	2.2.5
Project Representatives	4.2.10
Property Insurance	10.2.5, **11.3**
PROTECTION OF PERSONS AND PROPERTY	**10**
Regulations and Laws	1.3, 3.6, 3.7, 3.13, 4.1.1, 4.5.5, 4.5.7, 10.2.2, 11.1, 11.3, 13.1, 13.4, 13.5.1, 13.5.2, 13.6, 14
Rejection of Work	3.5.1, 4.2.6, 12.2
Releases of Waivers and Liens	9.10.2
Representations	1.2.2, 3.5.1, 3.12.7, 6.2.2, 8.2.1, 9.3.3, 9.4.2, 9.5.1, 9.8.2, 9.10.1
Representatives	2.1.1, 3.1.1, 3.9, 4.1.1, 4.2.1, 4.2.10, 5.1.1, 5.1.2, 13.2.1
Resolution of Claims and Disputes	**4.4**, 4.5
Responsibility for Those Performing the Work	3.3.2, 4.2.3, 6.1.3, 6.2, 10
Retainage	9.3.1, 9.6.2, 9.8.3, 9.9.1, 9.10.2, 9.10.3
Review of Contract Documents and Field Conditions by Contractor	1.2.2, **3.2**, 3.7.3, 3.12.7
Review of Contractor's Submittals by Owner and Architect	3.10.1, 3.10.2, 3.11, 3.12, 4.2.7, 4.2.9, 5.2.1, 5.2.3, 9.2, 9.8.2
Review of Shop Drawings, Product Data and Samples by Contractor	3.12.5
Rights and Remedies	1.1.2, 2.3, 2.4, 3.5.1, 3.15.2, 4.2.6, 4.3.6, 4.5, 5.3, 6.1, 6.3, 7.3.1, 8.3.1, 9.5.1, 9.7, 10.2.5, 10.3, 12.2.2, 12.2.4, **13.4**, 14
Royalties and Patents	3.17

Rules and Notices for Arbitration	**4.5.2**	**Suspension by the Owner for Convenience**	**14.3**
Safety of Persons and Property	**10.2**	Suspension of the Work	4.3.7, 5.4.2, 14.1.1.4, 14.3
Safety Precautions and Programs	4.2.3, 4.2.7, **10.1**	Suspension or Termination of the Contract	4.3.7, 5.4.1.1, 14
Samples, Definition of	3.12.3	**Taxes**	**3.6**, 7.3.6.4
Samples, Shop Drawings, Product Data and	3.11, **3.12**, 4.2.7	**Termination by the Contractor**	**14.1**
Samples at the Site, Documents and	3.11	**Termination by the Owner for Cause**	5.4.1.1, **14.2**
Schedule of Values	**9.2**, 9.3.1	Termination of the Architect	4.1.3
Schedules, Construction	3.10	Termination of the Contractor	14.2.2
Separate Contracts and Contractors	1.1.4, 3.14.2, 4.2.4, 4.5.5, 6, 11.3.7, 12.1.2, 12.2.5	**TERMINATION OR SUSPENSION OF THE CONTRACT**	**14**
Shop Drawings, Definition of	3.12.1	Tests and Inspections	3.3.3, 4.2.6, 4.2.9, 9.4.2, 12.2.1, **13.5**
Shop Drawings, Product Data and Samples	3.11, **3.12**, 4.2.7	**TIME**	**8**
Site, Use of	**3.13**, 6.1.1, 6.2.1	Time, Delays and Extensions of	4.3.8, 7.2.1, **8.3**
Site Inspections	1.2.2, 3.3.4, 4.2.2, 4.2.9, 4.3.6, 9.8.2, 9.10.1, 13.5	Time Limits, Specific	2.1.2, 2.2.1, 2.4, 3.10, 3.11, 3.15.1, 4.2.1, 4.2.11, 4.3, 4.4, 4.5, 5.3, 5.4, 7.3.5, 7.3.9, 8.2, 9.2, 9.3.1, 9.3.3, 9.4.1, 9.6.1, 9.7, 9.8.2, 9.10.2, 11.1.3, 11.3.6, 11.3.10, 11.3.11, 12.2.2, 12.2.4, 12.2.6, 13.7, 14
Site Visits, Architect's	4.2.2, 4.2.5, 4.2.9, 4.3.6, 9.4.2, 9.5.1, 9.8.2, 9.9.2, 9.10.1, 13.5		
Special Inspections and Testing	4.2.6, 12.2.1, 13.5	Time Limits on Claims	4.3.2, **4.3.3**, 4.3.6, 4.3.9, 4.4, 4.5
Specifications, Definition of the	**1.1.6**	Title to Work	9.3.2, 9.3.3
Specifications, The	1.1.1, **1.1.6**, 1.1.7, 1.2.4, 1.3, 3.11	**UNCOVERING AND CORRECTION OF WORK**	**12**
Statutes of Limitations	4.5.4.2, 12.2.6, 13.7	**Uncovering of Work**	**12.1**
Stopping the Work	2.3, 4.3.7, 9.7, 10.1.2, 10.3, 14.1	Unforeseen Conditions	4.3.6, 8.3.1, 10.1
Stored Materials	6.2.1, 9.3.2, 10.2.1.2, 11.3.1.4, 12.2.4	Unit Prices	7.1.4, 7.3.3.2
Subcontractor, Definition of	5.1.1	Use of Documents	1.1.1, 1.3, 2.2.5, 3.12.7, 5.3
SUBCONTRACTORS	**5**	**Use of Site**	**3.13**, 6.1.1, 6.2.1
Subcontractors, Work by	1.2.4, 3.3.2, 3.12.1, 4.2.3, 5.3, 5.4	Values, Schedule of	**9.2**, 9.3.1
Subcontractual Relations	**5.3**, 5.4, 9.3.1.2, 9.6.2, 9.6.3, 9.6.4, 10.2.1, 11.3.7, 11.3.8, 14.1.1, 14.2.1.2, 14.3.2	Waiver of Claims: Final Payment	4.3.5, 4.5.1, 9.10.3
Submittals	1.3, 3.2.3, 3.10, 3.11, 3.12, 4.2.7, 5.2.1, 5.2.3, 7.3.6, 9.2, 9.3.1, 9.8.2, 9.9.1, 9.10.2, 9.10.3, 10.1.2, 11.1.3	Waiver of Claims by the Architect	13.4.2
		Waiver of Claims by the Contractor	9.10.4, 11.3.7, 13.4.2
Subrogation, Waivers of	6.1.1, 11.3.5, **11.3.7**	Waiver of Claims by the Owner	4.3.5, 4.5.1, 9.9.3, 9.10.3, 11.3.3, 11.3.5, 11.3.7, 13.4.2
Substantial Completion	4.2.9, 4.3.5.2, 8.1.1, 8.1.3, 8.2.3, **9.8**, 9.9.1, 12.2.1, 12.2.2, 13.7	Waiver of Liens	9.10.2
Substantial Completion, Definition of	9.8.1	Waivers of Subrogation	6.1.1, 11.3.5, 11.3.7
Substitution of Subcontractors	5.2.3, 5.2.4	**Warranty** and Warranties	**3.5**, 4.2.9, 4.3.5.3, 9.3.3, 9.8.2, 9.9.1, 12.2.2, 13.7.1.3
Substitution of the Architect	4.1.3	Weather Delays	4.3.8.2
Substitutions of Materials	3.5.1	**When Arbitration May Be Demanded**	**4.5.4**
Sub-subcontractor, Definition of	5.1.2	Work, Definition of	1.1.3
Subsurface Conditions	4.3.6	Written Consent	1.3.1, 3.12.8, 3.14.2, 4.1.2, 4.3.4, 4.5.5, 9.3.2, 9.8.2, 9.9.1, 9.10.2, 9.10.3, 10.1.2, 10.1.3, 11.3.1, 11.3.1.4, 11.3.11, 13.2, 13.4.2
Successors and Assigns	13.2		
Superintendent	3.9, 10.2.6		
Supervision and Construction Procedures	1.2.4, **3.3**, 3.4, 4.2.3, 4.3.4, 6.1.3, 6.2.4, 7.1.3, 7.3.4, 8.2, 8.3.1, 10, 12, 14	Written Interpretations	4.2.11, 4.2.12, 4.3.7
		Written Notice	2.3, 2.4, 3.9, 3.12.8, 3.12.9, 4.3, 4.4.4, 4.5, 5.2.1, 5.3, 5.4.1.1, 8.2.2, 9.4.1, 9.5.1, 9.7, 9.10, 10.1.2, 10.2.6, 11.1.3, 11.3, 12.2.2, 12.2.4, **13.3**, 13.5.2, 14
Surety	4.4.1, 4.4.4, 5.4.1.2, 9.10.2, 9.10.3, 14.2.2		
Surety, Consent of	9.9.1, 9.10.2, 9.10.3	Written Orders	2.3, 3.9, 4.3.7, 7, 8.2.2, 11.3.9, 12.1, 12.2, 13.5.2, 14.3.1
Surveys	2.2.2, 3.18.3		

GENERAL CONDITIONS OF THE CONTRACT FOR CONSTRUCTION

ARTICLE 1
GENERAL PROVISIONS

1.1 BASIC DEFINITIONS

1.1.1 THE CONTRACT DOCUMENTS

The Contract Documents consist of the Agreement between Owner and Contractor (hereinafter the Agreement), Conditions of the Contract (General, Supplementary and other Conditions), Drawings, Specifications, addenda issued prior to execution of the Contract, other documents listed in the Agreement and Modifications issued after execution of the Contract. A Modification is (1) a written amendment to the Contract signed by both parties, (2) a Change Order, (3) a Construction Change Directive or (4) a written order for a minor change in the Work issued by the Architect. Unless specifically enumerated in the Agreement, the Contract Documents do not include other documents such as bidding requirements (advertisement or invitation to bid, Instructions to Bidders, sample forms, the Contractor's bid or portions of addenda relating to bidding requirements).

1.1.2 THE CONTRACT

The Contract Documents form the Contract for Construction. The Contract represents the entire and integrated agreement between the parties hereto and supersedes prior negotiations, representations or agreements, either written or oral. The Contract may be amended or modified only by a Modification. The Contract Documents shall not be construed to create a contractual relationship of any kind (1) between the Architect and Contractor, (2) between the Owner and a Subcontractor or Sub-subcontractor or (3) between any persons or entities other than the Owner and Contractor. The Architect shall, however, be entitled to performance and enforcement of obligations under the Contract intended to facilitate performance of the Architect's duties.

1.1.3 THE WORK

The term "Work" means the construction and services required by the Contract Documents, whether completed or partially completed, and includes all other labor, materials, equipment and services provided or to be provided by the Contractor to fulfill the Contractor's obligations. The Work may constitute the whole or a part of the Project.

1.1.4 THE PROJECT

The Project is the total construction of which the Work performed under the Contract Documents may be the whole or a part and which may include construction by the Owner or by separate contractors.

1.1.5 THE DRAWINGS

The Drawings are the graphic and pictorial portions of the Contract Documents, wherever located and whenever issued, showing the design, location and dimensions of the Work, generally including plans, elevations, sections, details, schedules and diagrams.

1.1.6 THE SPECIFICATIONS

The Specifications are that portion of the Contract Documents consisting of the written requirements for materials, equipment, construction systems, standards and workmanship for the Work, and performance of related services.

1.1.7 THE PROJECT MANUAL

The Project Manual is the volume usually assembled for the Work which may include the bidding requirements, sample forms, Conditions of the Contract and Specifications.

1.2 EXECUTION, CORRELATION AND INTENT

1.2.1 The Contract Documents shall be signed by the Owner and Contractor as provided in the Agreement. If either the Owner or Contractor or both do not sign all the Contract Documents, the Architect shall identify such unsigned Documents upon request.

1.2.2 Execution of the Contract by the Contractor is a representation that the Contractor has visited the site, become familiar with local conditions under which the Work is to be performed and correlated personal observations with requirements of the Contract Documents.

1.2.3 The intent of the Contract Documents is to include all items necessary for the proper execution and completion of the Work by the Contractor. The Contract Documents are complementary, and what is required by one shall be as binding as if required by all; performance by the Contractor shall be required only to the extent consistent with the Contract Documents and reasonably inferable from them as being necessary to produce the intended results.

1.2.4 Organization of the Specifications into divisions, sections and articles, and arrangement of Drawings shall not control the Contractor in dividing the Work among Subcontractors or in establishing the extent of Work to be performed by any trade.

1.2.5 Unless otherwise stated in the Contract Documents, words which have well-known technical or construction industry meanings are used in the Contract Documents in accordance with such recognized meanings.

1.3 OWNERSHIP AND USE OF ARCHITECT'S DRAWINGS, SPECIFICATIONS AND OTHER DOCUMENTS

1.3.1 The Drawings, Specifications and other documents prepared by the Architect are instruments of the Architect's service through which the Work to be executed by the Contractor is described. The Contractor may retain one contract record set. Neither the Contractor nor any Subcontractor, Sub-subcontractor or material or equipment supplier shall own or claim a copyright in the Drawings, Specifications and other documents prepared by the Architect, and unless otherwise indicated the Architect shall be deemed the author of them and will retain all common law, statutory and other reserved rights, in addition to the copyright. All copies of them, except the Contractor's record set, shall be returned or suitably accounted for to the Architect, on request, upon completion of the Work. The Drawings, Specifications and other documents prepared by the Architect, and copies thereof furnished to the Contractor, are for use solely with respect to this Project. They are not to be used by the Contractor or any Subcontractor, Sub-subcontractor or material or equipment supplier on other projects or for additions to this Project outside the scope of the

Work without the specific written consent of the Owner and Architect. The Contractor, Subcontractors, Sub-subcontractors and material or equipment suppliers are granted a limited license to use and reproduce applicable portions of the Drawings, Specifications and other documents prepared by the Architect appropriate to and for use in the execution of their Work under the Contract Documents. All copies made under this license shall bear the statutory copyright notice, if any, shown on the Drawings, Specifications and other documents prepared by the Architect. Submittal or distribution to meet official regulatory requirements or for other purposes in connection with this Project is not to be construed as publication in derogation of the Architect's copyright or other reserved rights.

1.4 CAPITALIZATION

1.4.1 Terms capitalized in these General Conditions include those which are (1) specifically defined, (2) the titles of numbered articles and identified references to Paragraphs, Subparagraphs and Clauses in the document or (3) the titles of other documents published by the American Institute of Architects.

1.5 INTERPRETATION

1.5.1 In the interest of brevity the Contract Documents frequently omit modifying words such as "all" and "any" and articles such as "the" and "an," but the fact that a modifier or an article is absent from one statement and appears in another is not intended to affect the interpretation of either statement.

ARTICLE 2

OWNER

2.1 DEFINITION

2.1.1 The Owner is the person or entity identified as such in the Agreement and is referred to throughout the Contract Documents as if singular in number. The term "Owner" means the Owner or the Owner's authorized representative.

2.1.2 The Owner upon reasonable written request shall furnish to the Contractor in writing information which is necessary and relevant for the Contractor to evaluate, give notice of or enforce mechanic's lien rights. Such information shall include a correct statement of the record legal title to the property on which the Project is located, usually referred to as the site, and the Owner's interest therein at the time of execution of the Agreement and, within five days after any change, information of such change in title, recorded or unrecorded.

2.2 INFORMATION AND SERVICES REQUIRED OF THE OWNER

2.2.1 The Owner shall, at the request of the Contractor, prior to execution of the Agreement and promptly from time to time thereafter, furnish to the Contractor reasonable evidence that financial arrangements have been made to fulfill the Owner's obligations under the Contract. *[Note: Unless such reasonable evidence were furnished on request prior to the execution of the Agreement, the prospective contractor would not be required to execute the Agreement or to commence the Work.]*

2.2.2 The Owner shall furnish surveys describing physical characteristics, legal limitations and utility locations for the site of the Project, and a legal description of the site.

2.2.3 Except for permits and fees which are the responsibility of the Contractor under the Contract Documents, the Owner shall secure and pay for necessary approvals, easements, assessments and charges required for construction, use or occupancy of permanent structures or for permanent changes in existing facilities.

2.2.4 Information or services under the Owner's control shall be furnished by the Owner with reasonable promptness to avoid delay in orderly progress of the Work.

2.2.5 Unless otherwise provided in the Contract Documents, the Contractor will be furnished, free of charge, such copies of Drawings and Project Manuals as are reasonably necessary for execution of the Work.

2.2.6 The foregoing are in addition to other duties and responsibilities of the Owner enumerated herein and especially those in respect to Article 6 (Construction by Owner or by Separate Contractors), Article 9 (Payments and Completion) and Article 11 (Insurance and Bonds).

2.3 OWNER'S RIGHT TO STOP THE WORK

2.3.1 If the Contractor fails to correct Work which is not in accordance with the requirements of the Contract Documents as required by Paragraph 12.2 or persistently fails to carry out Work in accordance with the Contract Documents, the Owner, by written order signed personally or by an agent specifically so empowered by the Owner in writing, may order the Contractor to stop the Work, or any portion thereof, until the cause for such order has been eliminated; however, the right of the Owner to stop the Work shall not give rise to a duty on the part of the Owner to exercise this right for the benefit of the Contractor or any other person or entity, except to the extent required by Subparagraph 6.1.3.

2.4 OWNER'S RIGHT TO CARRY OUT THE WORK

2.4.1 If the Contractor defaults or neglects to carry out the Work in accordance with the Contract Documents and fails within a seven-day period after receipt of written notice from the Owner to commence and continue correction of such default or neglect with diligence and promptness, the Owner may after such seven-day period give the Contractor a second written notice to correct such deficiencies within a second seven-day period. If the Contractor within such second seven-day period after receipt of such second notice fails to commence and continue to correct any deficiencies, the Owner may without prejudice to other remedies the Owner may have, correct such deficiencies. In such case an appropriate Change Order shall be issued deducting from payments then or thereafter due the Contractor the cost of correcting such deficiencies, including compensation for the Architect's additional services and expenses made necessary by such default, neglect or failure. Such action by the Owner and amounts charged to the Contractor are both subject to prior approval of the Architect. If payments then or thereafter due the Contractor are not sufficient to cover such amounts, the Contractor shall pay the difference to the Owner.

ARTICLE 3

CONTRACTOR

3.1 DEFINITION

3.1.1 The Contractor is the person or entity identified as such in the Agreement and is referred to throughout the Contract Documents as if singular in number. The term "Contractor" means the Contractor or the Contractor's authorized representative.

3.2 REVIEW OF CONTRACT DOCUMENTS AND FIELD CONDITIONS BY CONTRACTOR

3.2.1 The Contractor shall carefully study and compare the Contract Documents with each other and with information furnished by the Owner pursuant to Subparagraph 2.2.2 and shall at once report to the Architect errors, inconsistencies or omissions discovered. The Contractor shall not be liable to the Owner or Architect for damage resulting from errors, inconsistencies or omissions in the Contract Documents unless the Contractor recognized such error, inconsistency or omission and knowingly failed to report it to the Architect. If the Contractor performs any construction activity knowing it involves a recognized error, inconsistency or omission in the Contract Documents without such notice to the Architect, the Contractor shall assume appropriate responsibility for such performance and shall bear an appropriate amount of the attributable costs for correction.

3.2.2 The Contractor shall take field measurements and verify field conditions and shall carefully compare such field measurements and conditions and other information known to the Contractor with the Contract Documents before commencing activities. Errors, inconsistencies or omissions discovered shall be reported to the Architect at once.

3.2.3 The Contractor shall perform the Work in accordance with the Contract Documents and submittals approved pursuant to Paragraph 3.12.

3.3 SUPERVISION AND CONSTRUCTION PROCEDURES

3.3.1 The Contractor shall supervise and direct the Work, using the Contractor's best skill and attention. The Contractor shall be solely responsible for and have control over construction means, methods, techniques, sequences and procedures and for coordinating all portions of the Work under the Contract, unless Contract Documents give other specific instructions concerning these matters.

3.3.2 The Contractor shall be responsible to the Owner for acts and omissions of the Contractor's employees, Subcontractors and their agents and employees, and other persons performing portions of the Work under a contract with the Contractor.

3.3.3 The Contractor shall not be relieved of obligations to perform the Work in accordance with the Contract Documents either by activities or duties of the Architect in the Architect's administration of the Contract, or by tests, inspections or approvals required or performed by persons other than the Contractor.

3.3.4 The Contractor shall be responsible for inspection of portions of Work already performed under this Contract to determine that such portions are in proper condition to receive subsequent Work.

3.4 LABOR AND MATERIALS

3.4.1 Unless otherwise provided in the Contract Documents, the Contractor shall provide and pay for labor, materials, equipment, tools, construction equipment and machinery, water, heat, utilities, transportation, and other facilities and services necessary for proper execution and completion of the Work, whether temporary or permanent and whether or not incorporated or to be incorporated in the Work.

3.4.2 The Contractor shall enforce strict discipline and good order among the Contractor's employees and other persons carrying out the Contract. The Contractor shall not permit employment of unfit persons or persons not skilled in tasks assigned to them.

3.5 WARRANTY

3.5.1 The Contractor warrants to the Owner and Architect that materials and equipment furnished under the Contract will be of good quality and new unless otherwise required or permitted by the Contract Documents, that the Work will be free from defects not inherent in the quality required or permitted, and that the Work will conform with the requirements of the Contract Documents. Work not conforming to these requirements, including substitutions not properly approved and authorized, may be considered defective. The Contractor's warranty excludes remedy for damage or defect caused by abuse, modifications not executed by the Contractor, improper or insufficient maintenance, improper operation, or normal wear and tear under normal usage. If required by the Architect, the Contractor shall furnish satisfactory evidence as to the kind and quality of materials and equipment.

3.6 TAXES

3.6.1 The Contractor shall pay sales, consumer, use and similar taxes for the Work or portions thereof provided by the Contractor which are legally enacted when bids are received or negotiations concluded, whether or not yet effective or merely scheduled to go into effect.

3.7 PERMITS, FEES AND NOTICES

3.7.1 Unless otherwise provided in the Contract Documents, the Contractor shall secure and pay for the building permit and other permits and governmental fees, licenses and inspections necessary for proper execution and completion of the Work which are customarily secured after execution of the Contract and which are legally required when bids are received or negotiations concluded.

3.7.2 The Contractor shall comply with and give notices required by laws, ordinances, rules, regulations and lawful orders of public authorities bearing on performance of the Work.

3.7.3 It is not the Contractor's responsibility to ascertain that the Contract Documents are in accordance with applicable laws, statutes, ordinances, building codes, and rules and regulations. However, if the Contractor observes that portions of the Contract Documents are at variance therewith, the Contractor shall promptly notify the Architect and Owner in writing, and necessary changes shall be accomplished by appropriate Modification.

3.7.4 If the Contractor performs Work knowing it to be contrary to laws, statutes, ordinances, building codes, and rules and regulations without such notice to the Architect and Owner, the Contractor shall assume full responsibility for such Work and shall bear the attributable costs.

3.8 ALLOWANCES

3.8.1 The Contractor shall include in the Contract Sum all allowances stated in the Contract Documents. Items covered by allowances shall be supplied for such amounts and by such persons or entities as the Owner may direct, but the Contractor shall not be required to employ persons or entities against which the Contractor makes reasonable objection.

3.8.2 Unless otherwise provided in the Contract Documents:

.1 materials and equipment under an allowance shall be selected promptly by the Owner to avoid delay in the Work;

.2 allowances shall cover the cost to the Contractor of materials and equipment delivered at the site and all required taxes, less applicable trade discounts;

.3 Contractor's costs for unloading and handling at the site, labor, installation costs, overhead, profit and other expenses contemplated for stated allowance amounts shall be included in the Contract Sum and not in the allowances;

.4 whenever costs are more than or less than allowances, the Contract Sum shall be adjusted accordingly by Change Order. The amount of the Change Order shall reflect (1) the difference between actual costs and the allowances under Clause 3.8.2.2 and (2) changes in Contractor's costs under Clause 3.8.2.3.

3.9 SUPERINTENDENT

3.9.1 The Contractor shall employ a competent superintendent and necessary assistants who shall be in attendance at the Project site during performance of the Work. The superintendent shall represent the Contractor, and communications given to the superintendent shall be as binding as if given to the Contractor. Important communications shall be confirmed in writing. Other communications shall be similarly confirmed on written request in each case.

3.10 CONTRACTOR'S CONSTRUCTION SCHEDULES

3.10.1 The Contractor, promptly after being awarded the Contract, shall prepare and submit for the Owner's and Architect's information a Contractor's construction schedule for the Work. The schedule shall not exceed time limits current under the Contract Documents, shall be revised at appropriate intervals as required by the conditions of the Work and Project, shall be related to the entire Project to the extent required by the Contract Documents, and shall provide for expeditious and practicable execution of the Work.

3.10.2 The Contractor shall prepare and keep current, for the Architect's approval, a schedule of submittals which is coordinated with the Contractor's construction schedule and allows the Architect reasonable time to review submittals.

3.10.3 The Contractor shall conform to the most recent schedules.

3.11 DOCUMENTS AND SAMPLES AT THE SITE

3.11.1 The Contractor shall maintain at the site for the Owner one record copy of the Drawings, Specifications, addenda, Change Orders and other Modifications, in good order and marked currently to record changes and selections made during construction, and in addition approved Shop Drawings, Product Data, Samples and similar required submittals. These shall be available to the Architect and shall be delivered to the Architect for submittal to the Owner upon completion of the Work.

3.12 SHOP DRAWINGS, PRODUCT DATA AND SAMPLES

3.12.1 Shop Drawings are drawings, diagrams, schedules and other data specially prepared for the Work by the Contractor or a Subcontractor, Sub-subcontractor, manufacturer, supplier or distributor to illustrate some portion of the Work.

3.12.2 Product Data are illustrations, standard schedules, performance charts, instructions, brochures, diagrams and other information furnished by the Contractor to illustrate materials or equipment for some portion of the Work.

3.12.3 Samples are physical examples which illustrate materials, equipment or workmanship and establish standards by which the Work will be judged.

3.12.4 Shop Drawings, Product Data, Samples and similar submittals are not Contract Documents. The purpose of their submittal is to demonstrate for those portions of the Work for which submittals are required the way the Contractor proposes to conform to the information given and the design concept expressed in the Contract Documents. Review by the Architect is subject to the limitations of Subparagraph 4.2.7.

3.12.5 The Contractor shall review, approve and submit to the Architect Shop Drawings, Product Data, Samples and similar submittals required by the Contract Documents with reasonable promptness and in such sequence as to cause no delay in the Work or in the activities of the Owner or of separate contractors. Submittals made by the Contractor which are not required by the Contract Documents may be returned without action.

3.12.6 The Contractor shall perform no portion of the Work requiring submittal and review of Shop Drawings, Product Data, Samples or similar submittals until the respective submittal has been approved by the Architect. Such Work shall be in accordance with approved submittals.

3.12.7 By approving and submitting Shop Drawings, Product Data, Samples and similar submittals, the Contractor represents that the Contractor has determined and verified materials, field measurements and field construction criteria related thereto, or will do so, and has checked and coordinated the information contained within such submittals with the requirements of the Work and of the Contract Documents.

3.12.8 The Contractor shall not be relieved of responsibility for deviations from requirements of the Contract Documents by the Architect's approval of Shop Drawings, Product Data, Samples or similar submittals unless the Contractor has specifically informed the Architect in writing of such deviation at the time of submittal and the Architect has given written approval to the specific deviation. The Contractor shall not be relieved of responsibility for errors or omissions in Shop Drawings, Product Data, Samples or similar submittals by the Architect's approval thereof.

3.12.9 The Contractor shall direct specific attention, in writing or on resubmitted Shop Drawings, Product Data, Samples or similar submittals, to revisions other than those requested by the Architect on previous submittals.

3.12.10 Informational submittals upon which the Architect is not expected to take responsive action may be so identified in the Contract Documents.

3.12.11 When professional certification of performance criteria of materials, systems or equipment is required by the Contract Documents, the Architect shall be entitled to rely upon the accuracy and completeness of such calculations and certifications.

3.13 USE OF SITE

3.13.1 The Contractor shall confine operations at the site to areas permitted by law, ordinances, permits and the Contract Documents and shall not unreasonably encumber the site with materials or equipment.

3.14 CUTTING AND PATCHING

3.14.1 The Contractor shall be responsible for cutting, fitting or patching required to complete the Work or to make its parts fit together properly.

3.14.2 The Contractor shall not damage or endanger a portion of the Work or fully or partially completed construction of the Owner or separate contractors by cutting, patching or otherwise altering such construction, or by excavation. The Contractor shall not cut or otherwise alter such construction by the

Owner or a separate contractor except with written consent of the Owner and of such separate contractor; such consent shall not be unreasonably withheld. The Contractor shall not unreasonably withhold from the Owner or a separate contractor the Contractor's consent to cutting or otherwise altering the Work.

3.15 CLEANING UP

3.15.1 The Contractor shall keep the premises and surrounding area free from accumulation of waste materials or rubbish caused by operations under the Contract. At completion of the Work the Contractor shall remove from and about the Project waste materials, rubbish, the Contractor's tools, construction equipment, machinery and surplus materials.

3.15.2 If the Contractor fails to clean up as provided in the Contract Documents, the Owner may do so and the cost thereof shall be charged to the Contractor.

3.16 ACCESS TO WORK

3.16.1 The Contractor shall provide the Owner and Architect access to the Work in preparation and progress wherever located.

3.17 ROYALTIES AND PATENTS

3.17.1 The Contractor shall pay all royalties and license fees. The Contractor shall defend suits or claims for infringement of patent rights and shall hold the Owner and Architect harmless from loss on account thereof, but shall not be responsible for such defense or loss when a particular design, process or product of a particular manufacturer or manufacturers is required by the Contract Documents. However, if the Contractor has reason to believe that the required design, process or product is an infringement of a patent, the Contractor shall be responsible for such loss unless such information is promptly furnished to the Architect.

3.18 INDEMNIFICATION

3.18.1 To the fullest extent permitted by law, the Contractor shall indemnify and hold harmless the Owner, Architect, Architect's consultants, and agents and employees of any of them from and against claims, damages, losses and expenses, including but not limited to attorneys' fees, arising out of or resulting from performance of the Work, provided that such claim, damage, loss or expense is attributable to bodily injury, sickness, disease or death, or to injury to or destruction of tangible property (other than the Work itself) including loss of use resulting therefrom, but only to the extent caused in whole or in part by negligent acts or omissions of the Contractor, a Subcontractor, anyone directly or indirectly employed by them or anyone for whose acts they may be liable, regardless of whether or not such claim, damage, loss or expense is caused in part by a party indemnified hereunder. Such obligation shall not be construed to negate, abridge, or reduce other rights or obligations of indemnity which would otherwise exist as to a party or person described in this Paragraph 3.18.

3.18.2 In claims against any person or entity indemnified under this Paragraph 3.18 by an employee of the Contractor, a Subcontractor, anyone directly or indirectly employed by them or anyone for whose acts they may be liable, the indemnification obligation under this Paragraph 3.18 shall not be limited by a limitation on amount or type of damages, compensation or benefits payable by or for the Contractor or a Subcontractor under workers' or workmen's compensation acts, disability benefit acts or other employee benefit acts.

3.18.3 The obligations of the Contractor under this Paragraph 3.18 shall not extend to the liability of the Architect, the Architect's consultants, and agents and employees of any of them arising out of (1) the preparation or approval of maps, drawings, opinions, reports, surveys, Change Orders, designs or specifications, or (2) the giving of or the failure to give directions or instructions by the Architect, the Architect's consultants, and agents and employees of any of them provided such giving or failure to give is the primary cause of the injury or damage.

ARTICLE 4

ADMINISTRATION OF THE CONTRACT

4.1 ARCHITECT

4.1.1 The Architect is the person lawfully licensed to practice architecture or an entity lawfully practicing architecture identified as such in the Agreement and is referred to throughout the Contract Documents as if singular in number. The term "Architect" means the Architect or the Architect's authorized representative.

4.1.2 Duties, responsibilities and limitations of authority of the Architect as set forth in the Contract Documents shall not be restricted, modified or extended without written consent of the Owner, Contractor and Architect. Consent shall not be unreasonably withheld.

4.1.3 In case of termination of employment of the Architect, the Owner shall appoint an architect against whom the Contractor makes no reasonable objection and whose status under the Contract Documents shall be that of the former architect.

4.1.4 Disputes arising under Subparagraphs 4.1.2 and 4.1.3 shall be subject to arbitration.

4.2 ARCHITECT'S ADMINISTRATION OF THE CONTRACT

4.2.1 The Architect will provide administration of the Contract as described in the Contract Documents, and will be the Owner's representative (1) during construction, (2) until final payment is due and (3) with the Owner's concurrence, from time to time during the correction period described in Paragraph 12.2. The Architect will advise and consult with the Owner. The Architect will have authority to act on behalf of the Owner only to the extent provided in the Contract Documents, unless otherwise modified by written instrument in accordance with other provisions of the Contract.

4.2.2 The Architect will visit the site at intervals appropriate to the stage of construction to become generally familiar with the progress and quality of the completed Work and to determine in general if the Work is being performed in a manner indicating that the Work, when completed, will be in accordance with the Contract Documents. However, the Architect will not be required to make exhaustive or continuous on-site inspections to check quality or quantity of the Work. On the basis of on-site observations as an architect, the Architect will keep the Owner informed of progress of the Work, and will endeavor to guard the Owner against defects and deficiencies in the Work.

4.2.3 The Architect will not have control over or charge of and will not be responsible for construction means, methods, techniques, sequences or procedures, or for safety precautions and programs in connection with the Work, since these are solely the Contractor's responsibility as provided in Paragraph 3.3. The Architect will not be responsible for the Contractor's failure to carry out the Work in accordance with the Contract Documents. The Architect will not have control over or charge of and will not be responsible for acts or omissions of the Contractor, Subcontractors, or their agents or employees, or of any other persons performing portions of the Work.

4.2.4 Communications Facilitating Contract Administration. Except as otherwise provided in the Contract Documents or when direct communications have been specially authorized, the Owner and Contractor shall endeavor to communicate through the Architect. Communications by and with the Architect's consultants shall be through the Architect. Communications by and with Subcontractors and material suppliers shall be through the Contractor. Communications by and with separate contractors shall be through the Owner.

4.2.5 Based on the Architect's observations and evaluations of the Contractor's Applications for Payment, the Architect will review and certify the amounts due the Contractor and will issue Certificates for Payment in such amounts.

4.2.6 The Architect will have authority to reject Work which does not conform to the Contract Documents. Whenever the Architect considers it necessary or advisable for implementation of the intent of the Contract Documents, the Architect will have authority to require additional inspection or testing of the Work in accordance with Subparagraphs 13.5.2 and 13.5.3, whether or not such Work is fabricated, installed or completed. However, neither this authority of the Architect nor a decision made in good faith either to exercise or not to exercise such authority shall give rise to a duty or responsibility of the Architect to the Contractor, Subcontractors, material and equipment suppliers, their agents or employees, or other persons performing portions of the Work.

4.2.7 The Architect will review and approve or take other appropriate action upon the Contractor's submittals such as Shop Drawings, Product Data and Samples, but only for the limited purpose of checking for conformance with information given and the design concept expressed in the Contract Documents. The Architect's action will be taken with such reasonable promptness as to cause no delay in the Work or in the activities of the Owner, Contractor or separate contractors, while allowing sufficient time in the Architect's professional judgment to permit adequate review. Review of such submittals is not conducted for the purpose of determining the accuracy and completeness of other details such as dimensions and quantities, or for substantiating instructions for installation or performance of equipment or systems, all of which remain the responsibility of the Contractor as required by the Contract Documents. The Architect's review of the Contractor's submittals shall not relieve the Contractor of the obligations under Paragraphs 3.3, 3.5 and 3.12. The Architect's review shall not constitute approval of safety precautions or, unless otherwise specifically stated by the Architect, of any construction means, methods, techniques, sequences or procedures. The Architect's approval of a specific item shall not indicate approval of an assembly of which the item is a component.

4.2.8 The Architect will prepare Change Orders and Construction Change Directives, and may authorize minor changes in the Work as provided in Paragraph 7.4.

4.2.9 The Architect will conduct inspections to determine the date or dates of Substantial Completion and the date of final completion, will receive and forward to the Owner for the Owner's review and records written warranties and related documents required by the Contract and assembled by the Contractor, and will issue a final Certificate for Payment upon compliance with the requirements of the Contract Documents.

4.2.10 If the Owner and Architect agree, the Architect will provide one or more project representatives to assist in carrying out the Architect's responsibilities at the site. The duties, responsibilities and limitations of authority of such project representatives shall be as set forth in an exhibit to be incorporated in the Contract Documents.

4.2.11 The Architect will interpret and decide matters concerning performance under and requirements of the Contract Documents on written request of either the Owner or Contractor. The Architect's response to such requests will be made with reasonable promptness and within any time limits agreed upon. If no agreement is made concerning the time within which interpretations required of the Architect shall be furnished in compliance with this Paragraph 4.2, then delay shall not be recognized on account of failure by the Architect to furnish such interpretations until 15 days after written request is made for them.

4.2.12 Interpretations and decisions of the Architect will be consistent with the intent of and reasonably inferable from the Contract Documents and will be in writing or in the form of drawings. When making such interpretations and decisions, the Architect will endeavor to secure faithful performance by both Owner and Contractor, will not show partiality to either and will not be liable for results of interpretations or decisions so rendered in good faith.

4.2.13 The Architect's decisions on matters relating to aesthetic effect will be final if consistent with the intent expressed in the Contract Documents.

4.3 CLAIMS AND DISPUTES

4.3.1 Definition. A Claim is a demand or assertion by one of the parties seeking, as a matter of right, adjustment or interpretation of Contract terms, payment of money, extension of time or other relief with respect to the terms of the Contract. The term "Claim" also includes other disputes and matters in question between the Owner and Contractor arising out of or relating to the Contract. Claims must be made by written notice. The responsibility to substantiate Claims shall rest with the party making the Claim.

4.3.2 Decision of Architect. Claims, including those alleging an error or omission by the Architect, shall be referred initially to the Architect for action as provided in Paragraph 4.4. A decision by the Architect, as provided in Subparagraph 4.4.4, shall be required as a condition precedent to arbitration or litigation of a Claim between the Contractor and Owner as to all such matters arising prior to the date final payment is due, regardless of (1) whether such matters relate to execution and progress of the Work or (2) the extent to which the Work has been completed. The decision by the Architect in response to a Claim shall not be a condition precedent to arbitration or litigation in the event (1) the position of Architect is vacant, (2) the Architect has not received evidence or has failed to render a decision within agreed time limits, (3) the Architect has failed to take action required under Subparagraph 4.4.4 within 30 days after the Claim is made, (4) 45 days have passed after the Claim has been referred to the Architect or (5) the Claim relates to a mechanic's lien.

4.3.3 Time Limits on Claims. Claims by either party must be made within 21 days after occurrence of the event giving rise to such Claim or within 21 days after the claimant first recognizes the condition giving rise to the Claim, whichever is later. Claims must be made by written notice. An additional Claim made after the initial Claim has been implemented by Change Order will not be considered unless submitted in a timely manner.

AIA DOCUMENT A201 • GENERAL CONDITIONS OF THE CONTRACT FOR CONSTRUCTION • FOURTEENTH EDITION
AIA® • ©1987 THE AMERICAN INSTITUTE OF ARCHITECTS, 1735 NEW YORK AVENUE, N.W., WASHINGTON, D.C. 20006   **A201-1987**   **11**

4.3.4 Continuing Contract Performance. Pending final resolution of a Claim including arbitration, unless otherwise agreed in writing the Contractor shall proceed diligently with performance of the Contract and the Owner shall continue to make payments in accordance with the Contract Documents.

4.3.5 Waiver of Claims: Final Payment. The making of final payment shall constitute a waiver of Claims by the Owner except those arising from:

- **.1** liens, Claims, security interests or encumbrances arising out of the Contract and unsettled;
- **.2** failure of the Work to comply with the requirements of the Contract Documents; or
- **.3** terms of special warranties required by the Contract Documents.

4.3.6 Claims for Concealed or Unknown Conditions. If conditions are encountered at the site which are (1) subsurface or otherwise concealed physical conditions which differ materially from those indicated in the Contract Documents or (2) unknown physical conditions of an unusual nature, which differ materially from those ordinarily found to exist and generally recognized as inherent in construction activities of the character provided for in the Contract Documents, then notice by the observing party shall be given to the other party promptly before conditions are disturbed and in no event later than 21 days after first observance of the conditions. The Architect will promptly investigate such conditions and, if they differ materially and cause an increase or decrease in the Contractor's cost of, or time required for, performance of any part of the Work, will recommend an equitable adjustment in the Contract Sum or Contract Time, or both. If the Architect determines that the conditions at the site are not materially different from those indicated in the Contract Documents and that no change in the terms of the Contract is justified, the Architect shall so notify the Owner and Contractor in writing, stating the reasons. Claims by either party in opposition to such determination must be made within 21 days after the Architect has given notice of the decision. If the Owner and Contractor cannot agree on an adjustment in the Contract Sum or Contract Time, the adjustment shall be referred to the Architect for initial determination, subject to further proceedings pursuant to Paragraph 4.4.

4.3.7 Claims for Additional Cost. If the Contractor wishes to make Claim for an increase in the Contract Sum, written notice as provided herein shall be given before proceeding to execute the Work. Prior notice is not required for Claims relating to an emergency endangering life or property arising under Paragraph 10.3. If the Contractor believes additional cost is involved for reasons including but not limited to (1) a written interpretation from the Architect, (2) an order by the Owner to stop the Work where the Contractor was not at fault, (3) a written order for a minor change in the Work issued by the Architect, (4) failure of payment by the Owner, (5) termination of the Contract by the Owner, (6) Owner's suspension or (7) other reasonable grounds, Claim shall be filed in accordance with the procedure established herein.

4.3.8 Claims for Additional Time

4.3.8.1 If the Contractor wishes to make Claim for an increase in the Contract Time, written notice as provided herein shall be given. The Contractor's Claim shall include an estimate of cost and of probable effect of delay on progress of the Work. In the case of a continuing delay only one Claim is necessary.

4.3.8.2 If adverse weather conditions are the basis for a Claim for additional time, such Claim shall be documented by data substantiating that weather conditions were abnormal for the period of time and could not have been reasonably anticipated, and that weather conditions had an adverse effect on the scheduled construction.

4.3.9 Injury or Damage to Person or Property. If either party to the Contract suffers injury or damage to person or property because of an act or omission of the other party, of any of the other party's employees or agents, or of others for whose acts such party is legally liable, written notice of such injury or damage, whether or not insured, shall be given to the other party within a reasonable time not exceeding 21 days after first observance. The notice shall provide sufficient detail to enable the other party to investigate the matter. If a Claim for additional cost or time related to this Claim is to be asserted, it shall be filed as provided in Subparagraphs 4.3.7 or 4.3.8.

4.4 RESOLUTION OF CLAIMS AND DISPUTES

4.4.1 The Architect will review Claims and take one or more of the following preliminary actions within ten days of receipt of a Claim: (1) request additional supporting data from the claimant, (2) submit a schedule to the parties indicating when the Architect expects to take action, (3) reject the Claim in whole or in part, stating reasons for rejection, (4) recommend approval of the Claim by the other party or (5) suggest a compromise. The Architect may also, but is not obligated to, notify the surety, if any, of the nature and amount of the Claim.

4.4.2 If a Claim has been resolved, the Architect will prepare or obtain appropriate documentation.

4.4.3 If a Claim has not been resolved, the party making the Claim shall, within ten days after the Architect's preliminary response, take one or more of the following actions: (1) submit additional supporting data requested by the Architect, (2) modify the initial Claim or (3) notify the Architect that the initial Claim stands.

4.4.4 If a Claim has not been resolved after consideration of the foregoing and of further evidence presented by the parties or requested by the Architect, the Architect will notify the parties in writing that the Architect's decision will be made within seven days, which decision shall be final and binding on the parties but subject to arbitration. Upon expiration of such time period, the Architect will render to the parties the Architect's written decision relative to the Claim, including any change in the Contract Sum or Contract Time or both. If there is a surety and there appears to be a possibility of a Contractor's default, the Architect may, but is not obligated to, notify the surety and request the surety's assistance in resolving the controversy.

4.5 ARBITRATION

4.5.1 Controversies and Claims Subject to Arbitration. Any controversy or Claim arising out of or related to the Contract, or the breach thereof, shall be settled by arbitration in accordance with the Construction Industry Arbitration Rules of the American Arbitration Association, and judgment upon the award rendered by the arbitrator or arbitrators may be entered in any court having jurisdiction thereof, except controversies or Claims relating to aesthetic effect and except those waived as provided for in Subparagraph 4.3.5. Such controversies or Claims upon which the Architect has given notice and rendered a decision as provided in Subparagraph 4.4.4 shall be subject to arbitration upon written demand of either party. Arbitration may be commenced when 45 days have passed after a Claim has been referred to the Architect as provided in Paragraph 4.3 and no decision has been rendered.

4.5.2 Rules and Notices for Arbitration. Claims between the Owner and Contractor not resolved under Paragraph 4.4 shall, if subject to arbitration under Subparagraph 4.5.1, be decided by arbitration in accordance with the Construction Industry Arbitration Rules of the American Arbitration Association currently in effect, unless the parties mutually agree otherwise. Notice of demand for arbitration shall be filed in writing with the other party to the Agreement between the Owner and Contractor and with the American Arbitration Association, and a copy shall be filed with the Architect.

4.5.3 Contract Performance During Arbitration. During arbitration proceedings, the Owner and Contractor shall comply with Subparagraph 4.3.4.

4.5.4 When Arbitration May Be Demanded. Demand for arbitration of any Claim may not be made until the earlier of (1) the date on which the Architect has rendered a final written decision on the Claim, (2) the tenth day after the parties have presented evidence to the Architect or have been given reasonable opportunity to do so, if the Architect has not rendered a final written decision by that date, or (3) any of the five events described in Subparagraph 4.3.2.

4.5.4.1 When a written decision of the Architect states that (1) the decision is final but subject to arbitration and (2) a demand for arbitration of a Claim covered by such decision must be made within 30 days after the date on which the party making the demand receives the final written decision, then failure to demand arbitration within said 30 days' period shall result in the Architect's decision becoming final and binding upon the Owner and Contractor. If the Architect renders a decision after arbitration proceedings have been initiated, such decision may be entered as evidence, but shall not supersede arbitration proceedings unless the decision is acceptable to all parties concerned.

4.5.4.2 A demand for arbitration shall be made within the time limits specified in Subparagraphs 4.5.1 and 4.5.4 and Clause 4.5.4.1 as applicable, and in other cases within a reasonable time after the Claim has arisen, and in no event shall it be made after the date when institution of legal or equitable proceedings based on such Claim would be barred by the applicable statute of limitations as determined pursuant to Paragraph 13.7.

4.5.5 Limitation on Consolidation or Joinder. No arbitration arising out of or relating to the Contract Documents shall include, by consolidation or joinder or in any other manner, the Architect, the Architect's employees or consultants, except by written consent containing specific reference to the Agreement and signed by the Architect, Owner, Contractor and any other person or entity sought to be joined. No arbitration shall include, by consolidation or joinder or in any other manner, parties other than the Owner, Contractor, a separate contractor as described in Article 6 and other persons substantially involved in a common question of fact or law whose presence is required if complete relief is to be accorded in arbitration. No person or entity other than the Owner, Contractor or a separate contractor as described in Article 6 shall be included as an original third party or additional third party to an arbitration whose interest or responsibility is insubstantial. Consent to arbitration involving an additional person or entity shall not constitute consent to arbitration of a dispute not described therein or with a person or entity not named or described therein. The foregoing agreement to arbitrate and other agreements to arbitrate with an additional person or entity duly consented to by parties to the Agreement shall be specifically enforceable under applicable law in any court having jurisdiction thereof.

4.5.6 Claims and Timely Assertion of Claims. A party who files a notice of demand for arbitration must assert in the demand all Claims then known to that party on which arbitration is permitted to be demanded. When a party fails to include a Claim through oversight, inadvertence or excusable neglect, or when a Claim has matured or been acquired subsequently, the arbitrator or arbitrators may permit amendment.

4.5.7 Judgment on Final Award. The award rendered by the arbitrator or arbitrators shall be final and judgment may be entered upon it in accordance with applicable law in any court having jurisdiction thereof.

ARTICLE 5

SUBCONTRACTORS

5.1 DEFINITIONS

5.1.1 A Subcontractor is a person or entity who has a direct contract with the Contractor to perform a portion of the Work at the site. The term "Subcontractor" is referred to throughout the Contract Documents as if singular in number and means a Subcontractor or an authorized representative of the Subcontractor. The term "Subcontractor" does not include a separate contractor or subcontractors of a separate contractor.

5.1.2 A Sub-subcontractor is a person or entity who has a direct or indirect contract with a Subcontractor to perform a portion of the Work at the site. The term "Sub-subcontractor" is referred to throughout the Contract Documents as if singular in number and means a Sub-subcontractor or an authorized representative of the Sub-subcontractor.

5.2 AWARD OF SUBCONTRACTS AND OTHER CONTRACTS FOR PORTIONS OF THE WORK

5.2.1 Unless otherwise stated in the Contract Documents or the bidding requirements, the Contractor, as soon as practicable after award of the Contract, shall furnish in writing to the Owner through the Architect the names of persons or entities (including those who are to furnish materials or equipment fabricated to a special design) proposed for each principal portion of the Work. The Architect will promptly reply to the Contractor in writing stating whether or not the Owner or the Architect, after due investigation, has reasonable objection to any such proposed person or entity. Failure of the Owner or Architect to reply promptly shall constitute notice of no reasonable objection.

5.2.2 The Contractor shall not contract with a proposed person or entity to whom the Owner or Architect has made reasonable and timely objection. The Contractor shall not be required to contract with anyone to whom the Contractor has made reasonable objection.

5.2.3 If the Owner or Architect has reasonable objection to a person or entity proposed by the Contractor, the Contractor shall propose another to whom the Owner or Architect has no reasonable objection. The Contract Sum shall be increased or decreased by the difference in cost occasioned by such change and an appropriate Change Order shall be issued. However, no increase in the Contract Sum shall be allowed for such change unless the Contractor has acted promptly and responsively in submitting names as required.

5.2.4 The Contractor shall not change a Subcontractor, person or entity previously selected if the Owner or Architect makes reasonable objection to such change.

5.3 SUBCONTRACTUAL RELATIONS

5.3.1 By appropriate agreement, written where legally required for validity, the Contractor shall require each Subcontractor, to the extent of the Work to be performed by the Subcontractor, to be bound to the Contractor by terms of the Contract Documents, and to assume toward the Contractor all the obligations and responsibilities which the Contractor, by these Documents, assumes toward the Owner and Architect. Each subcontract agreement shall preserve and protect the rights of the Owner and Architect under the Contract Documents with respect to the Work to be performed by the Subcontractor so that subcontracting thereof will not prejudice such rights, and shall allow to the Subcontractor, unless specifically provided otherwise in the subcontract agreement, the benefit of all rights, remedies and redress against the Contractor that the Contractor, by the Contract Documents, has against the Owner. Where appropriate, the Contractor shall require each Subcontractor to enter into similar agreements with Sub-subcontractors. The Contractor shall make available to each proposed Subcontractor, prior to the execution of the subcontract agreement, copies of the Contract Documents to which the Subcontractor will be bound, and, upon written request of the Subcontractor, identify to the Subcontractor terms and conditions of the proposed subcontract agreement which may be at variance with the Contract Documents. Subcontractors shall similarly make copies of applicable portions of such documents available to their respective proposed Sub-subcontractors.

5.4 CONTINGENT ASSIGNMENT OF SUBCONTRACTS

5.4.1 Each subcontract agreement for a portion of the Work is assigned by the Contractor to the Owner provided that:

.1 assignment is effective only after termination of the Contract by the Owner for cause pursuant to Paragraph 14.2 and only for those subcontract agreements which the Owner accepts by notifying the Subcontractor in writing; and

.2 assignment is subject to the prior rights of the surety, if any, obligated under bond relating to the Contract.

5.4.2 If the Work has been suspended for more than 30 days, the Subcontractor's compensation shall be equitably adjusted.

ARTICLE 6

CONSTRUCTION BY OWNER OR BY SEPARATE CONTRACTORS

6.1 OWNER'S RIGHT TO PERFORM CONSTRUCTION AND TO AWARD SEPARATE CONTRACTS

6.1.1 The Owner reserves the right to perform construction or operations related to the Project with the Owner's own forces, and to award separate contracts in connection with other portions of the Project or other construction or operations on the site under Conditions of the Contract identical or substantially similar to these including those portions related to insurance and waiver of subrogation. If the Contractor claims that delay or additional cost is involved because of such action by the Owner, the Contractor shall make such Claim as provided elsewhere in the Contract Documents.

6.1.2 When separate contracts are awarded for different portions of the Project or other construction or operations on the site, the term "Contractor" in the Contract Documents in each case shall mean the Contractor who executes each separate Owner-Contractor Agreement.

6.1.3 The Owner shall provide for coordination of the activities of the Owner's own forces and of each separate contractor with the Work of the Contractor, who shall cooperate with them. The Contractor shall participate with other separate contractors and the Owner in reviewing their construction schedules when directed to do so. The Contractor shall make any revisions to the construction schedule and Contract Sum deemed necessary after a joint review and mutual agreement. The construction schedules shall then constitute the schedules to be used by the Contractor, separate contractors and the Owner until subsequently revised.

6.1.4 Unless otherwise provided in the Contract Documents, when the Owner performs construction or operations related to the Project with the Owner's own forces, the Owner shall be deemed to be subject to the same obligations and to have the same rights which apply to the Contractor under the Conditions of the Contract, including, without excluding others, those stated in Article 3, this Article 6 and Articles 10, 11 and 12.

6.2 MUTUAL RESPONSIBILITY

6.2.1 The Contractor shall afford the Owner and separate contractors reasonable opportunity for introduction and storage of their materials and equipment and performance of their activities and shall connect and coordinate the Contractor's construction and operations with theirs as required by the Contract Documents.

6.2.2 If part of the Contractor's Work depends for proper execution or results upon construction or operations by the Owner or a separate contractor, the Contractor shall, prior to proceeding with that portion of the Work, promptly report to the Architect apparent discrepancies or defects in such other construction that would render it unsuitable for such proper execution and results. Failure of the Contractor so to report shall constitute an acknowledgment that the Owner's or separate contractors' completed or partially completed construction is fit and proper to receive the Contractor's Work, except as to defects not then reasonably discoverable.

6.2.3 Costs caused by delays or by improperly timed activities or defective construction shall be borne by the party responsible therefor.

6.2.4 The Contractor shall promptly remedy damage wrongfully caused by the Contractor to completed or partially completed construction or to property of the Owner or separate contractors as provided in Subparagraph 10.2.5.

6.2.5 Claims and other disputes and matters in question between the Contractor and a separate contractor shall be subject to the provisions of Paragraph 4.3 provided the separate contractor has reciprocal obligations.

6.2.6 The Owner and each separate contractor shall have the same responsibilities for cutting and patching as are described for the Contractor in Paragraph 3.14.

6.3 OWNER'S RIGHT TO CLEAN UP

6.3.1 If a dispute arises among the Contractor, separate contractors and the Owner as to the responsibility under their respective contracts for maintaining the premises and surrounding area free from waste materials and rubbish as described in Paragraph 3.15, the Owner may clean up and allocate the cost among those responsible as the Architect determines to be just.

ARTICLE 7

CHANGES IN THE WORK

7.1 CHANGES

7.1.1 Changes in the Work may be accomplished after execution of the Contract, and without invalidating the Contract, by Change Order, Construction Change Directive or order for a minor change in the Work, subject to the limitations stated in this Article 7 and elsewhere in the Contract Documents.

7.1.2 A Change Order shall be based upon agreement among the Owner, Contractor and Architect; a Construction Change Directive requires agreement by the Owner and Architect and may or may not be agreed to by the Contractor; an order for a minor change in the Work may be issued by the Architect alone.

7.1.3 Changes in the Work shall be performed under applicable provisions of the Contract Documents, and the Contractor shall proceed promptly, unless otherwise provided in the Change Order, Construction Change Directive or order for a minor change in the Work.

7.1.4 If unit prices are stated in the Contract Documents or subsequently agreed upon, and if quantities originally contemplated are so changed in a proposed Change Order or Construction Change Directive that application of such unit prices to quantities of Work proposed will cause substantial inequity to the Owner or Contractor, the applicable unit prices shall be equitably adjusted.

7.2 CHANGE ORDERS

7.2.1 A Change Order is a written instrument prepared by the Architect and signed by the Owner, Contractor and Architect, stating their agreement upon all of the following:

.1 a change in the Work;

.2 the amount of the adjustment in the Contract Sum, if any; and

.3 the extent of the adjustment in the Contract Time, if any.

7.2.2 Methods used in determining adjustments to the Contract Sum may include those listed in Subparagraph 7.3.3.

7.3 CONSTRUCTION CHANGE DIRECTIVES

7.3.1 A Construction Change Directive is a written order prepared by the Architect and signed by the Owner and Architect, directing a change in the Work and stating a proposed basis for adjustment, if any, in the Contract Sum or Contract Time, or both. The Owner may by Construction Change Directive, without invalidating the Contract, order changes in the Work within the general scope of the Contract consisting of additions, deletions or other revisions, the Contract Sum and Contract Time being adjusted accordingly.

7.3.2 A Construction Change Directive shall be used in the absence of total agreement on the terms of a Change Order.

7.3.3 If the Construction Change Directive provides for an adjustment to the Contract Sum, the adjustment shall be based on one of the following methods:

.1 mutual acceptance of a lump sum properly itemized and supported by sufficient substantiating data to permit evaluation;

.2 unit prices stated in the Contract Documents or subsequently agreed upon;

.3 cost to be determined in a manner agreed upon by the parties and a mutually acceptable fixed or percentage fee; or

.4 as provided in Subparagraph 7.3.6.

7.3.4 Upon receipt of a Construction Change Directive, the Contractor shall promptly proceed with the change in the Work involved and advise the Architect of the Contractor's agreement or disagreement with the method, if any, provided in the Construction Change Directive for determining the proposed adjustment in the Contract Sum or Contract Time.

7.3.5 A Construction Change Directive signed by the Contractor indicates the agreement of the Contractor therewith, including adjustment in Contract Sum and Contract Time or the method for determining them. Such agreement shall be effective immediately and shall be recorded as a Change Order.

7.3.6 If the Contractor does not respond promptly or disagrees with the method for adjustment in the Contract Sum, the method and the adjustment shall be determined by the Architect on the basis of reasonable expenditures and savings of those performing the Work attributable to the change, including, in case of an increase in the Contract Sum, a reasonable allowance for overhead and profit. In such case, and also under Clause 7.3.3.3, the Contractor shall keep and present, in such form as the Architect may prescribe, an itemized accounting together with appropriate supporting data. Unless otherwise provided in the Contract Documents, costs for the purposes of this Subparagraph 7.3.6 shall be limited to the following:

.1 costs of labor, including social security, old age and unemployment insurance, fringe benefits required by agreement or custom, and workers' or workmen's compensation insurance;

.2 costs of materials, supplies and equipment, including cost of transportation, whether incorporated or consumed;

.3 rental costs of machinery and equipment, exclusive of hand tools, whether rented from the Contractor or others;

.4 costs of premiums for all bonds and insurance, permit fees, and sales, use or similar taxes related to the Work; and

.5 additional costs of supervision and field office personnel directly attributable to the change.

7.3.7 Pending final determination of cost to the Owner, amounts not in dispute may be included in Applications for Payment. The amount of credit to be allowed by the Contractor to the Owner for a deletion or change which results in a net decrease in the Contract Sum shall be actual net cost as confirmed by the Architect. When both additions and credits covering related Work or substitutions are involved in a change, the allowance for overhead and profit shall be figured on the basis of net increase, if any, with respect to that change.

7.3.8 If the Owner and Contractor do not agree with the adjustment in Contract Time or the method for determining it, the adjustment or the method shall be referred to the Architect for determination.

7.3.9 When the Owner and Contractor agree with the determination made by the Architect concerning the adjustments in the Contract Sum and Contract Time, or otherwise reach agreement upon the adjustments, such agreement shall be effective immediately and shall be recorded by preparation and execution of an appropriate Change Order.

7.4 MINOR CHANGES IN THE WORK

7.4.1 The Architect will have authority to order minor changes in the Work not involving adjustment in the Contract Sum or extension of the Contract Time and not inconsistent with the intent of the Contract Documents. Such changes shall be effected by written order and shall be binding on the Owner and Contractor. The Contractor shall carry out such written orders promptly.

ARTICLE 8

TIME

8.1 DEFINITIONS

8.1.1 Unless otherwise provided, Contract Time is the period of time, including authorized adjustments, allotted in the Contract Documents for Substantial Completion of the Work.

8.1.2 The date of commencement of the Work is the date established in the Agreement. The date shall not be postponed by the failure to act of the Contractor or of persons or entities for whom the Contractor is responsible.

8.1.3 The date of Substantial Completion is the date certified by the Architect in accordance with Paragraph 9.8.

8.1.4 The term "day" as used in the Contract Documents shall mean calendar day unless otherwise specifically defined.

8.2 PROGRESS AND COMPLETION

8.2.1 Time limits stated in the Contract Documents are of the essence of the Contract. By executing the Agreement the Contractor confirms that the Contract Time is a reasonable period for performing the Work.

8.2.2 The Contractor shall not knowingly, except by agreement or instruction of the Owner in writing, prematurely commence operations on the site or elsewhere prior to the effective date of insurance required by Article 11 to be furnished by the Contractor. The date of commencement of the Work shall not be changed by the effective date of such insurance. Unless the date of commencement is established by a notice to proceed given by the Owner, the Contractor shall notify the Owner in writing not less than five days or other agreed period before commencing the Work to permit the timely filing of mortgages, mechanic's liens and other security interests.

8.2.3 The Contractor shall proceed expeditiously with adequate forces and shall achieve Substantial Completion within the Contract Time.

8.3 DELAYS AND EXTENSIONS OF TIME

8.3.1 If the Contractor is delayed at any time in progress of the Work by an act or neglect of the Owner or Architect, or of an employee of either, or of a separate contractor employed by the Owner, or by changes ordered in the Work, or by labor disputes, fire, unusual delay in deliveries, unavoidable casualties or other causes beyond the Contractor's control, or by delay authorized by the Owner pending arbitration, or by other causes which the Architect determines may justify delay, then the Contract Time shall be extended by Change Order for such reasonable time as the Architect may determine.

8.3.2 Claims relating to time shall be made in accordance with applicable provisions of Paragraph 4.3.

8.3.3 This Paragraph 8.3 does not preclude recovery of damages for delay by either party under other provisions of the Contract Documents.

ARTICLE 9

PAYMENTS AND COMPLETION

9.1 CONTRACT SUM

9.1.1 The Contract Sum is stated in the Agreement and, including authorized adjustments, is the total amount payable by the Owner to the Contractor for performance of the Work under the Contract Documents.

9.2 SCHEDULE OF VALUES

9.2.1 Before the first Application for Payment, the Contractor shall submit to the Architect a schedule of values allocated to various portions of the Work, prepared in such form and supported by such data to substantiate its accuracy as the Architect may require. This schedule, unless objected to by the Architect, shall be used as a basis for reviewing the Contractor's Applications for Payment.

9.3 APPLICATIONS FOR PAYMENT

9.3.1 At least ten days before the date established for each progress payment, the Contractor shall submit to the Architect an itemized Application for Payment for operations completed in accordance with the schedule of values. Such application shall be notarized, if required, and supported by such data substantiating the Contractor's right to payment as the Owner or Architect may require, such as copies of requisitions from Subcontractors and material suppliers, and reflecting retainage if provided for elsewhere in the Contract Documents.

9.3.1.1 Such applications may include requests for payment on account of changes in the Work which have been properly authorized by Construction Change Directives but not yet included in Change Orders.

9.3.1.2 Such applications may not include requests for payment of amounts the Contractor does not intend to pay to a Subcontractor or material supplier because of a dispute or other reason.

9.3.2 Unless otherwise provided in the Contract Documents, payments shall be made on account of materials and equipment delivered and suitably stored at the site for subsequent incorporation in the Work. If approved in advance by the Owner, payment may similarly be made for materials and equipment suitably stored off the site at a location agreed upon in writing. Payment for materials and equipment stored on or off the site shall be conditioned upon compliance by the Contractor with procedures satisfactory to the Owner to establish the Owner's title to such materials and equipment or otherwise protect the Owner's interest, and shall include applicable insurance, storage and transportation to the site for such materials and equipment stored off the site.

9.3.3 The Contractor warrants that title to all Work covered by an Application for Payment will pass to the Owner no later than the time of payment. The Contractor further warrants that upon submittal of an Application for Payment all Work for which Certificates for Payment have been previously issued and payments received from the Owner shall, to the best of the Contractor's knowledge, information and belief, be free and clear of liens, claims, security interests or encumbrances in favor of the Contractor, Subcontractors, material suppliers, or other persons or entities making a claim by reason of having provided labor, materials and equipment relating to the Work.

9.4 CERTIFICATES FOR PAYMENT

9.4.1 The Architect will, within seven days after receipt of the Contractor's Application for Payment, either issue to the

Owner a Certificate for Payment, with a copy to the Contractor, for such amount as the Architect determines is properly due, or notify the Contractor and Owner in writing of the Architect's reasons for withholding certification in whole or in part as provided in Subparagraph 9.5.1.

9.4.2 The issuance of a Certificate for Payment will constitute a representation by the Architect to the Owner, based on the Architect's observations at the site and the data comprising the Application for Payment, that the Work has progressed to the point indicated and that, to the best of the Architect's knowledge, information and belief, quality of the Work is in accordance with the Contract Documents. The foregoing representations are subject to an evaluation of the Work for conformance with the Contract Documents upon Substantial Completion, to results of subsequent tests and inspections, to minor deviations from the Contract Documents correctable prior to completion and to specific qualifications expressed by the Architect. The issuance of a Certificate for Payment will further constitute a representation that the Contractor is entitled to payment in the amount certified. However, the issuance of a Certificate for Payment will not be a representation that the Architect has (1) made exhaustive or continuous on-site inspections to check the quality or quantity of the Work, (2) reviewed construction means, methods, techniques, sequences or procedures, (3) reviewed copies of requisitions received from Subcontractors and material suppliers and other data requested by the Owner to substantiate the Contractor's right to payment or (4) made examination to ascertain how or for what purpose the Contractor has used money previously paid on account of the Contract Sum.

9.5 DECISIONS TO WITHHOLD CERTIFICATION

9.5.1 The Architect may decide not to certify payment and may withhold a Certificate for Payment in whole or in part, to the extent reasonably necessary to protect the Owner, if in the Architect's opinion the representations to the Owner required by Subparagraph 9.4.2 cannot be made. If the Architect is unable to certify payment in the amount of the Application, the Architect will notify the Contractor and Owner as provided in Subparagraph 9.4.1. If the Contractor and Architect cannot agree on a revised amount, the Architect will promptly issue a Certificate for Payment for the amount for which the Architect is able to make such representations to the Owner. The Architect may also decide not to certify payment or, because of subsequently discovered evidence or subsequent observations, may nullify the whole or a part of a Certificate for Payment previously issued, to such extent as may be necessary in the Architect's opinion to protect the Owner from loss because of:

.1 defective Work not remedied;
.2 third party claims filed or reasonable evidence indicating probable filing of such claims;
.3 failure of the Contractor to make payments properly to Subcontractors or for labor, materials or equipment;
.4 reasonable evidence that the Work cannot be completed for the unpaid balance of the Contract Sum;
.5 damage to the Owner or another contractor;
.6 reasonable evidence that the Work will not be completed within the Contract Time, and that the unpaid balance would not be adequate to cover actual or liquidated damages for the anticipated delay; or
.7 persistent failure to carry out the Work in accordance with the Contract Documents.

9.5.2 When the above reasons for withholding certification are removed, certification will be made for amounts previously withheld.

9.6 PROGRESS PAYMENTS

9.6.1 After the Architect has issued a Certificate for Payment, the Owner shall make payment in the manner and within the time provided in the Contract Documents, and shall so notify the Architect.

9.6.2 The Contractor shall promptly pay each Subcontractor, upon receipt of payment from the Owner, out of the amount paid to the Contractor on account of such Subcontractor's portion of the Work, the amount to which said Subcontractor is entitled, reflecting percentages actually retained from payments to the Contractor on account of such Subcontractor's portion of the Work. The Contractor shall, by appropriate agreement with each Subcontractor, require each Subcontractor to make payments to Sub-subcontractors in similar manner.

9.6.3 The Architect will, on request, furnish to a Subcontractor, if practicable, information regarding percentages of completion or amounts applied for by the Contractor and action taken thereon by the Architect and Owner on account of portions of the Work done by such Subcontractor.

9.6.4 Neither the Owner nor Architect shall have an obligation to pay or to see to the payment of money to a Subcontractor except as may otherwise be required by law.

9.6.5 Payment to material suppliers shall be treated in a manner similar to that provided in Subparagraphs 9.6.2, 9.6.3 and 9.6.4.

9.6.6 A Certificate for Payment, a progress payment, or partial or entire use or occupancy of the Project by the Owner shall not constitute acceptance of Work not in accordance with the Contract Documents.

9.7 FAILURE OF PAYMENT

9.7.1 If the Architect does not issue a Certificate for Payment, through no fault of the Contractor, within seven days after receipt of the Contractor's Application for Payment, or if the Owner does not pay the Contractor within seven days after the date established in the Contract Documents the amount certified by the Architect or awarded by arbitration, then the Contractor may, upon seven additional days' written notice to the Owner and Architect, stop the Work until payment of the amount owing has been received. The Contract Time shall be extended appropriately and the Contract Sum shall be increased by the amount of the Contractor's reasonable costs of shut-down, delay and start-up, which shall be accomplished as provided in Article 7.

9.8 SUBSTANTIAL COMPLETION

9.8.1 Substantial Completion is the stage in the progress of the Work when the Work or designated portion thereof is sufficiently complete in accordance with the Contract Documents so the Owner can occupy or utilize the Work for its intended use.

9.8.2 When the Contractor considers that the Work, or a portion thereof which the Owner agrees to accept separately, is substantially complete, the Contractor shall prepare and submit to the Architect a comprehensive list of items to be completed or corrected. The Contractor shall proceed promptly to complete and correct items on the list. Failure to include an item on such list does not alter the responsibility of the Contractor to complete all Work in accordance with the Contract Documents. Upon receipt of the Contractor's list, the Architect will make an inspection to determine whether the Work or designated portion thereof is substantially complete. If the Architect's inspection discloses any item, whether or not included on the Contractor's list, which is not in accordance with the requirements of the Contract Documents, the Contractor shall, before issuance of the Certificate of Substantial Completion, complete or correct such item upon notification by the Architect. The Contractor shall then submit a request for another inspection by the Architect to determine Substantial Completion. When the Work or designated portion thereof is substantially complete, the Architect will prepare a Certificate of Substantial Completion which shall establish the date of Substantial Completion, shall establish responsibilities of the Owner and Contractor for security, maintenance, heat, utilities, damage to the Work and insurance, and shall fix the time within which the Contractor shall finish all items on the list accompanying the Certificate. Warranties required by the Contract Documents shall commence on the date of Substantial Completion of the Work or designated portion thereof unless otherwise provided in the Certificate of Substantial Completion. The Certificate of Substantial Completion shall be submitted to the Owner and Contractor for their written acceptance of responsibilities assigned to them in such Certificate.

9.8.3 Upon Substantial Completion of the Work or designated portion thereof and upon application by the Contractor and certification by the Architect, the Owner shall make payment, reflecting adjustment in retainage, if any, for such Work or portion thereof as provided in the Contract Documents.

9.9 PARTIAL OCCUPANCY OR USE

9.9.1 The Owner may occupy or use any completed or partially completed portion of the Work at any stage when such portion is designated by separate agreement with the Contractor, provided such occupancy or use is consented to by the insurer as required under Subparagraph 11.3.11 and authorized by public authorities having jurisdiction over the Work. Such partial occupancy or use may commence whether or not the portion is substantially complete, provided the Owner and Contractor have accepted in writing the responsibilities assigned to each of them for payments, retainage if any, security, maintenance, heat, utilities, damage to the Work and insurance, and have agreed in writing concerning the period for correction of the Work and commencement of warranties required by the Contract Documents. When the Contractor considers a portion substantially complete, the Contractor shall prepare and submit a list to the Architect as provided under Subparagraph 9.8.2. Consent of the Contractor to partial occupancy or use shall not be unreasonably withheld. The stage of the progress of the Work shall be determined by written agreement between the Owner and Contractor or, if no agreement is reached, by decision of the Architect.

9.9.2 Immediately prior to such partial occupancy or use, the Owner, Contractor and Architect shall jointly inspect the area to be occupied or portion of the Work to be used in order to determine and record the condition of the Work.

9.9.3 Unless otherwise agreed upon, partial occupancy or use of a portion or portions of the Work shall not constitute acceptance of Work not complying with the requirements of the Contract Documents.

9.10 FINAL COMPLETION AND FINAL PAYMENT

9.10.1 Upon receipt of written notice that the Work is ready for final inspection and acceptance and upon receipt of a final Application for Payment, the Architect will promptly make such inspection and, when the Architect finds the Work acceptable under the Contract Documents and the Contract fully performed, the Architect will promptly issue a final Certificate for Payment stating that to the best of the Architect's knowledge, information and belief, and on the basis of the Architect's observations and inspections, the Work has been completed in accordance with terms and conditions of the Contract Documents and that the entire balance found to be due the Contractor and noted in said final Certificate is due and payable. The Architect's final Certificate for Payment will constitute a further representation that conditions listed in Subparagraph 9.10.2 as precedent to the Contractor's being entitled to final payment have been fulfilled.

9.10.2 Neither final payment nor any remaining retained percentage shall become due until the Contractor submits to the Architect (1) an affidavit that payrolls, bills for materials and equipment, and other indebtedness connected with the Work for which the Owner or the Owner's property might be responsible or encumbered (less amounts withheld by Owner) have been paid or otherwise satisfied, (2) a certificate evidencing that insurance required by the Contract Documents to remain in force after final payment is currently in effect and will not be cancelled or allowed to expire until at least 30 days' prior written notice has been given to the Owner, (3) a written statement that the Contractor knows of no substantial reason that the insurance will not be renewable to cover the period required by the Contract Documents, (4) consent of surety, if any, to final payment and (5), if required by the Owner, other data establishing payment or satisfaction of obligations, such as receipts, releases and waivers of liens, claims, security interests or encumbrances arising out of the Contract, to the extent and in such form as may be designated by the Owner. If a Subcontractor refuses to furnish a release or waiver required by the Owner, the Contractor may furnish a bond satisfactory to the Owner to indemnify the Owner against such lien. If such lien remains unsatisfied after payments are made, the Contractor shall refund to the Owner all money that the Owner may be compelled to pay in discharging such lien, including all costs and reasonable attorneys' fees.

9.10.3 If, after Substantial Completion of the Work, final completion thereof is materially delayed through no fault of the Contractor or by issuance of Change Orders affecting final completion, and the Architect so confirms, the Owner shall, upon application by the Contractor and certification by the Architect, and without terminating the Contract, make payment of the balance due for that portion of the Work fully completed and accepted. If the remaining balance for Work not fully completed or corrected is less than retainage stipulated in the Contract Documents, and if bonds have been furnished, the written consent of surety to payment of the balance due for that portion of the Work fully completed and accepted shall be submitted by the Contractor to the Architect prior to certification of such payment. Such payment shall be made under terms and conditions governing final payment, except that it shall not constitute a waiver of claims. The making of final payment shall constitute a waiver of claims by the Owner as provided in Subparagraph 4.3.5.

9.10.4 Acceptance of final payment by the Contractor, a Subcontractor or material supplier shall constitute a waiver of claims by that payee except those previously made in writing and identified by that payee as unsettled at the time of final Application for Payment. Such waivers shall be in addition to the waiver described in Subparagraph 4.3.5.

ARTICLE 10

PROTECTION OF PERSONS AND PROPERTY

10.1 SAFETY PRECAUTIONS AND PROGRAMS

10.1.1 The Contractor shall be responsible for initiating, maintaining and supervising all safety precautions and programs in connection with the performance of the Contract.

10.1.2 In the event the Contractor encounters on the site material reasonably believed to be asbestos or polychlorinated biphenyl (PCB) which has not been rendered harmless, the Contractor shall immediately stop Work in the area affected and report the condition to the Owner and Architect in writing. The Work in the affected area shall not thereafter be resumed except by written agreement of the Owner and Contractor if in fact the material is asbestos or polychlorinated biphenyl (PCB) and has not been rendered harmless. The Work in the affected area shall be resumed in the absence of asbestos or polychlorinated biphenyl (PCB), or when it has been rendered harmless, by written agreement of the Owner and Contractor, or in accordance with final determination by the Architect on which arbitration has not been demanded, or by arbitration under Article 4.

10.1.3 The Contractor shall not be required pursuant to Article 7 to perform without consent any Work relating to asbestos or polychlorinated biphenyl (PCB).

10.1.4 To the fullest extent permitted by law, the Owner shall indemnify and hold harmless the Contractor, Architect, Architect's consultants and agents and employees of any of them from and against claims, damages, losses and expenses, including but not limited to attorneys' fees, arising out of or resulting from performance of the Work in the affected area if in fact the material is asbestos or polychlorinated biphenyl (PCB) and has not been rendered harmless, provided that such claim, damage, loss or expense is attributable to bodily injury, sickness, disease or death, or to injury to or destruction of tangible property (other than the Work itself) including loss of use resulting therefrom, but only to the extent caused in whole or in part by negligent acts or omissions of the Owner, anyone directly or indirectly employed by the Owner or anyone for whose acts the Owner may be liable, regardless of whether or not such claim, damage, loss or expense is caused in part by a party indemnified hereunder. Such obligation shall not be construed to negate, abridge, or reduce other rights or obligations of indemnity which would otherwise exist as to a party or person described in this Subparagraph 10.1.4.

10.2 SAFETY OF PERSONS AND PROPERTY

10.2.1 The Contractor shall take reasonable precautions for safety of, and shall provide reasonable protection to prevent damage, injury or loss to:

- .1 employees on the Work and other persons who may be affected thereby;
- .2 the Work and materials and equipment to be incorporated therein, whether in storage on or off the site, under care, custody or control of the Contractor or the Contractor's Subcontractors or Sub-subcontractors; and
- .3 other property at the site or adjacent thereto, such as trees, shrubs, lawns, walks, pavements, roadways, structures and utilities not designated for removal, relocation or replacement in the course of construction.

10.2.2 The Contractor shall give notices and comply with applicable laws, ordinances, rules, regulations and lawful orders of public authorities bearing on safety of persons or property or their protection from damage, injury or loss.

10.2.3 The Contractor shall erect and maintain, as required by existing conditions and performance of the Contract, reasonable safeguards for safety and protection, including posting danger signs and other warnings against hazards, promulgating safety regulations and notifying owners and users of adjacent sites and utilities.

10.2.4 When use or storage of explosives or other hazardous materials or equipment or unusual methods are necessary for execution of the Work, the Contractor shall exercise utmost care and carry on such activities under supervision of properly qualified personnel.

10.2.5 The Contractor shall promptly remedy damage and loss (other than damage or loss insured under property insurance required by the Contract Documents) to property referred to in Clauses 10.2.1.2 and 10.2.1.3 caused in whole or in part by the Contractor, a Subcontractor, a Sub-subcontractor, or anyone directly or indirectly employed by any of them, or by anyone for whose acts they may be liable and for which the Contractor is responsible under Clauses 10.2.1.2 and 10.2.1.3, except damage or loss attributable to acts or omissions of the Owner or Architect or anyone directly or indirectly employed by either of them, or by anyone for whose acts either of them may be liable, and not attributable to the fault or negligence of the Contractor. The foregoing obligations of the Contractor are in addition to the Contractor's obligations under Paragraph 3.18.

10.2.6 The Contractor shall designate a responsible member of the Contractor's organization at the site whose duty shall be the prevention of accidents. This person shall be the Contractor's superintendent unless otherwise designated by the Contractor in writing to the Owner and Architect.

10.2.7 The Contractor shall not load or permit any part of the construction or site to be loaded so as to endanger its safety.

10.3 EMERGENCIES

10.3.1 In an emergency affecting safety of persons or property, the Contractor shall act, at the Contractor's discretion, to prevent threatened damage, injury or loss. Additional compensation or extension of time claimed by the Contractor on account of an emergency shall be determined as provided in Paragraph 4.3 and Article 7.

ARTICLE 11

INSURANCE AND BONDS

11.1 CONTRACTOR'S LIABILITY INSURANCE

11.1.1 The Contractor shall purchase from and maintain in a company or companies lawfully authorized to do business in the jurisdiction in which the Project is located such insurance as will protect the Contractor from claims set forth below which may arise out of or result from the Contractor's operations under the Contract and for which the Contractor may be legally liable, whether such operations be by the Contractor or by a Subcontractor or by anyone directly or indirectly employed by any of them, or by anyone for whose acts any of them may be liable:

- .1 claims under workers' or workmen's compensation, disability benefit and other similar employee benefit acts which are applicable to the Work to be performed;

.2 claims for damages because of bodily injury, occupational sickness or disease, or death of the Contractor's employees;

.3 claims for damages because of bodily injury, sickness or disease, or death of any person other than the Contractor's employees;

.4 claims for damages insured by usual personal injury liability coverage which are sustained (1) by a person as a result of an offense directly or indirectly related to employment of such person by the Contractor, or (2) by another person;

.5 claims for damages, other than to the Work itself, because of injury to or destruction of tangible property, including loss of use resulting therefrom;

.6 claims for damages because of bodily injury, death of a person or property damage arising out of ownership, maintenance or use of a motor vehicle; and

.7 claims involving contractual liability insurance applicable to the Contractor's obligations under Paragraph 3.18.

11.1.2 The insurance required by Subparagraph 11.1.1 shall be written for not less than limits of liability specified in the Contract Documents or required by law, whichever coverage is greater. Coverages, whether written on an occurrence or claims-made basis, shall be maintained without interruption from date of commencement of the Work until date of final payment and termination of any coverage required to be maintained after final payment.

11.1.3 Certificates of Insurance acceptable to the Owner shall be filed with the Owner prior to commencement of the Work. These Certificates and the insurance policies required by this Paragraph 11.1 shall contain a provision that coverages afforded under the policies will not be cancelled or allowed to expire until at least 30 days' prior written notice has been given to the Owner. If any of the foregoing insurance coverages are required to remain in force after final payment and are reasonably available, an additional certificate evidencing continuation of such coverage shall be submitted with the final Application for Payment as required by Subparagraph 9.10.2. Information concerning reduction of coverage shall be furnished by the Contractor with reasonable promptness in accordance with the Contractor's information and belief.

11.2 OWNER'S LIABILITY INSURANCE

11.2.1 The Owner shall be responsible for purchasing and maintaining the Owner's usual liability insurance. Optionally, the Owner may purchase and maintain other insurance for self-protection against claims which may arise from operations under the Contract. The Contractor shall not be responsible for purchasing and maintaining this optional Owner's liability insurance unless specifically required by the Contract Documents.

11.3 PROPERTY INSURANCE

11.3.1 Unless otherwise provided, the Owner shall purchase and maintain, in a company or companies lawfully authorized to do business in the jurisdiction in which the Project is located, property insurance in the amount of the initial Contract Sum as well as subsequent modifications thereto for the entire Work at the site on a replacement cost basis without voluntary deductibles. Such property insurance shall be maintained, unless otherwise provided in the Contract Documents or otherwise agreed in writing by all persons and entities who are beneficiaries of such insurance, until final payment has been made as provided in Paragraph 9.10 or until no person or entity other than the Owner has an insurable interest in the property required by this Paragraph 11.3 to be covered, whichever is earlier. This insurance shall include interests of the Owner, the Contractor, Subcontractors and Sub-subcontractors in the Work.

11.3.1.1 Property insurance shall be on an all-risk policy form and shall insure against the perils of fire and extended coverage and physical loss or damage including, without duplication of coverage, theft, vandalism, malicious mischief, collapse, falsework, temporary buildings and debris removal including demolition occasioned by enforcement of any applicable legal requirements, and shall cover reasonable compensation for Architect's services and expenses required as a result of such insured loss. Coverage for other perils shall not be required unless otherwise provided in the Contract Documents.

11.3.1.2 If the Owner does not intend to purchase such property insurance required by the Contract and with all of the coverages in the amount described above, the Owner shall so inform the Contractor in writing prior to commencement of the Work. The Contractor may then effect insurance which will protect the interests of the Contractor, Subcontractors and Sub-subcontractors in the Work, and by appropriate Change Order the cost thereof shall be charged to the Owner. If the Contractor is damaged by the failure or neglect of the Owner to purchase or maintain insurance as described above, without so notifying the Contractor, then the Owner shall bear all reasonable costs properly attributable thereto.

11.3.1.3 If the property insurance requires minimum deductibles and such deductibles are identified in the Contract Documents, the Contractor shall pay costs not covered because of such deductibles. If the Owner or insurer increases the required minimum deductibles above the amounts so identified or if the Owner elects to purchase this insurance with voluntary deductible amounts, the Owner shall be responsible for payment of the additional costs not covered because of such increased or voluntary deductibles. If deductibles are not identified in the Contract Documents, the Owner shall pay costs not covered because of deductibles.

11.3.1.4 Unless otherwise provided in the Contract Documents, this property insurance shall cover portions of the Work stored off the site after written approval of the Owner at the value established in the approval, and also portions of the Work in transit.

11.3.2 Boiler and Machinery Insurance. The Owner shall purchase and maintain boiler and machinery insurance required by the Contract Documents or by law, which shall specifically cover such insured objects during installation and until final acceptance by the Owner; this insurance shall include interests of the Owner, Contractor, Subcontractors and Sub-subcontractors in the Work, and the Owner and Contractor shall be named insureds.

11.3.3 Loss of Use Insurance. The Owner, at the Owner's option, may purchase and maintain such insurance as will insure the Owner against loss of use of the Owner's property due to fire or other hazards, however caused. The Owner waives all rights of action against the Contractor for loss of use of the Owner's property, including consequential losses due to fire or other hazards however caused.

11.3.4 If the Contractor requests in writing that insurance for risks other than those described herein or for other special hazards be included in the property insurance policy, the Owner shall, if possible, include such insurance, and the cost thereof shall be charged to the Contractor by appropriate Change Order.

11.3.5 If during the Project construction period the Owner insures properties, real or personal or both, adjoining or adjacent to the site by property insurance under policies separate from those insuring the Project, or if after final payment property insurance is to be provided on the completed Project through a policy or policies other than those insuring the Project during the construction period, the Owner shall waive all rights in accordance with the terms of Subparagraph 11.3.7 for damages caused by fire or other perils covered by this separate property insurance. All separate policies shall provide this waiver of subrogation by endorsement or otherwise.

11.3.6 Before an exposure to loss may occur, the Owner shall file with the Contractor a copy of each policy that includes insurance coverages required by this Paragraph 11.3. Each policy shall contain all generally applicable conditions, definitions, exclusions and endorsements related to this Project. Each policy shall contain a provision that the policy will not be cancelled or allowed to expire until at least 30 days' prior written notice has been given to the Contractor.

11.3.7 Waivers of Subrogation. The Owner and Contractor waive all rights against (1) each other and any of their subcontractors, sub-subcontractors, agents and employees, each of the other, and (2) the Architect, Architect's consultants, separate contractors described in Article 6, if any, and any of their subcontractors, sub-subcontractors, agents and employees, for damages caused by fire or other perils to the extent covered by property insurance obtained pursuant to this Paragraph 11.3 or other property insurance applicable to the Work, except such rights as they have to proceeds of such insurance held by the Owner as fiduciary. The Owner or Contractor, as appropriate, shall require of the Architect, Architect's consultants, separate contractors described in Article 6, if any, and the subcontractors, sub-subcontractors, agents and employees of any of them, by appropriate agreements, written where legally required for validity, similar waivers each in favor of other parties enumerated herein. The policies shall provide such waivers of subrogation by endorsement or otherwise. A waiver of subrogation shall be effective as to a person or entity even though that person or entity would otherwise have a duty of indemnification, contractual or otherwise, did not pay the insurance premium directly or indirectly, and whether or not the person or entity had an insurable interest in the property damaged.

11.3.8 A loss insured under Owner's property insurance shall be adjusted by the Owner as fiduciary and made payable to the Owner as fiduciary for the insureds, as their interests may appear, subject to requirements of any applicable mortgagee clause and of Subparagraph 11.3.10. The Contractor shall pay Subcontractors their just shares of insurance proceeds received by the Contractor, and by appropriate agreements, written where legally required for validity, shall require Subcontractors to make payments to their Sub-subcontractors in similar manner.

11.3.9 If required in writing by a party in interest, the Owner as fiduciary shall, upon occurrence of an insured loss, give bond for proper performance of the Owner's duties. The cost of required bonds shall be charged against proceeds received as fiduciary. The Owner shall deposit in a separate account proceeds so received, which the Owner shall distribute in accordance with such agreement as the parties in interest may reach, or in accordance with an arbitration award in which case the procedure shall be as provided in Paragraph 4.5. If after such loss no other special agreement is made, replacement of damaged property shall be covered by appropriate Change Order.

11.3.10 The Owner as fiduciary shall have power to adjust and settle a loss with insurers unless one of the parties in interest shall object in writing within five days after occurrence of loss to the Owner's exercise of this power; if such objection be made, arbitrators shall be chosen as provided in Paragraph 4.5. The Owner as fiduciary shall, in that case, make settlement with insurers in accordance with directions of such arbitrators. If distribution of insurance proceeds by arbitration is required, the arbitrators will direct such distribution.

11.3.11 Partial occupancy or use in accordance with Paragraph 9.9 shall not commence until the insurance company or companies providing property insurance have consented to such partial occupancy or use by endorsement or otherwise. The Owner and the Contractor shall take reasonable steps to obtain consent of the insurance company or companies and shall, without mutual written consent, take no action with respect to partial occupancy or use that would cause cancellation, lapse or reduction of insurance.

11.4 PERFORMANCE BOND AND PAYMENT BOND

11.4.1 The Owner shall have the right to require the Contractor to furnish bonds covering faithful performance of the Contract and payment of obligations arising thereunder as stipulated in bidding requirements or specifically required in the Contract Documents on the date of execution of the Contract.

11.4.2 Upon the request of any person or entity appearing to be a potential beneficiary of bonds covering payment of obligations arising under the Contract, the Contractor shall promptly furnish a copy of the bonds or shall permit a copy to be made.

ARTICLE 12

UNCOVERING AND CORRECTION OF WORK

12.1 UNCOVERING OF WORK

12.1.1 If a portion of the Work is covered contrary to the Architect's request or to requirements specifically expressed in the Contract Documents, it must, if required in writing by the Architect, be uncovered for the Architect's observation and be replaced at the Contractor's expense without change in the Contract Time.

12.1.2 If a portion of the Work has been covered which the Architect has not specifically requested to observe prior to its being covered, the Architect may request to see such Work and it shall be uncovered by the Contractor. If such Work is in accordance with the Contract Documents, costs of uncovering and replacement shall, by appropriate Change Order, be charged to the Owner. If such Work is not in accordance with the Contract Documents, the Contractor shall pay such costs unless the condition was caused by the Owner or a separate contractor in which event the Owner shall be responsible for payment of such costs.

12.2 CORRECTION OF WORK

12.2.1 The Contractor shall promptly correct Work rejected by the Architect or failing to conform to the requirements of the Contract Documents, whether observed before or after Substantial Completion and whether or not fabricated, installed or completed. The Contractor shall bear costs of correcting such rejected Work, including additional testing and inspections and compensation for the Architect's services and expenses made necessary thereby.

12.2.2 If, within one year after the date of Substantial Completion of the Work or designated portion thereof, or after the date for commencement of warranties established under Subparagraph 9.9.1, or by terms of an applicable special warranty required by the Contract Documents, any of the Work is found to be not in accordance with the requirements of the Contract Documents, the Contractor shall correct it promptly after receipt of written notice from the Owner to do so unless the Owner has previously given the Contractor a written acceptance of such condition. This period of one year shall be extended with respect to portions of Work first performed after Substantial Completion by the period of time between Substantial Completion and the actual performance of the Work. This obligation under this Subparagraph 12.2.2 shall survive acceptance of the Work under the Contract and termination of the Contract. The Owner shall give such notice promptly after discovery of the condition.

12.2.3 The Contractor shall remove from the site portions of the Work which are not in accordance with the requirements of the Contract Documents and are neither corrected by the Contractor nor accepted by the Owner.

12.2.4 If the Contractor fails to correct nonconforming Work within a reasonable time, the Owner may correct it in accordance with Paragraph 2.4. If the Contractor does not proceed with correction of such nonconforming Work within a reasonable time fixed by written notice from the Architect, the Owner may remove it and store the salvable materials or equipment at the Contractor's expense. If the Contractor does not pay costs of such removal and storage within ten days after written notice, the Owner may upon ten additional days' written notice sell such materials and equipment at auction or at private sale and shall account for the proceeds thereof, after deducting costs and damages that should have been borne by the Contractor, including compensation for the Architect's services and expenses made necessary thereby. If such proceeds of sale do not cover costs which the Contractor should have borne, the Contract Sum shall be reduced by the deficiency. If payments then or thereafter due the Contractor are not sufficient to cover such amount, the Contractor shall pay the difference to the Owner.

12.2.5 The Contractor shall bear the cost of correcting destroyed or damaged construction, whether completed or partially completed, of the Owner or separate contractors caused by the Contractor's correction or removal of Work which is not in accordance with the requirements of the Contract Documents.

12.2.6 Nothing contained in this Paragraph 12.2 shall be construed to establish a period of limitation with respect to other obligations which the Contractor might have under the Contract Documents. Establishment of the time period of one year as described in Subparagraph 12.2.2 relates only to the specific obligation of the Contractor to correct the Work, and has no relationship to the time within which the obligation to comply with the Contract Documents may be sought to be enforced, nor to the time within which proceedings may be commenced to establish the Contractor's liability with respect to the Contractor's obligations other than specifically to correct the Work.

12.3 ACCEPTANCE OF NONCONFORMING WORK

12.3.1 If the Owner prefers to accept Work which is not in accordance with the requirements of the Contract Documents, the Owner may do so instead of requiring its removal and correction, in which case the Contract Sum will be reduced as appropriate and equitable. Such adjustment shall be effected whether or not final payment has been made.

ARTICLE 13

MISCELLANEOUS PROVISIONS

13.1 GOVERNING LAW

13.1.1 The Contract shall be governed by the law of the place where the Project is located.

13.2 SUCCESSORS AND ASSIGNS

13.2.1 The Owner and Contractor respectively bind themselves, their partners, successors, assigns and legal representatives to the other party hereto and to partners, successors, assigns and legal representatives of such other party in respect to covenants, agreements and obligations contained in the Contract Documents. Neither party to the Contract shall assign the Contract as a whole without written consent of the other. If either party attempts to make such an assignment without such consent, that party shall nevertheless remain legally responsible for all obligations under the Contract.

13.3 WRITTEN NOTICE

13.3.1 Written notice shall be deemed to have been duly served if delivered in person to the individual or a member of the firm or entity or to an officer of the corporation for which it was intended, or if delivered at or sent by registered or certified mail to the last business address known to the party giving notice.

13.4 RIGHTS AND REMEDIES

13.4.1 Duties and obligations imposed by the Contract Documents and rights and remedies available thereunder shall be in addition to and not a limitation of duties, obligations, rights and remedies otherwise imposed or available by law.

13.4.2 No action or failure to act by the Owner, Architect or Contractor shall constitute a waiver of a right or duty afforded them under the Contract, nor shall such action or failure to act constitute approval of or acquiescence in a breach thereunder, except as may be specifically agreed in writing.

13.5 TESTS AND INSPECTIONS

13.5.1 Tests, inspections and approvals of portions of the Work required by the Contract Documents or by laws, ordinances, rules, regulations or orders of public authorities having jurisdiction shall be made at an appropriate time. Unless otherwise provided, the Contractor shall make arrangements for such tests, inspections and approvals with an independent testing laboratory or entity acceptable to the Owner, or with the appropriate public authority, and shall bear all related costs of tests, inspections and approvals. The Contractor shall give the Architect timely notice of when and where tests and inspections are to be made so the Architect may observe such procedures. The Owner shall bear costs of tests, inspections or approvals which do not become requirements until after bids are received or negotiations concluded.

13.5.2 If the Architect, Owner or public authorities having jurisdiction determine that portions of the Work require additional testing, inspection or approval not included under Subparagraph 13.5.1, the Architect will, upon written authorization from the Owner, instruct the Contractor to make arrangements for such additional testing, inspection or approval by an entity acceptable to the Owner, and the Contractor shall give timely notice to the Architect of when and where tests and inspections are to be made so the Architect may observe such procedures.

The Owner shall bear such costs except as provided in Subparagraph 13.5.3.

13.5.3 If such procedures for testing, inspection or approval under Subparagraphs 13.5.1 and 13.5.2 reveal failure of the portions of the Work to comply with requirements established by the Contract Documents, the Contractor shall bear all costs made necessary by such failure including those of repeated procedures and compensation for the Architect's services and expenses.

13.5.4 Required certificates of testing, inspection or approval shall, unless otherwise required by the Contract Documents, be secured by the Contractor and promptly delivered to the Architect.

13.5.5 If the Architect is to observe tests, inspections or approvals required by the Contract Documents, the Architect will do so promptly and, where practicable, at the normal place of testing.

13.5.6 Tests or inspections conducted pursuant to the Contract Documents shall be made promptly to avoid unreasonable delay in the Work.

13.6 INTEREST

13.6.1 Payments due and unpaid under the Contract Documents shall bear interest from the date payment is due at such rate as the parties may agree upon in writing or, in the absence thereof, at the legal rate prevailing from time to time at the place where the Project is located.

13.7 COMMENCEMENT OF STATUTORY LIMITATION PERIOD

13.7.1 As between the Owner and Contractor:

.1 **Before Substantial Completion.** As to acts or failures to act occurring prior to the relevant date of Substantial Completion, any applicable statute of limitations shall commence to run and any alleged cause of action shall be deemed to have accrued in any and all events not later than such date of Substantial Completion;

.2 **Between Substantial Completion and Final Certificate for Payment.** As to acts or failures to act occurring subsequent to the relevant date of Substantial Completion and prior to issuance of the final Certificate for Payment, any applicable statute of limitations shall commence to run and any alleged cause of action shall be deemed to have accrued in any and all events not later than the date of issuance of the final Certificate for Payment; and

.3 **After Final Certificate for Payment.** As to acts or failures to act occurring after the relevant date of issuance of the final Certificate for Payment, any applicable statute of limitations shall commence to run and any alleged cause of action shall be deemed to have accrued in any and all events not later than the date of any act or failure to act by the Contractor pursuant to any warranty provided under Paragraph 3.5, the date of any correction of the Work or failure to correct the Work by the Contractor under Paragraph 12.2, or the date of actual commission of any other act or failure to perform any duty or obligation by the Contractor or Owner, whichever occurs last.

ARTICLE 14

TERMINATION OR SUSPENSION OF THE CONTRACT

14.1 TERMINATION BY THE CONTRACTOR

14.1.1 The Contractor may terminate the Contract if the Work is stopped for a period of 30 days through no act or fault of the Contractor or a Subcontractor, Sub-subcontractor or their agents or employees or any other persons performing portions of the Work under contract with the Contractor, for any of the following reasons:

.1 issuance of an order of a court or other public authority having jurisdiction;

.2 an act of government, such as a declaration of national emergency, making material unavailable;

.3 because the Architect has not issued a Certificate for Payment and has not notified the Contractor of the reason for withholding certification as provided in Subparagraph 9.4.1, or because the Owner has not made payment on a Certificate for Payment within the time stated in the Contract Documents;

.4 if repeated suspensions, delays or interruptions by the Owner as described in Paragraph 14.3 constitute in the aggregate more than 100 percent of the total number of days scheduled for completion, or 120 days in any 365-day period, whichever is less; or

.5 the Owner has failed to furnish to the Contractor promptly, upon the Contractor's request, reasonable evidence as required by Subparagraph 2.2.1.

14.1.2 If one of the above reasons exists, the Contractor may, upon seven additional days' written notice to the Owner and Architect, terminate the Contract and recover from the Owner payment for Work executed and for proven loss with respect to materials, equipment, tools, and construction equipment and machinery, including reasonable overhead, profit and damages.

14.1.3 If the Work is stopped for a period of 60 days through no act or fault of the Contractor or a Subcontractor or their agents or employees or any other persons performing portions of the Work under contract with the Contractor because the Owner has persistently failed to fulfill the Owner's obligations under the Contract Documents with respect to matters important to the progress of the Work, the Contractor may, upon seven additional days' written notice to the Owner and the Architect, terminate the Contract and recover from the Owner as provided in Subparagraph 14.1.2.

14.2 TERMINATION BY THE OWNER FOR CAUSE

14.2.1 The Owner may terminate the Contract if the Contractor:

.1 persistently or repeatedly refuses or fails to supply enough properly skilled workers or proper materials;

.2 fails to make payment to Subcontractors for materials or labor in accordance with the respective agreements between the Contractor and the Subcontractors;

.3 persistently disregards laws, ordinances, or rules, regulations or orders of a public authority having jurisdiction; or

.4 otherwise is guilty of substantial breach of a provision of the Contract Documents.

14.2.2 When any of the above reasons exist, the Owner, upon certification by the Architect that sufficient cause exists to justify such action, may without prejudice to any other rights or remedies of the Owner and after giving the Contractor and the Contractor's surety, if any, seven days' written notice, terminate employment of the Contractor and may, subject to any prior rights of the surety:

- **.1** take possession of the site and of all materials, equipment, tools, and construction equipment and machinery thereon owned by the Contractor;
- **.2** accept assignment of subcontracts pursuant to Paragraph 5.4; and
- **.3** finish the Work by whatever reasonable method the Owner may deem expedient.

14.2.3 When the Owner terminates the Contract for one of the reasons stated in Subparagraph 14.2.1, the Contractor shall not be entitled to receive further payment until the Work is finished.

14.2.4 If the unpaid balance of the Contract Sum exceeds costs of finishing the Work, including compensation for the Architect's services and expenses made necessary thereby, such excess shall be paid to the Contractor. If such costs exceed the unpaid balance, the Contractor shall pay the difference to the Owner. The amount to be paid to the Contractor or Owner, as the case may be, shall be certified by the Architect, upon application, and this obligation for payment shall survive termination of the Contract.

14.3 SUSPENSION BY THE OWNER FOR CONVENIENCE

14.3.1 The Owner may, without cause, order the Contractor in writing to suspend, delay or interrupt the Work in whole or in part for such period of time as the Owner may determine.

14.3.2 An adjustment shall be made for increases in the cost of performance of the Contract, including profit on the increased cost of performance, caused by suspension, delay or interruption. No adjustment shall be made to the extent:

- **.1** that performance is, was or would have been so suspended, delayed or interrupted by another cause for which the Contractor is responsible; or
- **.2** that an equitable adjustment is made or denied under another provision of this Contract.

14.3.3 Adjustments made in the cost of performance may have a mutually agreed fixed or percentage fee.

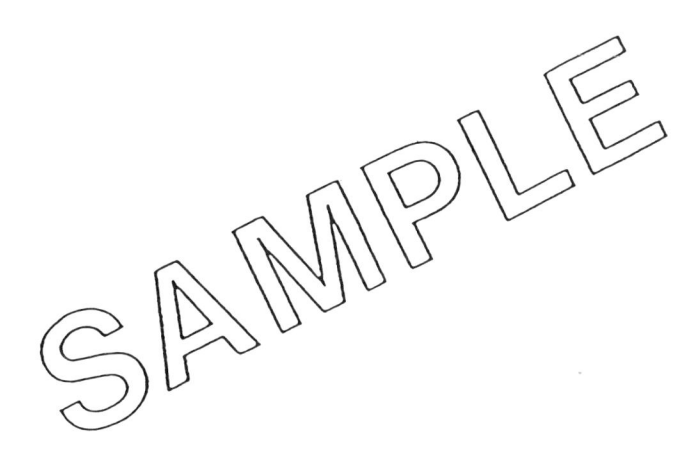

INSTRUCTION SHEET

FOR AIA DOCUMENT A201, GENERAL CONDITIONS OF THE
CONTRACT FOR CONSTRUCTION—1987 Edition

A. GENERAL INFORMATION

1. Purpose

AIA Document A201, a general conditions form, is intended to be used as one of the Contract Documents forming the Construction Contract. In addition, it is frequently adopted by reference into a variety of other agreements, including the Owner-Architect agreements and the Contractor-Subcontractor agreements, in order to establish a common basis for the primary and secondary relationships on the typical construction project.

2. Related Documents

The current edition of A201 is incorporated by specific reference into two AIA Owner-Contractor agreements (A101 and A111) and several AIA Owner-Architect agreements (B141, B151, B161 and B181). It may also be adopted by indirect reference when the prime Agreement between the Owner and Contractor is adopted into a Subcontract, such as AIA Document A401, or when the prime Agreement between the Owner and Architect is adopted into Architect-Consultant agreements such as AIA Documents C141, C142, C161 and C431. Such incorporation by reference is a valid legal drafting method, and documents so incorporated are generally interpreted as part of the respective contract.

The Contract Documents, including A201, record the Contract for Construction between the Owner and the Contractor. The other Contract Documents include:

Owner-Contractor Agreement Form (i.e., A101 or A111)
Supplementary and Other Conditions
Drawings
Specifications
Modifications

Also included in the Contract Documents are addenda issued prior to execution of the Contract and other documents listed in the Agreement. The A201 document is considered the keystone document coordinating the many parties involved in the construction process. As mentioned above and diagramed below, it is a vital document used to allocate the proper legal responsibilities of the parties.

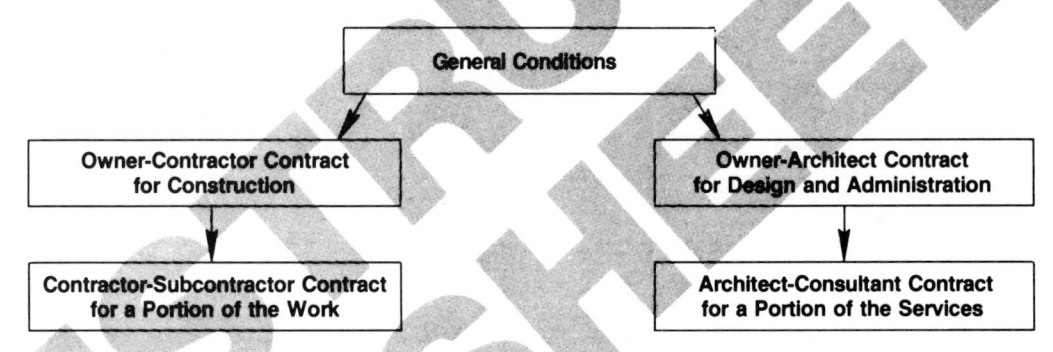

```
                    ┌─────────────────────┐
                    │ General Conditions  │
                    └──────────┬──────────┘
              ┌────────────────┴────────────────┐
              ▼                                 ▼
┌──────────────────────────┐        ┌──────────────────────────┐
│ Owner-Contractor Contract│        │ Owner-Architect Contract │
│     for Construction     │        │ for Design and Administration │
└─────────────┬────────────┘        └─────────────┬────────────┘
              ▼                                   ▼
┌──────────────────────────────┐    ┌──────────────────────────────┐
│ Contractor-Subcontractor Contract │ │ Architect-Consultant Contract │
│    for a Portion of the Work      │ │  for a Portion of the Services │
└──────────────────────────────┘    └──────────────────────────────┘
```

The AIA publishes other General Conditions that parallel A201 for the construction management family of documents (AIA Document A201/CM) and the interiors family of documents (AIA Document A271). For certain federal projects, the AIA publishes the A201 document with Federal Supplementary Conditions (AIA Document A201/SC).

3. Arbitration

The A201 document incorporates ARBITRATION according to the Construction Industry Arbitration Rules of the American Arbitration Association. Arbitration is BINDING AND MANDATORY in most states and under the federal Arbitration Act. In a minority of states, arbitration provisions related to future disputes are not enforceable, but arbitration is enforceable if agreed to after the dispute arises. A few states require that the contracting parties be especially notified that the written contract contains an arbitration provision by: a warning on the face of the document; specific placement of the arbitration provision within the document; or specific discussions among the parties prior to signing the document.

Arbitration provisions have been included in most AIA contract forms since 1888 in order to encourage alternative dispute resolution procedures and to provide users of AIA documents with legally enforceable arbitration provisions when the parties choose to adopt arbitration into their contract. Individuals may, however, choose to delete the arbitration provisions based upon their business decisions with the advice of counsel. To obtain a copy of the Construction Industry Arbitration Rules, write to the American Arbitration Association, 140 West 51st St., New York, NY 10020.

4. Use of Non-AIA Forms

If a combination of AIA documents and non-AIA documents is to be used, particular care must be taken to achieve consistency of language and intent. Certain owners require the use of owner-contractor agreements with general conditions and other contract forms which they prepare. Such forms should be carefully compared with the standard AIA forms for which they are being substituted before execution of an agreement. If there are any significant omissions, additions or variances from the terms of the related standard AIA forms, both legal and insurance counsel should be consulted.

5. Use of Current Documents

Prior to using any AIA document, the user should consult the AIA, an AIA component chapter or a current AIA Documents Price List to determine the current edition of each document.

6. Reproduction

AIA Document A201 is a copyrighted work and may not be reproduced or excerpted from in substantial part without the express written permission of the AIA. The A201 document is intended to be used as a consumable—that is, the original document purchased by the user is intended to be consumed in the course of being used. There is no implied permission to reproduce this document, nor does membership in The American Institute of Architects confer any further rights to reproduce them.

A201 may not be reproduced for Project Manuals. Rather, if a user wishes to include it in a Project Manual, the normal practice is to purchase a quantity of the pre-printed forms and bind one in each of the Project Manuals. Modifications may be accomplished through the use of separate Supplementary Conditions, such as those derived from AIA Document A511.

Unlike the instruction sheets accompanying some AIA documents, this A201 Instruction Sheet does not include a license granting permission to reproduce the A201 document. AIA will not permit the reproduction of this document or the use of substantial portions of language from it, except upon written request and receipt of written permission from the AIA.

B. CHANGES FROM THE PREVIOUS EDITION

1. Format Changes

The provisions dealing with the rights and responsibilities of the Architect have been moved from Article 2 to Article 4, retitled Administration of the Contract, in order to focus on the Owner and the Contractor as the parties to the Construction Contract. Miscellaneous Provisions, formerly Article 7, is now Article 13.

2. Changes in Content

The 1987 edition of A201 revises the 1976 edition to reflect changes in construction industry practices and the law. Comments and assistance in this revision were received from numerous individuals and organizations, including those representing owners, architects, engineers, specifiers, general contractors, subcontractors, sureties, attorneys and arbitrators.

Substantial changes have been made to the A201 document. The principal changes are as follows.

Article 3: Contractor

Warranty—The warranty provision now explicitly excludes damage or defect caused by abuse, modifications not executed by the Contractor, improper or insufficient maintenance, and normal wear and tear under normal usage.

Article 4: Administration of the Contract

Review of Shop Drawings—The provision governing architect's review of shop drawings has been expanded, and now requires that the architect be given sufficient time in his or her professional judgment to conduct an adequate review. The general limitation on the purpose of the Architect's review to checking for conformance with the information given and the design concept expressed in the Contract Documents has been retained. In addition, language has been added specifically excluding purposes of checking details that are the responsibility of the Contractor.

Claims and Disputes—Provisions governing the handling of Claims and disputes have been expanded and brought together in a single paragraph to spell out procedures more clearly and sequentially; diagrams of the Change Order and Claims processes may be found on the last page of this Instruction Sheet. In the interest of expediting arbitration proceedings, a notice of demand for arbitration is now required to include all causes of action then known to the party filing the demand. Limitations on consolidation or joinder in arbitration of the Architect or the Architect's employees or consultants have been retained.

Delays Due to Adverse Weather Conditions—Claims for delay due to adverse weather conditions must now be substantiated by data showing that such conditions were out of the ordinary and had an adverse effect on the scheduled construction.

Article 5: Subcontractors

Contingent Assignment of Subcontracts—A new provision assigns Subcontracts to the Owner in the event that the Contract is terminated, and also provides for adjustment of the Subcontractor's compensation if termination has resulted in suspension of the Work for more than 30 days. Both Owner and Subcontractors are thus given a measure of protection from the effects of termination.

Article 7: Changes in the Work

This article has undergone substantial revision, and provides for a new type of document. The Change Order is now required to be signed by the Owner, Contractor and Architect. In the event the Contractor's agreement cannot be obtained, a new document, a Construction Change Directive which is signed by the Owner and Architect, shall be issued. Both of these situations were previously covered by Change Orders. Now they are separated so that they can, if necessary, be handled independently. A diagram of the process may be found on the last page of this Instruction Sheet.

Article 9: Payments and Completion

Substantial Completion—The Substantial Completion provisions now explicitly allow for partial occupancy or use. A Certificate of Substantial Completion covering a portion of Work is provided for, and consent of the insurer of the property is required.

Article 10: Protection of Persons and Property

Asbestos, PCB and Other Hazardous Wastes—The problem of hazardous wastes is addressed, for the first time, in a paragraph prescribing procedures to be followed in the event such substances are encountered on the site. Under its provisions, the Work may only proceed in the affected area by written consent of the Owner and Contractor, or in accordance with a determination of the Architect upon which arbitration has not been demanded.

Article 11: Insurance and Bonds

This article has been expanded to cover bonds as well, and it is now provided that bonding requirements must be made known to the Contractor in the bidding requirements or at the time the Contract is signed. The Contractor, in turn, is required to furnish copies of the bonds on request to any person appearing to be a beneficiary of them.

Owner's property insurance is now required to be written in the full amount of the Contract Sum and adjusted for changes in the Contract Sum effected by Change Order. The coverages to be included on the "all-risk" policy form are given in much greater detail because "all-risk" merely means coverage of all risks not specifically excluded. In addition, the Owner is now required to insure materials stored off-site or in transit.

Article 12: Uncovering and Correction of Work

Correction of Work—The correction period has been extended with respect to Work performed after Substantial Completion, so that such Work is also covered by a one-year correction period.

Article 13: Miscellaneous Provisions

Statutory Limitation Period—A separate paragraph has been included under Miscellaneous Provisions giving the dates of commencement of the statutory limitation period with respect to acts or failures to act occurring at different points in the Project. This paragraph covers a range of situations and sets three commencement dates: one for occurrences before Substantial Completion, another for those taking place between Substantial Completion and issuance of the final Certificate for Payment, and a third for those taking place after the final Certificate has been issued.

Article 14: Termination or Suspension of the Contract

Procedures are set out for suspension of the Contract by the Owner for reasons other than the fault of the Contractor. A provision allowing for termination in like circumstances has been included in AIA Document A511, Guide for Supplementary Conditions.

Further details on these changes may be found in the *Architect's Handbook of Professional Practice* when revised. A side-by-side comparison of the 1976 and 1987 editions of A201 will be available for a limited time after publication of the 1987 edition.

C. USING THE A201 FORM

Modifications

Users are encouraged to consult an attorney before using an AIA document. Particularly with respect to licensing laws, duties imposed by building codes, interest charges, arbitration and indemnification, this document may require modification with the assistance of legal counsel to fully comply with state or local laws regulating these matters.

Generally, necessary modifications to the General Conditions may be accomplished by Supplementary Conditions included in the Project Manual and referenced in the Owner-Contractor Agreement. See AIA Document A511, Guide for Supplementary Conditions, for model provisions and suggested format for the Supplementary Conditions.

Because A201 is designed for general usage, it does not provide all the information and legal requirements needed for a specific Project and location. Necessary additional requirements must be provided in the other Contract Documents, such as the Supplementary Conditions. Consult AIA Document A521, Uniform Location of Subject Matter, to determine the proper location for such additional stipulations.

It is definitely not recommended practice to retype the standard document. Besides being a violation of copyright, retyping can introduce typographical errors and cloud the legal interpretation given to a standard clause when blended with modifications. Retyping eliminates one of the principal advantages of standard form documents. By merely reviewing the modifications to be made to a standard form document, parties familiar with that document can quickly understand the essence of the proposed relationship. Commercial exchanges are greatly simplified and expedited, good-faith dealing is encouraged, and otherwise latent clauses are exposed for scrutiny. In this way, contracting parties can more confidently and fairly measure their risks.

D. CHANGE ORDERS AND CLAIMS

The diagrams below are graphic examples of the Change Order and Claims processes under the 1987 edition of AIA Document A201. These diagrams are presented for instructional purposes only, and are not intended to augment or supersede any contract language contained in the document. Users are urged to read the document in its entirety and to consult the relevant contract language regarding the particulars of the processes diagrammed below.

A Change Order may be initiated by the Owner, Contractor or Architect. Typically, upon initiation of the Change Order process, the Architect prepares a copy of AIA Document G709, Proposal Request, and submits it to the Contractor for pricing. This is then conveyed back through the Architect to the Owner, beginning the process diagrammed below.

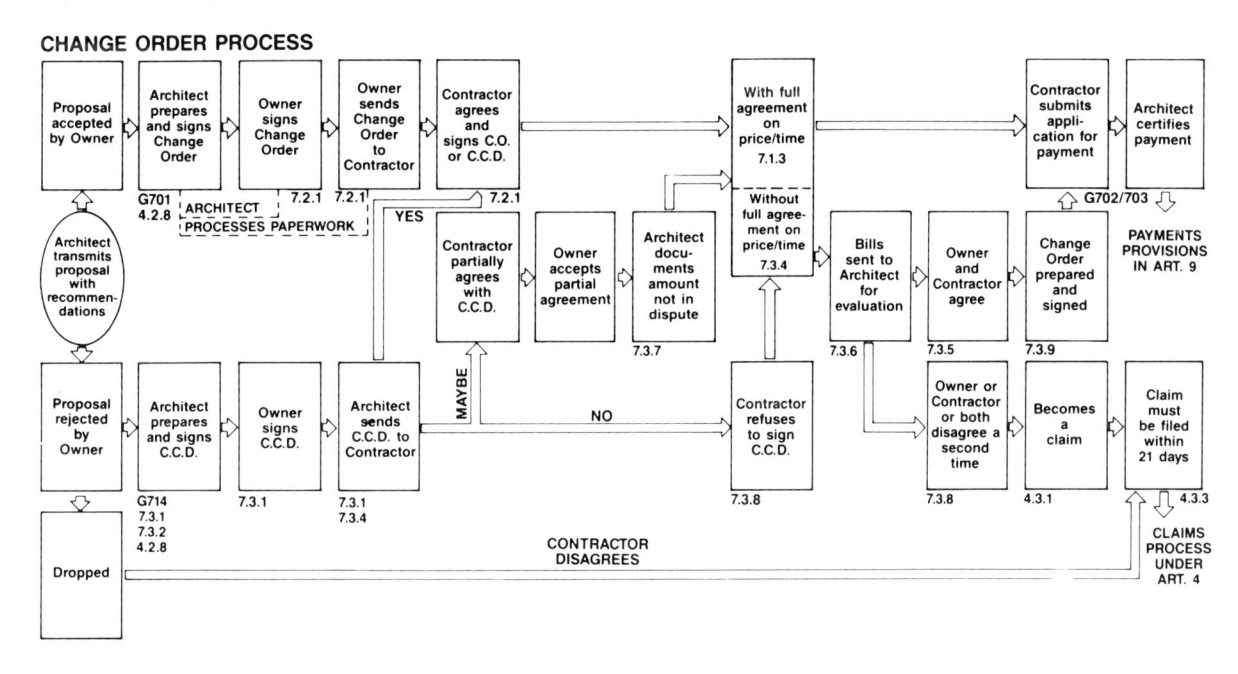

CHANGE ORDER PROCESS

The Claims process may be started through a variety of circumstances, including failure to agree upon the terms of a Change Order as shown in the diagram above. Once the Claim arises, the Owner and Contractor, together with the Architect, seek resolution of the dispute by following specific steps established in the Contract Documents and particularly in A201. These steps are generalized in the diagram below.

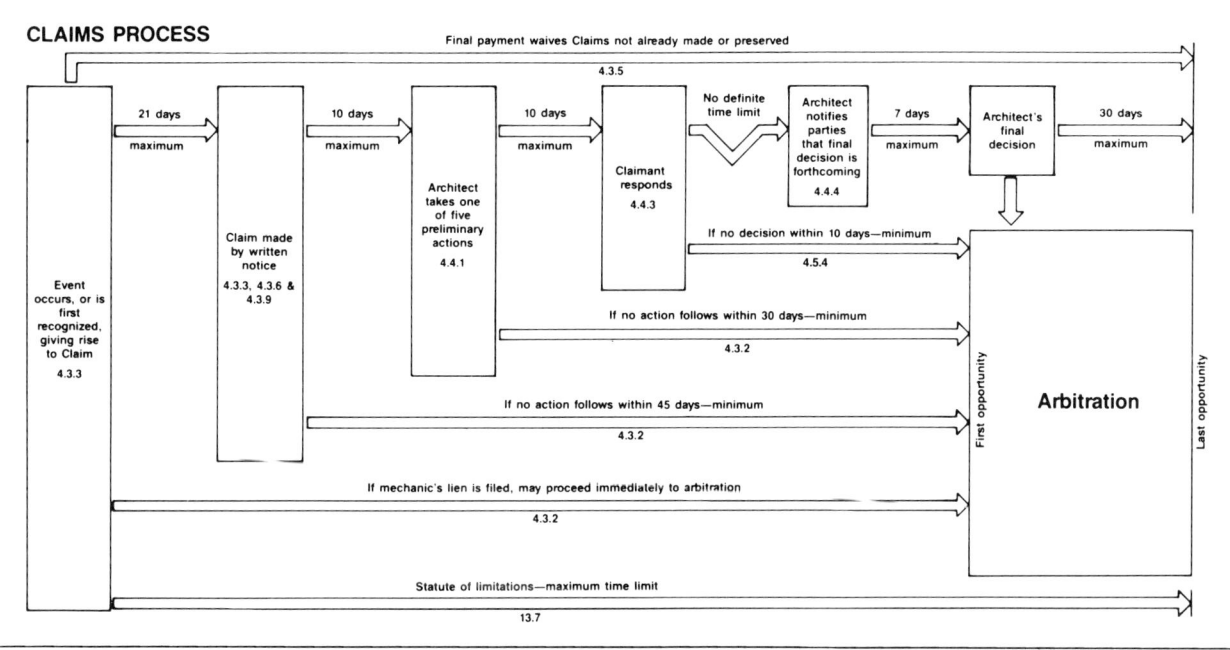

CLAIMS PROCESS

Appendix E:
Synopses of AIA Standard Form Documents Referred to in This Book

The following synopses of AIA documents have been created by the AIA Documents Committee to provide users of the documents with a quick reference for determining their specific applications. These synopses will also be of use to those unfamiliar with AIA documents by providing an overview of the types of agreements the documents cover.

While they will aid users in selecting the most suitable document for a given agreement, the synopses should not be used as the sole basis for selection. Users are advised to examine the actual documents and consult with legal counsel to ensure use of the most suitable ones.

These portions of AIA Document M100, Documents Synopses, 1987 Edition, copyrighted by the American Institute of Architects, have been reproduced here with the permission of the AIA under license number 90011. FURTHER REPRODUCTION IS PROHIBITED. Permission expires December 31, 1991.

AIA DOCUMENT A101, OWNER-CONTRACTOR AGREEMENT FORM—STIPULATED SUM

This is a standard form of agreement between owner and contractor, for use where the basis of payment is a stipulated sum (fixed price). The document has been prepared for use with AIA Document A201, General Conditions of the Contract for Construction, providing an integrated pair of documents. This pair of documents is suitable for most projects; however, for projects of limited scope, use of AIA Document A107 should be considered.

AIA DOCUMENT A111, OWNER-CONTRACTOR AGREEMENT FORM—COST OF THE WORK PLUS A FEE WITH OR WITHOUT A GUARANTEED MAXIMUM PRICE

This is a standard form of agreement between owner and contractor, for use where the basis of payment to the contractor is the cost of the work plus a fee, which may be a stipulated amount or a percentage of the construction cost. A guaranteed maximum price may be designated, with provisions, if any, for distribution of any savings below the guaranteed maximum price. The document has been prepared for use with AIA Document A201, General Conditions of the Contract for Construction, providing an integrated pair of documents. This pair of documents is suitable for most projects; however, for projects of limited scope, use of AIA Document A117 should be considered.

AIA DOCUMENT A201, GENERAL CONDITIONS OF THE CONTRACT FOR CONSTRUCTION

The General Conditions are a part of the contract for construction and set forth rights, responsibilities and relationships of the parties involved. Since conditions vary by locality and project, supplementary conditions are usually required to amend or supplement portions of the General Conditions as required by the individual project.

While not a party to the contract for construction between owner and contractor, the architect does participate in the preparation of the construction contract documents and performs certain duties and responsibilities described in detail in the general conditions.

AIA DOCUMENT A305, CONTRACTOR'S QUALIFICATION STATEMENT

An owner about to request bids or award a contract for a construction project needs a vehicle for verifying the background, history, references and financial stability of any contractor being considered. The construction time frame and the contractor's performance, history, previous experience, and financial capability are important factors for an owner to consider. This form provides a sworn, notarized statement with appropriate attachments to elaborate on the important facets of the contractor's qualifications.

AIA DOCUMENT A310, BID BOND

This simple one-page form was drafted with input from the major surety companies as to its legality and acceptability. A bid bond establishes the maximum penal amount that may be due the owner if the selected bidder fails to execute the contract and provide any required bonds.

AIA DOCUMENT A312, PERFORMANCE BOND AND PAYMENT BOND

This two-part bond form, when properly executed, guarantees the funds, up to the bond amount, to complete the contract in the event some unforeseen situation prevents the original contractor and subcontractors from finishing the work.

The Performance Bond allows the surety, in the event of the contractor's default, to assume the contract obligations and "perform" the contractor's function, obtaining a bid or bids to complete the work.

Should the contractor fail to make proper payments, the Payment Bond provides for payment up to the bond amount of those subcontractors and others whose labor and materials are required for complete performance of the contract.

AIA DOCUMENT A401, STANDARD FORM OF AGREEMENT BETWEEN CONTRACTOR AND SUBCONTRACTOR

This document establishes the contractual relationship between prime contractor and subcontractor. It spells out the responsibilities of both parties and lists their respective obligations as enumerated in the General Conditions, AIA Document A201. The appropriate sections of A201 are included as part of the document. Blank spaces are provided where the parties can supplement the details of their agreement for each project.

AIA DOCUMENT A501, RECOMMENDED GUIDE FOR COMPETITIVE BIDDING PROCEDURES AND CONTRACT AWARDS FOR BUILDING CONSTRUCTION

This guide is intended to establish desirable objectives in the bidding procedure and the award of contracts. The Guide is for use when competitive lump sum bids are requested in connection with building and related construction, and is a joint publication of the AIA and the Associated General Contractors of America (AGC).

AIA DOCUMENT A701, INSTRUCTIONS TO BIDDERS

This document provides a base which other documents and project requirements build upon. It is complementary to the AIA General Conditions; it is meant for general usage and anticipates some additions, modifications and other provisions. The usual, rather than specific, project provisions for instructions to bidders are included.

AIA DOCUMENT B141, STANDARD FORM OF AGREEMENT BETWEEN OWNER AND ARCHITECT

This is a standard form of agreement between owner and architect, for use where services are based on the five traditional phases. The document has been prepared for use when AIA Document A201, General Conditions of the Contract for Construction, is used in the contract between the owner and the contractor. It sets forth the duties and responsibilities of the architect and the owner in each phase of the project.

AIA DOCUMENT B151, ABBREVIATED OWNER-ARCHITECT AGREEMENT

This is an abbreviated owner-architect agreement for use on projects of limited scope where a concise, readable contract is needed but where the services and detail of B141 may not be appropriate. Three phases of services are provided for, rather than five as in B141. B151 should be used in lieu of oral or letter forms of agreement.

AIA DOCUMENT B161, STANDARD FORM OF AGREEMENT BETWEEN OWNER AND ARCHITECT FOR DESIGNATED SERVICES

This standard form of agreement between owner and architect for designated services is intended to be used in conjunction with AIA Document B162, Scope of Designated Services. These documents are designed to work together in describing the terms and conditions of the agreement and the amounts of compensation (B161), and the responsibilities and services to be undertaken by the owner and architect (B162). The B162 document may be used with other agreement forms. Similarly, B161 may be used as the terms and conditions with other forms of scope of services statements. However, neither document may be used alone.

B161 provides a description of the architect's construction phase services which is coordinated with AIA Document A201, General Conditions of the Contract for Construction.

AIA DOCUMENT B162, SCOPE OF DESIGNATED SERVICES

The Scope of Designated Services is intended to be used in conjunction with AIA Document B161, Owner-Architect Agreement for Designated Services. These documents are designed to work together in describing the terms and conditions of the agreement and the amounts of compensation (B161), and the responsibilities and services to be undertaken by the owner and architect (B162). The B162 document may be used with other agreement forms. Similarly, B161 may be used as the terms and conditions with other forms of scope of services statements. However, neither document may be used alone.

B162 provides for designated services to be performed by both the owner and the architect. Nine phases of services are listed, from pre-design and site analysis through the traditional five phases to post-construction and supplemental services. Within the nine phases, over 125 different services are listed and more may be added at the parties' discretion. Any or all may be designated as appropriate to the project.

AIA DOCUMENT B181, STANDARD FORM OF AGREEMENT BETWEEN OWNER AND ARCHITECT FOR HOUSING SERVICES WITH COST ESTIMATING SERVICES PROVIDED BY OWNER

The Standard Form of Agreement Between Owner and Architect for Housing Services with Cost Estimating Services Provided by Owner is intended for use on single and multifamily dwelling projects, including those for government agencies, and is essentially a modified version of AIA Document B151, Abbreviated Owner-Architect Agreement.

This document has been accepted by the U.S. Department of Housing and Urban Development and replaces former FHA Documents A, B and C.

AIA DOCUMENT C141, STANDARD FORM OF AGREEMENT BETWEEN ARCHITECT AND CONSULTANT

This is a standard form of agreement between architect and consultant, establishing their responsibilities to each other and their mutual rights under the agreement. The document is most applicable to engineers, but may be used by consultants in other disciplines providing services for architects who are providing the traditional five phases of "Basic Services" for owners under the provisions of AIA Document B141, Owner-Architect Agreement. Its provisions are in accord with those of B141 and of AIA Document A201, General Conditions of the Contract for Construction.

AIA DOCUMENT C142, ABBREVIATED ARCHITECT-CONSULTANT AGREEMENT

This is an abbreviated form of agreement between architect and consultant, and adopts the terms of a prime agreement between owner and architect by reference. It is intended that the prime agreement be based on AIA Document B141.

AIA DOCUMENT G612, OWNER'S INSTRUCTIONS REGARDING THE CONSTRUCTION CONTRACT, INSURANCE AND BONDS, AND BIDDING PROCEDURES

This is a standard form which the architect may use as a questionnaire to request instructions from the owner which will be needed by the architect in preparation of the contract documents. The form is in three parts: Part A, Owner's Instructions Regarding the Construction Contract; Part B, Owner's Instructions for Insurance and Bonds; and Part C, Owner's Instructions Regarding Bidding Instructions. It is expected that the owner would decide these matters with appropriate advice of legal and insurance counsel.

AIA DOCUMENT G701, CHANGE ORDER

A Change Order is the instrument by which changes in the work and adjustments in the contract sum or contract time under the owner-contractor agreement are formalized. The form provides space for a complete description of the change, modifications to the contract sum and adjustments in the contract time.

AIA DOCUMENT G702, APPLICATION AND CERTIFICATE FOR PAYMENT; AIA DOCUMENT G703, CONTINUATION SHEET

These documents provide convenient and complete forms on which the contractor can make application for payment and on which the architect can certify that payment is due. The forms require the contractor to show the status of the contract sum to date, including the total dollar amount of the work completed and stored to date, the amount of retainage, the total of previous payments, a summary of change orders, and the amount of current payment requested. G703, Continuation Sheet, breaks the contract sum into the portions of work in accordance with a schedule of values required by the general conditions. The form serves as both the contractor's application and the architect's certification. Its use can expedite payment and reduce the possibility of error. If the application is properly completed and acceptable to the architect, the architect's signature certifies to the owner that a payment in the amount indicated is due the contractor. The form also allows the architect to certify an amount different than the amount applied for, with explanation by the architect.

AIA DOCUMENT G704, CERTIFICATE OF SUBSTANTIAL COMPLETION

This is a standard form for recording the date of substantial completion of the work or designated portion thereof. The contractor prepares a list of items to be completed or corrected, and the architect verifies and amends this list. If the architect finds that the work is substantially complete, the form is completed for acceptance by the contractor and the owner. Appended thereto is the list of items to be completed or corrected. The form provides for agreement as to the time allowed for completion or correction of the items, the date upon which the owner will occupy the work or designated portion thereof, and description of responsibilities for maintenance, heat, utilities and insurance.

AIA DOCUMENT G705, CERTIFICATE OF INSURANCE

This is a standard form by which the contractor's insurers present to the owner a confirmation of insurance coverages relating to the project.

AIA DOCUMENT G706, CONTRACTOR'S AFFIDAVIT OF PAYMENT OF DEBTS AND CLAIMS

The contractor submits this affidavit with the final request for payment, stating that all payrolls, bills for materials and equipment, and other indebtedness connected with the work for which the owner might be responsible have been paid or otherwise satisfied. The form requires the contractor to list specifically any indebtedness or known claims in connection with the construction contract which have not been paid or otherwise satisfied and to furnish a lien bond or indemnity bond to protect the owner with respect to each exception.

AIA DOCUMENT G706A, CONTRACTOR'S AFFIDAVIT OF RELEASE OF LIENS

This document supports AIA Document G706 if the owner requires a sworn statement of the contractor that all releases or waivers of liens have been received. In such cases, it is normal for the contractor to submit G706 duly executed, together with G706A duly executed with attached releases or waivers of liens for the contractor, all subcontractors and others who may have lien rights against the property of the owner. The contractor is required to list any exceptions to this statement and furnish a lien bond or indemnity bond to protect the owner with respect to such exceptions.

AIA DOCUMENT G707, CONSENT OF SURETY TO FINAL PAYMENT

By obtaining the surety's approval of final payment to the contractor and its agreement that final payment will not relieve the surety of any of its obligations, the owner may preserve its rights under the bonds.

AIA DOCUMENT G707A, CONSENT OF SURETY TO REDUCTION IN OR PARTIAL RELEASE OF RETAINAGE

This is a standard form for use when a surety company is involved and the owner-contractor agreement contains a clause whereby retainage is reduced during the course of the construction project. The form, when duly executed, assures the owner that such reduction or partial release of retainage does not relieve the surety of its obligations.

AIA DOCUMENT G709, PROPOSAL REQUEST

This is a form used to secure price quotations which are necessary in the negotiation of change orders. The form is not a change order or a direction to proceed with the work; it is simply a request to the contractor for information related to a proposed change in the construction contract.

AIA DOCUMENT G711, ARCHITECT'S FIELD REPORT

The Architect's Field Report is a standard form for the architect's project representative to use to maintain a concise record of site visits or, in case of a full-time project representative, a daily log of construction activities.

AIA DOCUMENT G712, SHOP DRAWING AND SAMPLE RECORD

This is a standard form by which the architect can schedule and monitor shop drawings and samples. Since this process tends to be a complicated one, this schedule, showing the progress of a submittal, is an aid in the orderly processing of work and will serve as a permanent record of the chronology of the process.

AIA DOCUMENT G714, CONSTRUCTION CHANGE DIRECTIVE

This document was developed as a directive for changes in the work which, if not implemented expeditiously, might delay the project. In contrast to a Change Order (AIA Document G701), AIA Document G714 is to be used where the owner and contractor, for whatever reason, have not reached agreement upon the proposed changes in the contract sum or contract time. Upon receipt of the completed G714, this contractor *must* promptly proceed with the change in the work described therein.

Index

Acceleration, 77–78
Accident prevention procedures, 25, 94–95, 109–110
Accidental losses, financial responsibility for, 37
ACORD, 25-S, 38
Addenda to contract documents, 5, 106, 179
Additional agreements, 177–178
Additional meetings, 26
Advertisements to bid, 5
Advisors (see Consultants)
Aesthetic effect, 134–136, 140–141
Agency Company Organization for Research and Development, 38
Agreements between owners and contractors, 5, 177–178
AIA (see American Institute of Architects)
Allowances, 26–27, 47
Alternate bids, 14–15, 47
Amendments to contracts, 5, 179
American Arbitration Association, 143–144, 154
American Institute of Architects (AIA) documents:
   Abbreviated Agreement between Architect and Consultant (C142), 62, 65, 263
   Abbreviated Agreement between Owner and Architect (B151), 42, 263

American Institute of Architects (AIA) documents (Cont.):
   Application and Certificate for Payment (G702), 68, 85–86, 117, 170–171, 264
   Architect's Field Report (G711), 46, 264
   Bid Bond (A310), 15, 262
   Certificate of Insurance (G705), 38, 264
   Certificate of Substantial Completion (G704), 114, 171, 264
   Change Order (G701), 75, 263
   Consent of Surety to Final Payment (G707), 56, 72, 118, 264
   Consent of Surety to Reduction in or Partial Release of Retainage (G707A), 57, 72, 120, 264
   Construction Change Directive (G714), 75, 264
   Continuation Sheet (G703), 68, 86, 117, 264
   Contractor's Affidavit of Payment of Debts and Claims (G706), 72, 118, 264
   Contractor's Affidavit of Release of Liens (G706A), 72, 118, 264
   Contractor's Qualification Statement (A305), 12, 262

American Institute of Architects (AIA) documents (Cont.):
   Documents Synopses (M100), 261–264
   General Conditions of the Contract for Construction (A201), 5, 21–30, 33, 37–39, 44, 49, 51, 56, 60–62, 64–65, 67–69, 71–72, 74, 79, 82–89, 92–111, 113–121, 123–126, 132–136, 138–151, 161, 169–179, 231–259, 262
   Instructions to Bidders (A701), 12–13, 262
   Owner's Instructions Regarding the Construction Contract, Insurance and Bonds, and Bidding Procedures (G612), 10, 38, 263
   Performance Bond and Payment Bond (A312), 54, 126–127, 174, 262
   Proposal Request (G709), 75, 264
   Recommended Guide for Competitive Bidding Procedures and Contract Awards for Building Construction (A501), 11, 262
   Scope of Designated Services (B162), 42, 263
   Shop Drawing and Sample Record (G712), 44, 63, 65, 264

American Institute of Architects (AIA) documents (*Cont.*):
   Standard Form of Agreement between Architect and Consultant (C141), 33–34, 60, 62, 65, 263
   Standard Form of Agreement between Contractor and Subcontractor (A401), 262
   Standard Form of Agreement between Owner and Architect (B141), 5, 34, 38, 42–47, 49, 60, 62, 64–65, 72, 79, 97, 99–100, 113–114, 116, 121–122, 161, 181–195, 263
   Standard Form of Agreement between Owner and Architect for Designated Services (B161), 42, 263
   Standard Form of Agreement between Owner and Architect for Housing Services with Cost Estimating Services Provided by Owner (B181), 42, 263
   Standard Form of Agreement between Owner and Contractor (A101), 5, 16, 91, 197–209, 262
   Standard Form of Agreement between Owner and Contractor (A111), 5, 17, 91, 211–229, 262
Approvals, 178–179
Arbitration, about disputes, 142–144, 154
Architects:
   aesthetic effects decisions, 134–136, 140–141
   approval of shop drawings, 64–65
   certifications, 170
   changes in duties, 99–100
   claims against, 153–163
   and consultants, 34–35
   as contract administrators, 2–5
   decisions by, 26, 30, 121, 131–136, 140–141
   delays caused by, 147–148
   field reports, 44, 46–47
   final certificate and final payment, 117–118
   limitations of authority, 48–49
   minor changes by, 5, 79, 134, 141
   new, 99–100
   and personnel in office and field, 47, 64
   relationship with owners, 88–89, 121–122

Architects (*Cont.*):
   resolution of differences and claims, 121, 136–144
   and termination of construction contracts, 127
   visits to jobsites, 24, 46–47
Architectural services agreements, 42
Asbestos, 74, 97, 110–111
Associated General Contractors, 11
Authorizations, 178–179
Award of contract, 16–17
Awards, arbitration, 143–144

Base bids, 14–15
Bid bonds, 15
Bid packages, 13–14
Bidding:
   alternate bids, 14–15, 47
   award of contract, 16–17
   base bids, 14–15
   bid bonds, 15
   bid packages, 13–14
   competitive, 9
   determining low bidder, 15–16
   establishment of conditions, 10
   instructions to bidders, 12–13
   invitations to bid, 12
   and negotiated contracts, 9
   opening of bids, 15–16
   periods, 14
   practices, 10
   proposal forms, 15
   recommended procedures, 10–11
   requirements, 5
   selection of bidders, 11–12
   unit prices, 14–15
Bonds:
   bid, 15
   (*See also* Construction bonds)
Boundary surveys, 22
Budgeting of fees, construction phase services, 45
Building projects, successful, 19–20

Calendar days, 146–147
Cash allowances, 47
Certificates of insurance (*see* Insurance certificates)
Certificates of payment (*see* Payment certificates)
Certificates of substantial completion (*see* Substantial completion certificates)
Certifications, architect, 170
Change orders, 5, 45, 47, 106
   acceleration, 77–78
   for all contract changes, 79

Change orders (*Cont.*):
   and construction change directives, 74
   contractor claims for extra compensation, 78–79
   effect on architects, 78
   effect on surety, 78
   effect on time, 77
   impact claims, 77–78
   minor changes by architects, 79
   no benefits from, 73
   owner's right to make changes, 74
   pricing and billing, 76–77
   procedure, 74–75
Chemical toilets, 21
Claims:
   in disputes, 121, 139–140
   impact, 77–78
   and lawsuits, 153–163
Clarification drawings, 5
Communications, 24, 44, 96, 106–107
   (*See also* Written communications)
Competitive bidding, 9
Competitive proposals, 10
Completion of construction projects:
   architect's final certificate and final payment, 117–118
   certificate of substantial completion, 114–115
   final completion, 117
   final submittals, 116–117
   liquidated damages, 120–121
   notices of completion, 115–116
   owner-architect relationship, 121–122
   partial use or occupancy by owners, 119
   resolution of differences, architect role in, 121
   retainage, 120
   substantial completion, 114, 150
   termination of construction contract, 113–114, 121
   withholding certificates, 118–119
Completion notices, 115–116
Concealed conditions, claims for, 107
Conditions of contracts, 5
Conferences (*see* Preconstruction jobsite conferences)
Construction administration:
   architect as contract administrator, 2–3
   benefits of contracts, 2–3

266 / Index

Construction administration (*Cont.*):
  contract documents, 5
  of contracts, 4–5
  contractual relationships, 6–7
  general principles, 6, 8
  role of architect, 2–3
  standard construction documents, 1–2
Construction bonds, 5, 28, 51–52, 78, 84–85
  AIA standard forms, 54–55
  assistance from surety in disputes, 141
  commencing work before issuance of, 55
  consent of surety, 56–57
  contractor prequalification, 53
  costs, 52–53
  definitions, 52
  keeping surety informed, 55–56
  obligations of surety, 52
  overpayment of contractors, 57
  owner approval of contractor surety, 54
  owner claims against, 57
  owner instructions regarding, 38
  surety as adversary, 53–54
  surety as ally, 54
  and termination of construction contracts, 56, 126–127
  transmitting bonds to owners, 55
Construction change directives, 5, 47, 74
Construction contracts:
  administered by contractors, 4
  administered on owner's behalf, 4–5
  award of, 16–17
  benefits for owners and contractors, 3–4
  changes in, 73, 79
  competitive bidding, 9
  and contract documents, 5
  contractual relationships, 6–7
  copies of documents, 22
  cost-plus-fee, 17
  errors in documents, 21
  general principles, 6, 8
  negotiated, 9
  signing, 83, 92–93
  stipulated sum, 16–17
  suspension of, 126
  termination of, 56, 113–114, 121, 123–129
  (*See also* Bidding)
Construction defects (*see* Defects)
Construction disputes (*see* Disputes)

Construction documents, standard, 1–2
Construction drawings, 5
Construction Industry Arbitration Rules, 143–144, 154
Construction insurance:
  AIA General Conditions, 37–38
  financial responsibility for accidental losses, 37
  insurance certificates, 38–39
  owner instructions regarding, 38
Construction methods, 25
Construction observation (*see* Site observation)
Construction phase:
  budgeting fees for services, 45
  commencement of, 19
  misunderstandings during, 137–138
  services, 43–45
  and site observation, 42–43
  visits by architects, 46–47
Construction problems, defects from, 167
Construction projects, successful, 19–20
Construction schedules (*see* Progress schedules)
Construction superintendents (*see* Superintendents)
Consultants:
  liability for mistakes of, 31
  limiting exposure to liability, 32–33
  owners' versus architects', 34–35
  reviews of shop drawings, 62
  shortcomings of, limiting liability for, 33–34
Contract documents, 5, 106
  copies, 22
  errors in, 21, 93, 103
  intent of, 132–133
  (*See also* Written communications)
Contractors:
  accident prevention procedures, 94–95
  administration of contracts by, 4
  benefits of contracts for, 3–4
  bids by, 5
  bond qualification, 53
  claims against architects, 153–163
  claims for extra compensation due to change orders, 78–79
  communications by, 96
  construction quality, 94
  designation of superintendents, 101–103
  drawings, 93

Contractors (*Cont.*):
  hazardous waste materials, 74, 97
  indemnification of owners and architects, 99
  insurance, 26, 29
  licenses, 94
  and limitation on owner's right to make changes, 99–100
  overhead, 26–28
  owner claims against, 88
  payment requests by, 25, 44, 47, 57, 67–68, 72
  profits, 26–28
  responsibilities, in general, 91–92
  responsibility for results, 93–94
  reviews of shop drawings, 61–62
  safety procedures, 94–95
  separate, 26, 28, 87–88, 95, 108
  signing contracts, 92–93
  specifications, 93
  and subcontractors, 28, 96
  taxes, 94
  termination of construction contracts by, 123–125
  warranties, 44, 97–99
  (*See also* Selection of contractors)
Contracts (*see* Construction contracts)
Contractual relationships, 6–7
Copies of contract documents, 22
Correction of work, 111
Correspondence, 5
Cost-plus-fee contracts, 17
Cutting and patching, 106

Daily logs, 23, 104–105
Damages (*see* Liquidated damages)
Days, working versus calendar, 146–147
Debris storage, 21
Decisions by architects, 26, 30, 121, 133–134
  aesthetic effect, 134–136
  design concept, 22, 133
  imprecise standards for, 131–132
  intent of contract documents, 132–133
  minor changes by, 79, 134
Default, 57, 128
Defects, 88, 111
  analyses of, 166
  mediation regarding, 167–168
  responsibility for, 166–167
  types, 165–166
Delays, 23, 48, 77, 145, 151
  AIA General Conditions, 145–146
  caused by owners and architects, 147–148
  construction schedules, 148

Index / 267

Delays (Cont.):
   and critical path, 150
   and liquidated damages, 146, 151
   and substantial completion, 150
   unforeseen conditions, 147
   weather, 23, 48, 107–108, 148–150
   working days versus calendar days, 146–147
Deposits, bid, 13–14
Design concept, 22, 133
Design problems, defects from, 166
Disputes, 45, 144
   aesthetic effect decisions by architects, 140–141
   AIA General Conditions, 138–139, 145–146
   architect's failure to resolve, 141
   assistance from surety, 141
   continuing contract performance, 143
   minor changes by architects, 141
   misunderstandings during construction, 137–138
   resolution by arbitration, 142–144
   resolution by architects, 121, 138–141
   resolution by mediation, 142
   resolution by negotiation, 142
   time and delay, 145–151
   unsettled claims, 139–140
Drawings, 5, 48, 75, 93, 106, 116
   (See also Shop drawings)
Dust control, 22

Electrical facilities, 22
Emergencies, 110
Errors in contract documents, 21, 93, 103

Fees:
   budgeting, for construction phase services, 45
   contractor, 17
Fences, temporary, 22
Field reports, 44, 46–47
Final completion, 117
Final payments, 71–72
Final submittals, 116–117
Financial capability of owners, 26–27
Foundation investigation reports, 22
Front end loading, 70

General conditions of contracts, 5
General contractors (see Contractors)

Hazardous waste materials, 74, 97, 110–111
Hours of operation, 22

Impact claims, 77–78
Indemnification clauses, 99
Information bulletins, 5
Information requests, 5, 48
Inspections, 25–26, 111
Instruction sheets for standard AIA documents:
   A101, 206–209
   A111, 226–229
   A201, 256–259
   B141, 193–195
Instructions to bidders, 5, 12–13
Insurance:
   architect, 155
   owner and contractor, 26, 29, 38, 84–85
   (See also Construction insurance)
Insurance certificates, 5, 28, 38–39, 44
Intent of contract documents, 132–133
Invitations to bid, 5, 12

Jobsites:
   offices, 21
   record keeping at, 23
   superintendent's duties, 101–103
   (See also Preconstruction jobsite conferences)

Keys, 116

Lawsuits, 153–154
   and arbitration demands, 154
   assisting lawyers, 156–160
   legal counsel, 155
   professional liability insurance, 155
   record keeping, 160–161
   responding to complaints, 154
   selecting lawyers, 155–156
   settlement of, 162
   statutes of limitations, 161–162
   witnesses, 162–163
Legal description of property, 22
Legal matters, 44, 153–163
Liability insurance, 155
Licenses, 94
Liquidated damages, 26, 29, 115, 120–121, 146, 151
Logs, superintendent, 23, 104–105
Low bidders, 15–16

Maintenance problems, defects from, 167

Materials storage, 21
Mediation:
   and defects, 167–168
   of disputes, 142
Minor changes, by architects, 5, 79, 134, 141
Misunderstandings, 137–138
Models, 22
Modifications to contract documents, 5, 106

Negotiated contracts, 9
Negotiated disputes, 142
Noise control, 22
Noncompliance, prevention of, 44
Notices, 171–174
Notices of completion, 115–116
Notices to proceed, 26

Objections, 178–179
Observation of construction, 3
   (See also Site observation)
Occupancy, 119
Offices, jobsite, 21
Operating instructions, 116
Orders, 5, 178–179
Overcertification, 69–70
Overhead of contractors, 26–28
Owners:
   administration of contracts on behalf of, 4–5
   after signing of contracts, 83–84
   AIA General Conditions, 82
   approval of contractor surety, 54
   benefits of contracts for, 3–4
   and bonds, 84–85
   claims against architects, 153–163
   claims against contractors, 88
   and consultants, 34–35
   and defects, 88
   delays caused by, 147–148
   failure to pay, 86
   financial capability of, 26–27
   ideal, 89
   information furnished by, 84
   instructions regarding insurance and bonds, 38
   insurance, 26, 29, 38, 84–85
   keeping informed about site observations, 48
   limitations on rights, 99–100
   as member of construction team, 81–82
   partial use or occupancy, 119
   payments by, 85–86
   relationship with architects, 88–89, 121–122
   responsibilities, in general, 82–83
   right to carry out work, 87

Owners (Cont.):
 right to make changes, 74, 108
 right to stop work, 86–87
 and separate contractors, 26, 28, 87–88
 signing contracts, 83
 suspension of construction contracts by, 126
 termination of construction contracts by, 125–126

Packages, bid, 13–14
Parking, jobsite, 21–22
Partial use, 119
Parts lists, 116
Patching and cutting, 106
Payment:
 final, 71–72
 by owner, 85–86
 owner's failure to pay, 86
 requests by contractors, 25, 44, 47, 57, 67–68, 72
Payment certificates, 44, 170–171
 accord and satisfaction, 71–72
 contractor applications for payments, 67–68
 decisions to withhold, 69
 fairness of, 70–71
 and final payments, 71
 limitations, 68–69
 overcertification, 69–70
 representations, 68–69
 substantiation for payment requests, 72
Periods, bidding, 14
Perspective renderings, 22
Polychlorinated biphenyl (PCB), 74, 97, 110–111
Power facilities, 22
Preconstruction jobsite conferences:
 allowances, 27
 attendance by superintendents, 104
 and commencement of construction phase, 19
 communication tools, 20–21
 communications, 24
 construction methods, 25
 copies of contract documents, 22
 decisions by architects, 30
 design intent, 22
 errors in contract documents, 21
 financial capability of owners, 27
 inspections, 25–26
 insurance, 29
 liquidated damages, 29
 notices to proceed, 26
 overhead of contractors, 27–28

Preconstruction jobsite conferences (Cont.):
 payment requests by contractors, 25
 private meetings, 26
 profits of contractors, 27–28
 progress schedules, 23
 record keeping on jobsites, 23
 safety procedures, 25
 separate contractors, 28
 specification substitutions, 23
 submittals, 28–29
 and successful building projects, 19–20
 testing, 25–26
 unit prices, 27
 use of site, 21–22
 visits by architects, 24
Presentation drawings, 22
Price quotations, 5
Private meetings, 26
Product data, 5, 44, 47, 106
Professional liability insurance, 155
Profits of contractors, 26–28
Progress schedules, 23, 29, 44, 47, 105–106, 148
Proposal requests, 5, 75
Proposals, competitive, 10, 15

Quality, construction, 94
Quotation requests, 48

Record drawings, 116
Record keeping:
 for all documents and transactions, 44, 47–48
 jobsite, 23
 legal necessity, 160–161
Reports, field, 44, 46–47
Retainage, 57, 120
Roofing installations, 26

Safety procedures, 25, 94–95, 109–110
Sample forms, for bidding, 5
Samples, 5, 44, 47, 106
Schedules:
 progress, 23, 29, 44, 47, 105–106, 148
 submittal, 29
 of values, 29
Security provisions, 22
Selection of contractors:
 alternate bids, 14–15
 award of contract, 16–17
 base bids, 14–15
 bid bonds, 15
 bid packages, 13–14
 bidding periods, 14

Selection of contractors (Cont.):
 bidding practices, 10
 competitive bidding, 9
 determining low bidder, 15–16
 establishment of bidding conditions, 10
 instructions to bidders, 12–13
 invitations to bid, 12
 negotiated contracts, 9
 opening of bids, 15–16
 recommended bidding procedures, 10–11
 selection of bidders, 11–12
 unit prices, 14–15
Separate contractors, 26, 28, 87–88, 95, 108
Shop drawings, 5, 44, 47, 59, 106
 AIA documents for, 60
 architect approval of, 64–65
 consultant reviews of, 62
 contractor reviews of, 61–62
 improper use of, 65–66
 keeping clients informed, 63
 monitoring progress of submissions, 63
 necessity of, 60–61
 qualified personnel assigned to, 64
 stamps, 64
 submittals, in general, 60
 unneeded, specifying, 61
Signs, jobsite, 22
Site observation:
 by architect's personnel, 47
 architectural services agreements, 42
 budgeting fees for construction phase services, 45
 construction phase services, 43–45
 and construction phase, 42–43
 keeping owner informed, 48
 limitations of architect authority, 48–49
 record keeping, 47–48
 time involved in, 41
 visits by architect, 46–47
Sites, use of, 21–22
Spare parts, 116
Specification substitutions, 23
Specifications, 5, 48, 75, 93, 106, 116
Stamps, shop drawing, 64
Standard construction documents, 1–2
Statutes of limitations, 161–162
Stipulated sum contracts, 16–17
Storage, jobsite, 21
Strikes, 48

Index / 269

Subcontractors, 28, 96
Submittal schedules, 29
Submittals, 60, 106, 175–176
   construction phase, 44, 47
   final, 116–117
   preconstruction, 26, 28–29
Substantial completion, 109, 114, 150
Substantial completion certificates, 114–115, 171
Substantiating data, for payment requests, 72
Substitutions, specification, 23
Superintendents:
   accident prevention procedures, 109–110
   attendance at preconstruction jobsite conferences, 104
   changes in work, 108
   claims for concealed or unknown conditions, 107
   claims for time extensions, 107–108
   communications by, 106–107
   construction procedures, 105
   and construction of work, 105
   continuing contract performance, 107
   cooperation with owners and architects, 108
   correction of work, 111
   cutting and patching, 106
   daily logs, 23, 104–105
   documents at site, 106
   hazardous waste materials, 110–111
   inspections, 111
   preliminary site visits, 103

Superintendents (Cont.):
   progress schedules, 105–106
   responsibilities, 101–103
   reviews of contract documents and field conditions, 103–104
   safety procedures, 109–110
   samples at site, 106
   substantial completion stage, 109
   supervision by, 105
   testing, 111
   time of construction, 108–109
   uncovered work, 111
Supervision of construction, 3, 105
Supplementary conditions of contracts, 5
Suppliers, 28, 96
Surety bonds (*see* Construction bonds)
Surveys, jobsite, 22
Suspension of construction contracts, 126

Taxes, 94
Telephones, 22
Temporary fences, 22
Termination of construction contracts, 56, 121
   by contractors, 123–125
   orderly, 113–114
   by owners, 125–126
   position of architects, 127
   position of surety, 126–127
   practical considerations, 127–129
   provisions, in general, 123
   and suspension of contracts, 126
Testimony, 162–163
Testing, 25–26, 111

Time extensions, 23, 77, 107–108
   (*See also* Delays)
Toilet facilities, 21–22
Topographic surveys, 22
Truck parking, 22

Unavailability of materials, 48
Uncovered work, 111
Unexecuted change orders, 5
Unforeseen conditions, 147
Unit prices, 14–15, 26–27
Unknown conditions, claims for, 107
Usage problems, defects from, 167
Use of sites, 21–22
User manuals, 116

Values, schedules of, 29
Visits, by architects, 24, 46–47

Warranties, 44, 97–99, 114, 116
Water facilities, 22
Weather, 23, 48, 107–108, 148–150
Wiring diagrams, 116
Witnesses, 162–163
Worker parking, 21
Working days, 146–147
Written communications:
   additional agreements, 177–178
   approvals, 178–179
   authorizations, 178–179
   certifications, 170–171
   notices, 171–174
   objections, 178–179
   orders, 178–179
   other, 179
   required, 169
   submittals, 175–176
   (*See also* Contract documents)

ABOUT THE AUTHOR

Arthur F. O'Leary is a leading expert on construction industry arbitration and architectural practice. He founded the Los Angeles architectural firm of O'Leary Terasawa Partners in 1949, has served as arbitrator and consultant on more than 300 industry litigations, and has written, lectured, and published extensively in over 40 years of professional activity. He received his Bachelor of Architecture from the University of Southern California, where he served on the faculty for 10 years. Mr. O'Leary is a member of the National Panel of Arbitrators of the American Arbitration Association. He is also the recipient of the Distinguished Achievement Award from the American Institute of Architects. He currently resides near Dublin in Drogheda, County Louth, Ireland.